S T O R Y

When Shizuku Mizutani does a favor for problem child Haru Yoshida, who sits next to her in school, he develops a huge crush on her. Attracted to his innocence, she eventually falls for him too, but when she asks him out, he inexplicably turns her down. Shizuku locks away her romantic feelings. After that, she starts to change, and decides to face people more assertively. She finally tells him again that she likes him, but Haru is so worried about Yamaken's advances on Shizuku that her confession goes right over his head! And while these two constantly fail to get on the same page, Natsume-san's own love story begins to unfold.

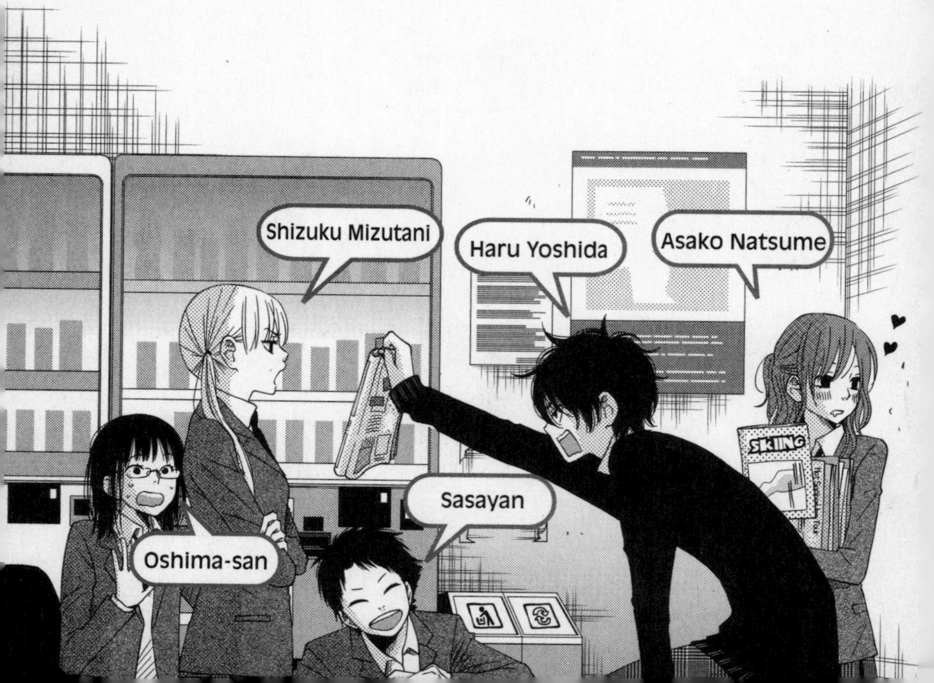
Asako Natsume
Haru Yoshida
Shizuku Mizutani
Sasayan
Oshima-san

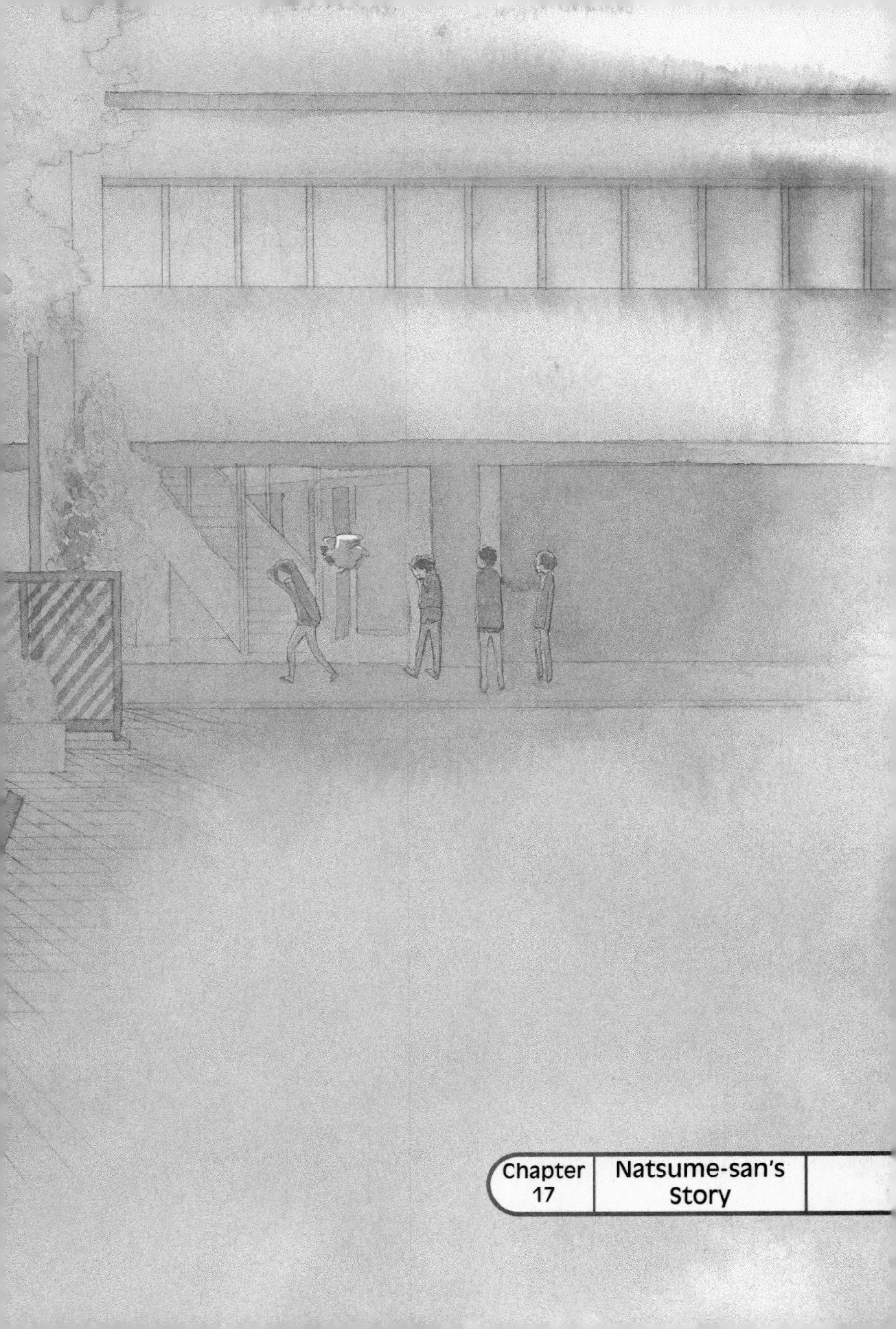

Chapter 17 Natsume-san's Story

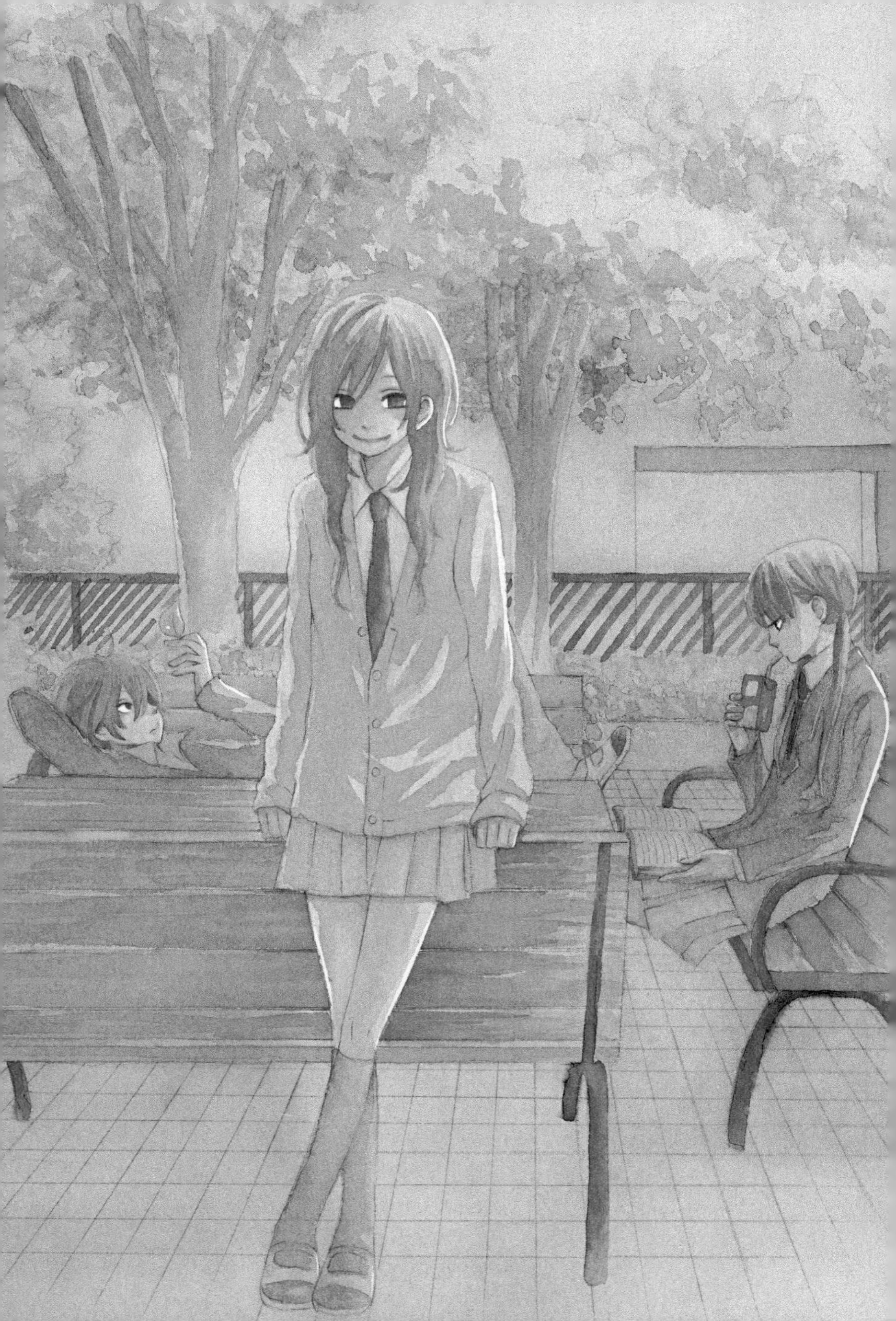

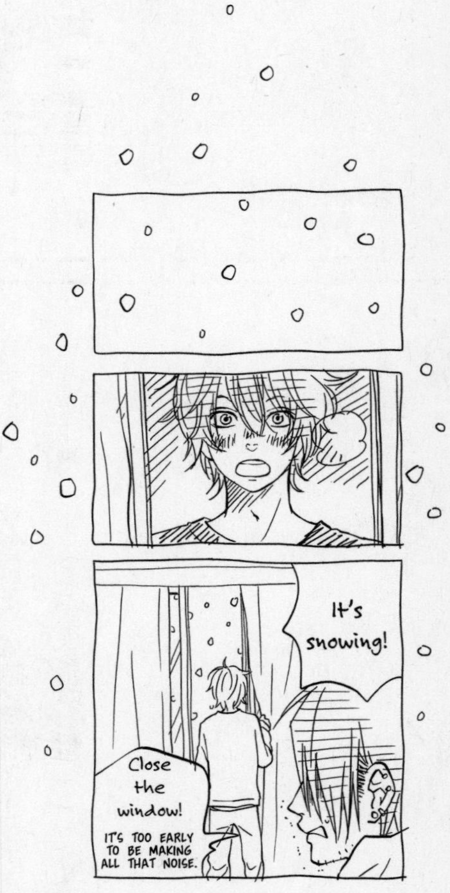
It's snowing!
Close the window!
IT'S TOO EARLY TO BE MAKING ALL THAT NOISE.

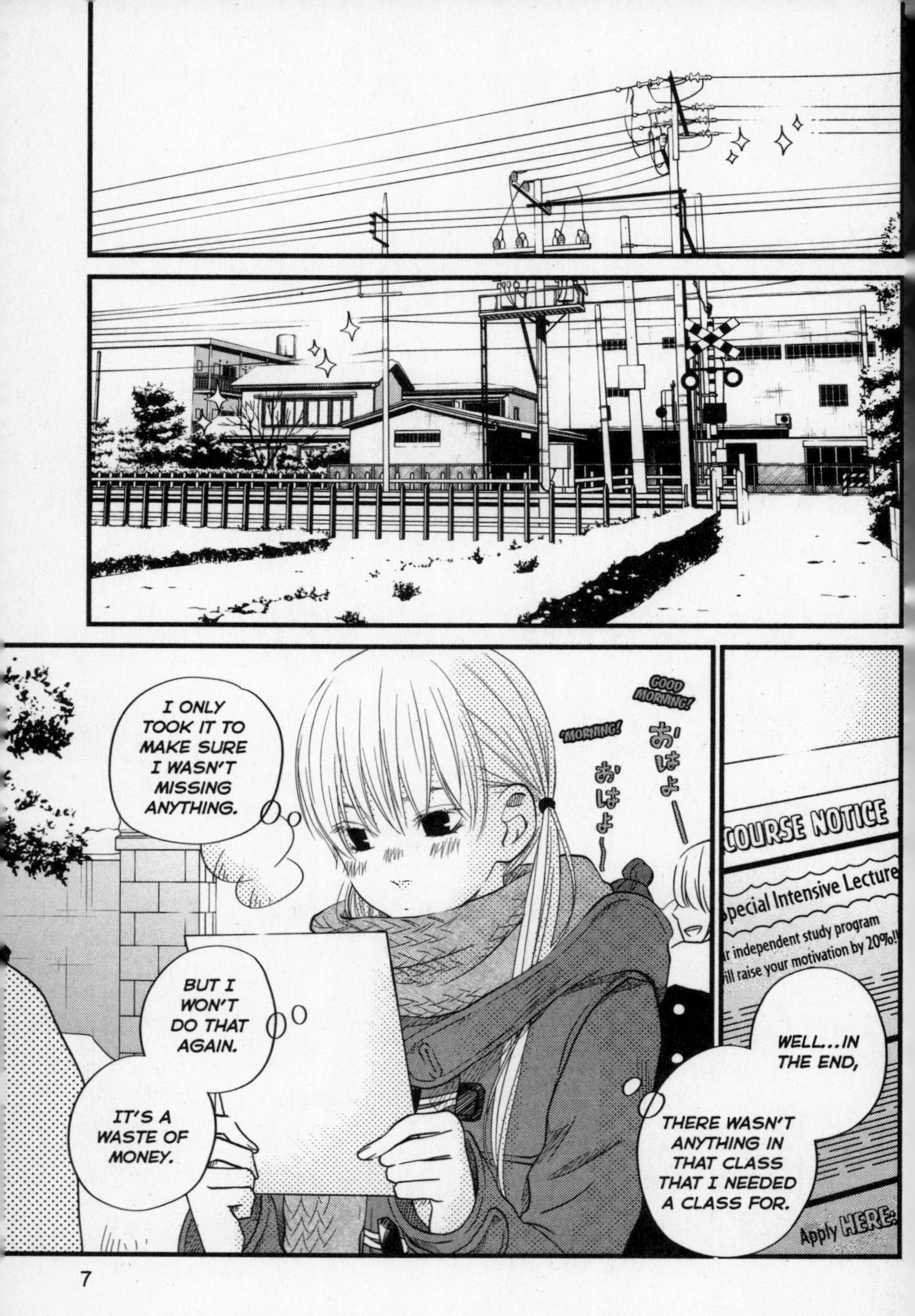
COURSE NOTICE
Special Intensive Lecture
r independent study program
ill raise your motivation by 20%!!
WELL...IN THE END,
THERE WASN'T ANYTHING IN THAT CLASS THAT I NEEDED A CLASS FOR.
Apply HERE:
GOOD MORNING!
おはよー
'MORNING!
おはよ〜
I ONLY TOOK IT TO MAKE SURE I WASN'T MISSING ANYTHING.
BUT I WON'T DO THAT AGAIN.
IT'S A WASTE OF MONEY.

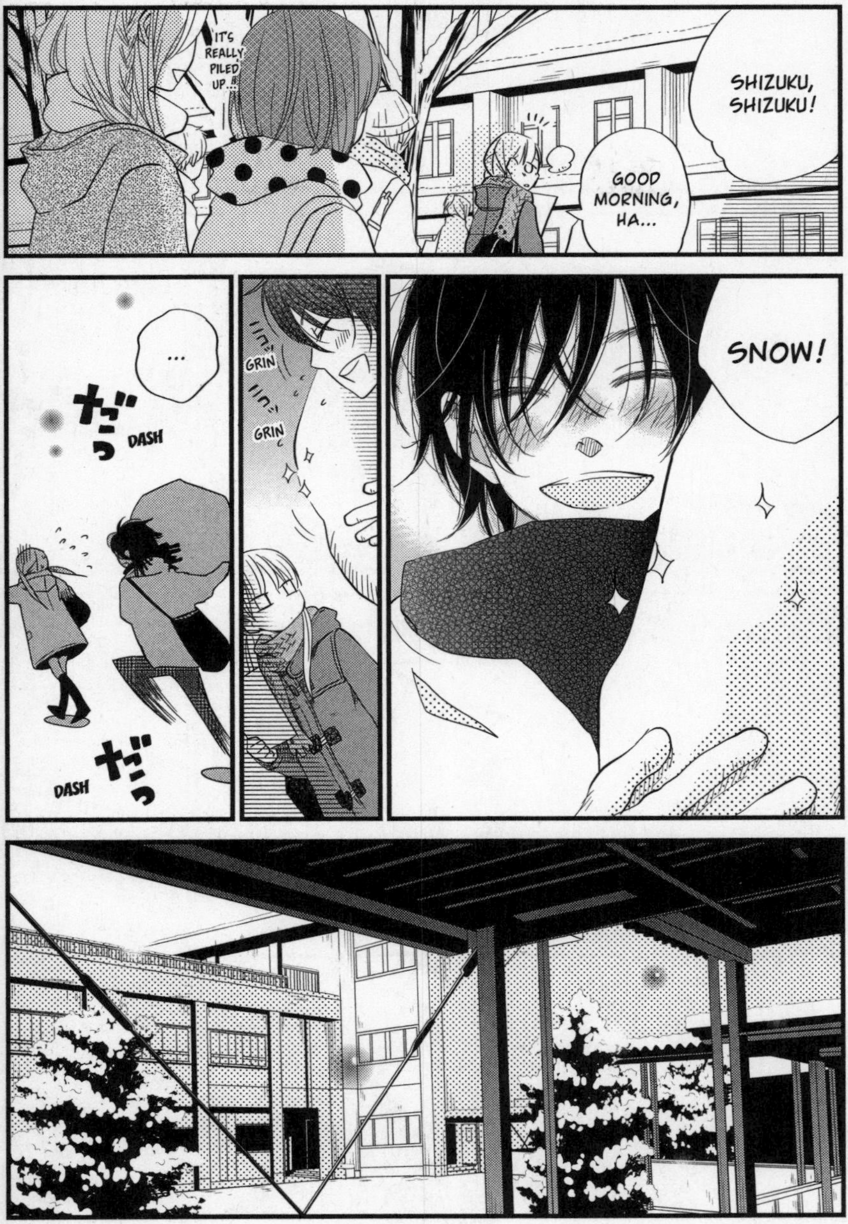
SHIZUKU, SHIZUKU!
GOOD MORNING, HA...
IT'S REALLY PILED UP...
SNOW!
GRIN
GRIN
...
だっ
DASH
だっ
DASH

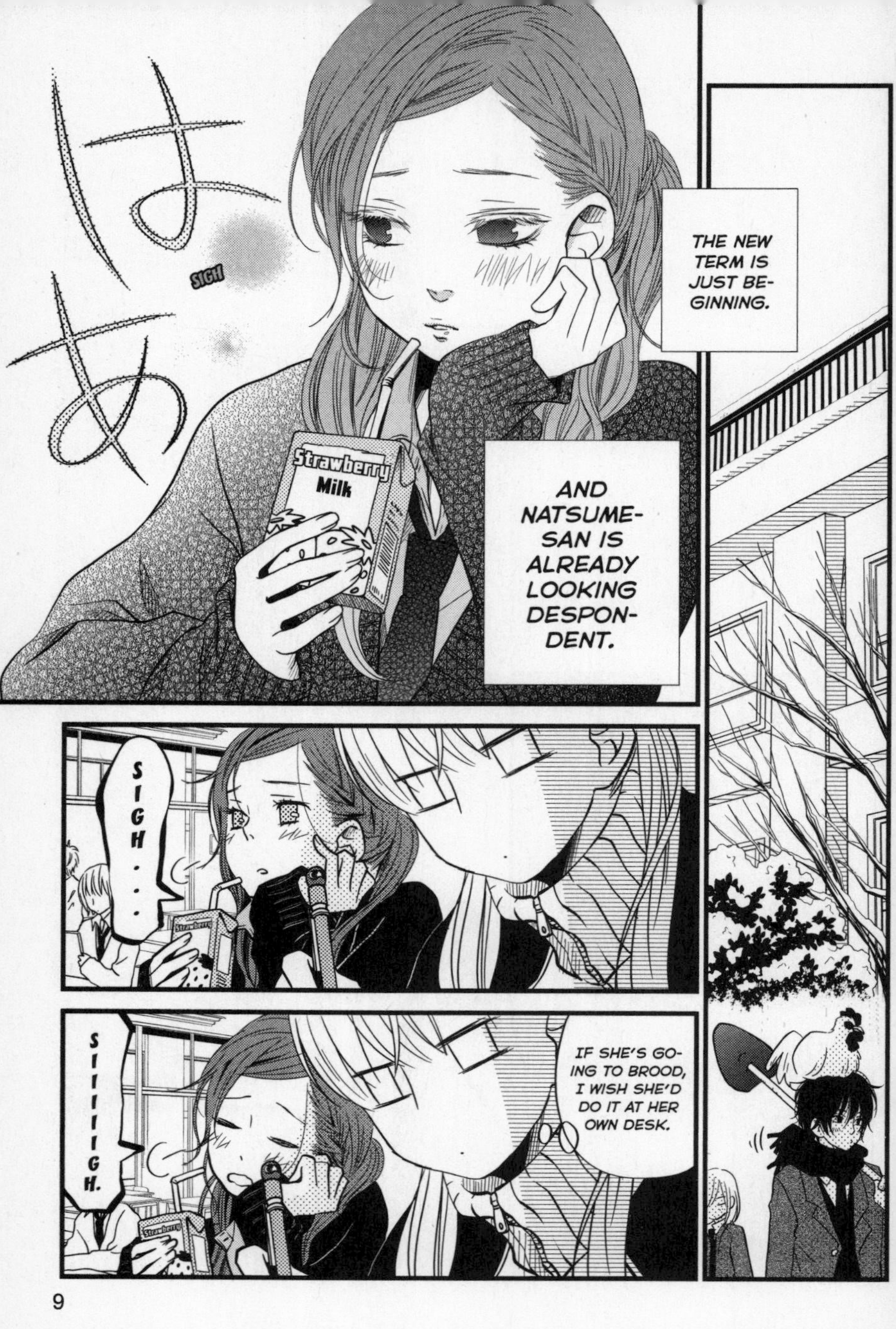
THE NEW TERM IS JUST BEGINNING.
はぁ
SIGH
Strawberry Milk
AND NATSUME-SAN IS ALREADY LOOKING DESPONDENT.
SIGH...
SIIIIIGH.
IF SHE'S GOING TO BROOD, I WISH SHE'D DO IT AT HER OWN DESK.

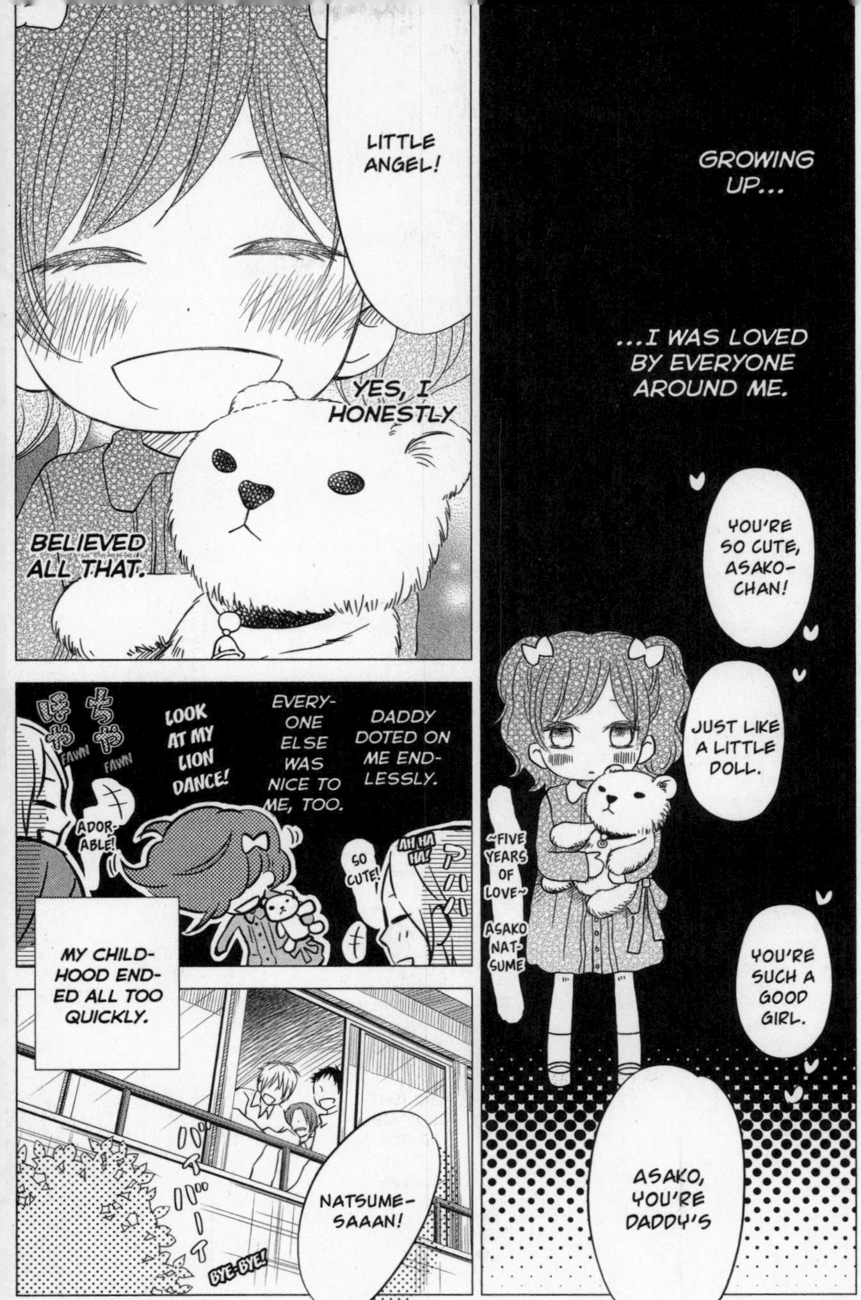
GROWING UP...
...I WAS LOVED BY EVERYONE AROUND ME.
YOU'RE SO CUTE, ASAKO-CHAN!
JUST LIKE A LITTLE DOLL.
~FIVE YEARS OF LOVE~
ASAKO NATSUME
YOU'RE SUCH A GOOD GIRL.
ASAKO, YOU'RE DADDY'S
LITTLE ANGEL!
YES, I HONESTLY
BELIEVED ALL THAT.
DADDY DOTED ON ME ENDLESSLY.
EVERYONE ELSE WAS NICE TO ME, TOO.
LOOK AT MY LION DANCE!
FAWN
FAWN
ADORABLE!
AH HA HA!
SO CUTE!
MY CHILDHOOD ENDED ALL TOO QUICKLY.
NATSUME-SAAAN!
BYE-BYE!

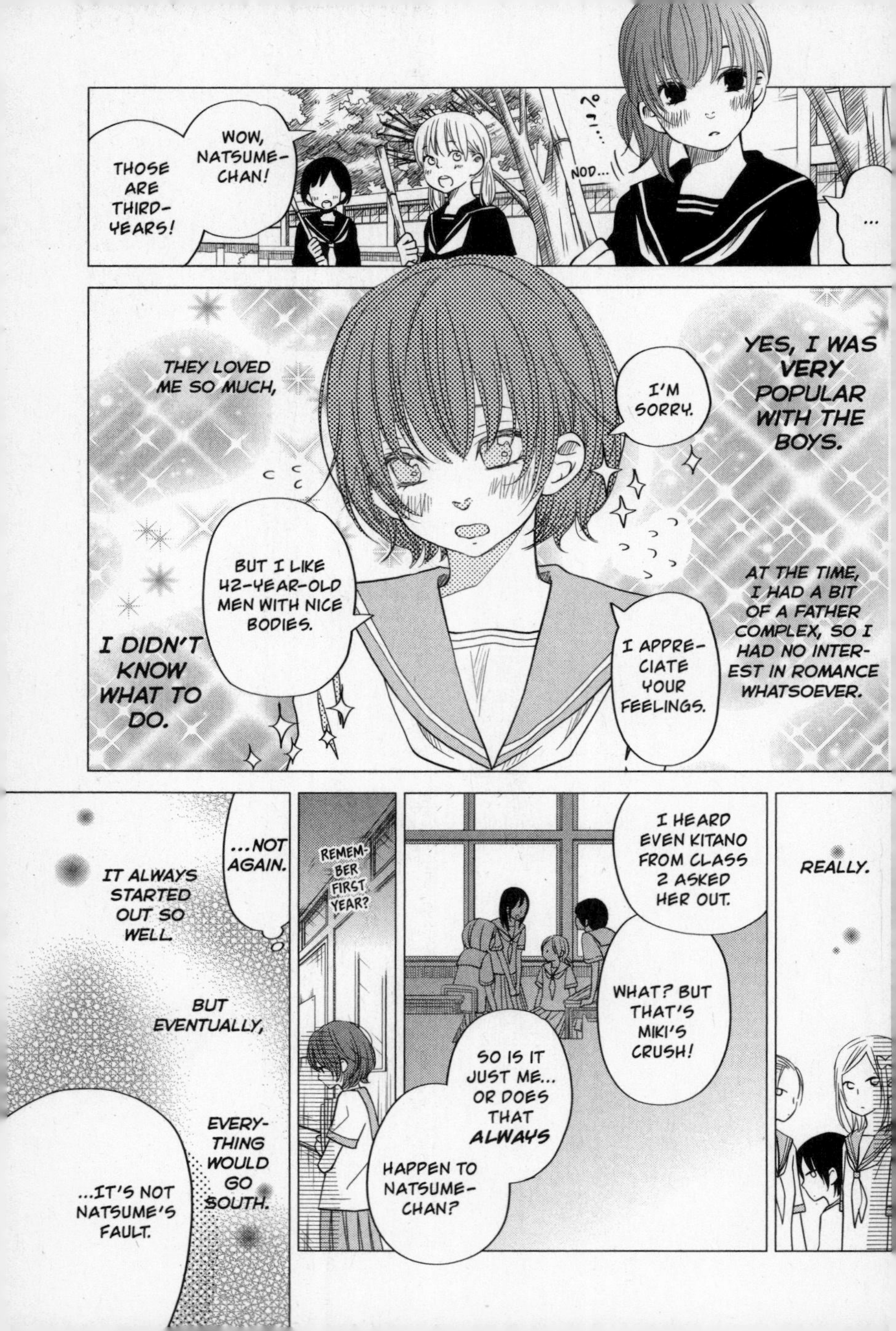
...
NOD...
WOW, NATSUME-CHAN!
THOSE ARE THIRD-YEARS!
YES, I WAS VERY POPULAR WITH THE BOYS.
I'M SORRY.
THEY LOVED ME SO MUCH,
AT THE TIME, I HAD A BIT OF A FATHER COMPLEX, SO I HAD NO INTEREST IN ROMANCE WHATSOEVER.
I APPRECIATE YOUR FEELINGS.
BUT I LIKE 42-YEAR-OLD MEN WITH NICE BODIES.
I DIDN'T KNOW WHAT TO DO.
REALLY.
I HEARD EVEN KITANO FROM CLASS 2 ASKED HER OUT.
WHAT? BUT THAT'S MIKI'S CRUSH!
SO IS IT JUST ME... OR DOES THAT ALWAYS HAPPEN TO NATSUME-CHAN?
REMEMBER FIRST YEAR?
...NOT AGAIN.
IT ALWAYS STARTED OUT SO WELL.
BUT EVENTUALLY,
EVERYTHING WOULD GO SOUTH.
...IT'S NOT NATSUME'S FAULT.

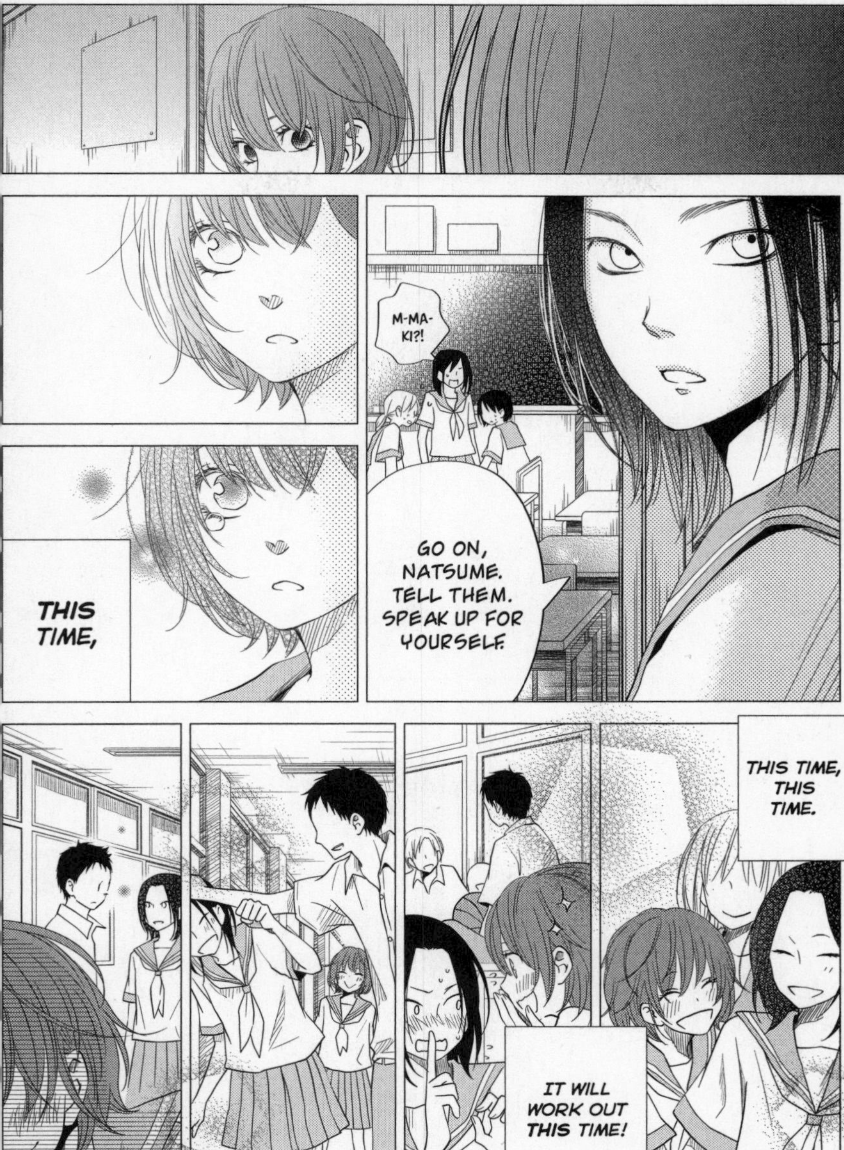
M-MA-KI?!
GO ON, NATSUME. TELL THEM. SPEAK UP FOR YOURSELF.
THIS TIME,
THIS TIME, THIS TIME.
IT WILL WORK OUT THIS TIME!

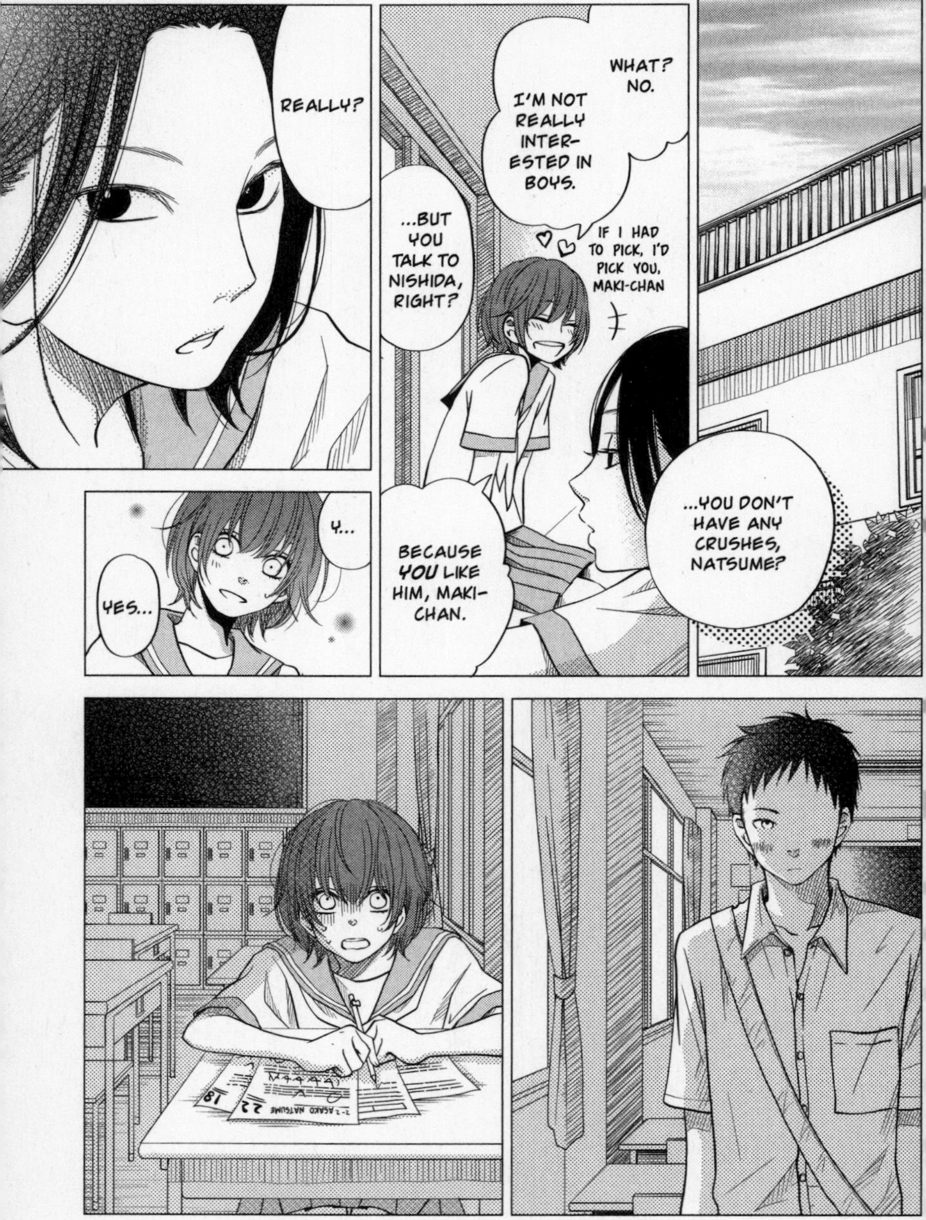
...YOU DON'T HAVE ANY CRUSHES, NATSUME?
WHAT? NO.
I'M NOT REALLY INTER-ESTED IN BOYS.
IF I HAD TO PICK, I'D PICK YOU, MAKI-CHAN
...BUT YOU TALK TO NISHIDA, RIGHT?
BECAUSE *YOU* LIKE HIM, MAKI-CHAN.
REALLY?
Y...
YES...

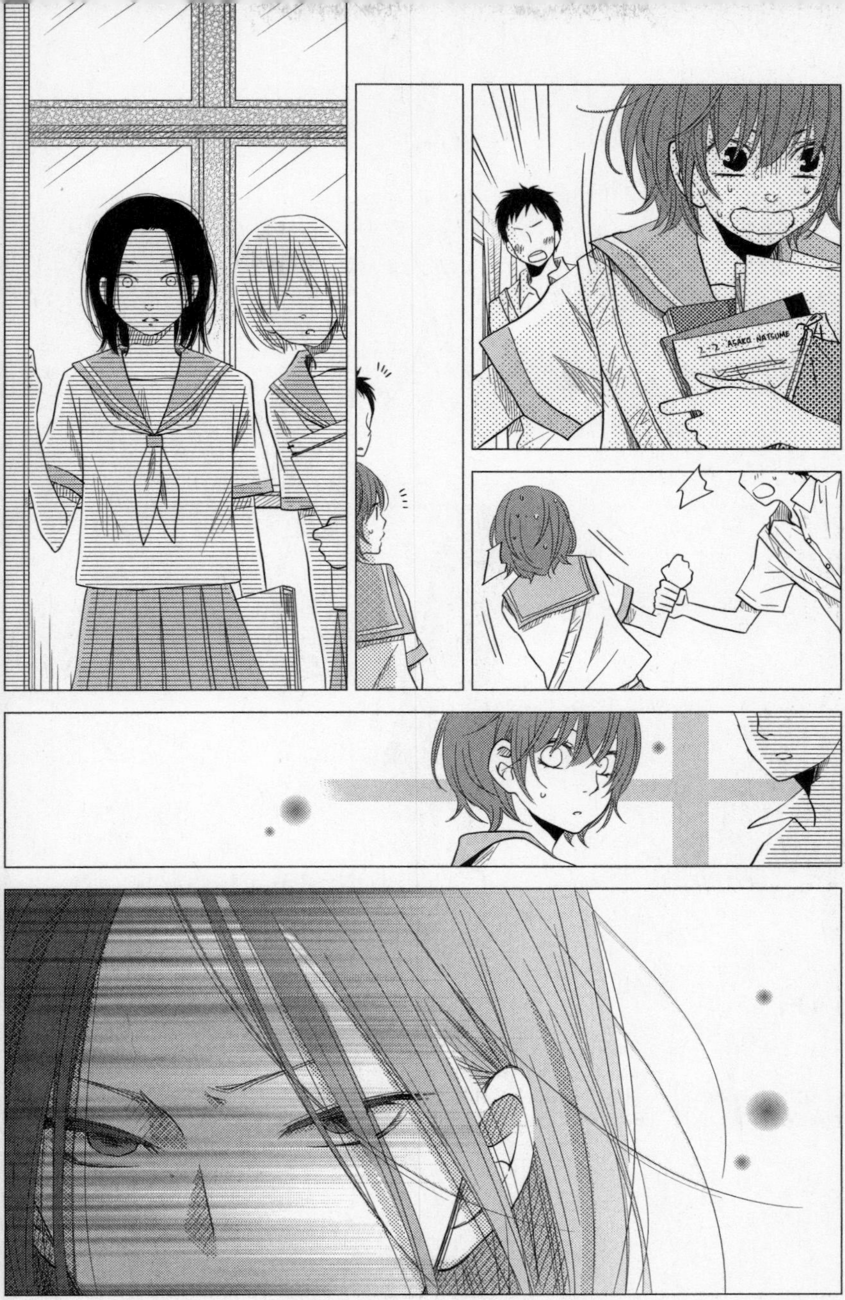
2-2 ASAKO NATSUME

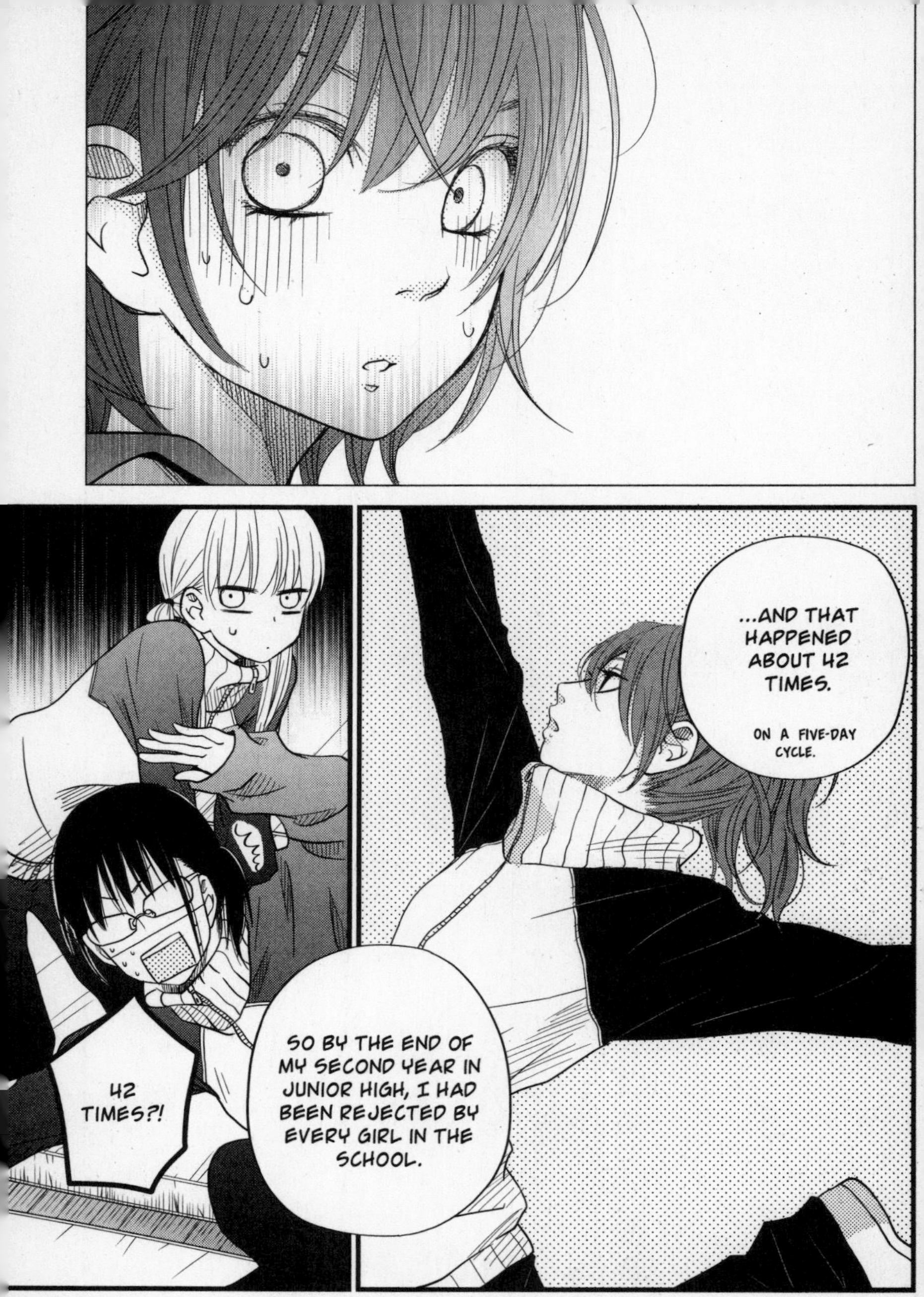
...AND THAT HAPPENED ABOUT 42 TIMES.
ON A FIVE-DAY CYCLE.
SO BY THE END OF MY SECOND YEAR IN JUNIOR HIGH, I HAD BEEN REJECTED BY EVERY GIRL IN THE SCHOOL.
42 TIMES?!

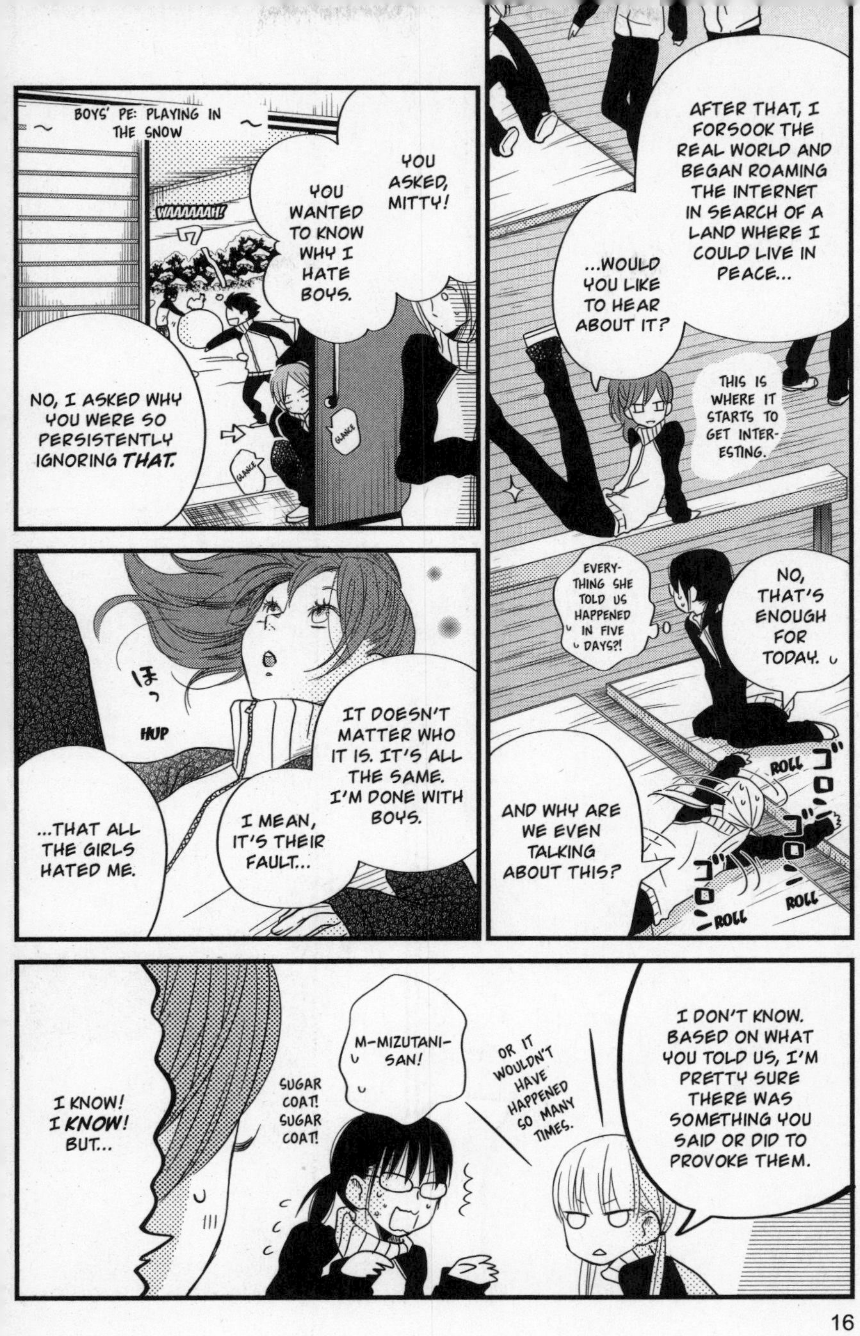
AFTER THAT, I FORSOOK THE REAL WORLD AND BEGAN ROAMING THE INTERNET IN SEARCH OF A LAND WHERE I COULD LIVE IN PEACE...
...WOULD YOU LIKE TO HEAR ABOUT IT?
THIS IS WHERE IT STARTS TO GET INTERESTING.
NO, THAT'S ENOUGH FOR TODAY.
EVERYTHING SHE TOLD US HAPPENED IN FIVE DAYS?!
AND WHY ARE WE EVEN TALKING ABOUT THIS?
ゴロン ROLL
ゴロン ROLL
ゴロン ROLL
BOYS' PE: PLAYING IN THE SNOW
YOU ASKED, MITTY!
YOU WANTED TO KNOW WHY I HATE BOYS.
WAAAAAAH!
GLANCE
GLANCE
NO, I ASKED WHY YOU WERE SO PERSISTENTLY IGNORING THAT.
ほっ
HUP
IT DOESN'T MATTER WHO IT IS. IT'S ALL THE SAME. I'M DONE WITH BOYS.
I MEAN, IT'S THEIR FAULT...
...THAT ALL THE GIRLS HATED ME.
I DON'T KNOW. BASED ON WHAT YOU TOLD US, I'M PRETTY SURE THERE WAS SOMETHING YOU SAID OR DID TO PROVOKE THEM.
OR IT WOULDN'T HAVE HAPPENED SO MANY TIMES.
M-MIZUTANI-SAN!
SUGAR COAT! SUGAR COAT!
I KNOW! I KNOW! BUT...

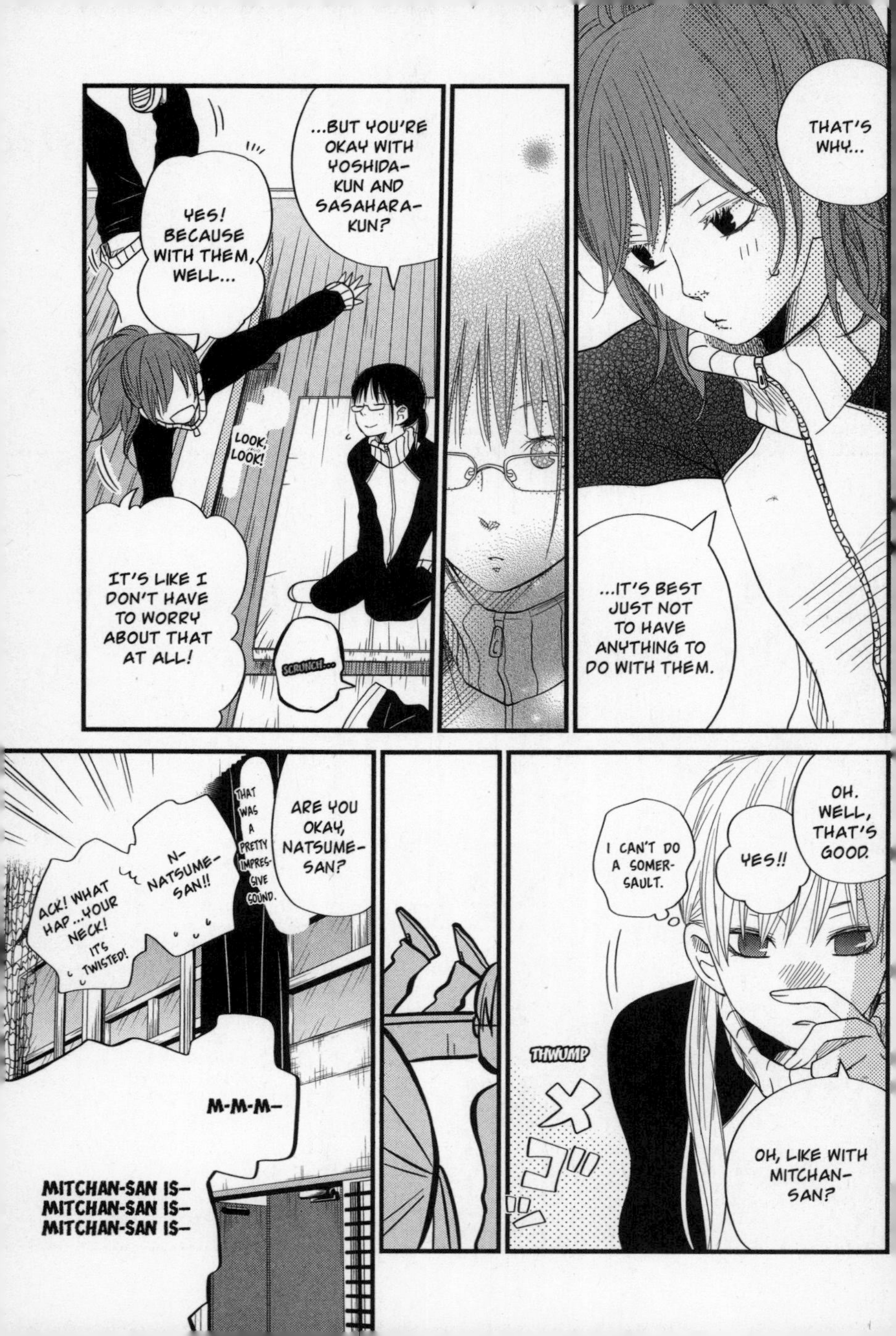
THAT'S WHY...
...IT'S BEST JUST NOT TO HAVE ANYTHING TO DO WITH THEM.
...BUT YOU'RE OKAY WITH YOSHIDA-KUN AND SASAHARA-KUN?
YES! BECAUSE WITH THEM, WELL...
LOOK, LOOK!
IT'S LIKE I DON'T HAVE TO WORRY ABOUT THAT AT ALL!
SCRUNCH...
OH. WELL, THAT'S GOOD.
YES!!
I CAN'T DO A SOMERSAULT.
OH, LIKE WITH MITCHAN-SAN?
THWUMP
ARE YOU OKAY, NATSUME-SAN?
THAT WAS A PRETTY IMPRESSIVE SOUND.
N-NATSUME-SAN!!
ACK! WHAT HAP...YOUR NECK! IT'S TWISTED!
M-M-M-
MITCHAN-SAN IS-
MITCHAN-SAN IS-
MITCHAN-SAN IS-

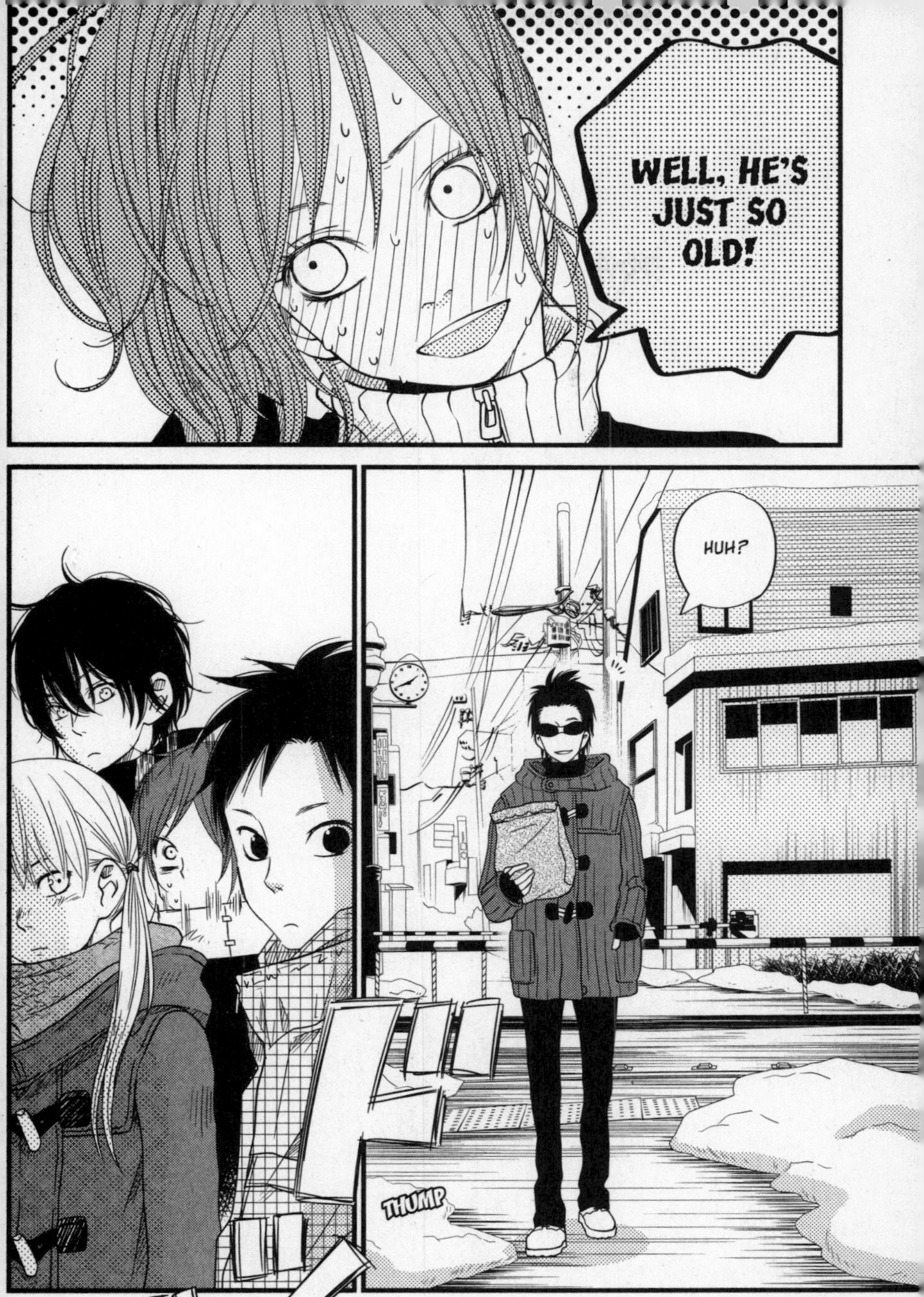
WELL, HE'S JUST SO OLD!
HUH?
THUMP

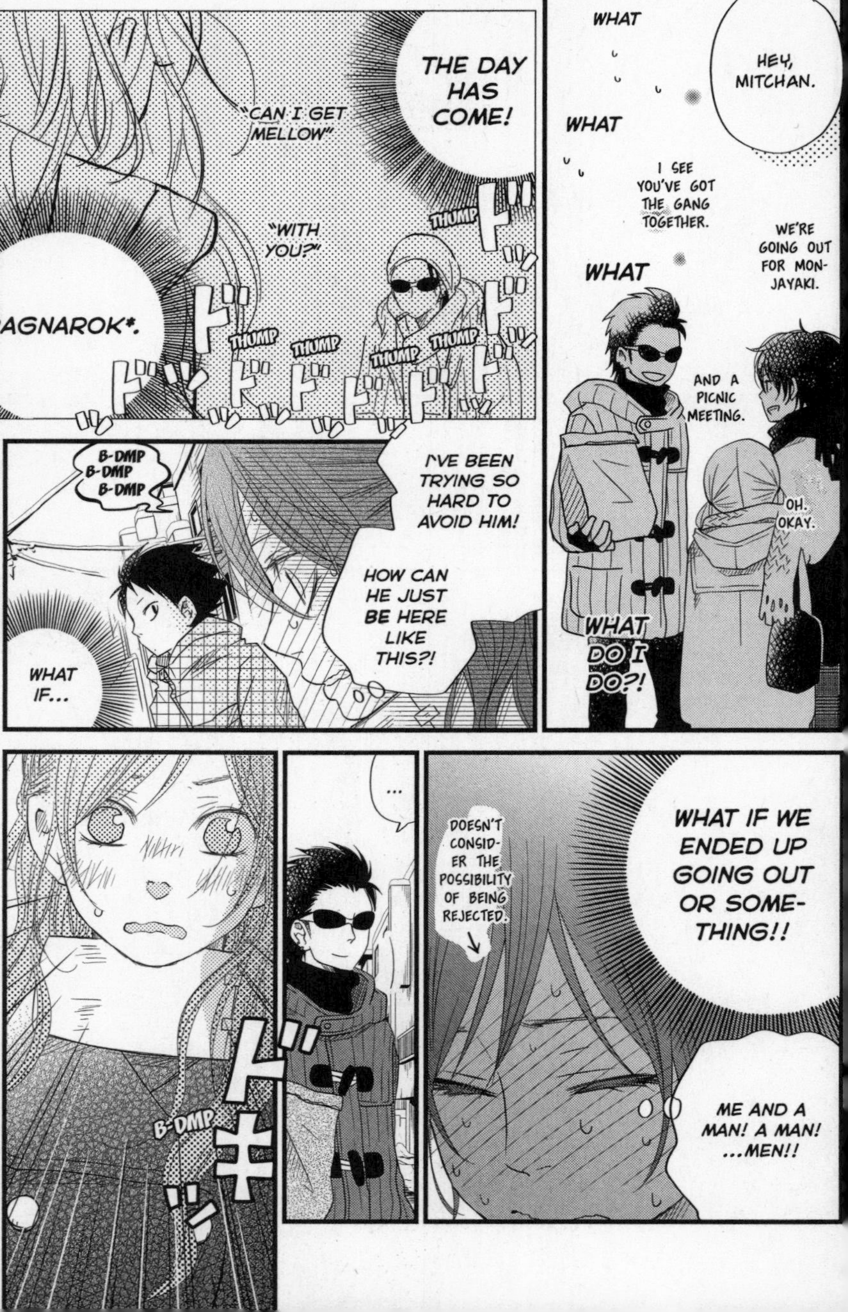
HEY, MITCHAN.
WHAT
WHAT
I SEE YOU'VE GOT THE GANG TOGETHER.
WE'RE GOING OUT FOR MON-JAYAKI.
WHAT
AND A PICNIC MEETING.
OH. OKAY.
WHAT DO I DO?!
THE DAY HAS COME!
"CAN I GET MELLOW"
"WITH YOU?"
THUMP
RAGNAROK*.
THUMP
THUMP
THUMP
THUMP
I'VE BEEN TRYING SO HARD TO AVOID HIM!
HOW CAN HE JUST BE HERE LIKE THIS?!
B-DMP B-DMP B-DMP
WHAT IF...
WHAT IF WE ENDED UP GOING OUT OR SOME-THING!!
DOESN'T CONSID-ER THE POSSIBILITY OF BEING REJECTED.
ME AND A MAN! A MAN! ...MEN!!
...
B-DMP

*RAGNAROK: SOMETHING LIKE "THE END OF THE WORLD."

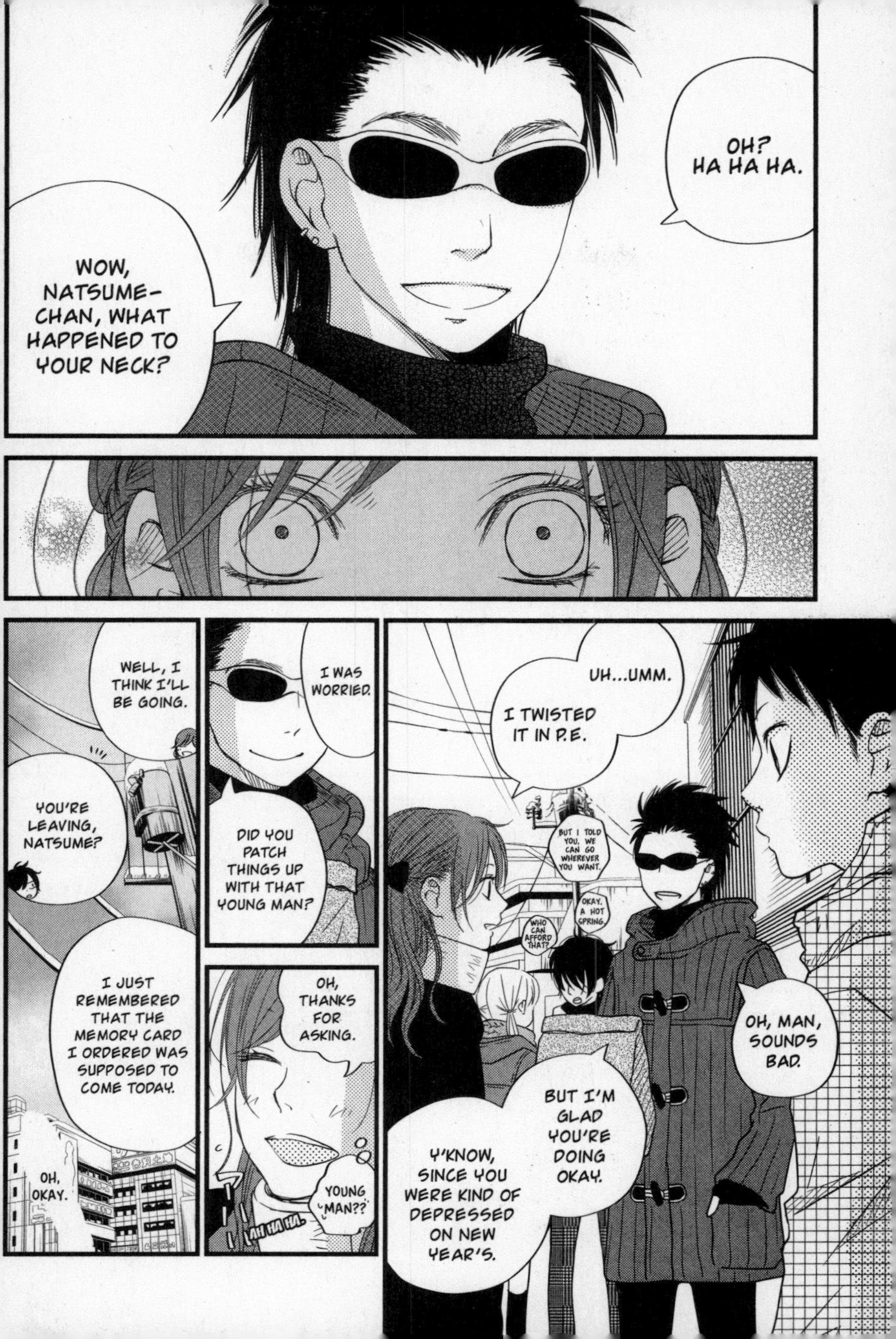
OH? HA HA HA.
WOW, NATSUME-CHAN, WHAT HAPPENED TO YOUR NECK?
UH...UMM.
I TWISTED IT IN P.E.
BUT I TOLD YOU, WE CAN GO WHEREVER YOU WANT.
OKAY, A HOT SPRING.
WHO CAN AFFORD THAT?
OH, MAN, SOUNDS BAD.
BUT I'M GLAD YOU'RE DOING OKAY.
Y'KNOW, SINCE YOU WERE KIND OF DEPRESSED ON NEW YEAR'S.
I WAS WORRIED.
DID YOU PATCH THINGS UP WITH THAT YOUNG MAN?
OH, THANKS FOR ASKING.
YOUNG MAN??
AH HA HA.
WELL, I THINK I'LL BE GOING.
YOU'RE LEAVING, NATSUME?
I JUST REMEMBERED THAT THE MEMORY CARD I ORDERED WAS SUPPOSED TO COME TODAY.
OH, OKAY.

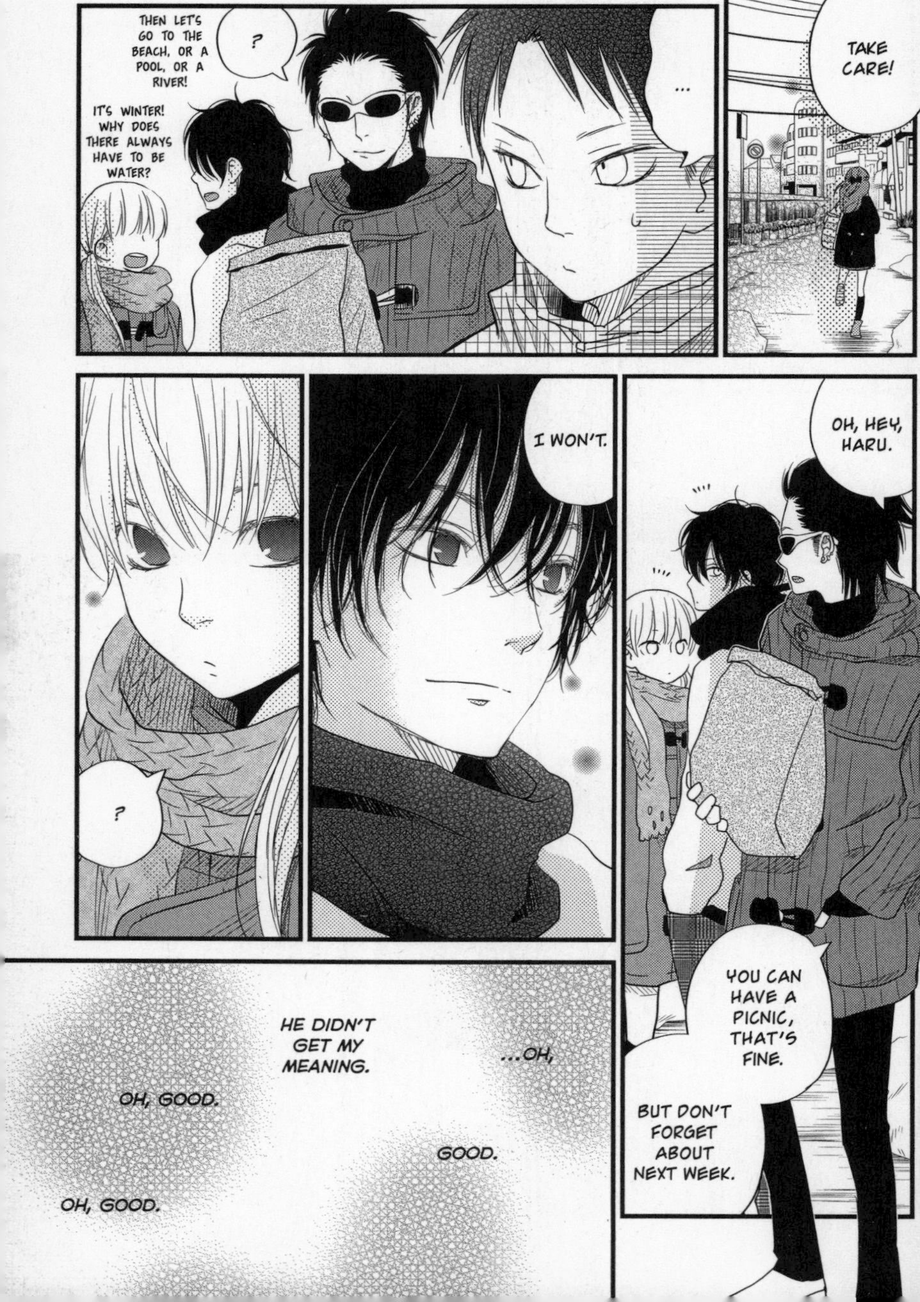
TAKE CARE!
...
?
THEN LET'S GO TO THE BEACH, OR A POOL, OR A RIVER!
IT'S WINTER! WHY DOES THERE ALWAYS HAVE TO BE WATER?
OH, HEY, HARU.
YOU CAN HAVE A PICNIC, THAT'S FINE.
BUT DON'T FORGET ABOUT NEXT WEEK.
I WON'T.
?
...OH,
HE DIDN'T GET MY MEANING.
GOOD.
OH, GOOD.
OH, GOOD.

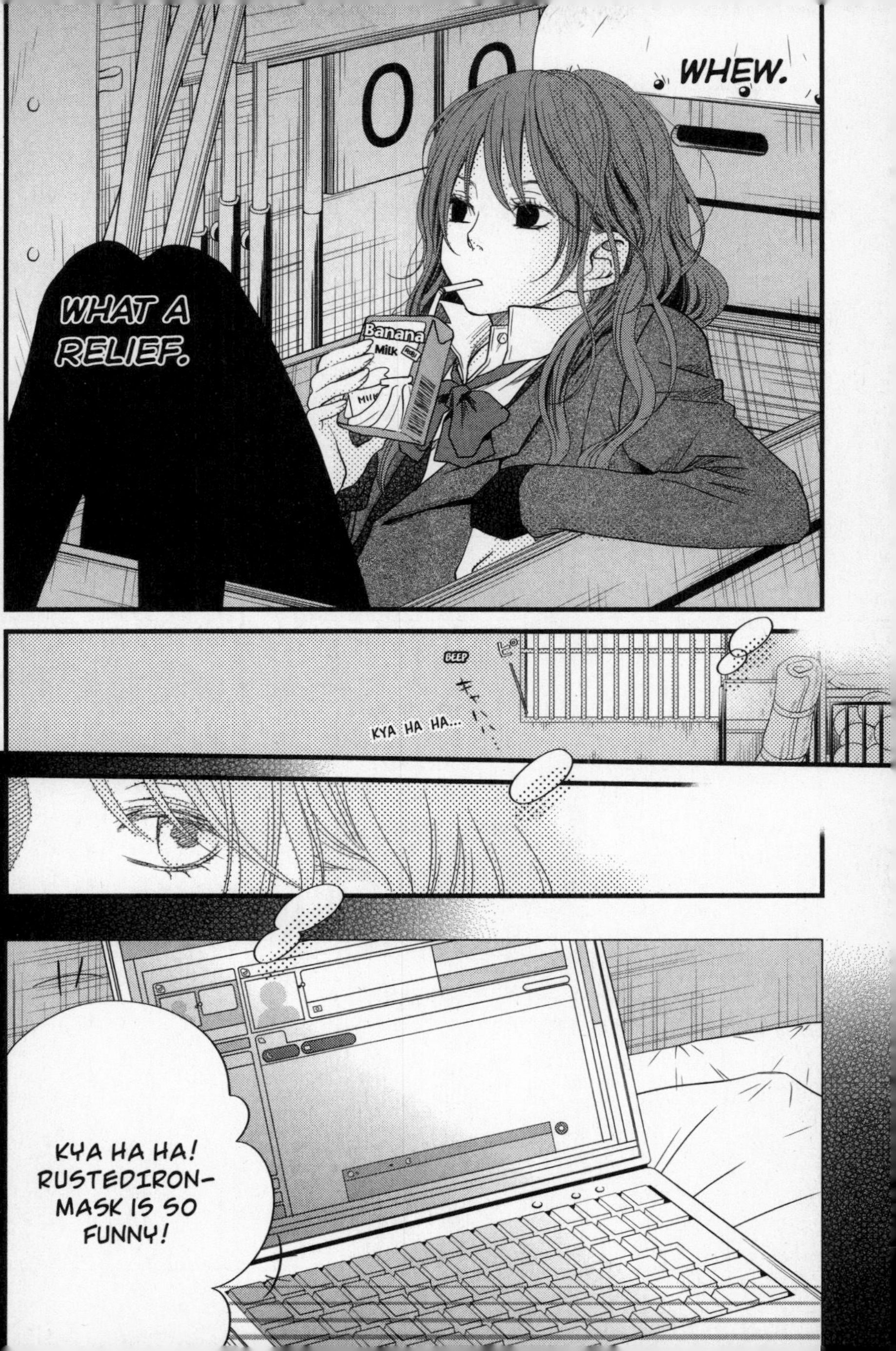
WHEW.
WHAT A RELIEF.
Banana Milk
BEEP
KYA HA HA...
KYA HA HA! RUSTEDIRON-MASK IS SO FUNNY!

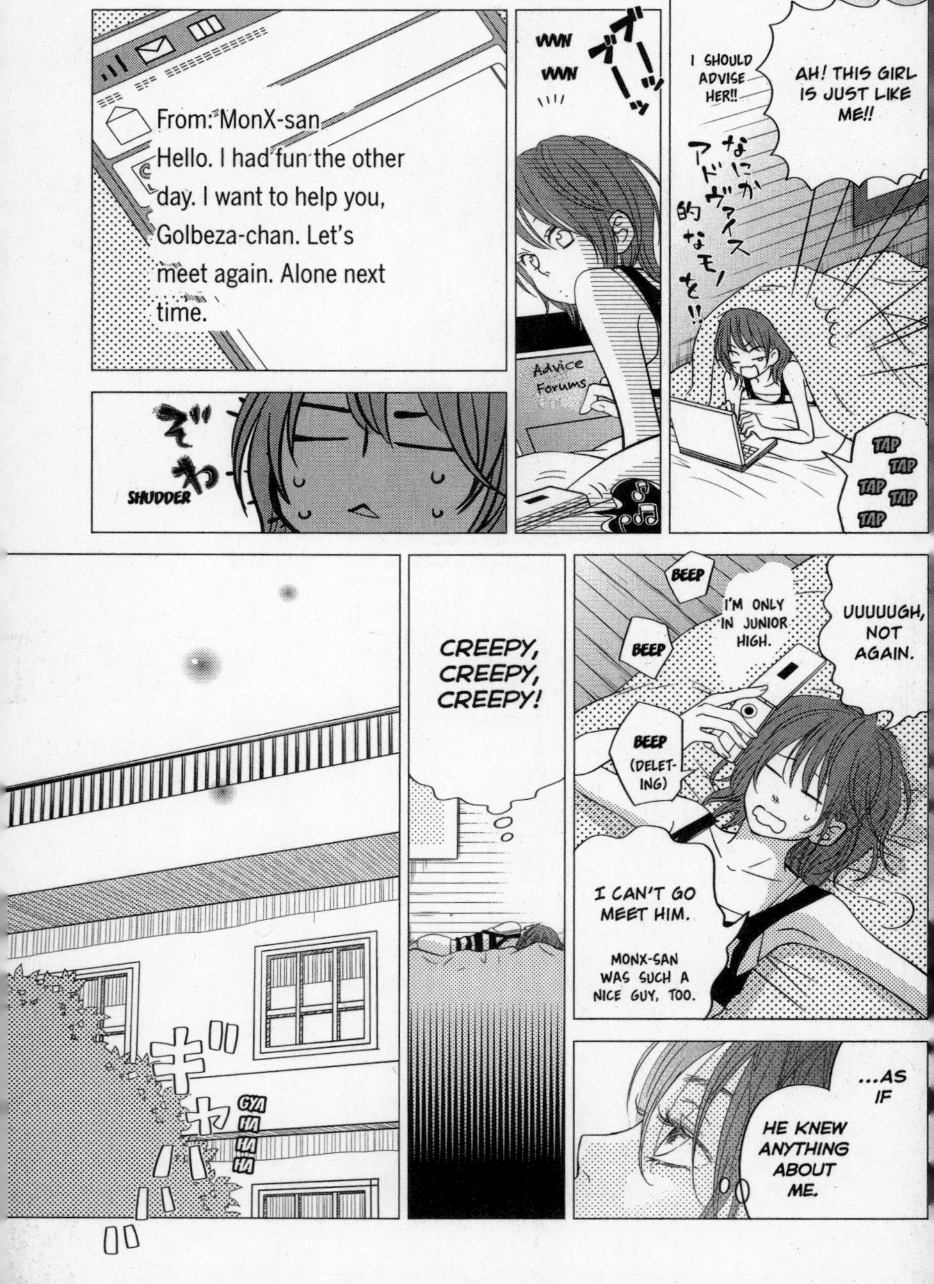
AH! THIS GIRL IS JUST LIKE ME!!
I SHOULD ADVISE HER!!
なにかアドヴァイス的なモノを!!
TAP TAP TAP TAP TAP
ブーッ ブーッ
WWN WWN
Advice Forums
From: MonX-san
Hello. I had fun the other day. I want to help you, Golbeza-chan. Let's meet again. Alone next time.
ぞわ
SHUDDER
UUUUUGH, NOT AGAIN.
I'M ONLY IN JUNIOR HIGH.
BEEP
BEEP
BEEP (DELETING)
I CAN'T GO MEET HIM.
MONX-SAN WAS SUCH A NICE GUY, TOO.
...AS IF
HE KNEW ANYTHING ABOUT ME.
CREEPY, CREEPY, CREEPY!
キャハハ
GYA HA HA HA

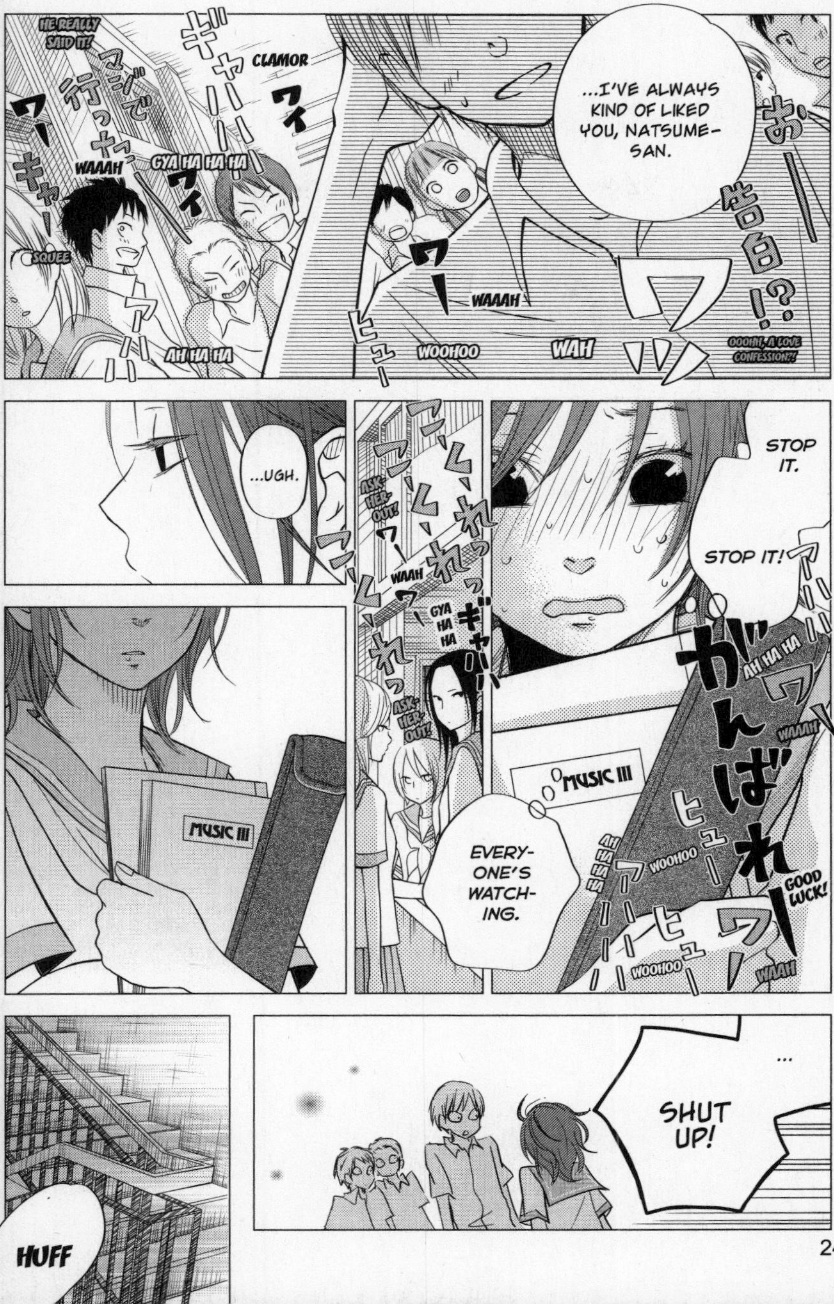
...I'VE ALWAYS KIND OF LIKED YOU, NATSUME-SAN.
おー 告白!?
OOOHH, A LOVE CONFESSION?!
ワ
WAH
ワー
WAAAH
ヒュー
WOOHOO
HE REALLY SAID IT!
マジで行ったっ
ギャハハハ
CLAMOR
ワイ
GYA HA HA HA
ワイ
ワー
WAAAH
キャー
SQUEE
アハハ
AH HA HA
STOP IT.
STOP IT!
アハハ
AH HA HA
がんばれー
GOOD LUCK!
ワー
WAAAH
ヒュー
WOOHOO
ワー
WAAH
アハハ
AH HA HA HA
MUSIC III
EVERY-ONE'S WATCH-ING.
コーくれっ
ASK-HER-OUT!
ワー
WAAH
ギャハ
GYA HA HA
ASK-HER-OUT!
...UGH.
MUSIC III
...
SHUT UP!
HUFF

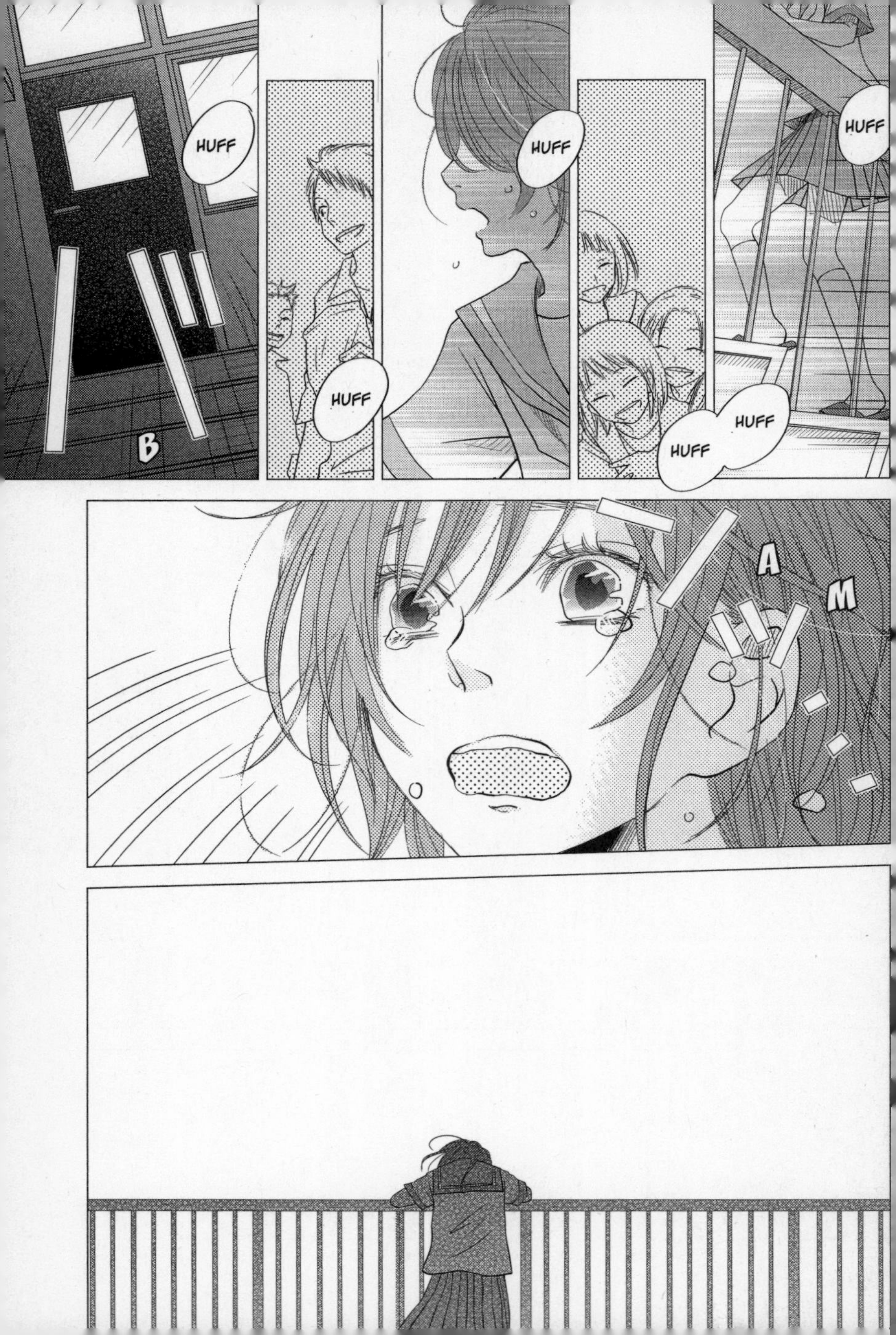
HUFF
HUFF
HUFF
HUFF
HUFF
HUFF
B
A
M

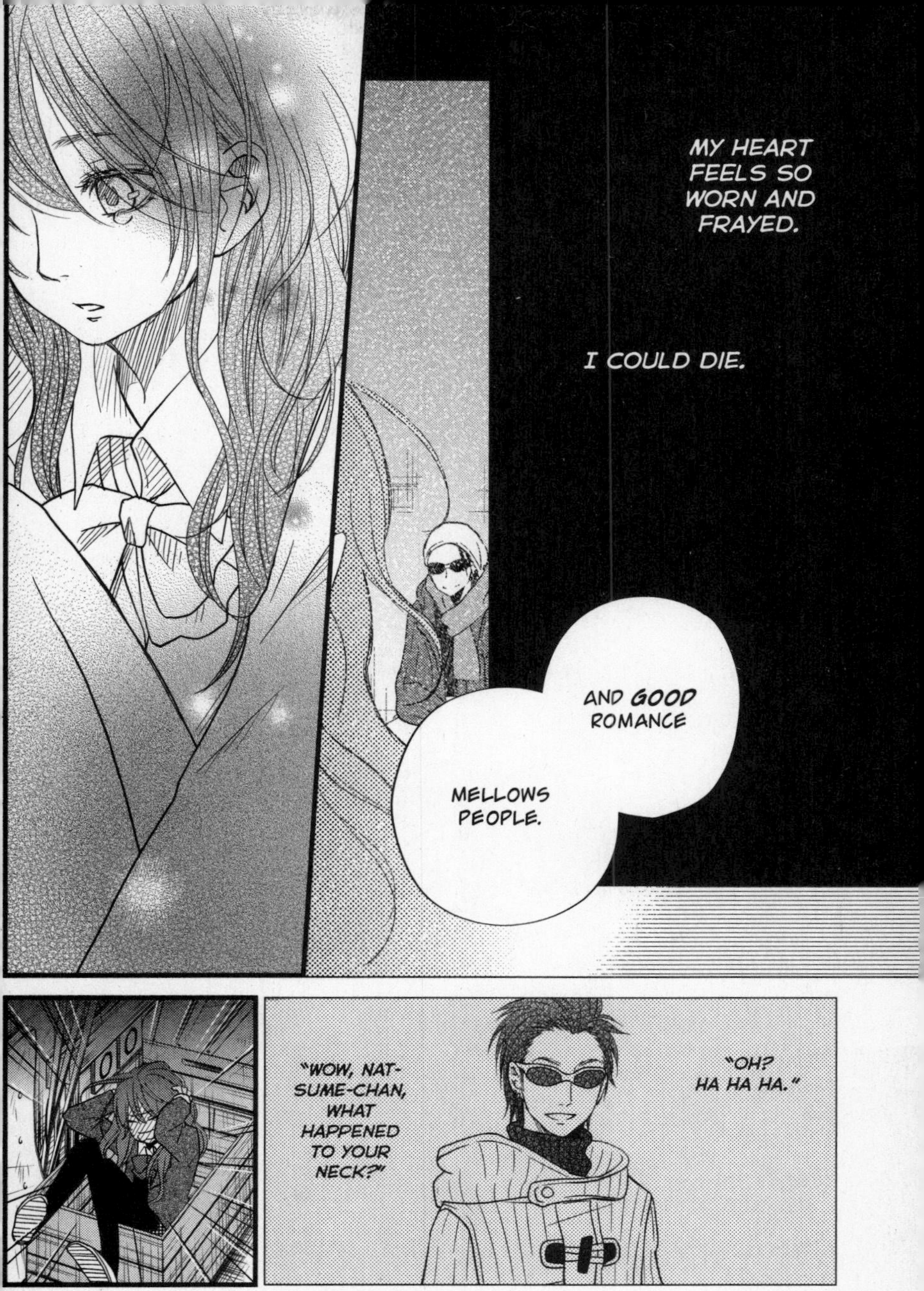
MY HEART FEELS SO WORN AND FRAYED.
I COULD DIE.
AND GOOD ROMANCE MELLOWS PEOPLE.
"OH? HA HA HA."
"WOW, NAT-SUME-CHAN, WHAT HAPPENED TO YOUR NECK?"

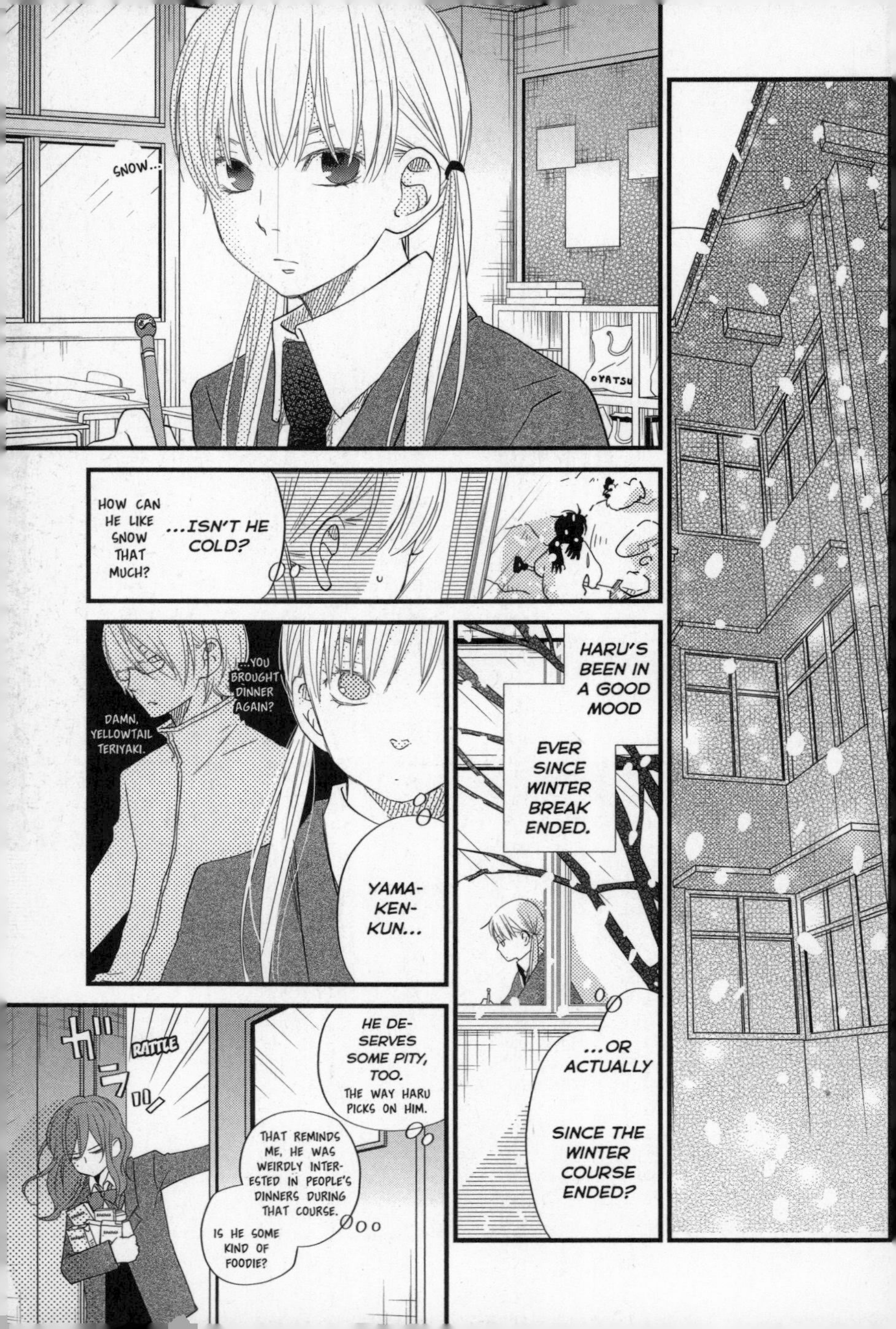
SNOW...
...ISN'T HE COLD?
HOW CAN HE LIKE SNOW THAT MUCH?
HARU'S BEEN IN A GOOD MOOD
EVER SINCE WINTER BREAK ENDED.
...OR ACTUALLY
SINCE THE WINTER COURSE ENDED?
...YOU BROUGHT DINNER AGAIN?
DAMN, YELLOWTAIL TERIYAKI.
YAMA-KEN-KUN...
HE DE-SERVES SOME PITY, TOO.
THE WAY HARU PICKS ON HIM.
THAT REMINDS ME, HE WAS WEIRDLY INTER-ESTED IN PEOPLE'S DINNERS DURING THAT COURSE.
IS HE SOME KIND OF FOODIE?
RATTLE

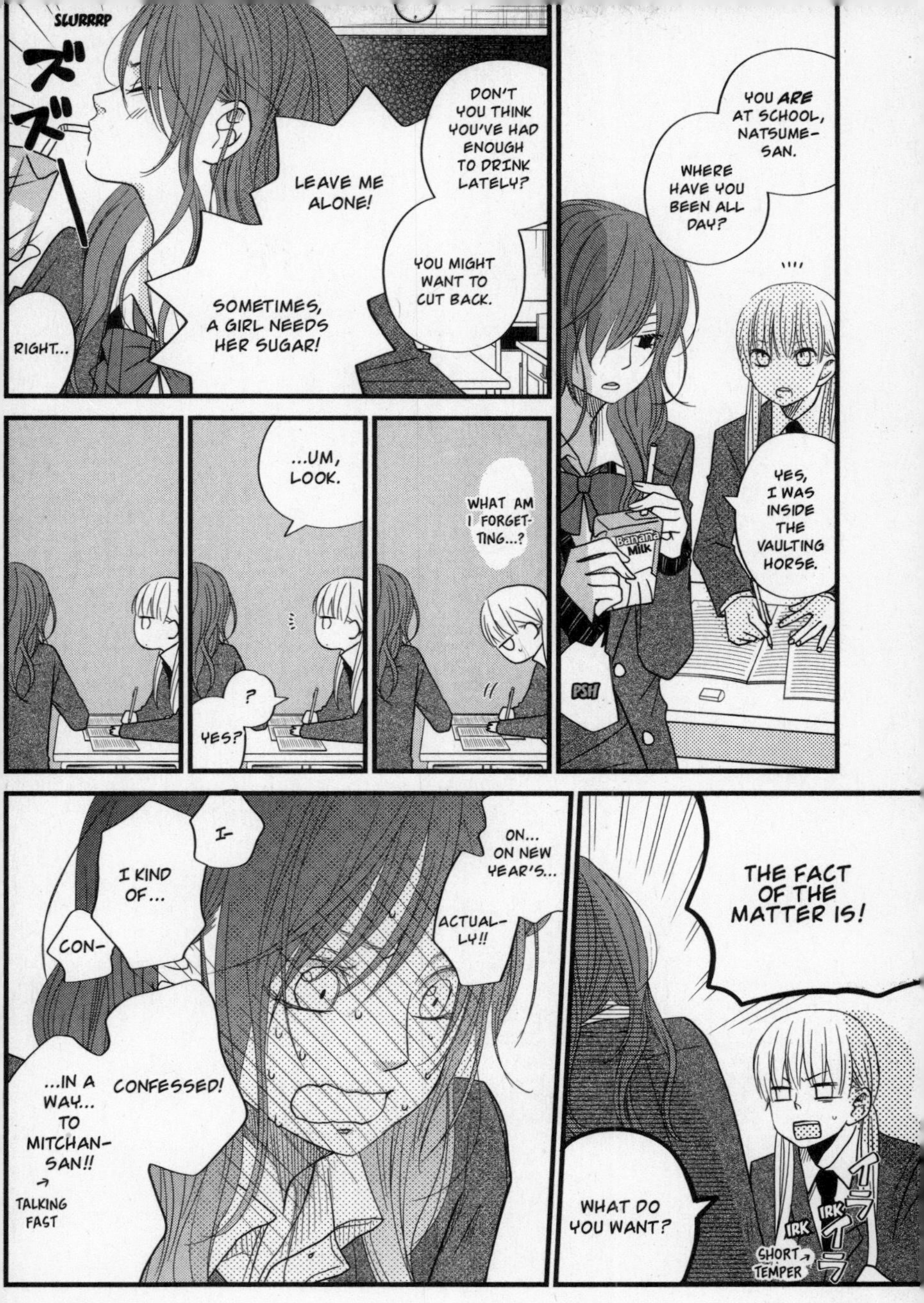
YOU ARE AT SCHOOL, NATSUME-SAN.
WHERE HAVE YOU BEEN ALL DAY?
'''
YES, I WAS INSIDE THE VAULTING HORSE.
Banana Milk
PSH
DON'T YOU THINK YOU'VE HAD ENOUGH TO DRINK LATELY?
YOU MIGHT WANT TO CUT BACK.
LEAVE ME ALONE!
SOMETIMES, A GIRL NEEDS HER SUGAR!
SLURRRP
ズズー
RIGHT...
WHAT AM I FORGET-TING...?
...UM, LOOK.
?
YES?
THE FACT OF THE MATTER IS!
WHAT DO YOU WANT?
IRK IRK
イライラ
SHORT TEMPER
ON... ON NEW YEAR'S...
ACTUAL-LY!!
I-
I KIND OF...
CON-
CONFESSED!
...IN A WAY... TO MITCHAN-SAN!!
TALKING FAST

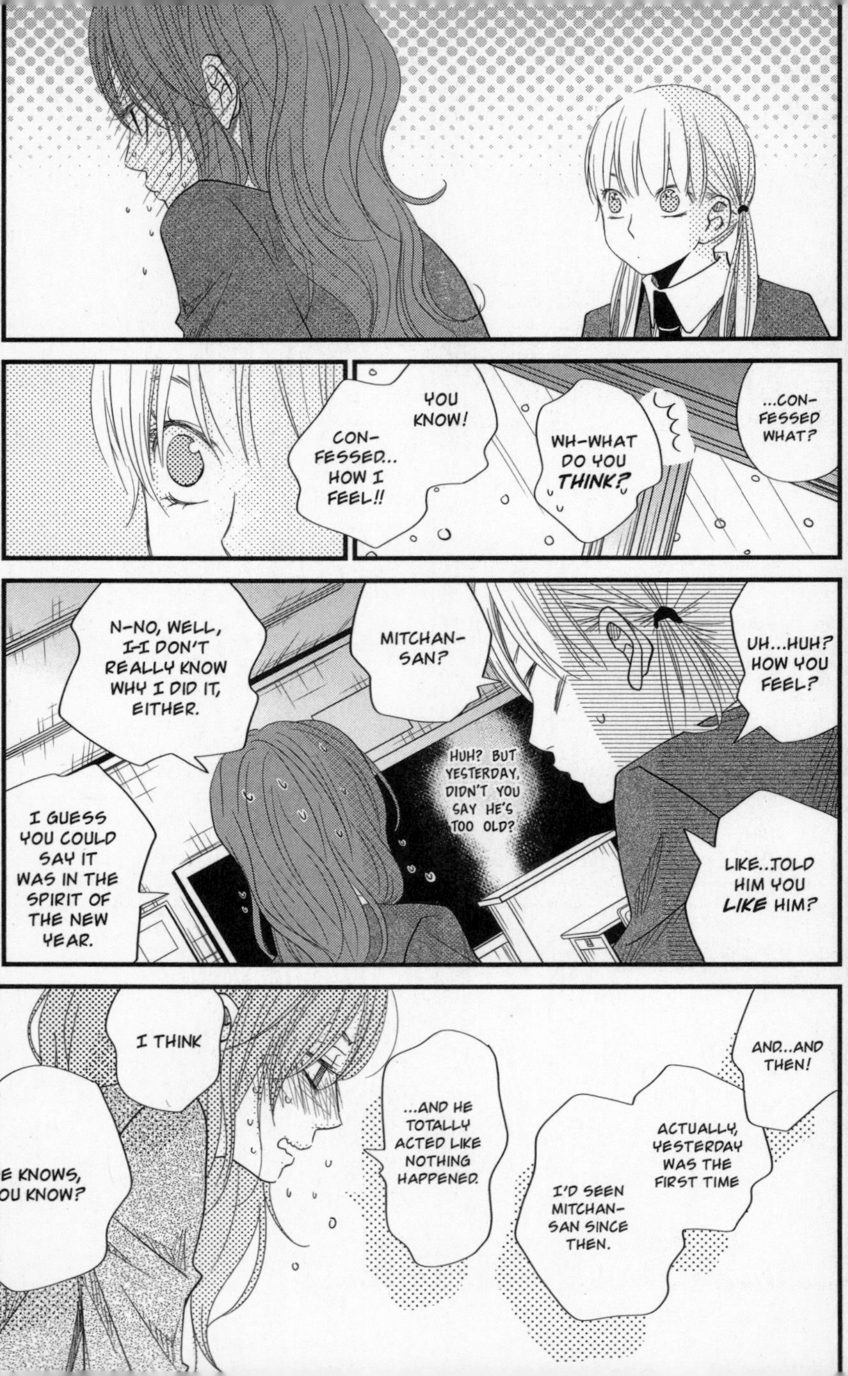
...CONFESSED WHAT?
WH-WHAT DO YOU THINK?
YOU KNOW! CONFESSED... HOW I FEEL!!
UH...HUH? HOW YOU FEEL?
MITCHAN-SAN?
N-NO, WELL, I-I DON'T REALLY KNOW WHY I DID IT, EITHER.
LIKE...TOLD HIM YOU LIKE HIM?
HUH? BUT YESTERDAY, DIDN'T YOU SAY HE'S TOO OLD?
I GUESS YOU COULD SAY IT WAS IN THE SPIRIT OF THE NEW YEAR.
AND...AND THEN!
ACTUALLY, YESTERDAY WAS THE FIRST TIME
I'D SEEN MITCHAN-SAN SINCE THEN.
...AND HE TOTALLY ACTED LIKE NOTHING HAPPENED.
I THINK
HE KNOWS, YOU KNOW?

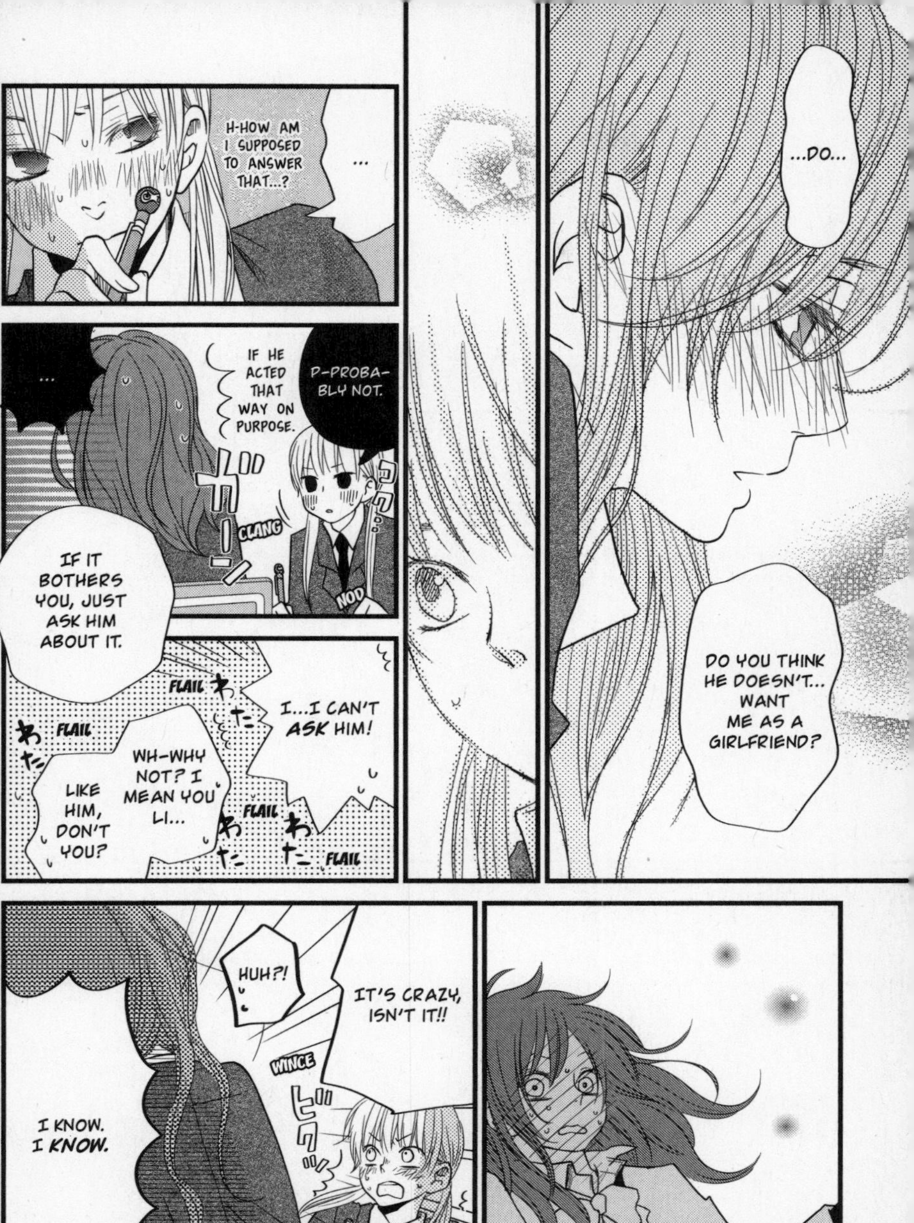
...DO...
DO YOU THINK HE DOESN'T... WANT ME AS A GIRLFRIEND?
...
H-HOW AM I SUPPOSED TO ANSWER THAT...?
P-PROBA-BLY NOT.
IF HE ACTED THAT WAY ON PURPOSE.
...
CLANG
NOD
IF IT BOTHERS YOU, JUST ASK HIM ABOUT IT.
I...I CAN'T ASK HIM!
FLAIL
FLAIL
WH-WHY NOT? I MEAN YOU LI...
LIKE HIM, DON'T YOU?
FLAIL
FLAIL
IT'S CRAZY, ISN'T IT!!
HUH?!
WINCE
I KNOW. I KNOW.

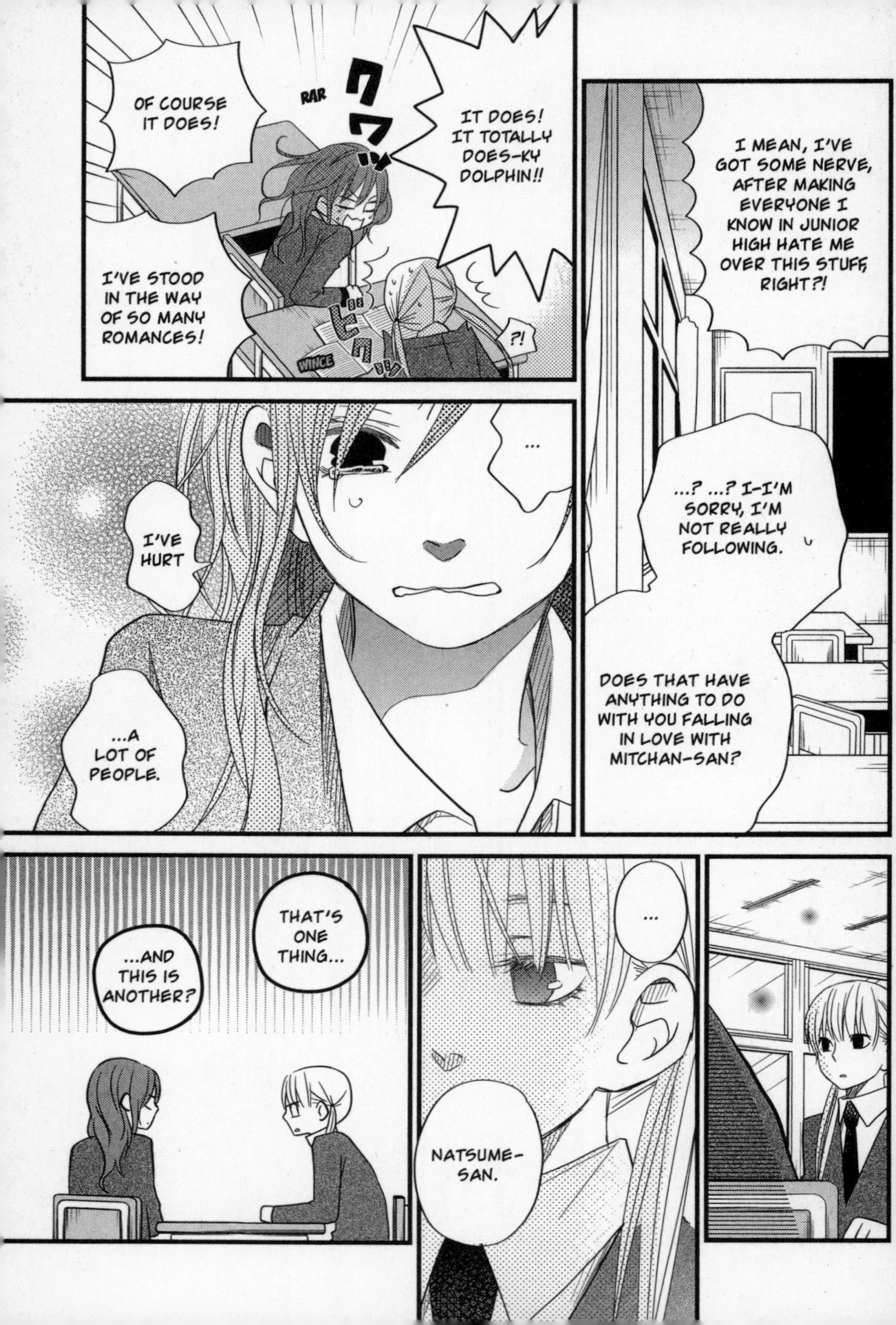
I MEAN, I'VE GOT SOME NERVE, AFTER MAKING EVERYONE I KNOW IN JUNIOR HIGH HATE ME OVER THIS STUFF, RIGHT?!
...? ...? I-I'M SORRY, I'M NOT REALLY FOLLOWING.
DOES THAT HAVE ANYTHING TO DO WITH YOU FALLING IN LOVE WITH MITCHAN-SAN?
IT DOES! IT TOTALLY DOES-KY DOLPHIN!!
RAR
OF COURSE IT DOES!
?!
I'VE STOOD IN THE WAY OF SO MANY ROMANCES!
WINCE
...
I'VE HURT
...A LOT OF PEOPLE.
...
NATSUME-SAN.
THAT'S ONE THING...
...AND THIS IS ANOTHER?

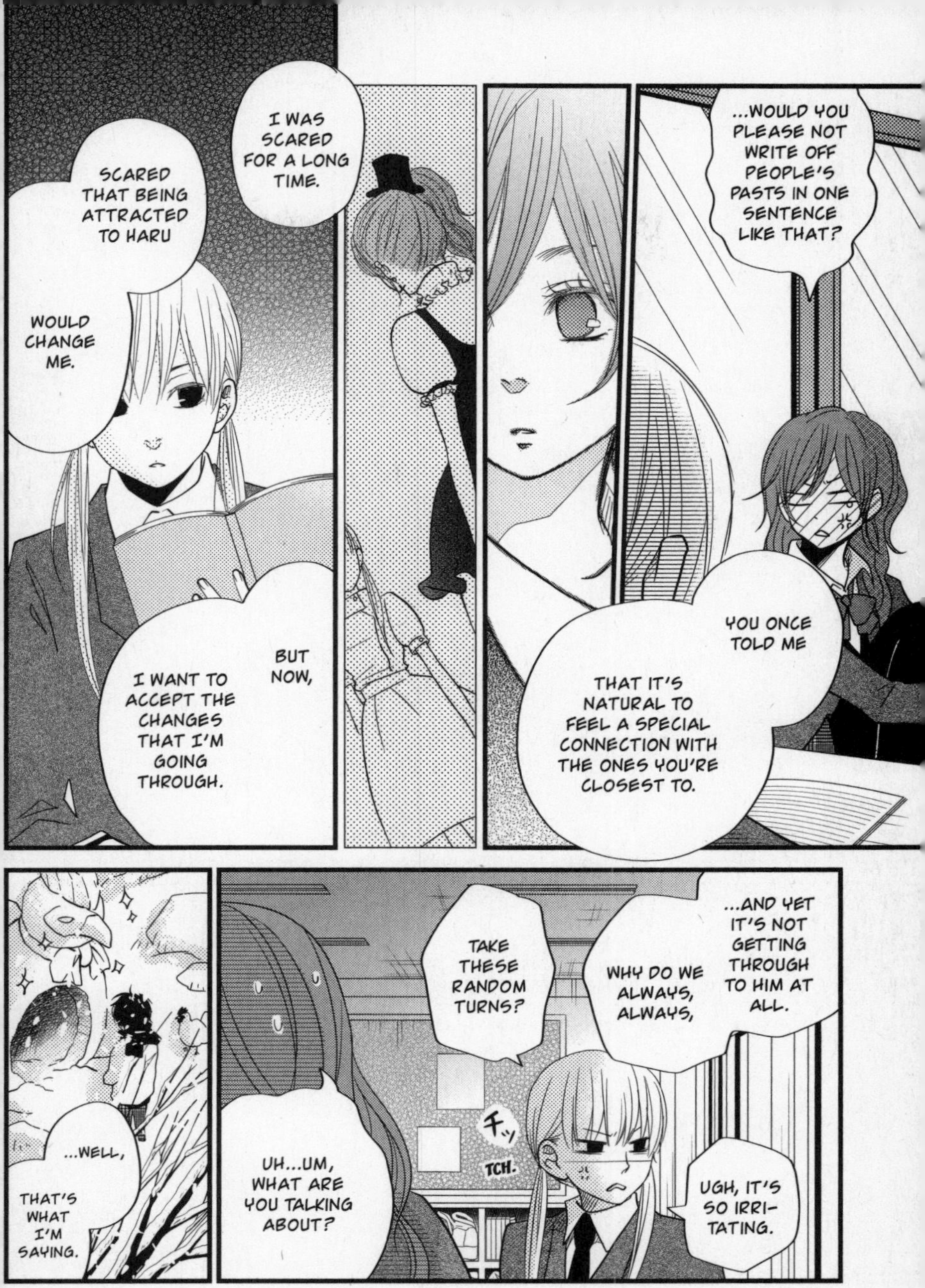
...WOULD YOU PLEASE NOT WRITE OFF PEOPLE'S PASTS IN ONE SENTENCE LIKE THAT?
YOU ONCE TOLD ME
THAT IT'S NATURAL TO FEEL A SPECIAL CONNECTION WITH THE ONES YOU'RE CLOSEST TO.
I WAS SCARED FOR A LONG TIME.
SCARED THAT BEING ATTRACTED TO HARU
WOULD CHANGE ME.
BUT NOW,
I WANT TO ACCEPT THE CHANGES THAT I'M GOING THROUGH.
...AND YET IT'S NOT GETTING THROUGH TO HIM AT ALL.
WHY DO WE ALWAYS, ALWAYS,
TAKE THESE RANDOM TURNS?
チッ
TCH.
UGH, IT'S SO IRRI-TATING.
UH...UM, WHAT ARE YOU TALKING ABOUT?
...WELL,
THAT'S WHAT I'M SAYING.

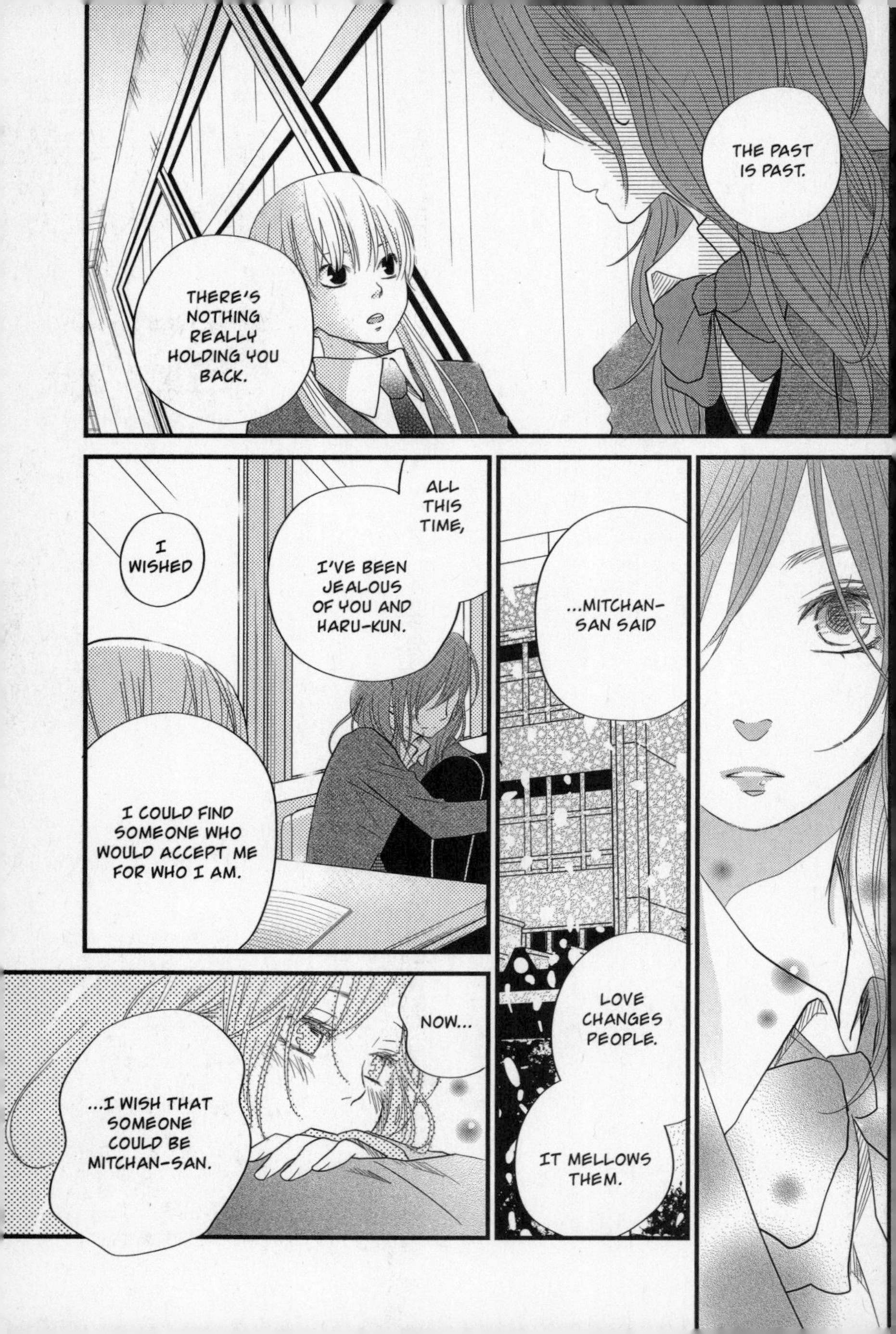
THE PAST IS PAST.
THERE'S NOTHING REALLY HOLDING YOU BACK.
...MITCHAN-SAN SAID
LOVE CHANGES PEOPLE.
IT MELLOWS THEM.
ALL THIS TIME,
I'VE BEEN JEALOUS OF YOU AND HARU-KUN.
I WISHED
I COULD FIND SOMEONE WHO WOULD ACCEPT ME FOR WHO I AM.
NOW...
...I WISH THAT SOMEONE COULD BE MITCHAN-SAN.

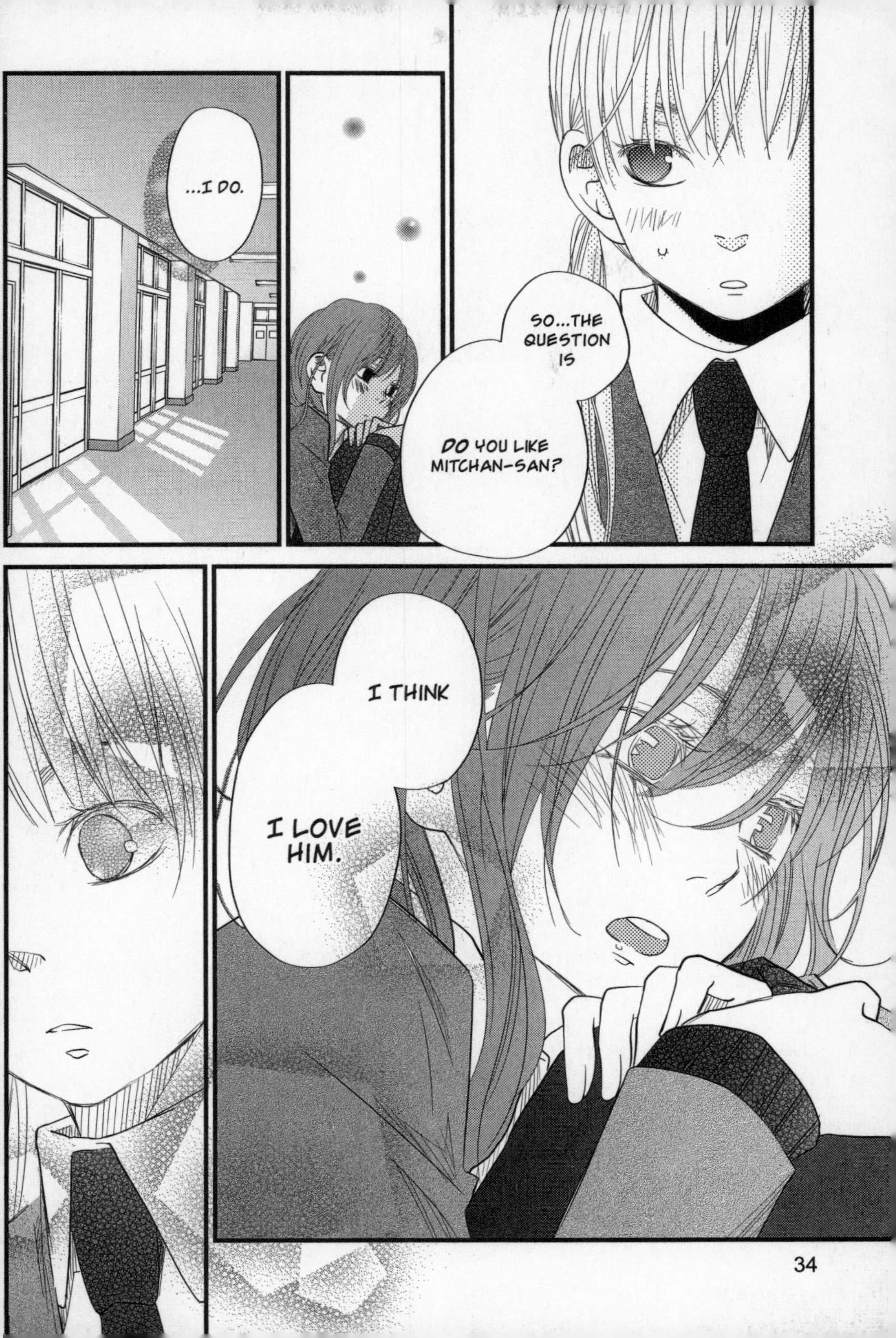
SO...THE QUESTION IS
DO YOU LIKE MITCHAN-SAN?
...I DO.
I THINK
I LOVE HIM.

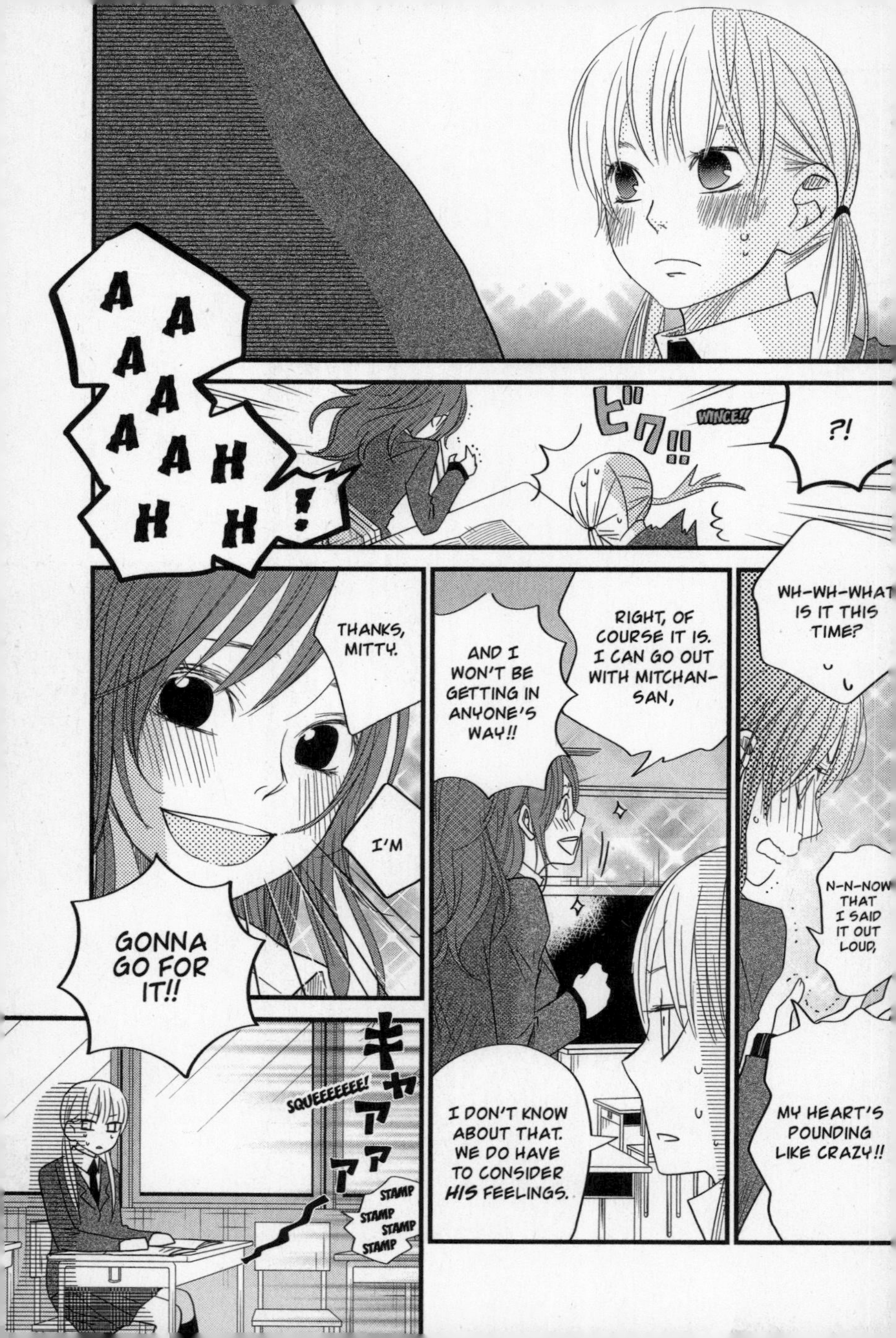
?!
ビクッ!!
WINCE!!
AAAAAAAHHH!
WH-WH-WHAT IS IT THIS TIME?
N-N-NOW THAT I SAID IT OUT LOUD,
MY HEART'S POUNDING LIKE CRAZY!!
RIGHT, OF COURSE IT IS. I CAN GO OUT WITH MITCHAN-SAN,
AND I WON'T BE GETTING IN ANYONE'S WAY!!
I DON'T KNOW ABOUT THAT. WE DO HAVE TO CONSIDER *HIS* FEELINGS.
THANKS, MITTY.
I'M
GONNA GO FOR IT!!
キャアアア
SQUEEEEEEE!
STAMP STAMP STAMP STAMP

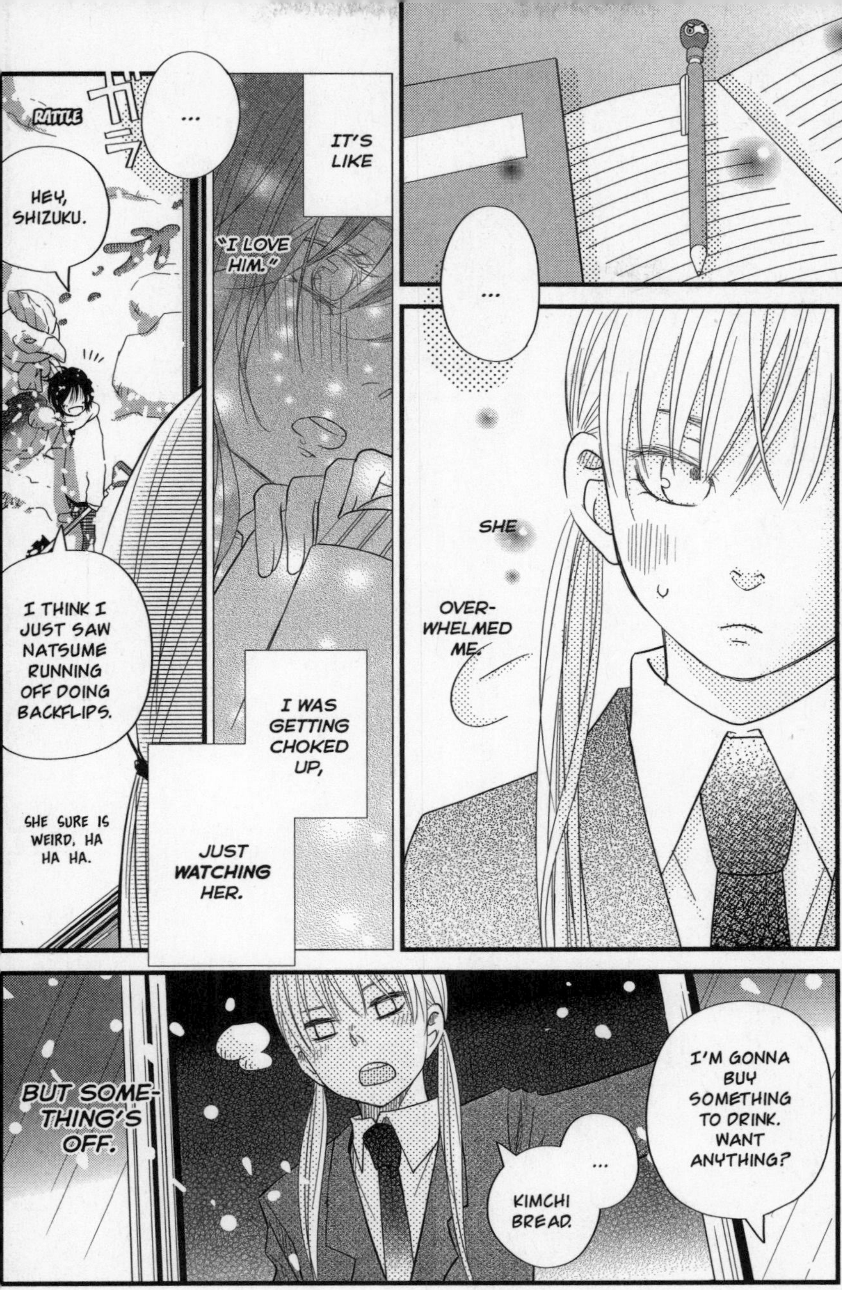
...
SHE OVERWHELMED ME.
IT'S LIKE
"I LOVE HIM."
I WAS GETTING CHOKED UP,
JUST WATCHING HER.
...
RATTLE
HEY, SHIZUKU.
I THINK I JUST SAW NATSUME RUNNING OFF DOING BACKFLIPS.
SHE SURE IS WEIRD, HA HA HA.
I'M GONNA BUY SOMETHING TO DRINK. WANT ANYTHING?
...
KIMCHI BREAD.
BUT SOME-THING'S OFF.

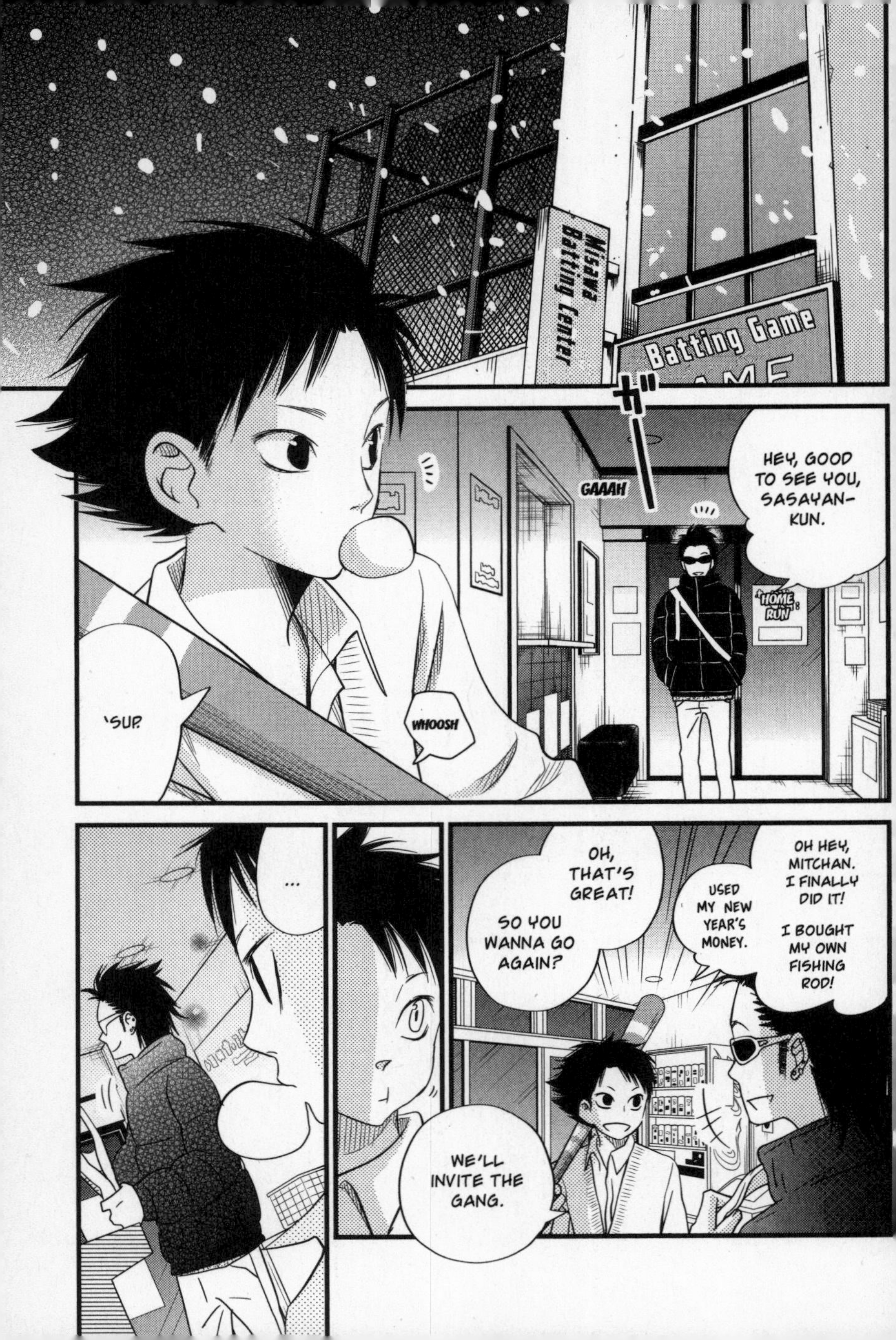
Misawa Batting Center
Batting Game
ガー
GAAAH
HEY, GOOD TO SEE YOU, SASAYAN-KUN.
HOME RUN
'SUP.
WHOOSH
OH HEY, MITCHAN. I FINALLY DID IT!
I BOUGHT MY OWN FISHING ROD!
USED MY NEW YEAR'S MONEY.
OH, THAT'S GREAT!
SO YOU WANNA GO AGAIN?
WE'LL INVITE THE GANG.
...

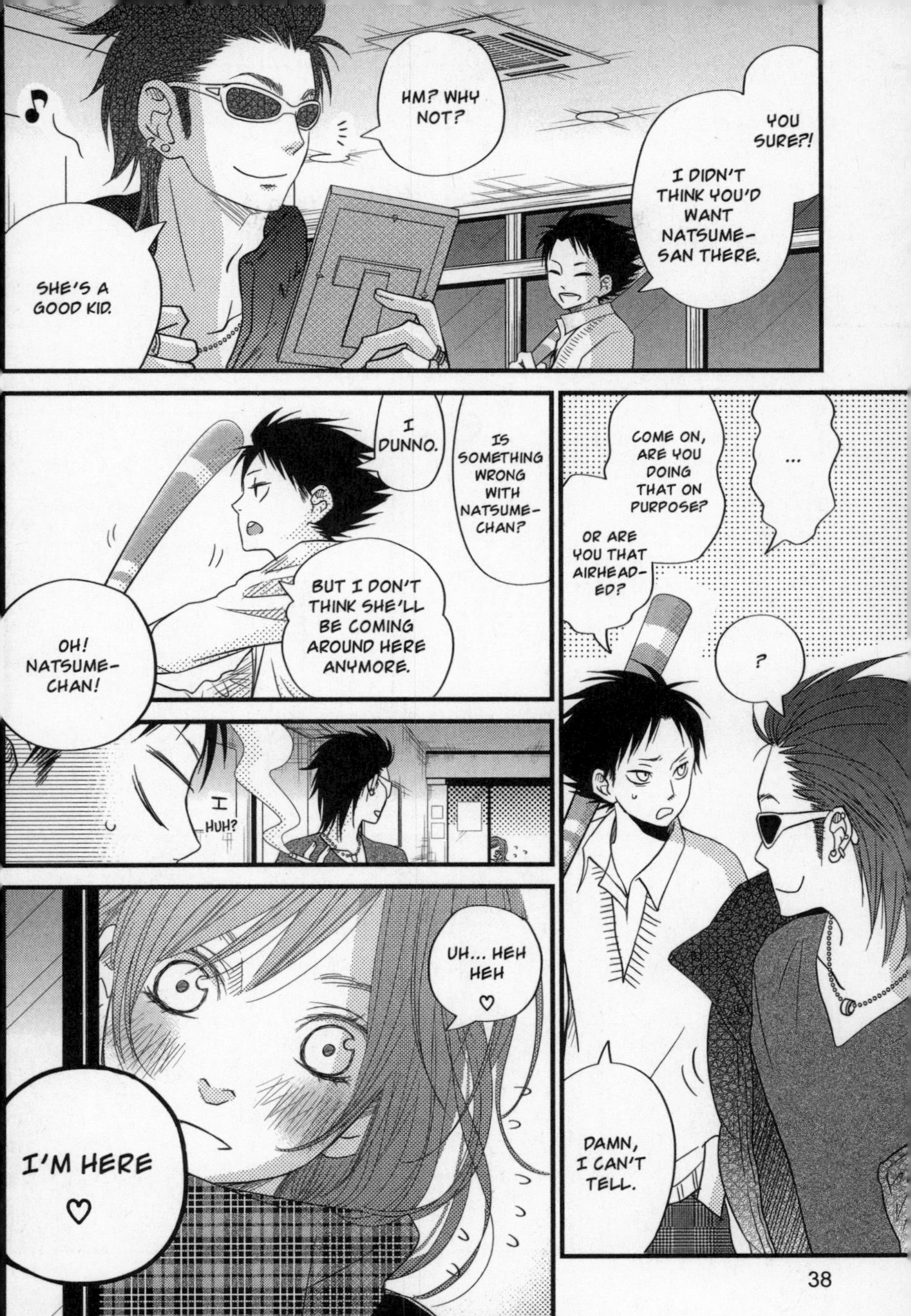
YOU SURE?!
I DIDN'T THINK YOU'D WANT NATSUME-SAN THERE.
HM? WHY NOT?
SHE'S A GOOD KID.
...
COME ON, ARE YOU DOING THAT ON PURPOSE?
OR ARE YOU THAT AIRHEAD-ED?
?
DAMN, I CAN'T TELL.
IS SOMETHING WRONG WITH NATSUME-CHAN?
I DUNNO.
BUT I DON'T THINK SHE'LL BE COMING AROUND HERE ANYMORE.
OH! NATSUME-CHAN!
I
HUH?
UH... HEH HEH ♡
I'M HERE ♡

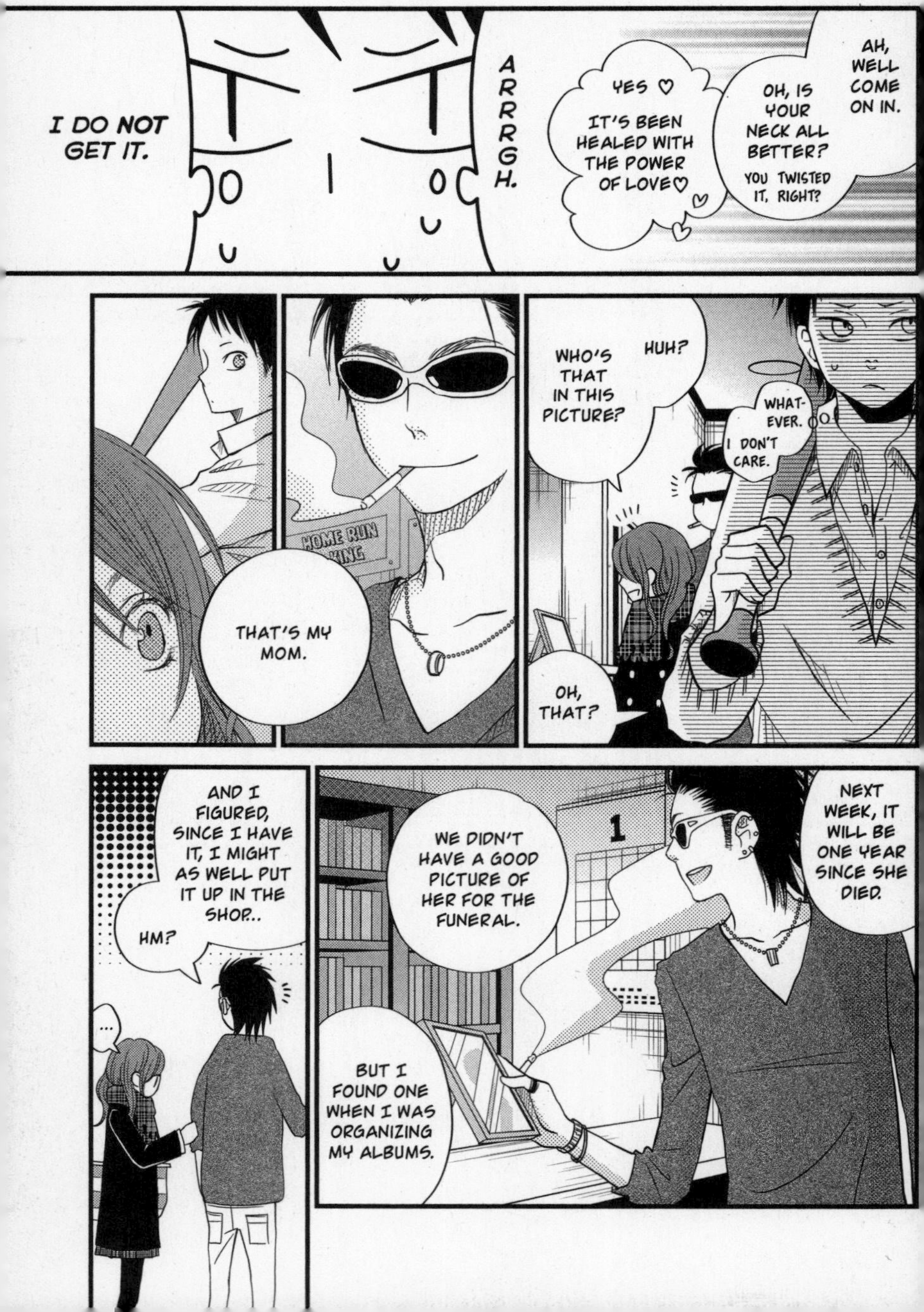
AH, WELL COME ON IN.
OH, IS YOUR NECK ALL BETTER?
YOU TWISTED IT, RIGHT?
YES ♡
IT'S BEEN HEALED WITH THE POWER OF LOVE♡
ARRRGH.
I DO NOT GET IT.
HUH?
WHO'S THAT IN THIS PICTURE?
WHAT-EVER.
I DON'T CARE.
OH, THAT?
HOME RUN KING
THAT'S MY MOM.
NEXT WEEK, IT WILL BE ONE YEAR SINCE SHE DIED.
1
WE DIDN'T HAVE A GOOD PICTURE OF HER FOR THE FUNERAL.
BUT I FOUND ONE WHEN I WAS ORGANIZING MY ALBUMS.
AND I FIGURED, SINCE I HAVE IT, I MIGHT AS WELL PUT IT UP IN THE SHOP..
HM?
...

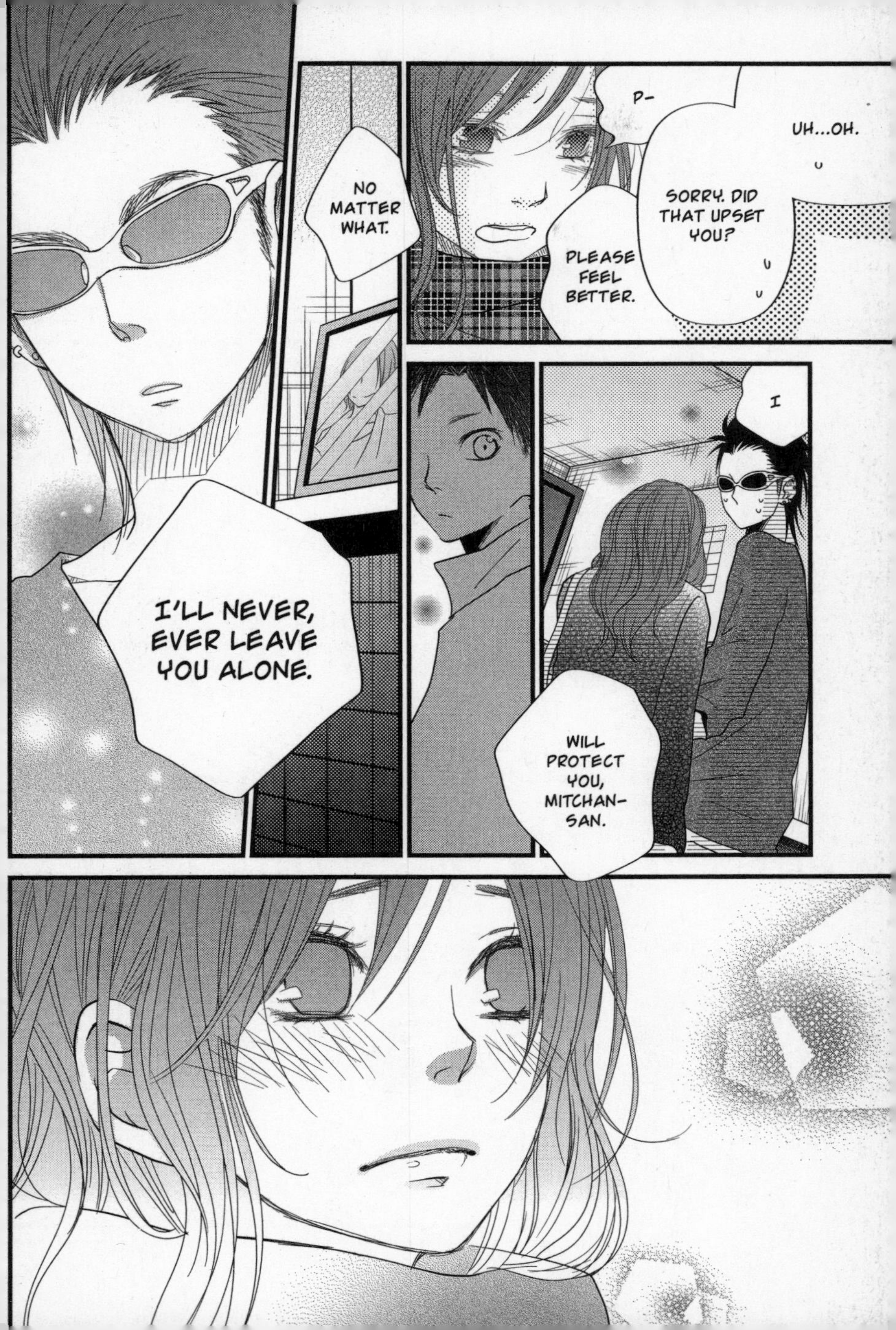
UH...OH.
SORRY. DID THAT UPSET YOU?
P-
PLEASE FEEL BETTER.
I
WILL PROTECT YOU, MITCHAN-SAN.
NO MATTER WHAT.
I'LL NEVER, EVER LEAVE YOU ALONE.

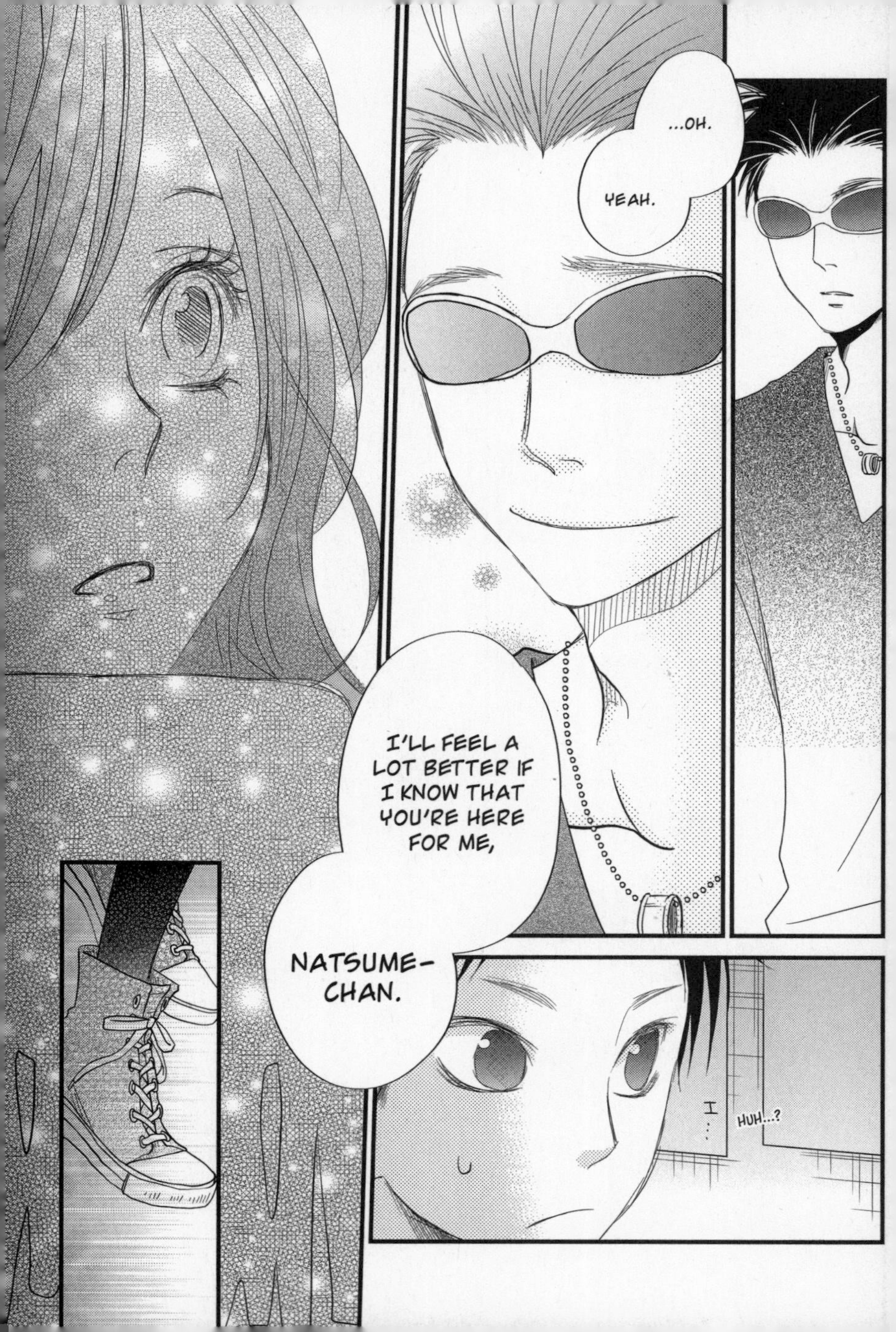
...OH.
YEAH.
I'LL FEEL A LOT BETTER IF I KNOW THAT YOU'RE HERE FOR ME,
NATSUME-CHAN.
I...
HUH...?

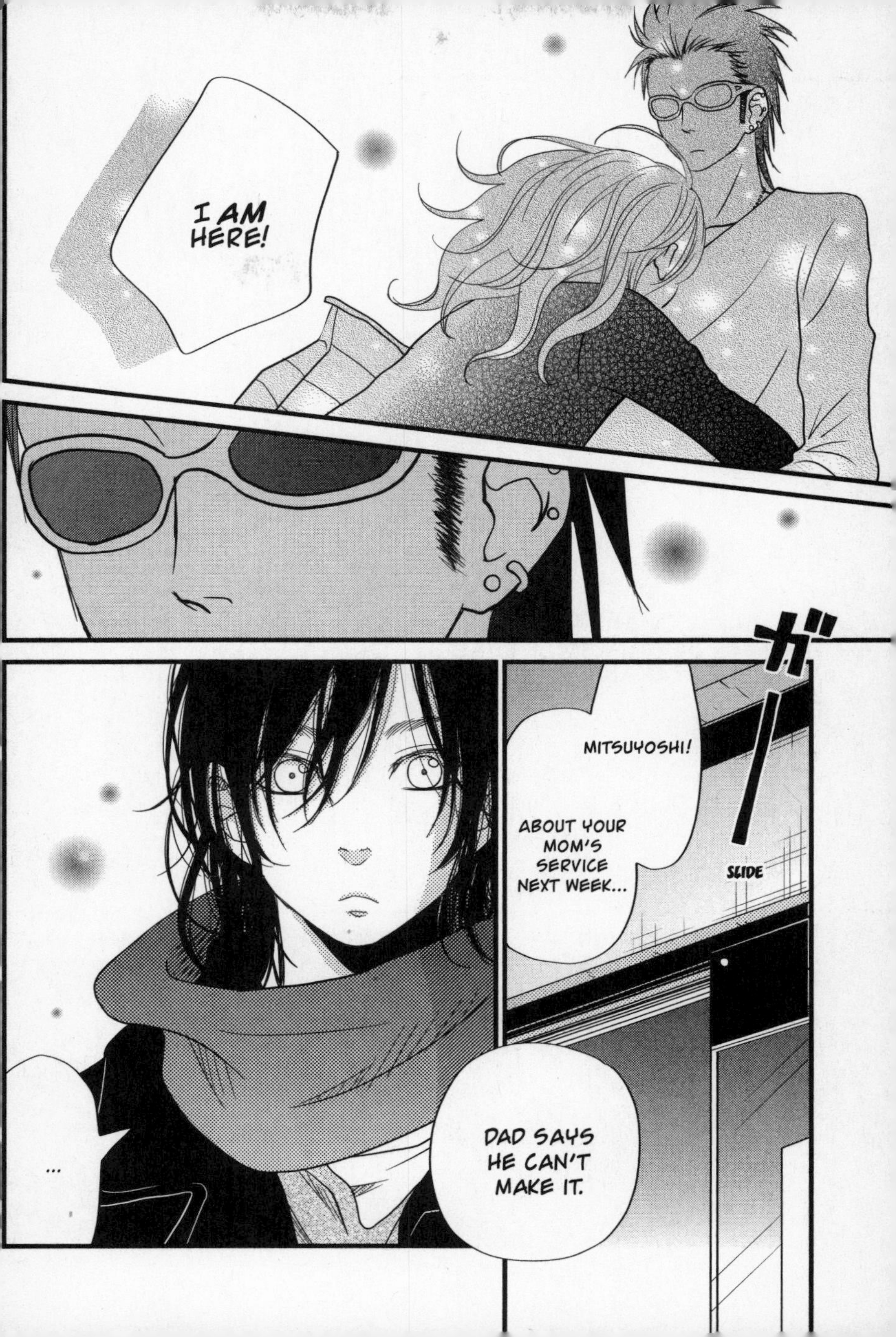
I AM HERE!
ガー
SLIDE
MITSUYOSHI!
ABOUT YOUR MOM'S SERVICE NEXT WEEK...
DAD SAYS HE CAN'T MAKE IT.
...

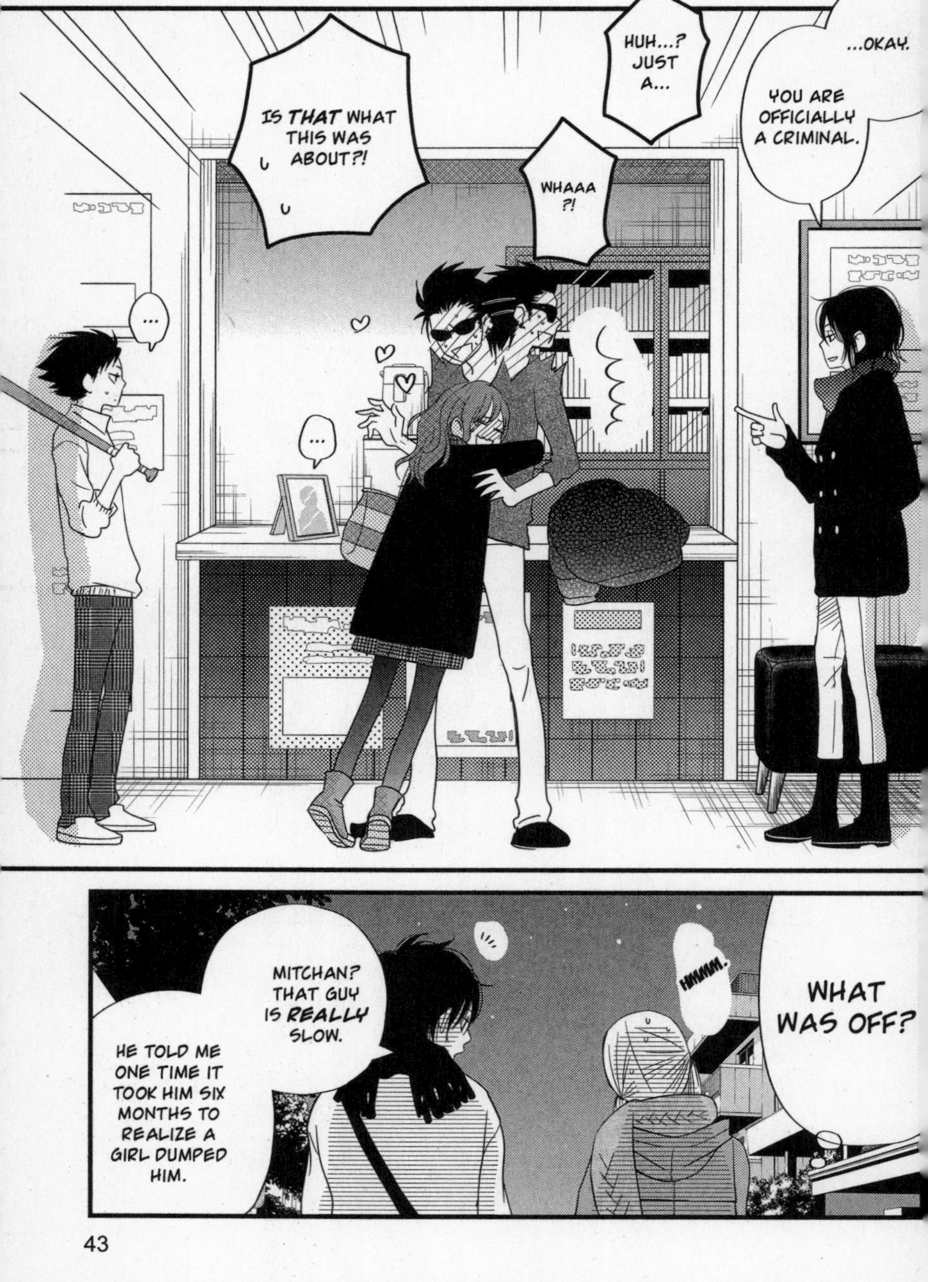
...OKAY.
YOU ARE OFFICIALLY A CRIMINAL.
HUH...? JUST A...
WHAAA?!
IS THAT WHAT THIS WAS ABOUT?!
...
...
WHAT WAS OFF?
HMMM.
MITCHAN? THAT GUY IS REALLY SLOW.
HE TOLD ME ONE TIME IT TOOK HIM SIX MONTHS TO REALIZE A GIRL DUMPED HIM.

My Net Persona

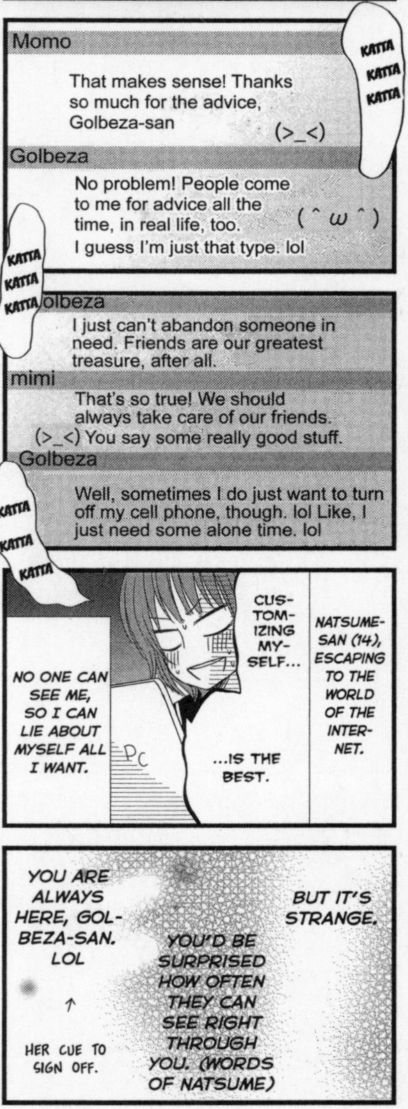
KATTA KATTA KATTA
Momo
That makes sense! Thanks so much for the advice, Golbeza-san
(>_<)
Golbeza
No problem! People come to me for advice all the time, in real life, too.
(^ ω ^)
I guess I'm just that type. lol
KATTA KATTA KATTA
olbeza
I just can't abandon someone in need. Friends are our greatest treasure, after all.
mimi
That's so true! We should always take care of our friends.
(>_<) You say some really good stuff.
KATTA KATTA KATTA
Golbeza
Well, sometimes I do just want to turn off my cell phone, though. lol Like, I just need some alone time. lol
NATSUME-SAN (14), ESCAPING TO THE WORLD OF THE INTERNET.
CUS-TOM-IZING MY-SELF...
...IS THE BEST.
NO ONE CAN SEE ME, SO I CAN LIE ABOUT MYSELF ALL I WANT.
PC
BUT IT'S STRANGE.
YOU'D BE SURPRISED HOW OFTEN THEY CAN SEE RIGHT THROUGH YOU. (WORDS OF NATSUME)
YOU ARE ALWAYS HERE, GOL-BEZA-SAN. LOL
↑
HER CUE TO SIGN OFF.

Snow

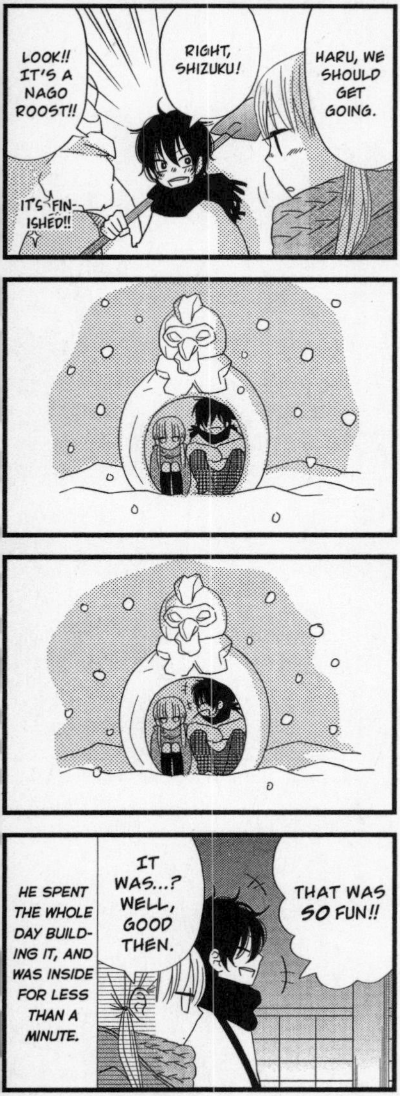
HARU, WE SHOULD GET GOING.
RIGHT, SHIZUKU!
LOOK!! IT'S A NAGO ROOST!!
IT'S FIN-ISHED!!
THAT WAS SO FUN!!
IT WAS...? WELL, GOOD THEN.
HE SPENT THE WHOLE DAY BUILD-ING IT, AND WAS INSIDE FOR LESS THAN A MINUTE.

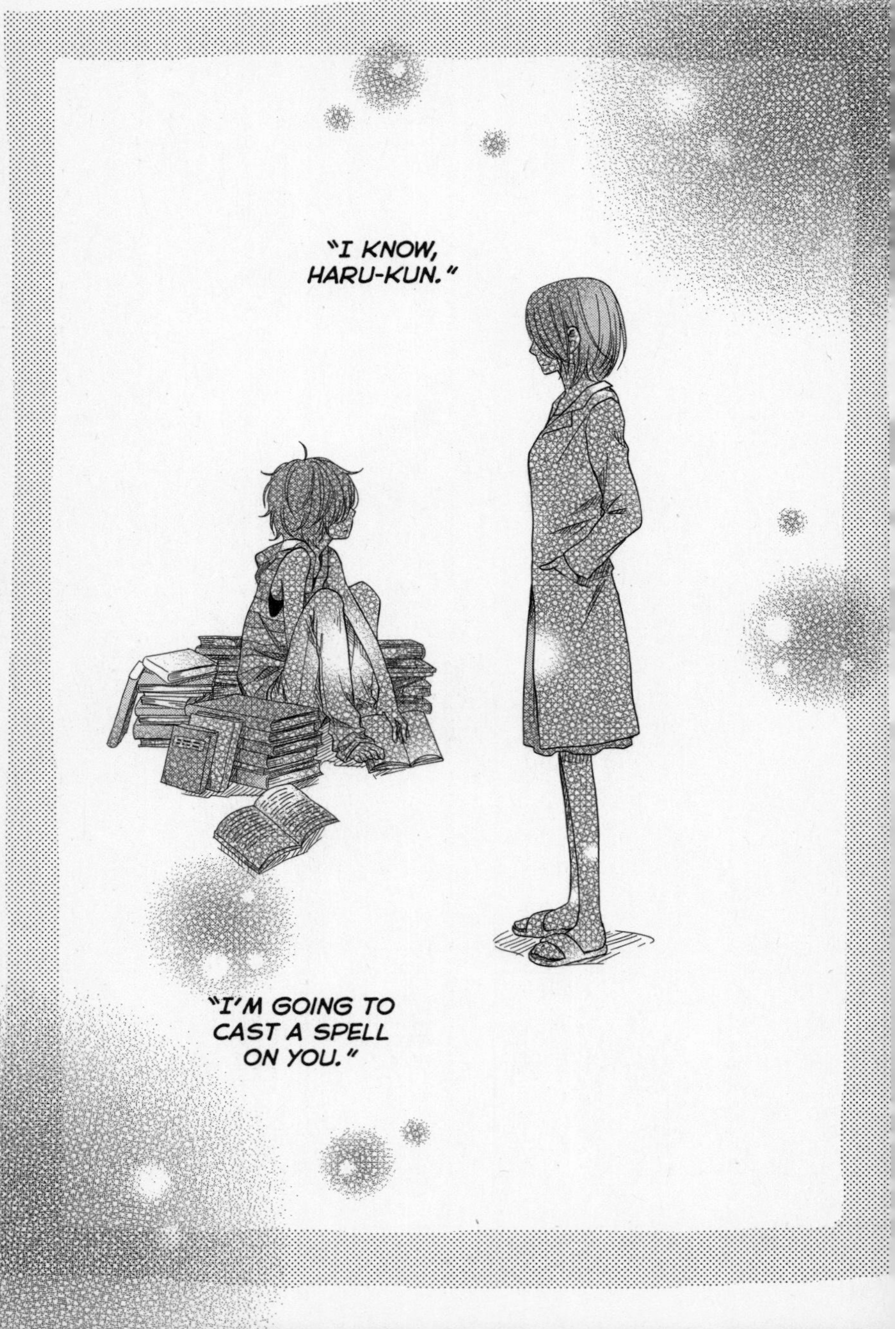
"I KNOW, HARU-KUN."
"I'M GOING TO CAST A SPELL ON YOU."

Chapter 18 A Dubious Day Off

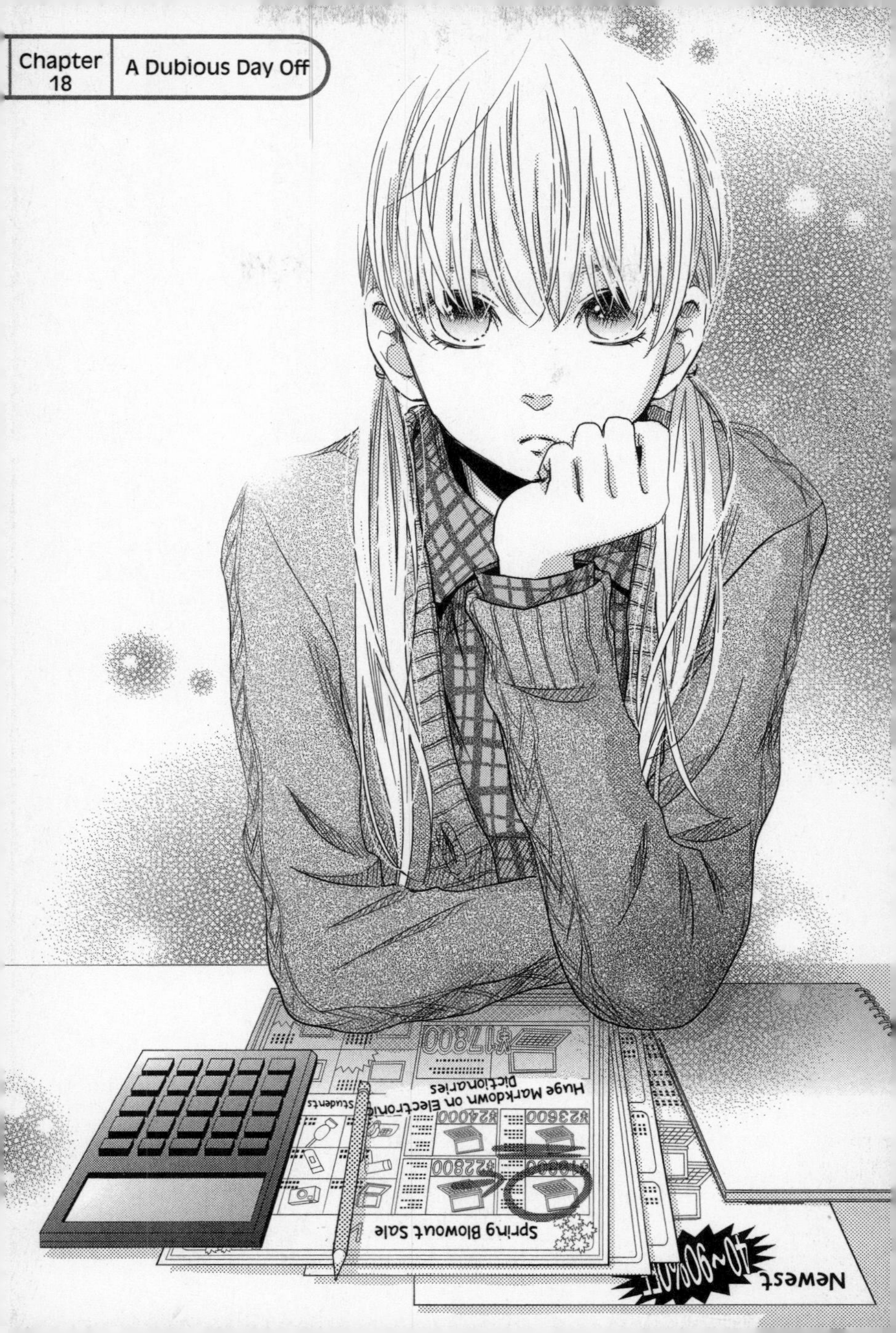

¥17800
Huge Markdown on Electronic Dictionaries
Students
¥23600
¥24000
¥10800
¥22800
Spring Blowout Sale
Newest
40~90% OFF

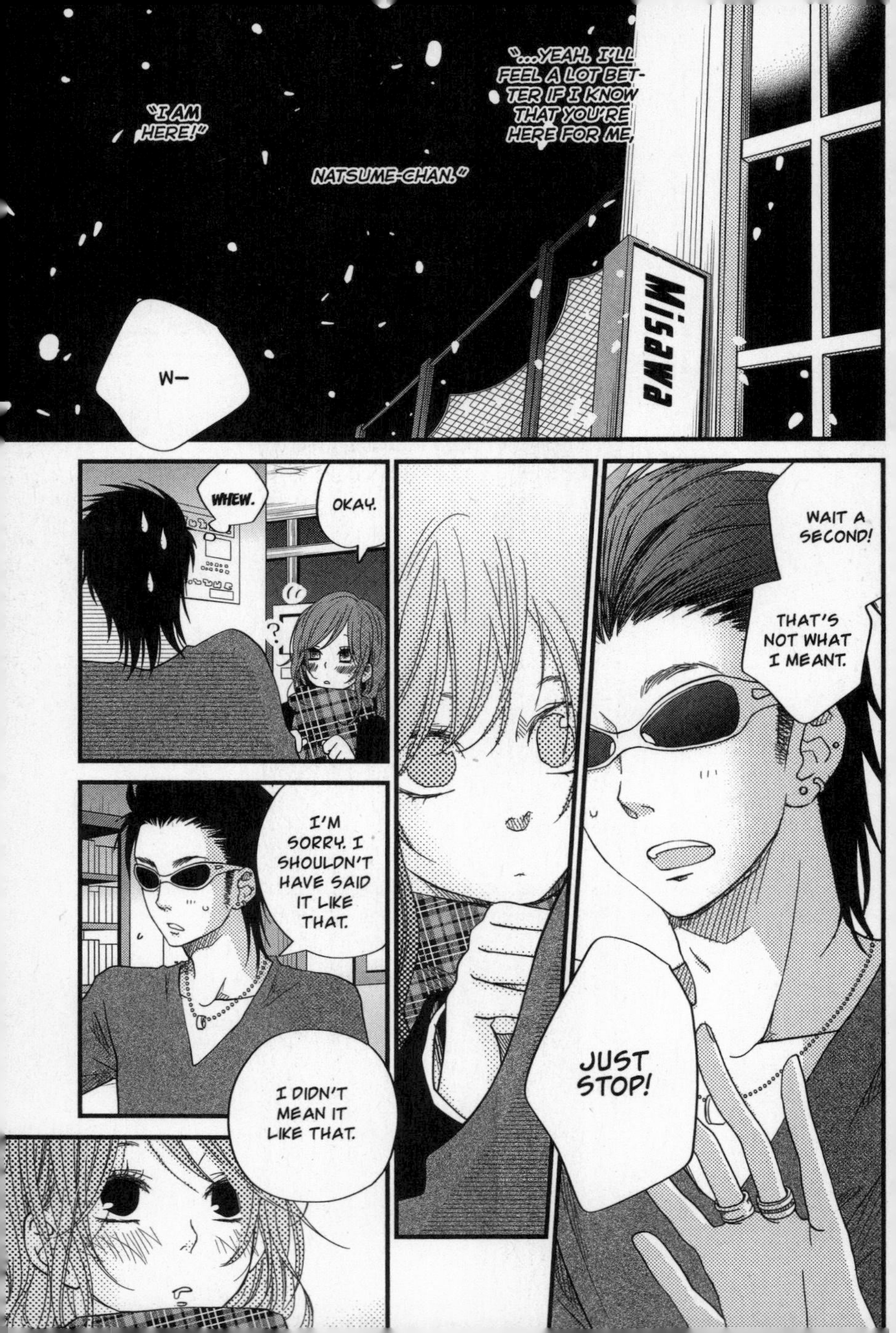
"...YEAH, I'LL FEEL A LOT BETTER IF I KNOW THAT YOU'RE HERE FOR ME,
NATSUME-CHAN."
"I AM HERE!"
Misawa
W—
WAIT A SECOND!
THAT'S NOT WHAT I MEANT.
JUST STOP!
OKAY.
WHEW.
I'M SORRY. I SHOULDN'T HAVE SAID IT LIKE THAT.
I DIDN'T MEAN IT LIKE THAT.

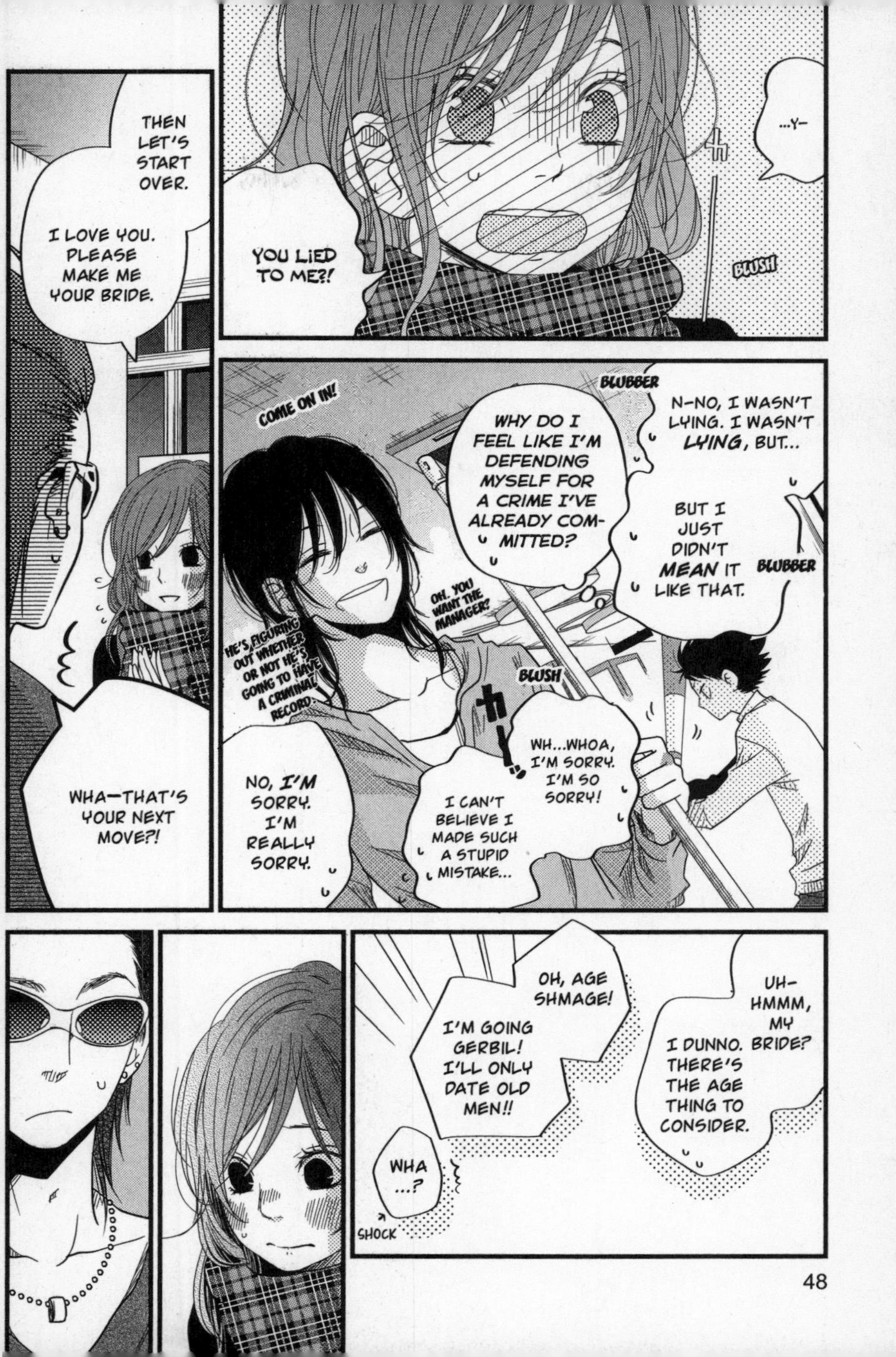
...Y-
BLUSH
YOU LIED TO ME?!
BLUBBER
N-NO, I WASN'T LYING. I WASN'T LYING, BUT...
BUT I JUST DIDN'T MEAN IT LIKE THAT.
BLUBBER
WHY DO I FEEL LIKE I'M DEFENDING MYSELF FOR A CRIME I'VE ALREADY COM-MITTED?
COME ON IN!
OH. YOU WANT THE MANAGER?
HE'S FIGURING OUT WHETHER OR NOT HE'S GOING TO HAVE A CRIMINAL RECORD.
BLUSH
WH...WHOA, I'M SORRY. I'M SO SORRY!
I CAN'T BELIEVE I MADE SUCH A STUPID MISTAKE...
NO, I'M SORRY. I'M REALLY SORRY.
THEN LET'S START OVER.
I LOVE YOU. PLEASE MAKE ME YOUR BRIDE.
WHA-THAT'S YOUR NEXT MOVE?!
UH-HMMM, MY BRIDE?
I DUNNO. THERE'S THE AGE THING TO CONSIDER.
OH, AGE SHMAGE!
I'M GOING GERBIL! I'LL ONLY DATE OLD MEN!!
WHA ...?
SHOCK

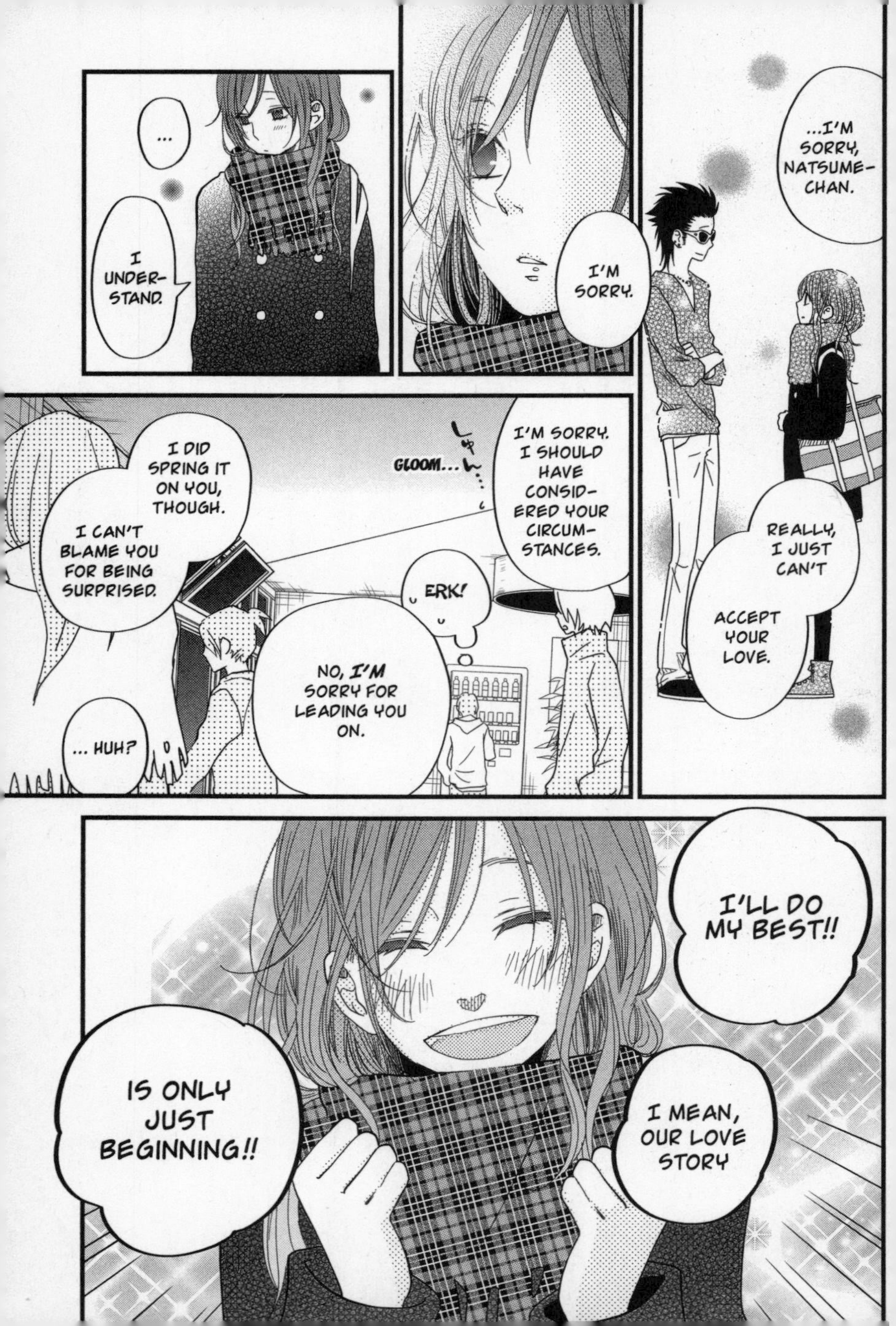
...I'M SORRY, NATSUME-CHAN.
REALLY, I JUST CAN'T
ACCEPT YOUR LOVE.
I'M SORRY.
...
I UNDER-STAND.
I'M SORRY. I SHOULD HAVE CONSID-ERED YOUR CIRCUM-STANCES.
しゅん…
GLOOM...
I DID SPRING IT ON YOU, THOUGH.
I CAN'T BLAME YOU FOR BEING SURPRISED.
ERK!
NO, *I'M* SORRY FOR LEADING YOU ON.
... HUH?
I'LL DO MY BEST!!
I MEAN, OUR LOVE STORY
IS ONLY JUST BEGINNING!!

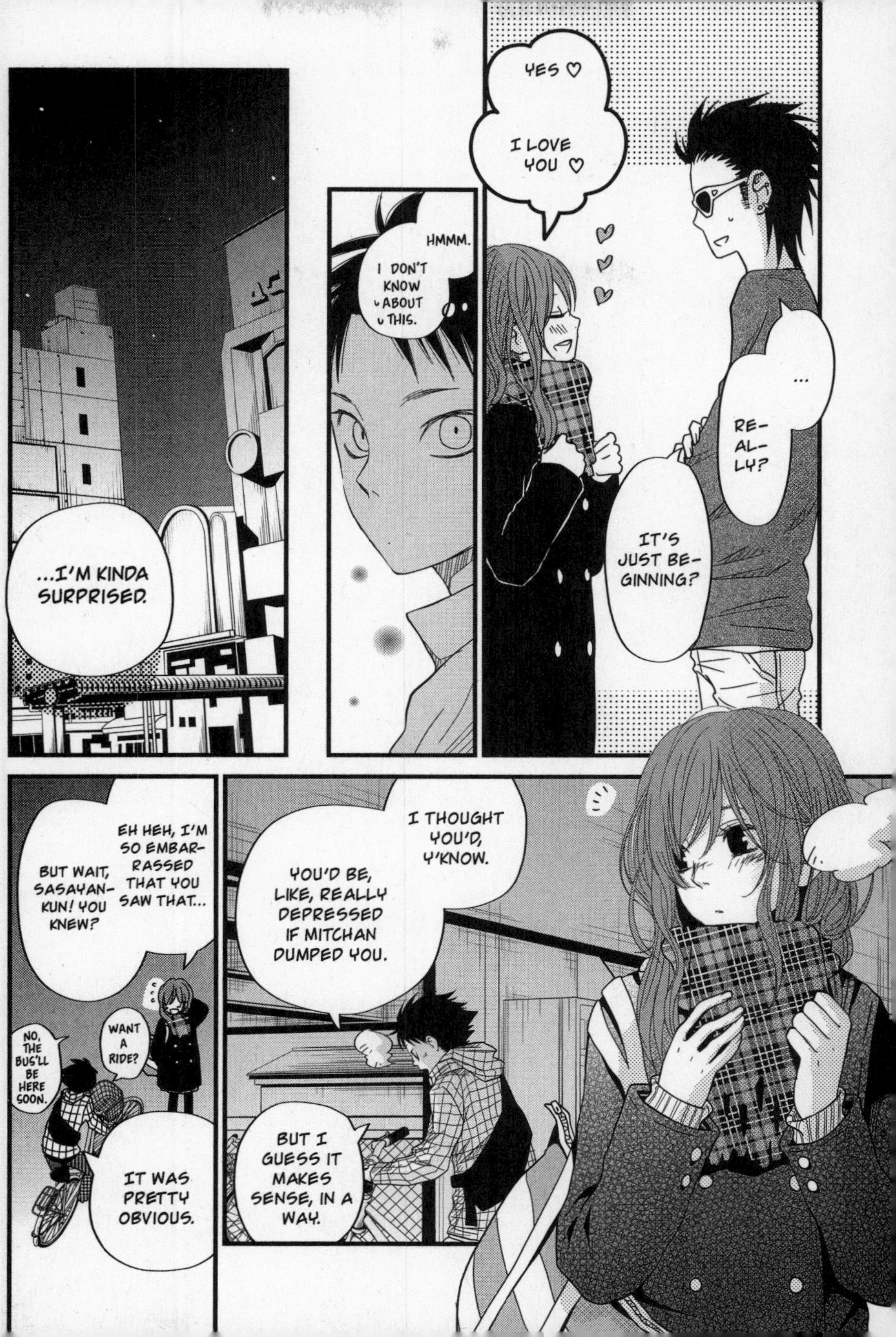
YES ♡ I LOVE YOU ♡
... RE-AL-LY?
IT'S JUST BE-GINNING?
HMMM. I DON'T KNOW ABOUT THIS.
...I'M KINDA SURPRISED.
I THOUGHT YOU'D, Y'KNOW.
YOU'D BE, LIKE, REALLY DEPRESSED IF MITCHAN DUMPED YOU.
BUT I GUESS IT MAKES SENSE, IN A WAY.
EH HEH, I'M SO EMBAR-RASSED THAT YOU SAW THAT...
BUT WAIT, SASAYAN-KUN! YOU KNEW?
WANT A RIDE?
NO, THE BUS'LL BE HERE SOON.
IT WAS PRETTY OBVIOUS.

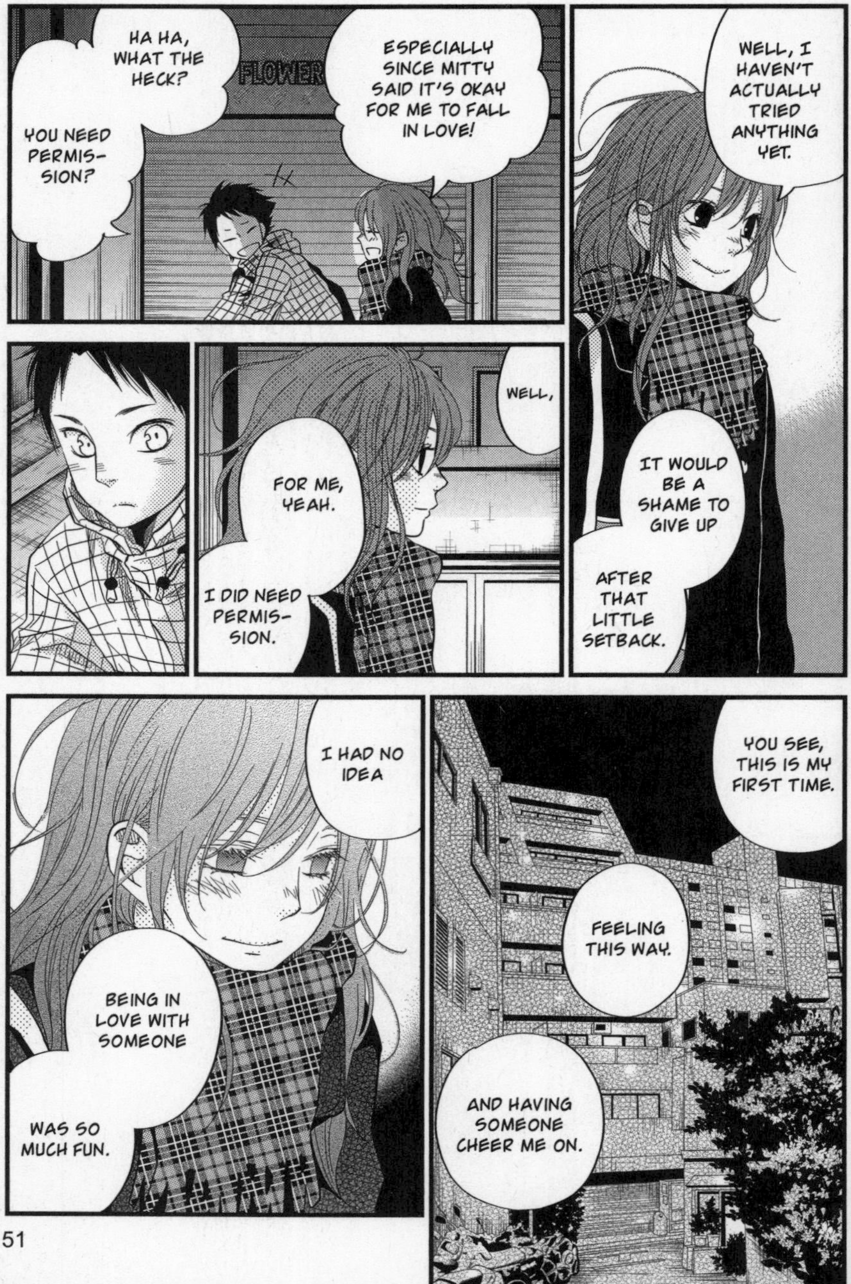
WELL, I HAVEN'T ACTUALLY TRIED ANYTHING YET.
IT WOULD BE A SHAME TO GIVE UP
AFTER THAT LITTLE SETBACK.
FLOWER
ESPECIALLY SINCE MITTY SAID IT'S OKAY FOR ME TO FALL IN LOVE!
HA HA, WHAT THE HECK?
YOU NEED PERMISSION?
WELL,
FOR ME, YEAH.
I DID NEED PERMISSION.
YOU SEE, THIS IS MY FIRST TIME.
FEELING THIS WAY.
AND HAVING SOMEONE CHEER ME ON.
I HAD NO IDEA
BEING IN LOVE WITH SOMEONE
WAS SO MUCH FUN.

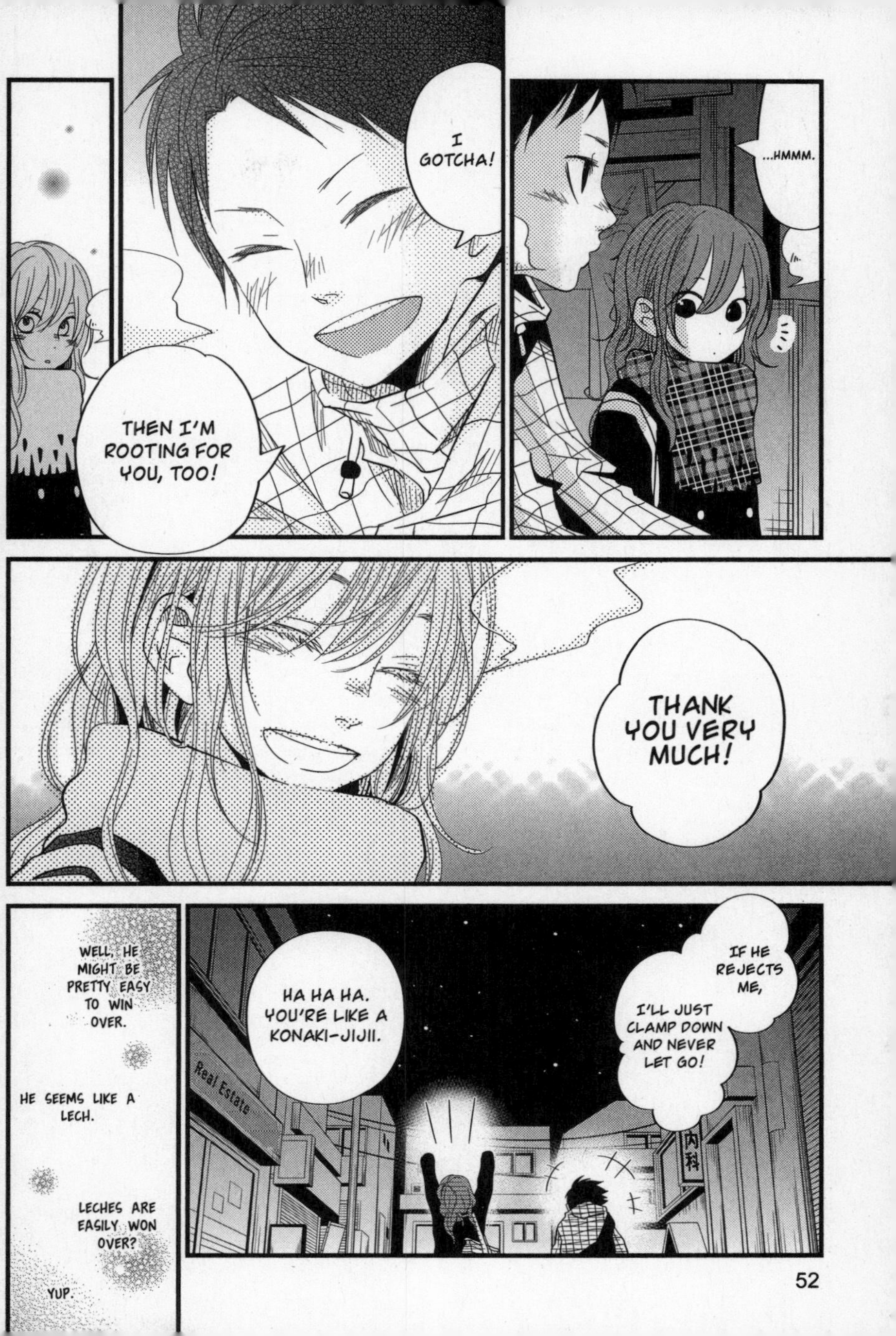
...HMMM.
I GOTCHA!
THEN I'M ROOTING FOR YOU, TOO!
THANK YOU VERY MUCH!
IF HE REJECTS ME,
I'LL JUST CLAMP DOWN AND NEVER LET GO!
HA HA HA. YOU'RE LIKE A KONAKI-JIJII.
内科
Real Estate
WELL, HE MIGHT BE PRETTY EASY TO WIN OVER.
HE SEEMS LIKE A LECH.
LECHES ARE EASILY WON OVER?
YUP.

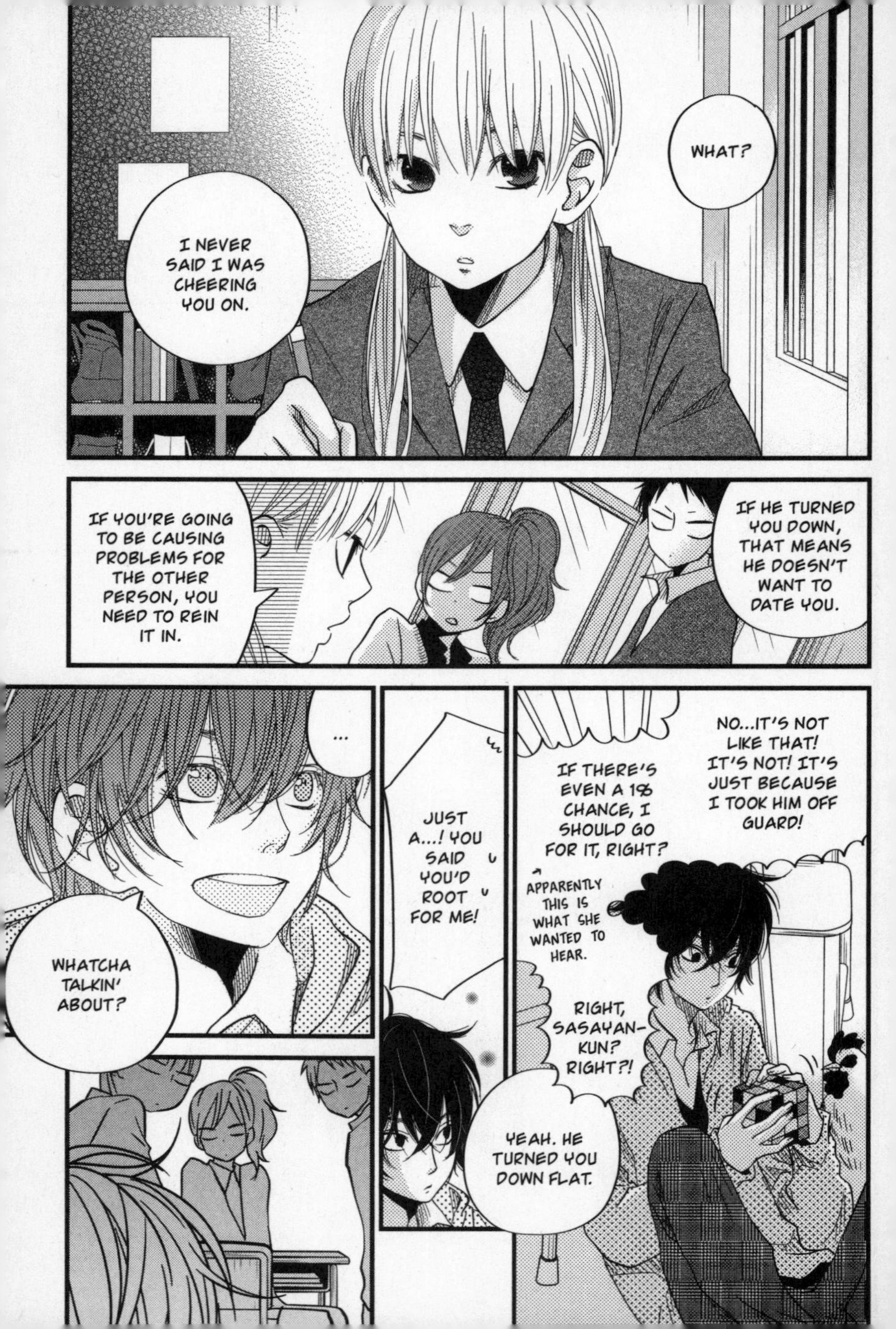
WHAT?
I NEVER SAID I WAS CHEERING YOU ON.
IF HE TURNED YOU DOWN, THAT MEANS HE DOESN'T WANT TO DATE YOU.
IF YOU'RE GOING TO BE CAUSING PROBLEMS FOR THE OTHER PERSON, YOU NEED TO REIN IT IN.
NO...IT'S NOT LIKE THAT! IT'S NOT! IT'S JUST BECAUSE I TOOK HIM OFF GUARD!
IF THERE'S EVEN A 1% CHANCE, I SHOULD GO FOR IT, RIGHT?
APPARENTLY THIS IS WHAT SHE WANTED TO HEAR.
RIGHT, SASAYAN-KUN? RIGHT?!
YEAH. HE TURNED YOU DOWN FLAT.
JUST A...! YOU SAID YOU'D ROOT FOR ME!
...
WHATCHA TALKIN' ABOUT?

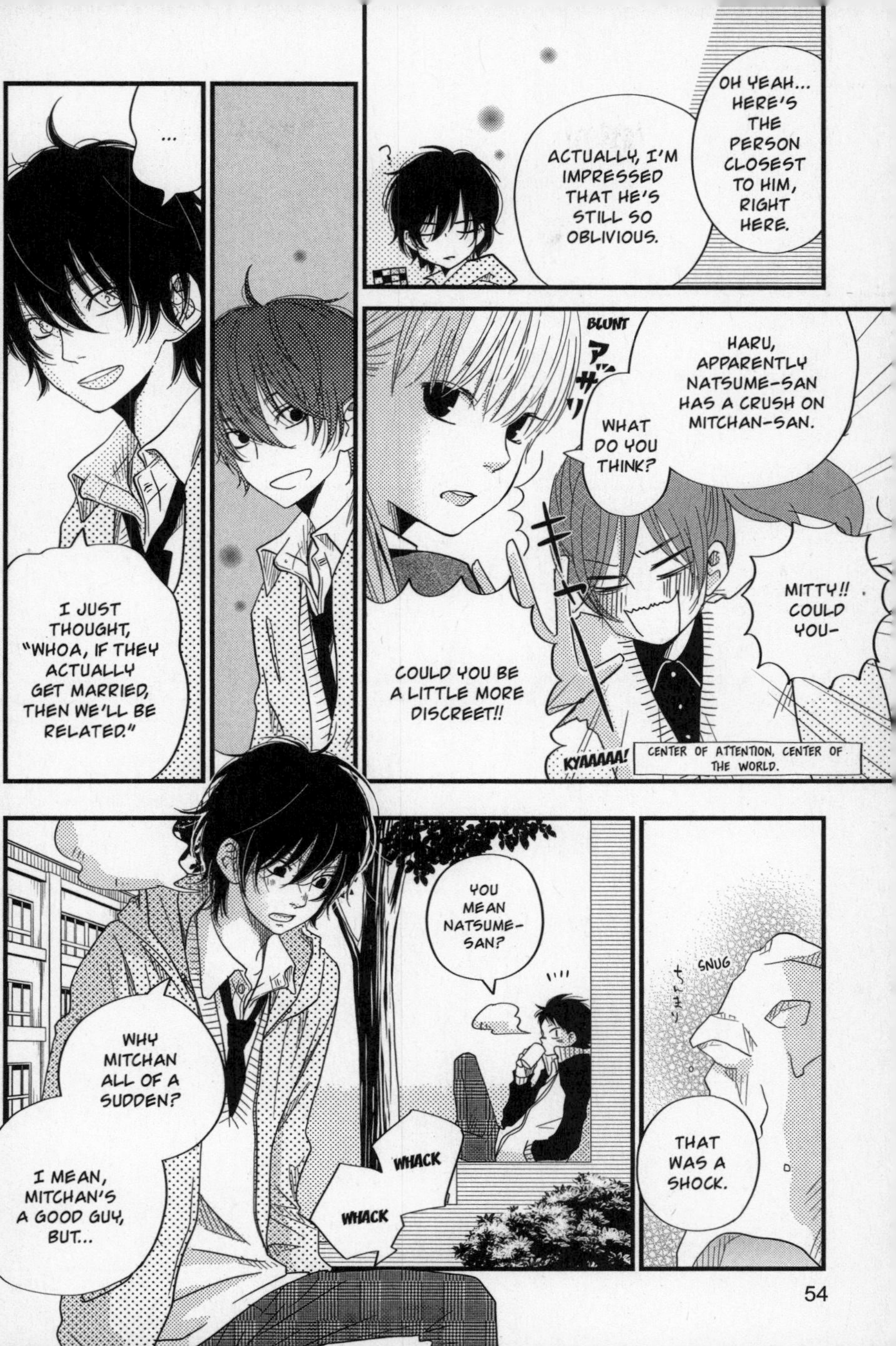
OH YEAH... HERE'S THE PERSON CLOSEST TO HIM, RIGHT HERE.
ACTUALLY, I'M IMPRESSED THAT HE'S STILL SO OBLIVIOUS.
HARU, APPARENTLY NATSUME-SAN HAS A CRUSH ON MITCHAN-SAN.
BLUNT
WHAT DO YOU THINK?
MITTY!! COULD YOU-
COULD YOU BE A LITTLE MORE DISCREET!!
KYAAAAA!
CENTER OF ATTENTION, CENTER OF THE WORLD.
...
I JUST THOUGHT, "WHOA, IF THEY ACTUALLY GET MARRIED, THEN WE'LL BE RELATED."
SNUG
THAT WAS A SHOCK.
YOU MEAN NATSUME-SAN?
WHY MITCHAN ALL OF A SUDDEN?
I MEAN, MITCHAN'S A GOOD GUY, BUT...
WHACK
WHACK

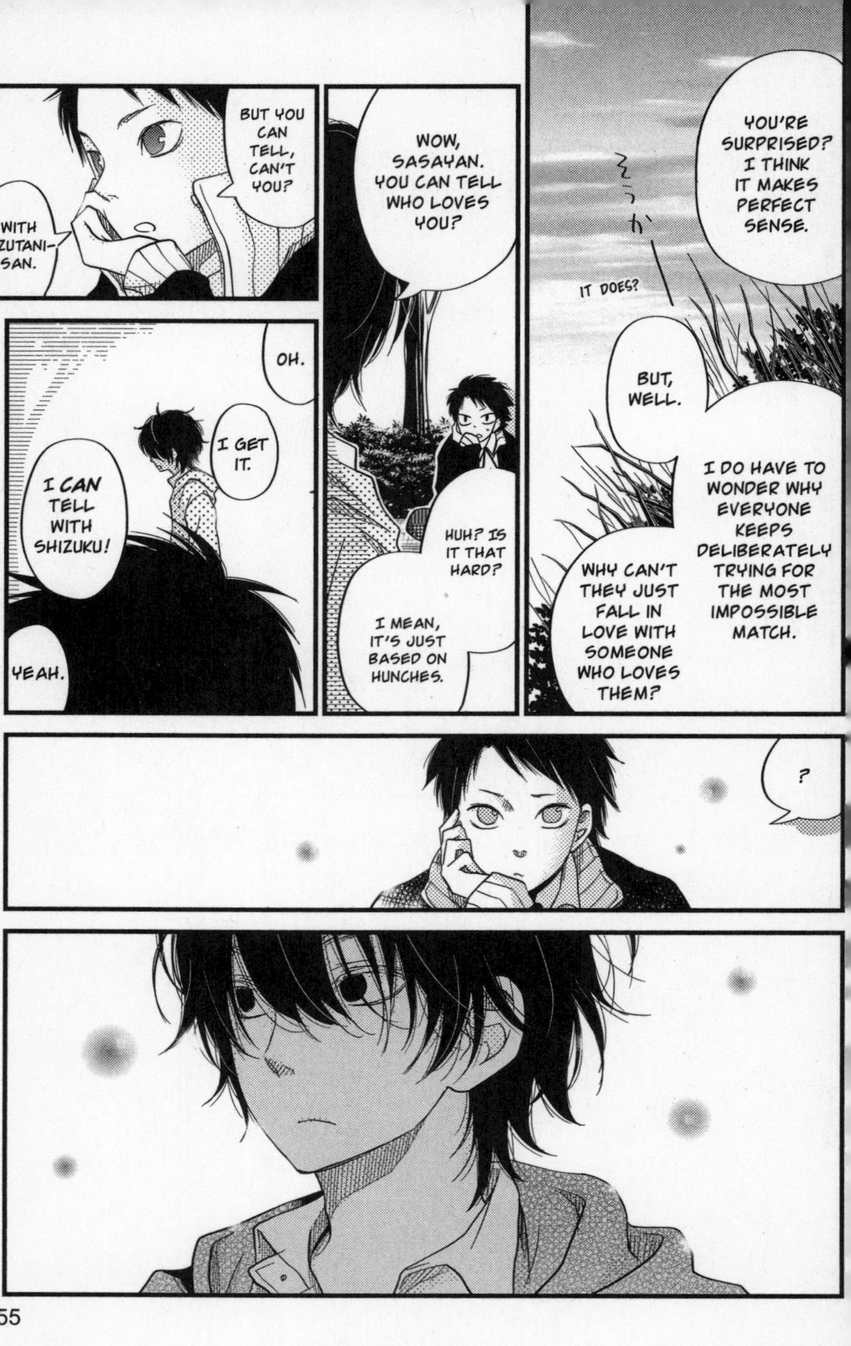
YOU'RE SURPRISED? I THINK IT MAKES PERFECT SENSE.
IT DOES?
BUT, WELL.
I DO HAVE TO WONDER WHY EVERYONE KEEPS DELIBERATELY TRYING FOR THE MOST IMPOSSIBLE MATCH.
WHY CAN'T THEY JUST FALL IN LOVE WITH SOMEONE WHO LOVES THEM?
WOW, SASAYAN. YOU CAN TELL WHO LOVES YOU?
HUH? IS IT THAT HARD?
I MEAN, IT'S JUST BASED ON HUNCHES.
BUT YOU CAN TELL, CAN'T YOU?
WITH MIZUTANI-SAN.
OH.
I GET IT.
I CAN TELL WITH SHIZUKU!
YEAH.
?

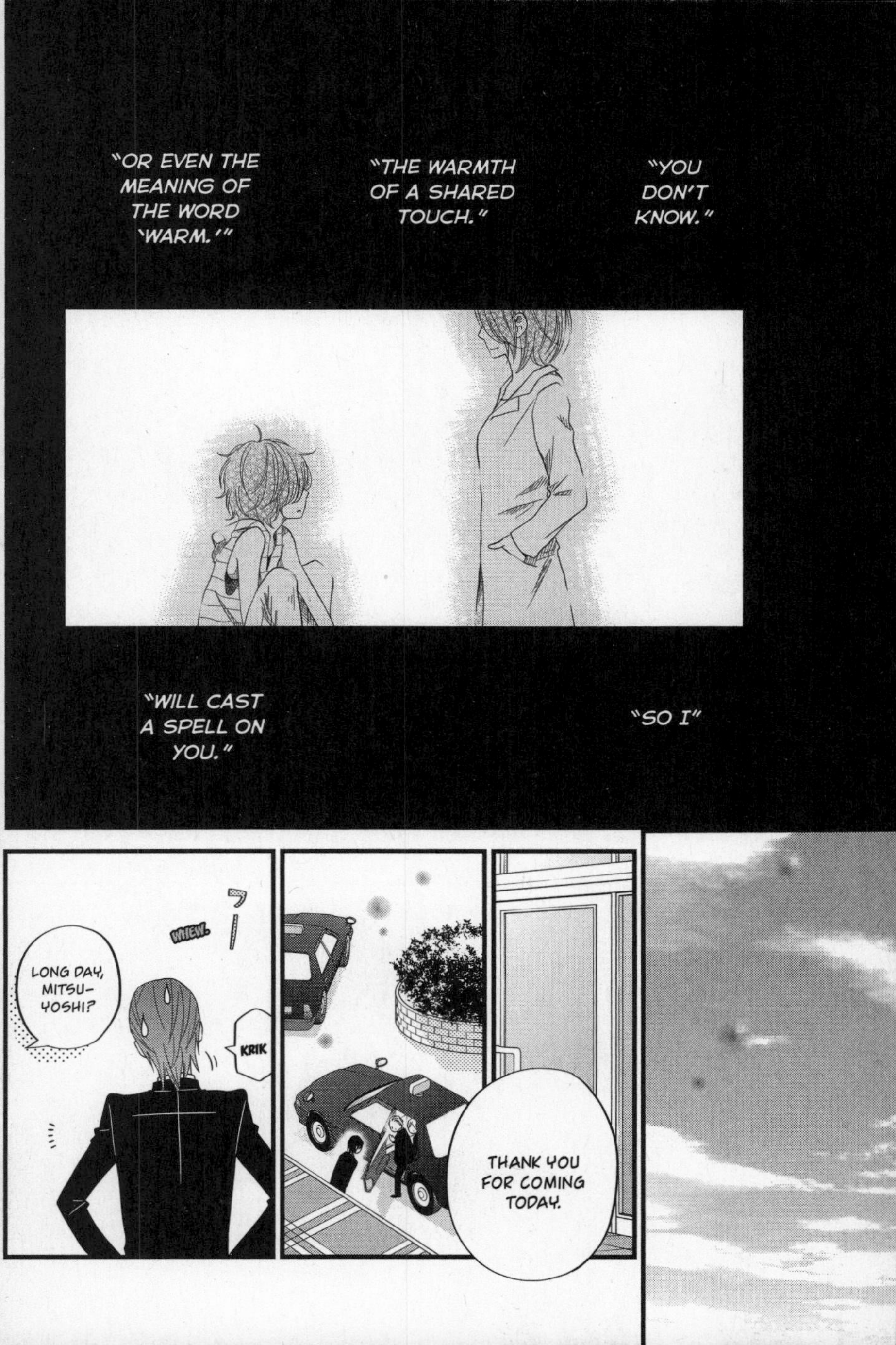
"YOU DON'T KNOW."
"THE WARMTH OF A SHARED TOUCH."
"OR EVEN THE MEANING OF THE WORD 'WARM.'"
"SO I"
"WILL CAST A SPELL ON YOU."
THANK YOU FOR COMING TODAY.
WHEW.
LONG DAY, MITSU-YOSHI?
KRIK

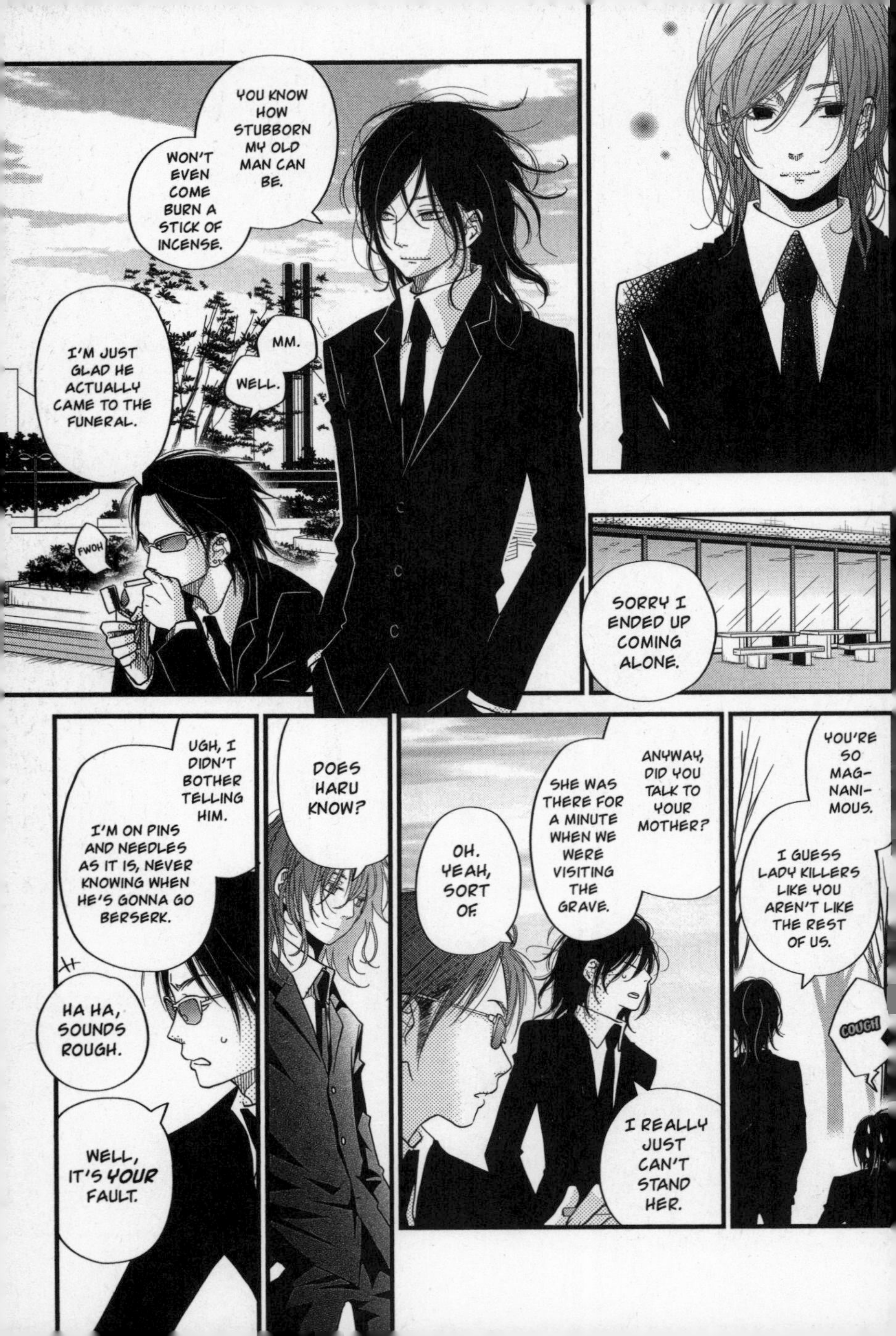

SORRY I ENDED UP COMING ALONE.
YOU KNOW HOW STUBBORN MY OLD MAN CAN BE.
WON'T EVEN COME BURN A STICK OF INCENSE.
MM.
WELL.
I'M JUST GLAD HE ACTUALLY CAME TO THE FUNERAL.
FWOH
YOU'RE SO MAG-NANI-MOUS.
I GUESS LADY KILLERS LIKE YOU AREN'T LIKE THE REST OF US.
COUGH
ANYWAY, DID YOU TALK TO YOUR MOTHER?
SHE WAS THERE FOR A MINUTE WHEN WE WERE VISITING THE GRAVE.
OH. YEAH, SORT OF.
I REALLY JUST CAN'T STAND HER.
DOES HARU KNOW?
UGH, I DIDN'T BOTHER TELLING HIM.
I'M ON PINS AND NEEDLES AS IT IS, NEVER KNOWING WHEN HE'S GONNA GO BERSERK.
HA HA, SOUNDS ROUGH.
WELL, IT'S YOUR FAULT.

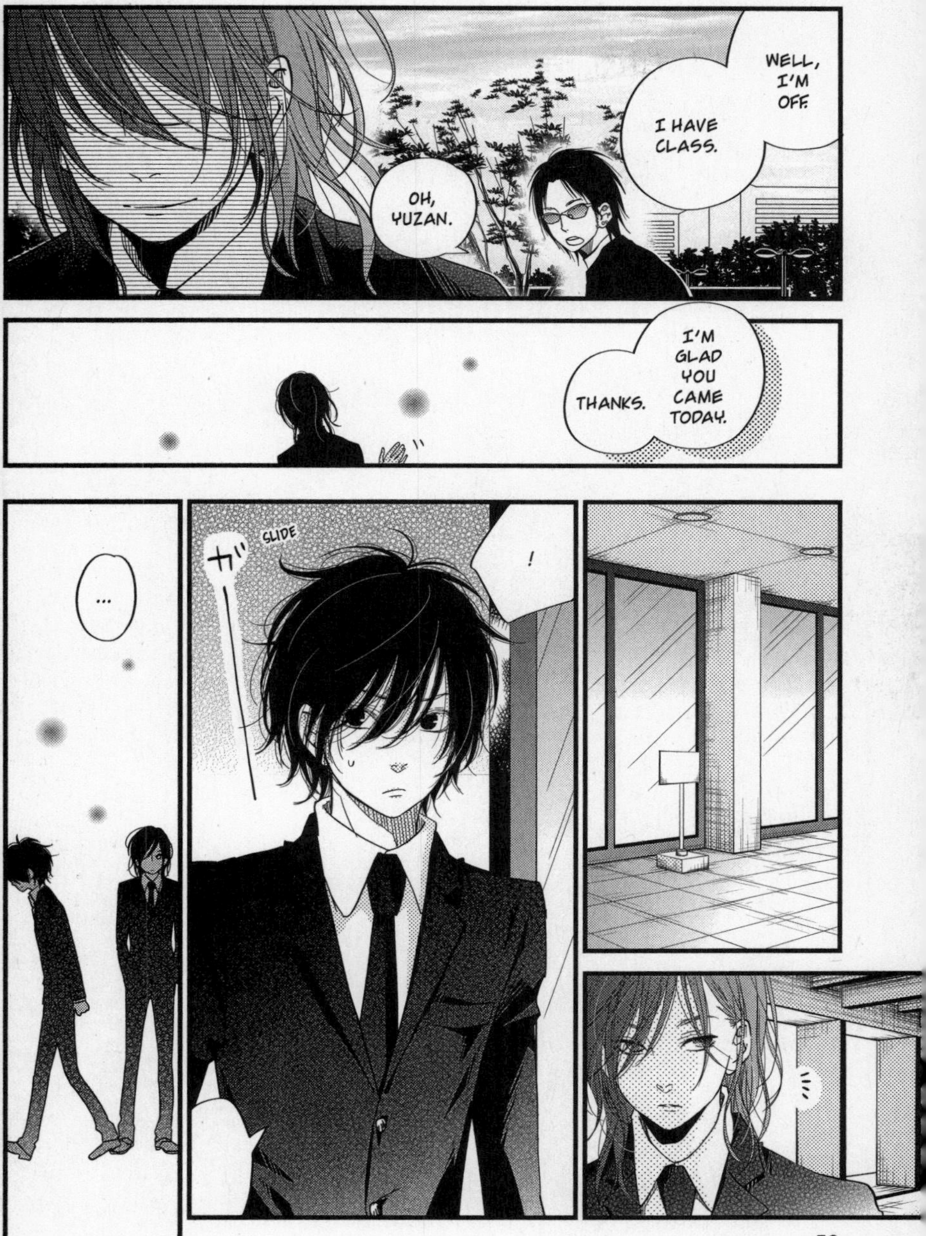
WELL, I'M OFF.
I HAVE CLASS.
OH, YUZAN.
I'M GLAD YOU CAME TODAY.
THANKS.
!
SLIDE
ガ
...

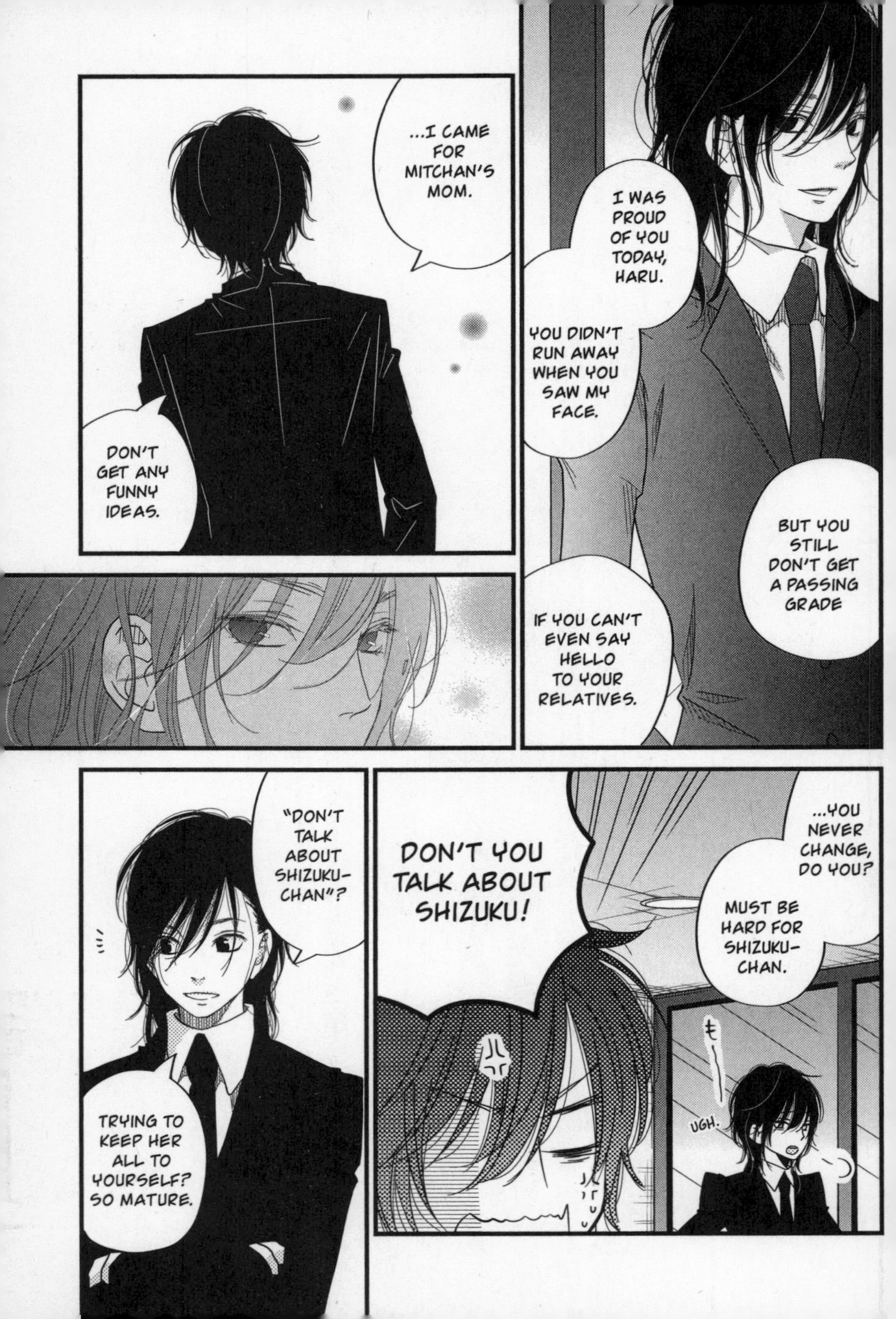
I WAS PROUD OF YOU TODAY, HARU.
YOU DIDN'T RUN AWAY WHEN YOU SAW MY FACE.
BUT YOU STILL DON'T GET A PASSING GRADE
IF YOU CAN'T EVEN SAY HELLO TO YOUR RELATIVES.
...I CAME FOR MITCHAN'S MOM.
DON'T GET ANY FUNNY IDEAS.
...YOU NEVER CHANGE, DO YOU?
MUST BE HARD FOR SHIZUKU-CHAN.
DON'T YOU TALK ABOUT SHIZUKU!
UGH.
"DON'T TALK ABOUT SHIZUKU-CHAN"?
TRYING TO KEEP HER ALL TO YOURSELF? SO MATURE.

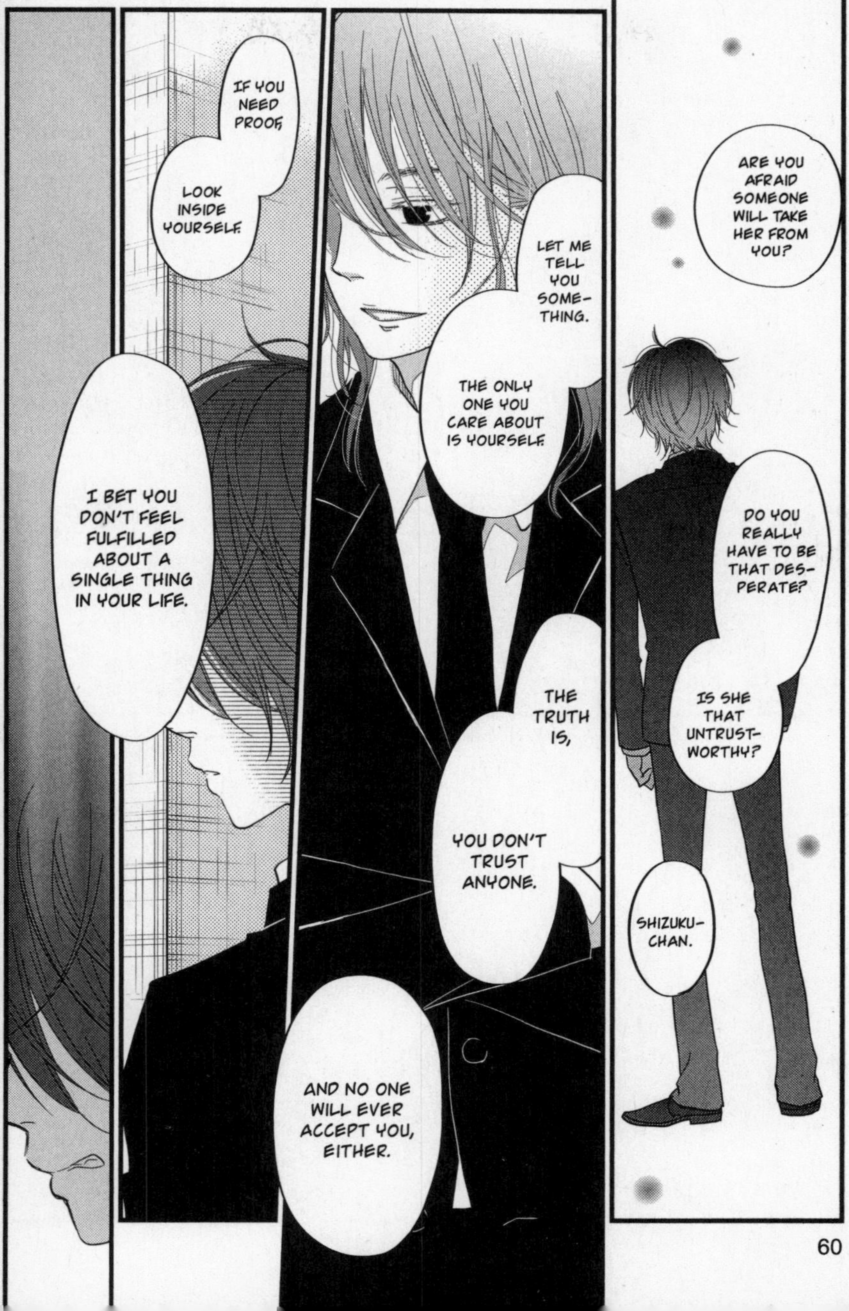
ARE YOU AFRAID SOMEONE WILL TAKE HER FROM YOU?
DO YOU REALLY HAVE TO BE THAT DESPERATE?
IS SHE THAT UNTRUSTWORTHY?
SHIZUKU-CHAN.
LET ME TELL YOU SOMETHING.
THE ONLY ONE YOU CARE ABOUT IS YOURSELF.
THE TRUTH IS,
YOU DON'T TRUST ANYONE.
AND NO ONE WILL EVER ACCEPT YOU, EITHER.
IF YOU NEED PROOF,
LOOK INSIDE YOURSELF.
I BET YOU DON'T FEEL FULFILLED ABOUT A SINGLE THING IN YOUR LIFE.

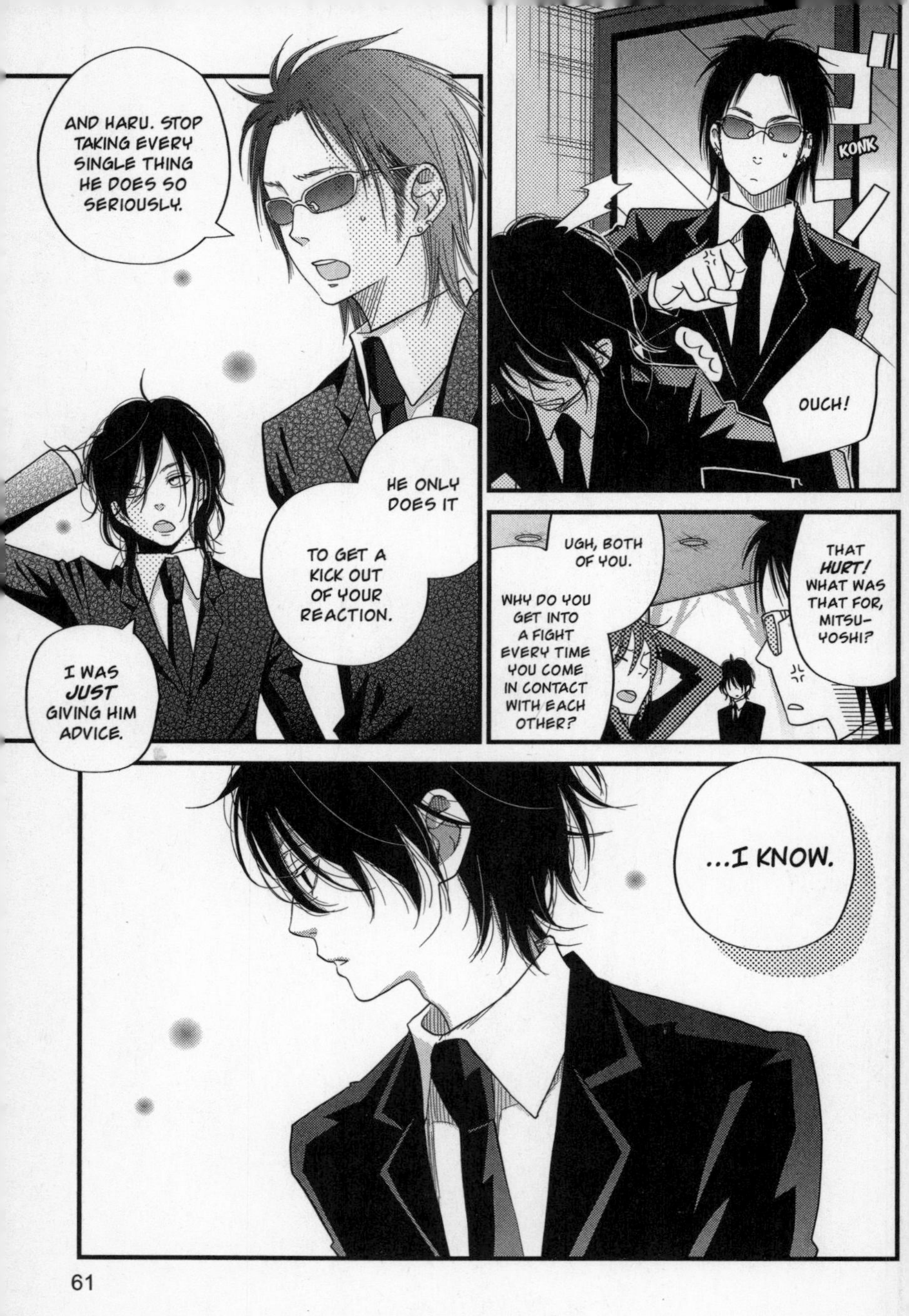
KONK
OUCH!
THAT HURT! WHAT WAS THAT FOR, MITSU-YOSHI?
UGH, BOTH OF YOU.
WHY DO YOU GET INTO A FIGHT EVERY TIME YOU COME IN CONTACT WITH EACH OTHER?
AND HARU. STOP TAKING EVERY SINGLE THING HE DOES SO SERIOUSLY.
HE ONLY DOES IT
TO GET A KICK OUT OF YOUR REACTION.
I WAS JUST GIVING HIM ADVICE.
...I KNOW.

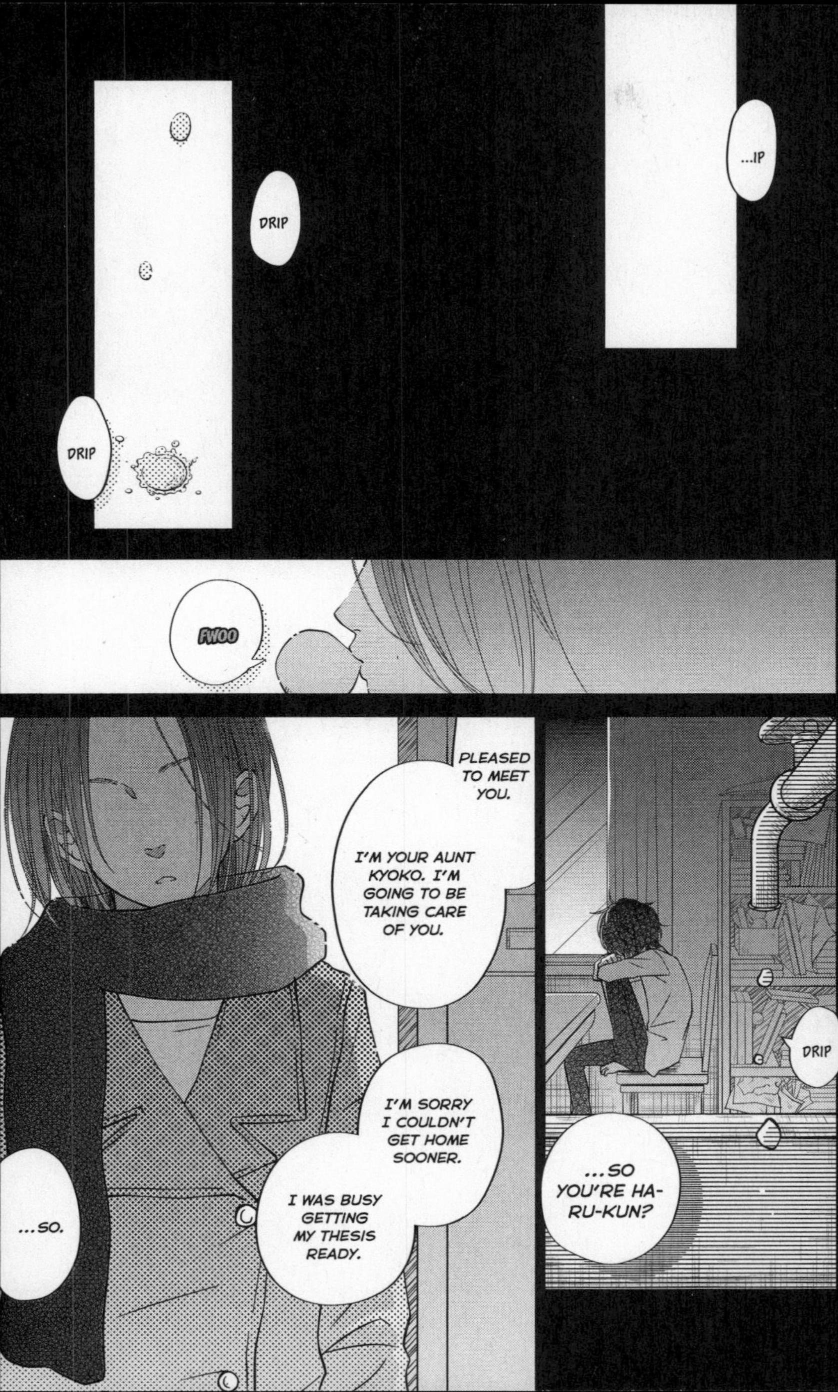

...IP
DRIP
DRIP
FWOO
DRIP
...SO YOU'RE HA-RU-KUN?
PLEASED TO MEET YOU.
I'M YOUR AUNT KYOKO. I'M GOING TO BE TAKING CARE OF YOU.
I'M SORRY I COULDN'T GET HOME SOONER.
I WAS BUSY GETTING MY THESIS READY.
...SO.

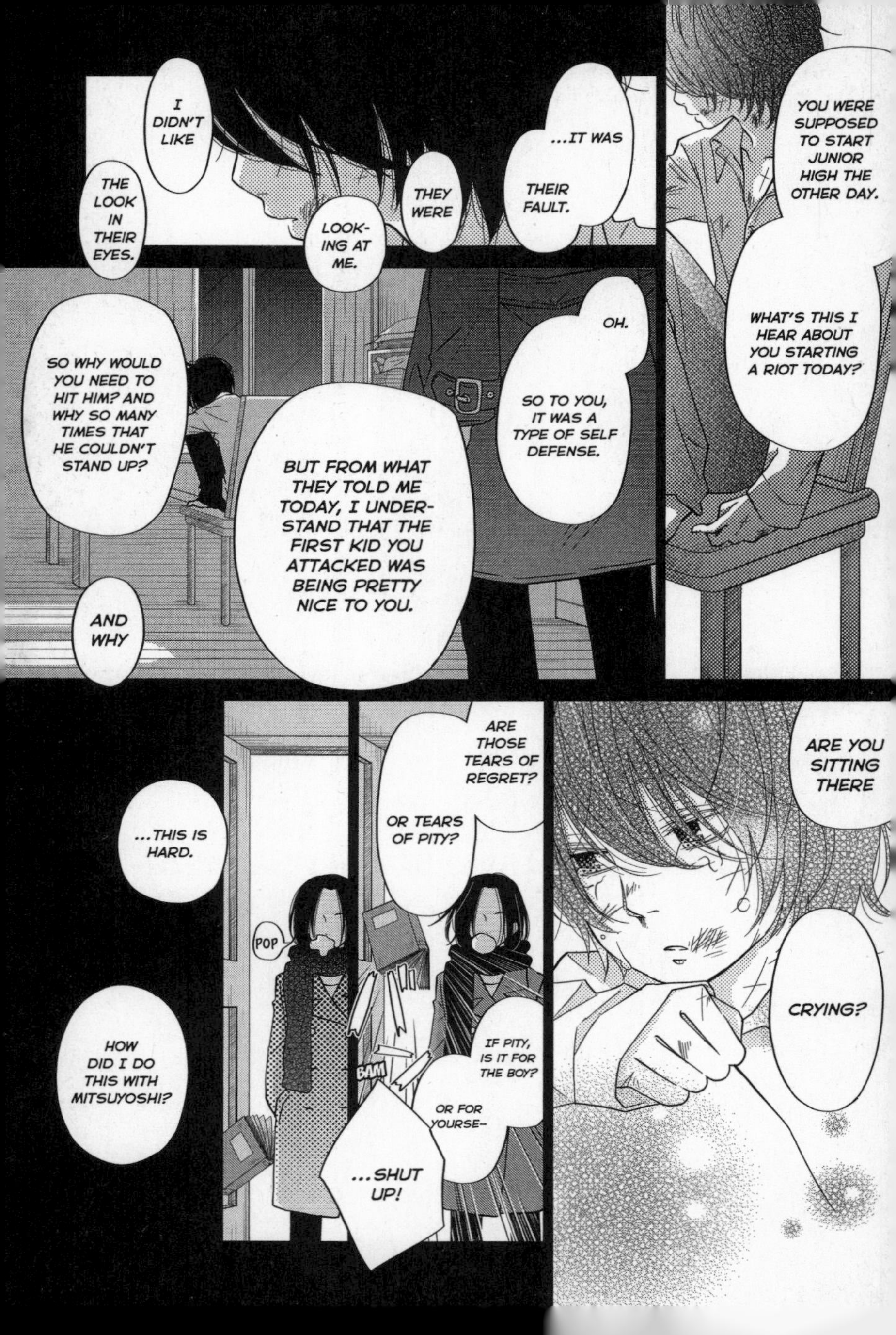
YOU WERE SUPPOSED TO START JUNIOR HIGH THE OTHER DAY.
WHAT'S THIS I HEAR ABOUT YOU STARTING A RIOT TODAY?
...IT WAS THEIR FAULT.
THEY WERE LOOKING AT ME.
I DIDN'T LIKE THE LOOK IN THEIR EYES.
OH.
SO TO YOU, IT WAS A TYPE OF SELF DEFENSE.
BUT FROM WHAT THEY TOLD ME TODAY, I UNDERSTAND THAT THE FIRST KID YOU ATTACKED WAS BEING PRETTY NICE TO YOU.
SO WHY WOULD YOU NEED TO HIT HIM? AND WHY SO MANY TIMES THAT HE COULDN'T STAND UP?
AND WHY
ARE YOU SITTING THERE
CRYING?
ARE THOSE TEARS OF REGRET?
OR TEARS OF PITY?
IF PITY, IS IT FOR THE BOY?
OR FOR YOURSE–
BAM
...SHUT UP!
POP
...THIS IS HARD.
HOW DID I DO THIS WITH MITSUYOSHI?

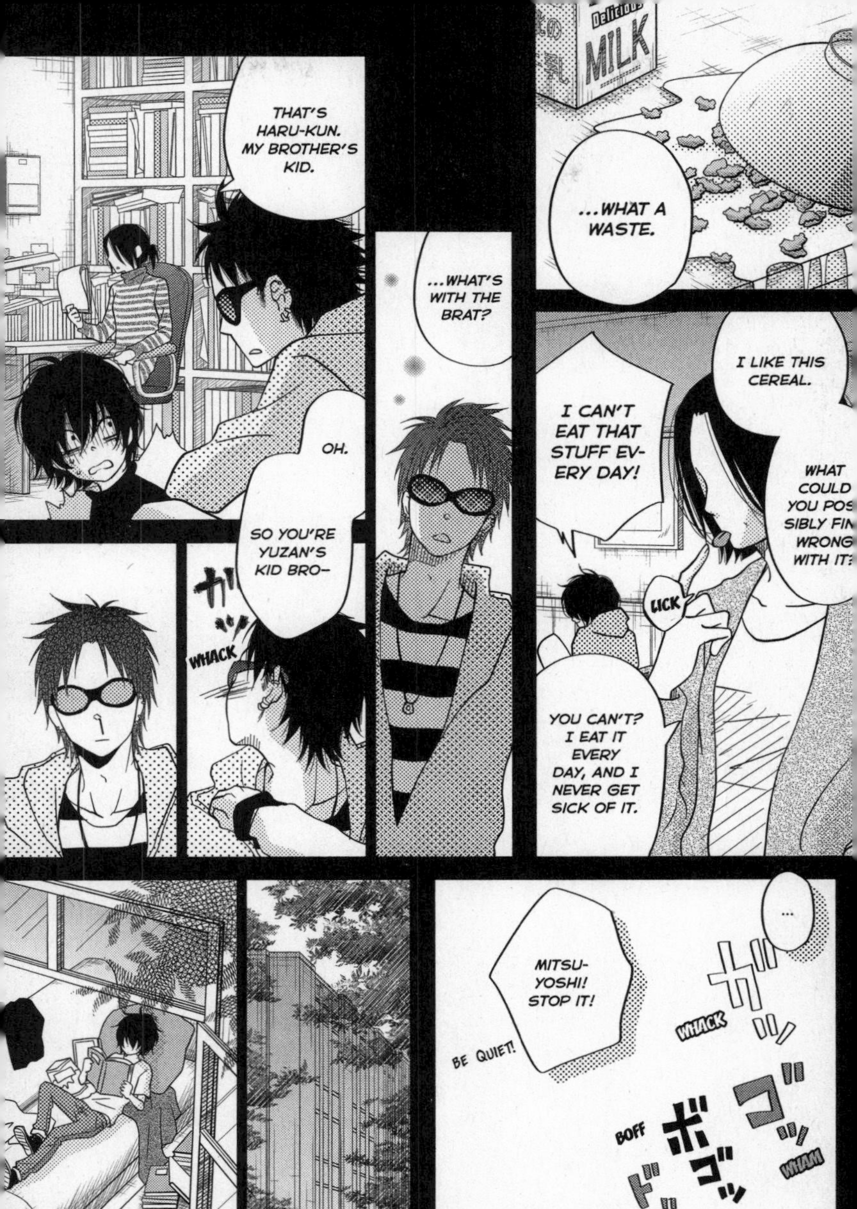
...WHAT A WASTE.
I LIKE THIS CEREAL.
WHAT COULD YOU POS SIBLY FIN WRONG WITH IT
I CAN'T EAT THAT STUFF EV- ERY DAY!
LICK
YOU CAN'T? I EAT IT EVERY DAY, AND I NEVER GET SICK OF IT.
...WHAT'S WITH THE BRAT?
THAT'S HARU-KUN. MY BROTHER'S KID.
OH.
SO YOU'RE YUZAN'S KID BRO-
WHACK
...
WHACK
MITSU- YOSHI! STOP IT!
BE QUIET!
WHAM
BOFF
BAM

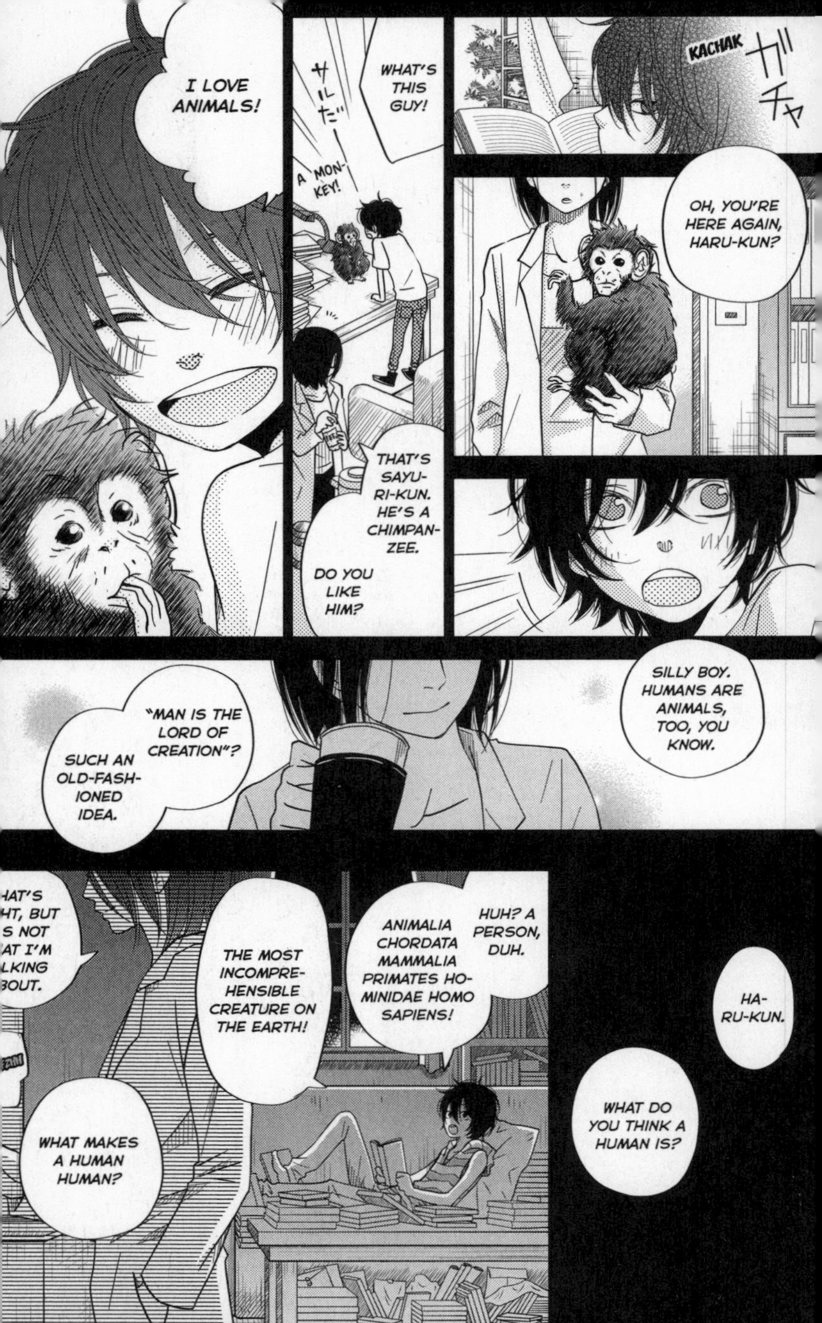
KACHAK
ガチャ
OH, YOU'RE HERE AGAIN, HARU-KUN?
WHAT'S THIS GUY!
サルだ
A MON-KEY!
THAT'S SAYU-RI-KUN. HE'S A CHIMPAN-ZEE.
DO YOU LIKE HIM?
I LOVE ANIMALS!
SILLY BOY. HUMANS ARE ANIMALS, TOO, YOU KNOW.
"MAN IS THE LORD OF CREATION"?
SUCH AN OLD-FASH-IONED IDEA.
HA-RU-KUN.
WHAT DO YOU THINK A HUMAN IS?
HUH? A PERSON, DUH.
ANIMALIA CHORDATA MAMMALIA PRIMATES HO-MINIDAE HOMO SAPIENS!
THE MOST INCOMPRE-HENSIBLE CREATURE ON THE EARTH!
HAT'S HT, BUT S NOT AT I'M LKING BOUT.
WHAT MAKES A HUMAN HUMAN?

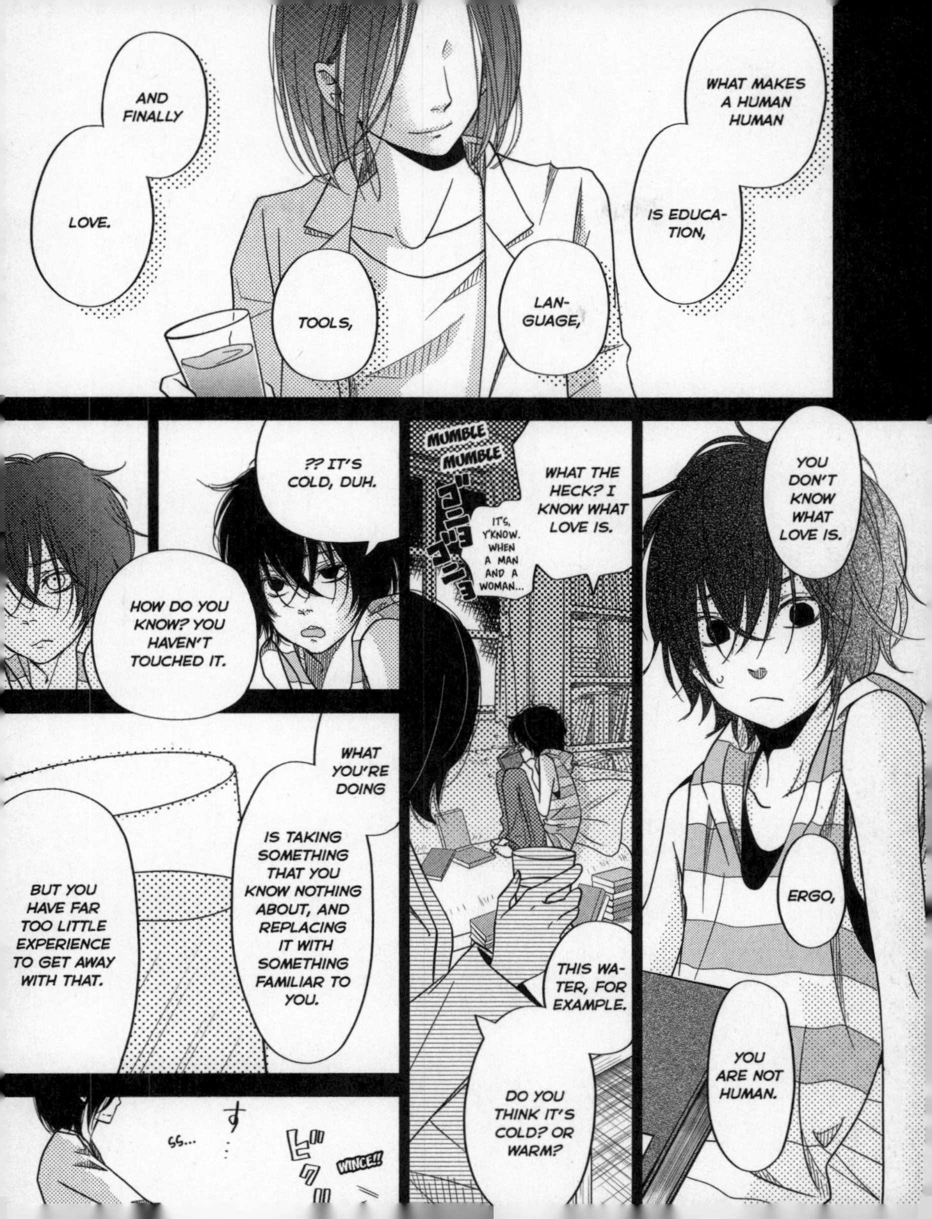
WHAT MAKES A HUMAN HUMAN
IS EDUCATION,
LANGUAGE,
TOOLS,
AND FINALLY
LOVE.
YOU DON'T KNOW WHAT LOVE IS.
ERGO,
YOU ARE NOT HUMAN.
MUMBLE MUMBLE
WHAT THE HECK? I KNOW WHAT LOVE IS.
IT'S, Y'KNOW. WHEN A MAN AND A WOMAN...
THIS WATER, FOR EXAMPLE.
DO YOU THINK IT'S COLD? OR WARM?
?? IT'S COLD, DUH.
HOW DO YOU KNOW? YOU HAVEN'T TOUCHED IT.
WHAT YOU'RE DOING
IS TAKING SOMETHING THAT YOU KNOW NOTHING ABOUT, AND REPLACING IT WITH SOMETHING FAMILIAR TO YOU.
BUT YOU HAVE FAR TOO LITTLE EXPERIENCE TO GET AWAY WITH THAT.
SS...
WINCE!!

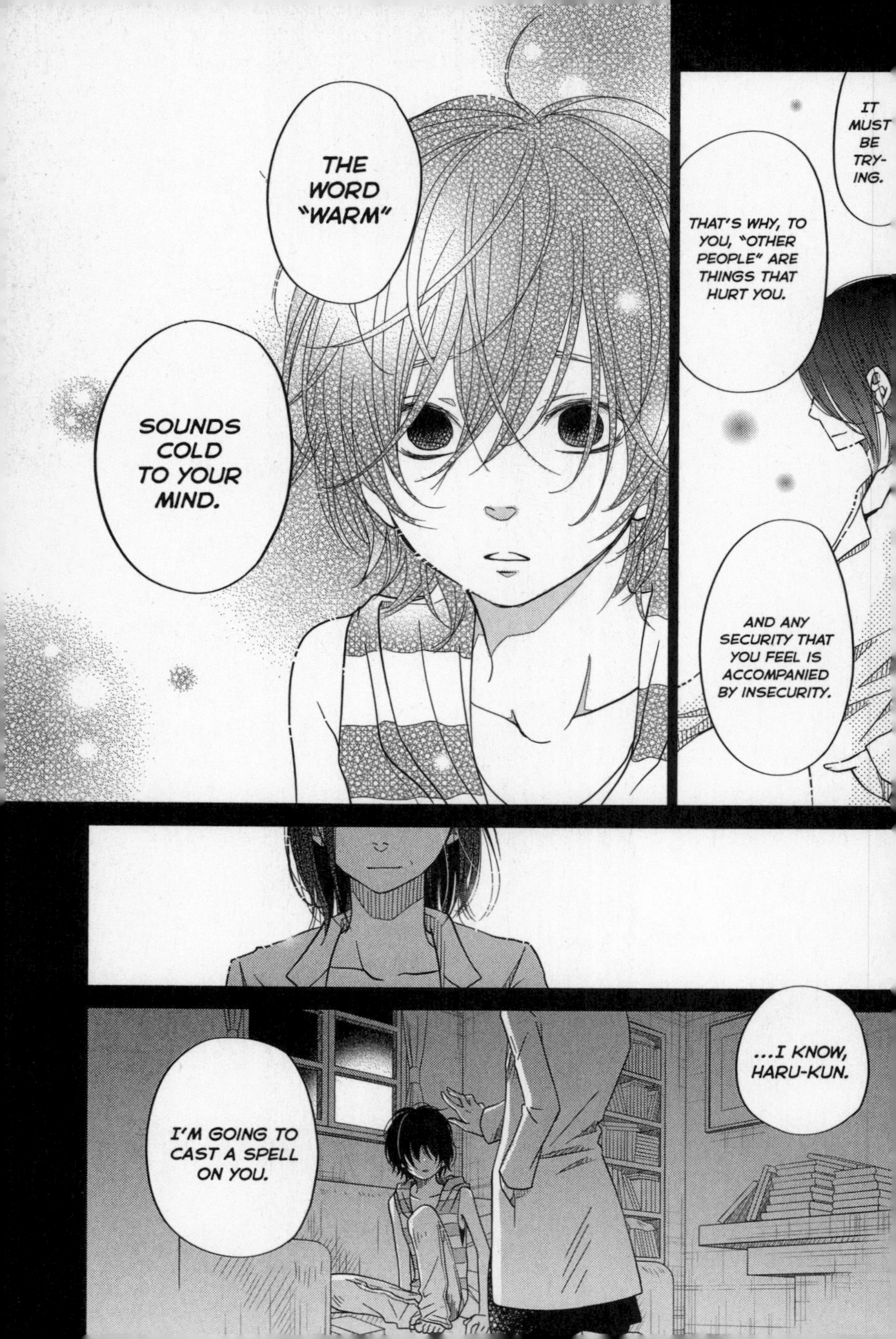
IT MUST BE TRY-ING.
THAT'S WHY, TO YOU, "OTHER PEOPLE" ARE THINGS THAT HURT YOU.
AND ANY SECURITY THAT YOU FEEL IS ACCOMPANIED BY INSECURITY.
THE WORD "WARM"
SOUNDS COLD TO YOUR MIND.
...I KNOW, HARU-KUN.
I'M GOING TO CAST A SPELL ON YOU.

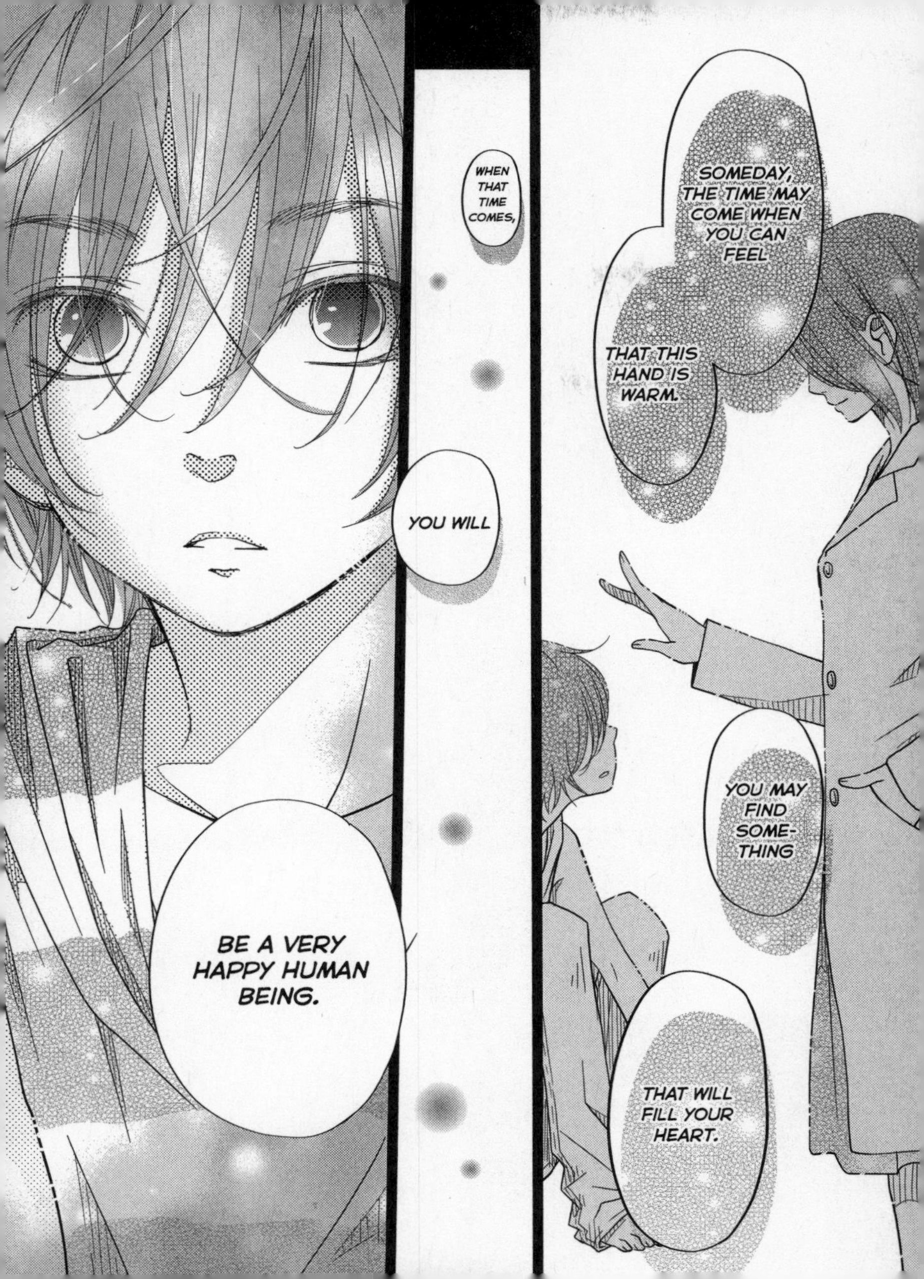
SOMEDAY, THE TIME MAY COME WHEN YOU CAN FEEL
THAT THIS HAND IS WARM.
YOU MAY FIND SOME-THING
THAT WILL FILL YOUR HEART.
WHEN THAT TIME COMES,
YOU WILL
BE A VERY HAPPY HUMAN BEING.

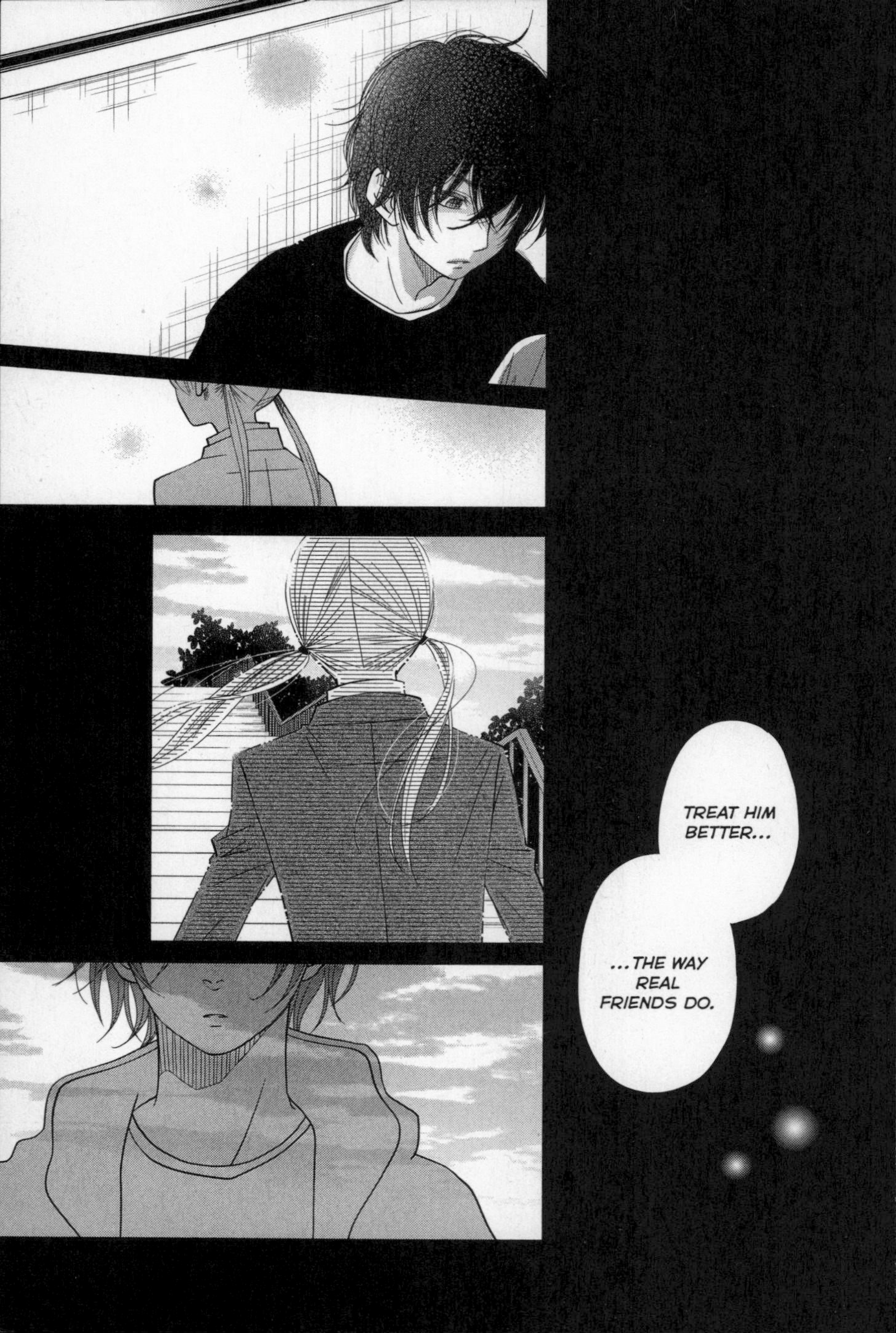
TREAT HIM BETTER...
...THE WAY REAL FRIENDS DO.

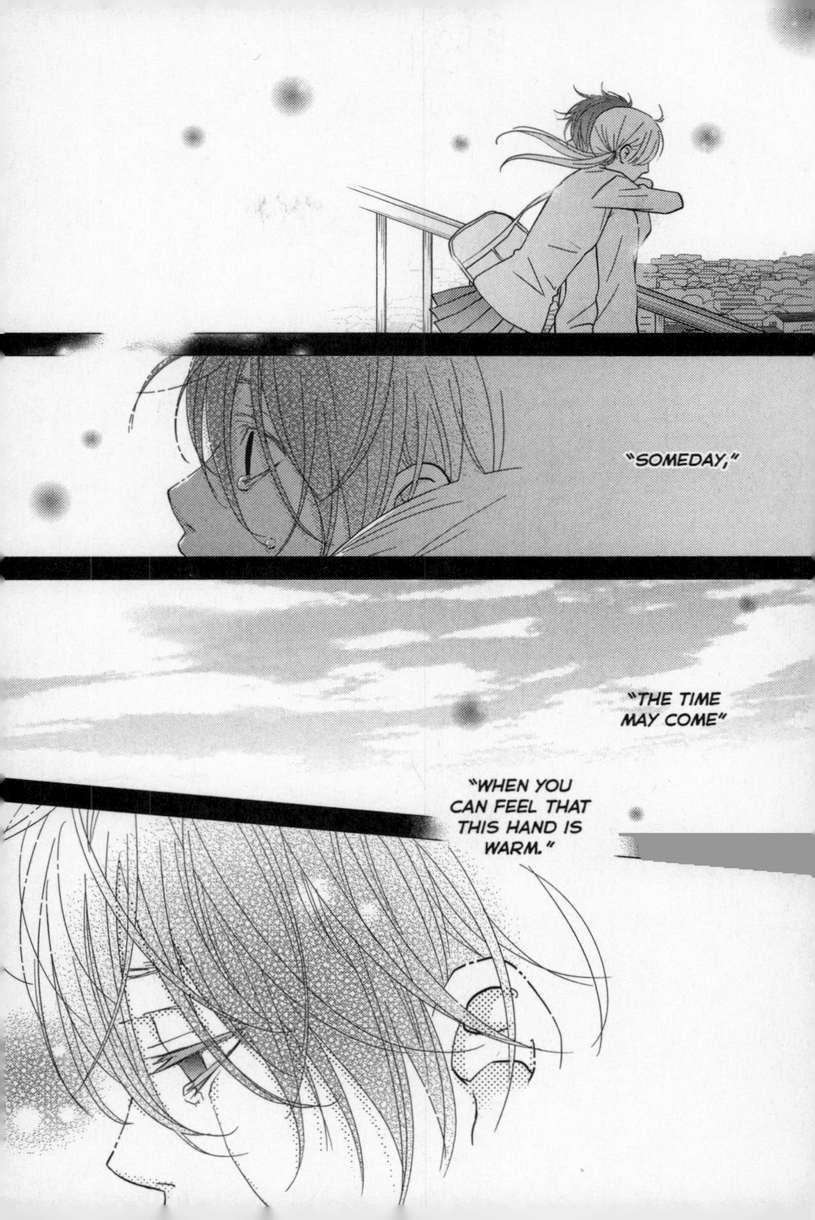
"SOMEDAY,"
"THE TIME MAY COME"
"WHEN YOU CAN FEEL THAT THIS HAND IS WARM."

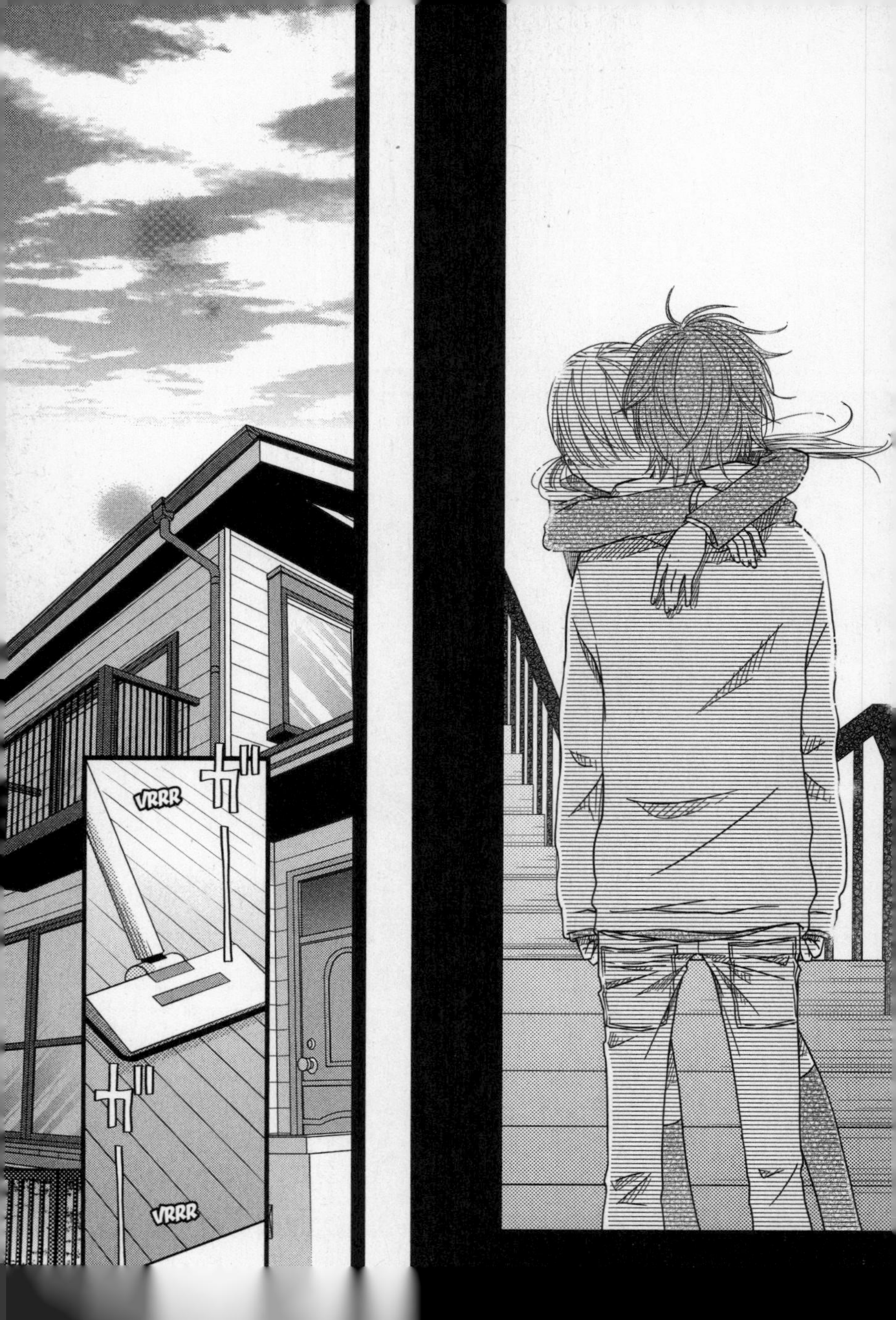
ガー
VRRR
ガー
VRRR

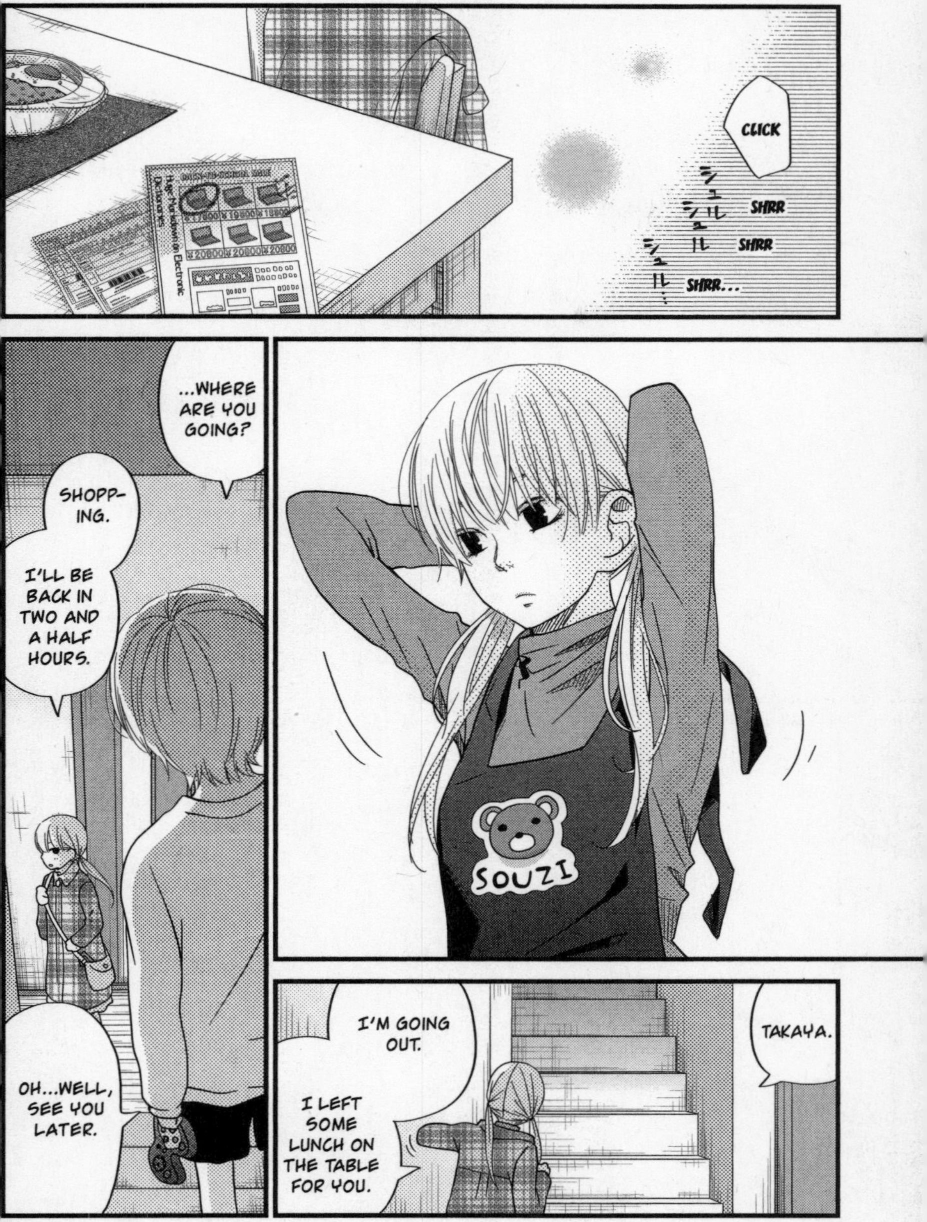

CLICK
シュ
SHRR
シュル
SHRR
シュル…
SHRR…
Huge Markdown on Electronic Dictionaries
¥19800
¥20800
¥20800
¥20800
SOUZI
TAKAYA.
I'M GOING OUT.
I LEFT SOME LUNCH ON THE TABLE FOR YOU.
...WHERE ARE YOU GOING?
SHOPPING.
I'LL BE BACK IN TWO AND A HALF HOURS.
OH...WELL, SEE YOU LATER.

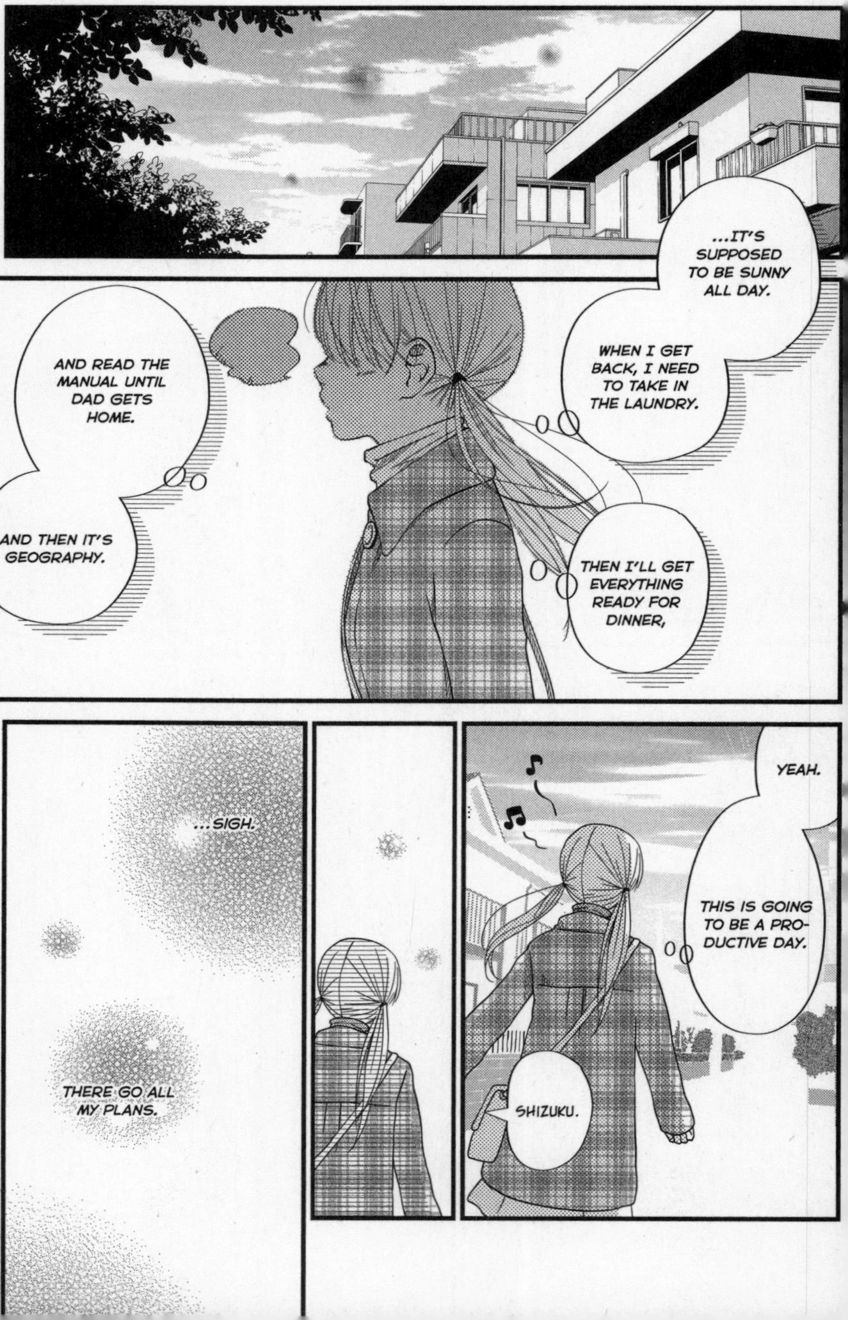
...IT'S SUPPOSED TO BE SUNNY ALL DAY.
WHEN I GET BACK, I NEED TO TAKE IN THE LAUNDRY.
THEN I'LL GET EVERYTHING READY FOR DINNER,
AND READ THE MANUAL UNTIL DAD GETS HOME.
AND THEN IT'S GEOGRAPHY.
YEAH.
THIS IS GOING TO BE A PRO-DUCTIVE DAY.
SHIZUKU.
...SIGH.
THERE GO ALL MY PLANS.

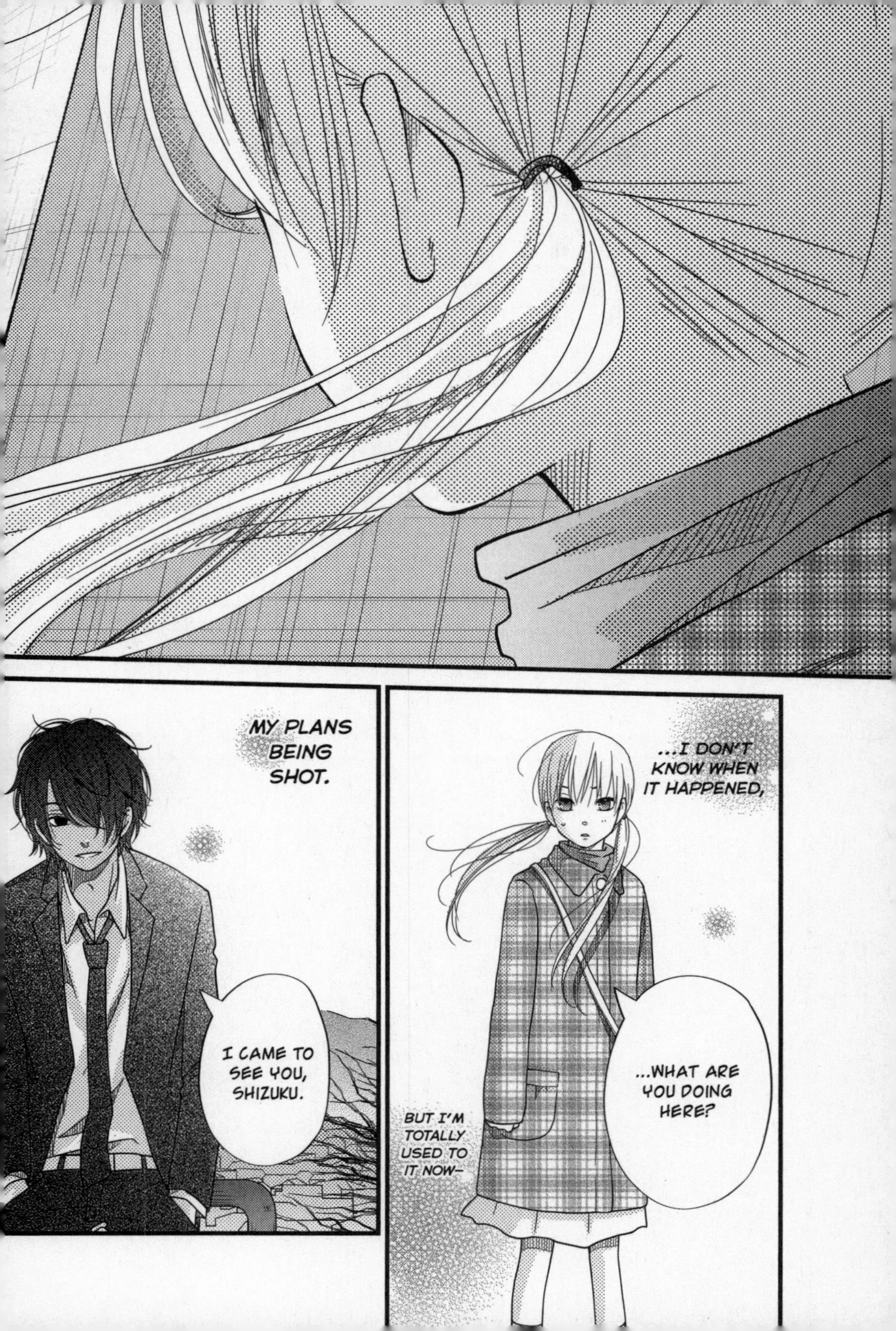
...I DON'T KNOW WHEN IT HAPPENED,
...WHAT ARE YOU DOING HERE?
BUT I'M TOTALLY USED TO IT NOW–
MY PLANS BEING SHOT.
I CAME TO SEE YOU, SHIZUKU.

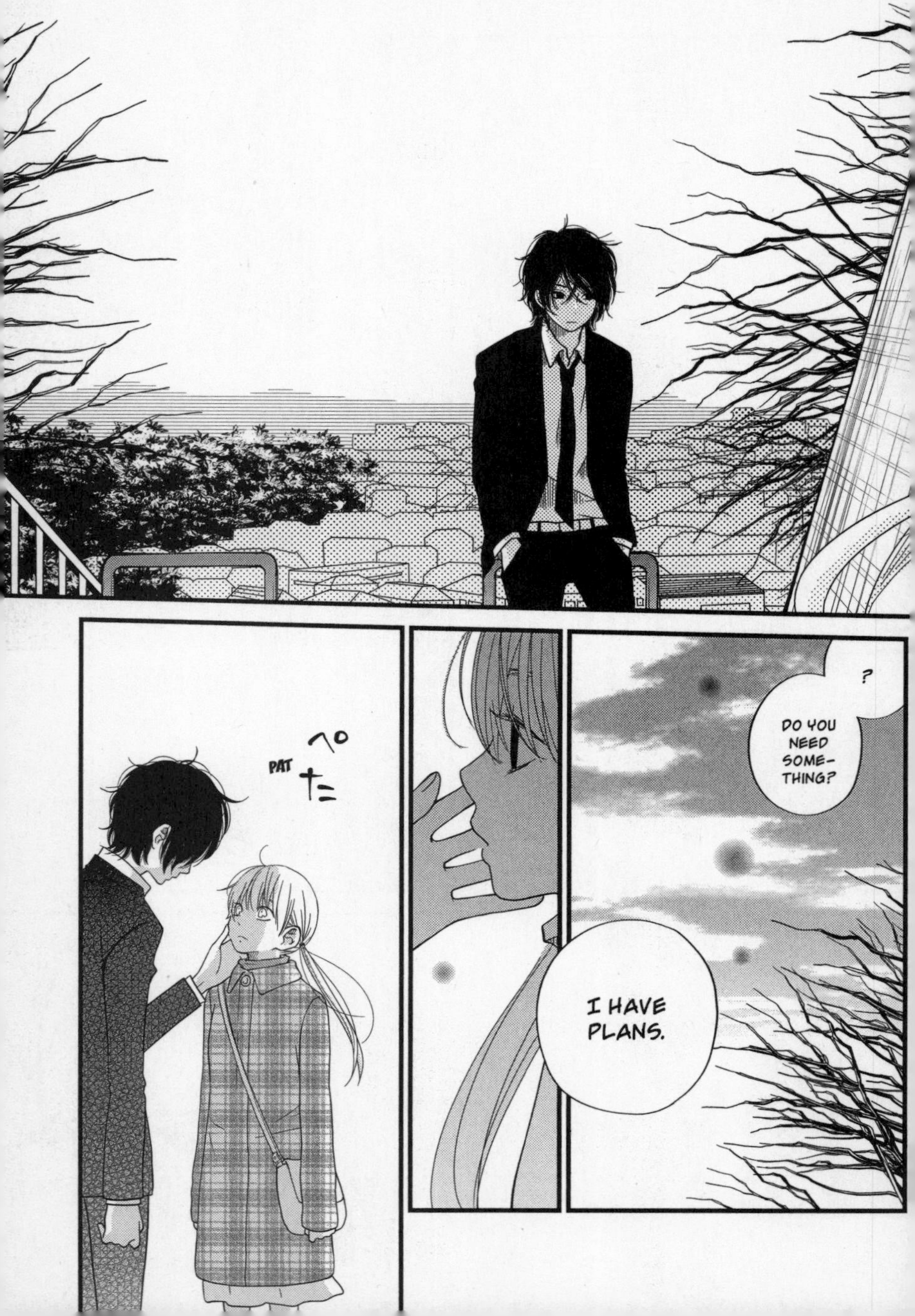
?
DO YOU NEED SOMETHING?
I HAVE PLANS.
ぺた
PAT

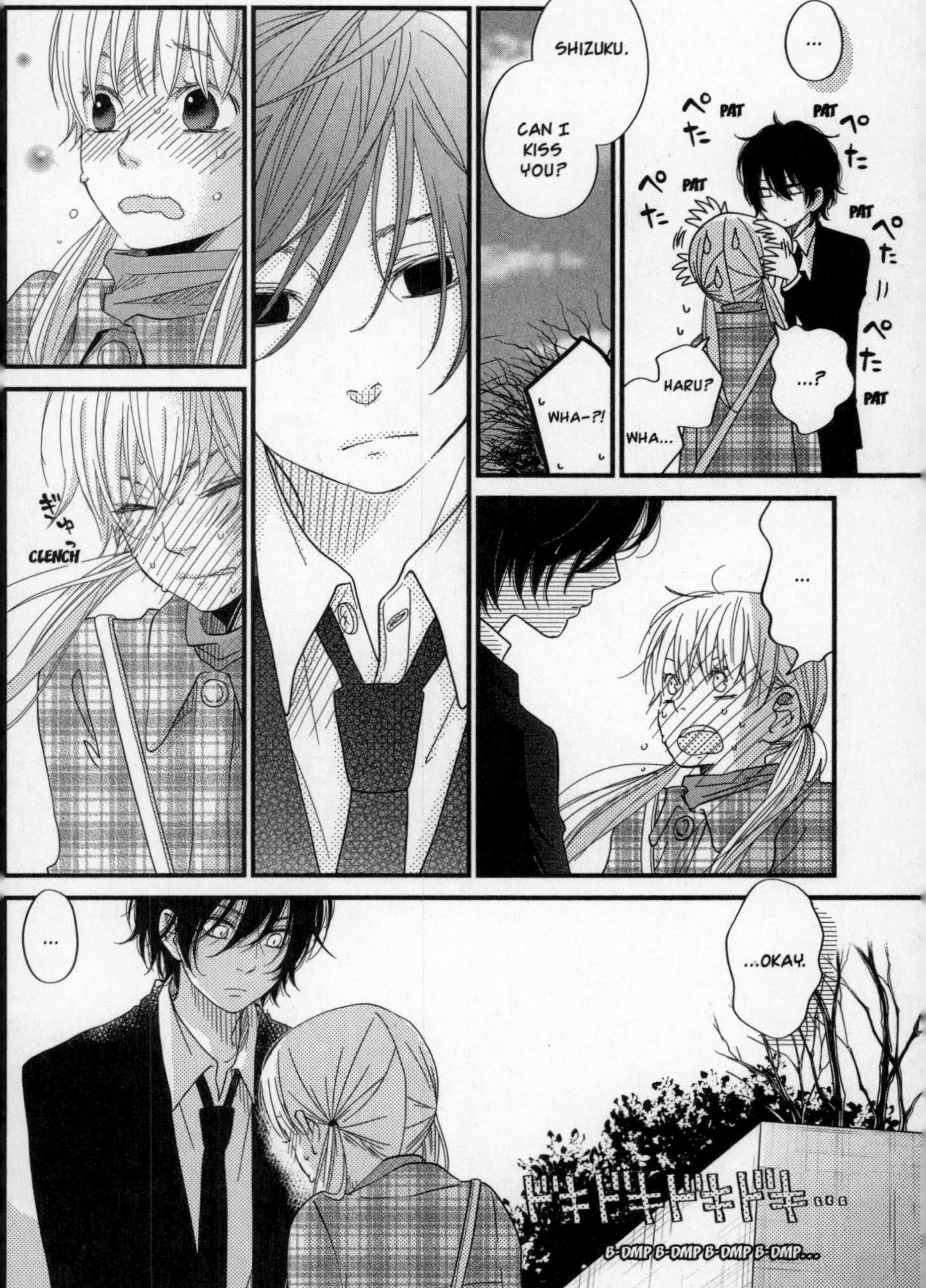
...
ぺた PAT
ぺた PAT
ぺた PAT
ぺた PAT
ぺた ぺた PAT
...?
HARU?
WHA...
SHIZUKU.
CAN I KISS YOU?
WHA-?!
ぎゅっ CLENCH
...
...OKAY.
...
ドキドキドキドキ...
B-DMP B-DMP B-DMP B-DMP...

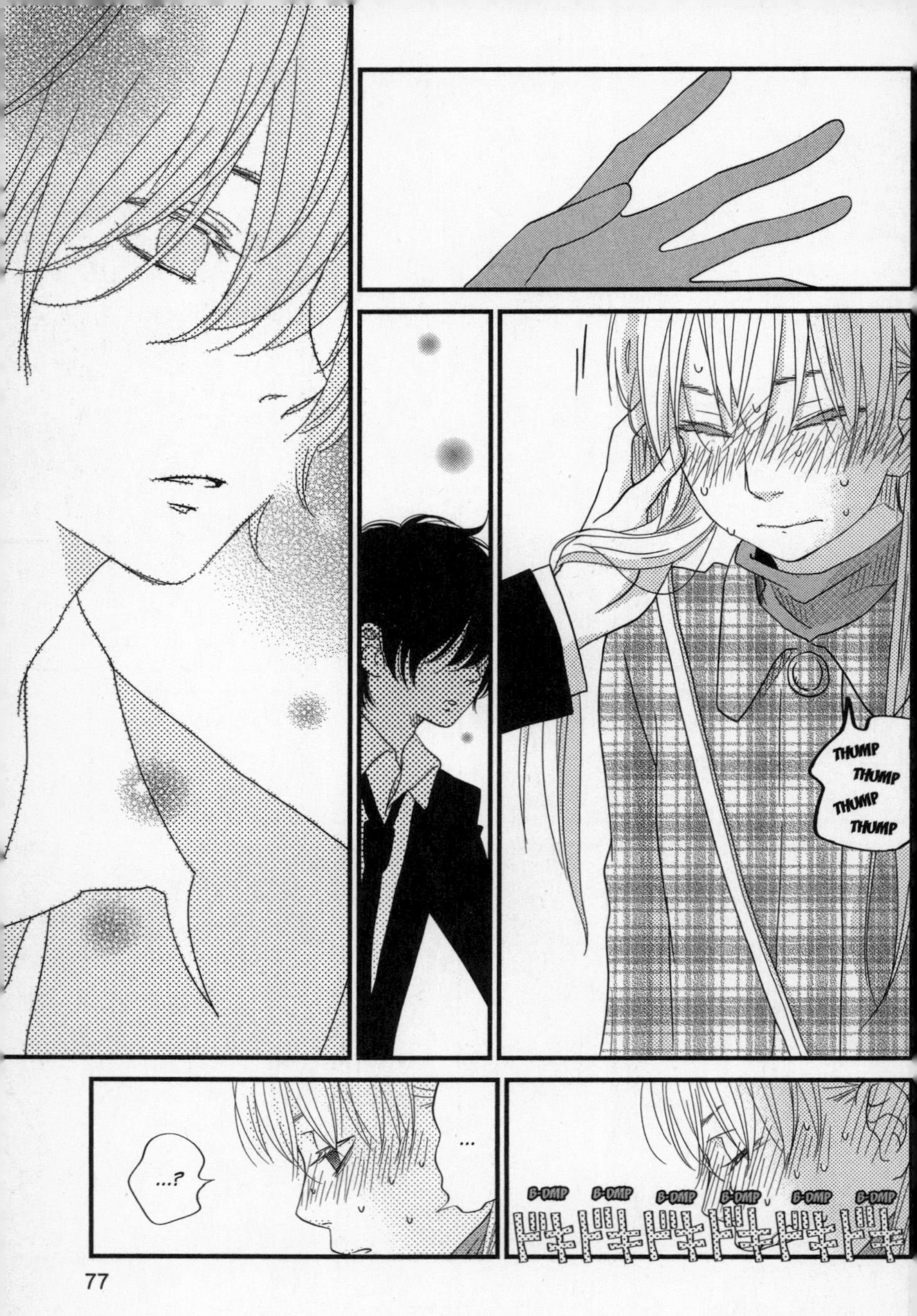
THUMP THUMP THUMP THUMP
B-DMP B-DMP B-DMP B-DMP B-DMP B-DMP
ドキドキドキドキドキドキ
...
...?

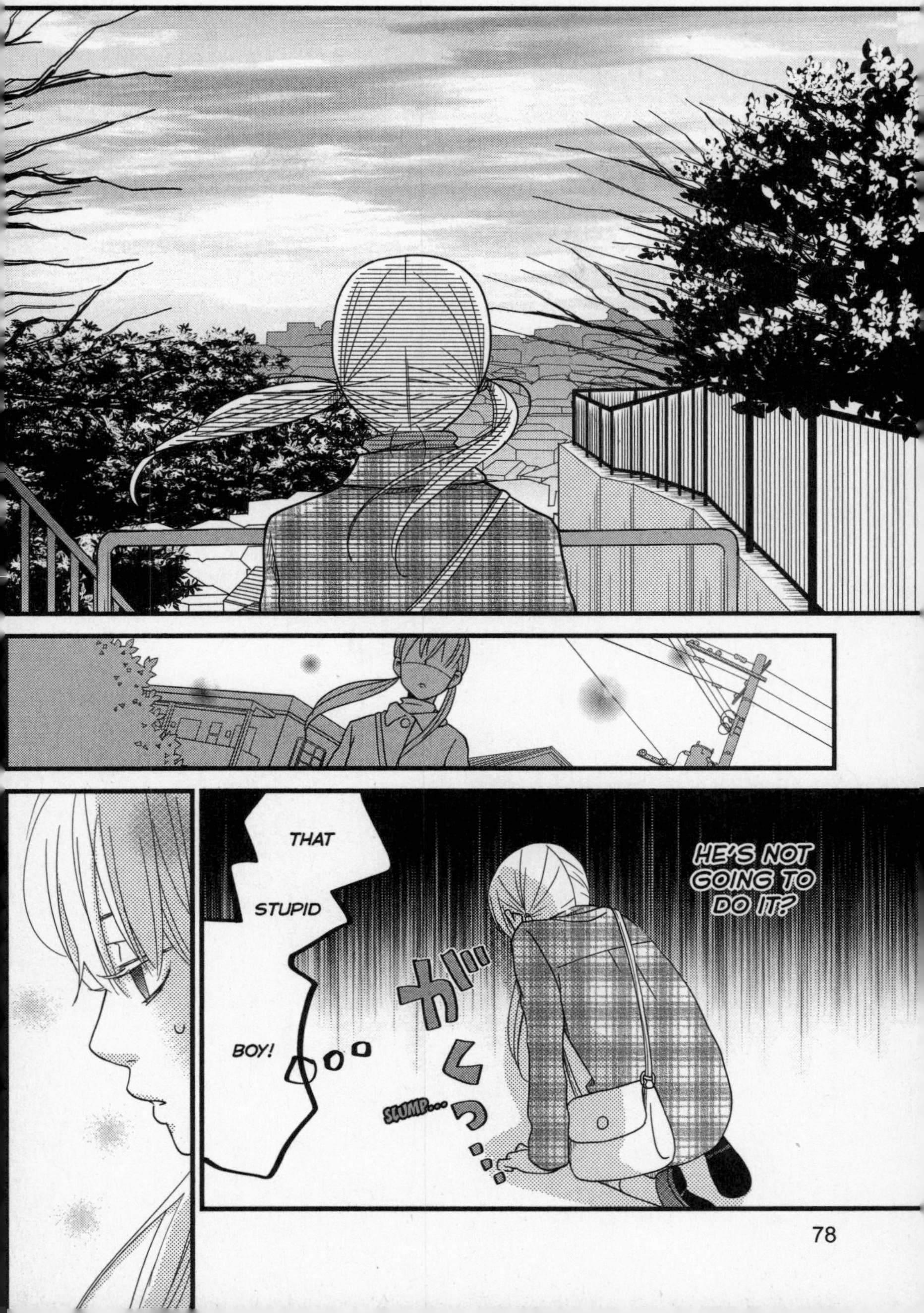
HE'S NOT GOING TO DO IT?
SLUMP...
THAT STUPID BOY!

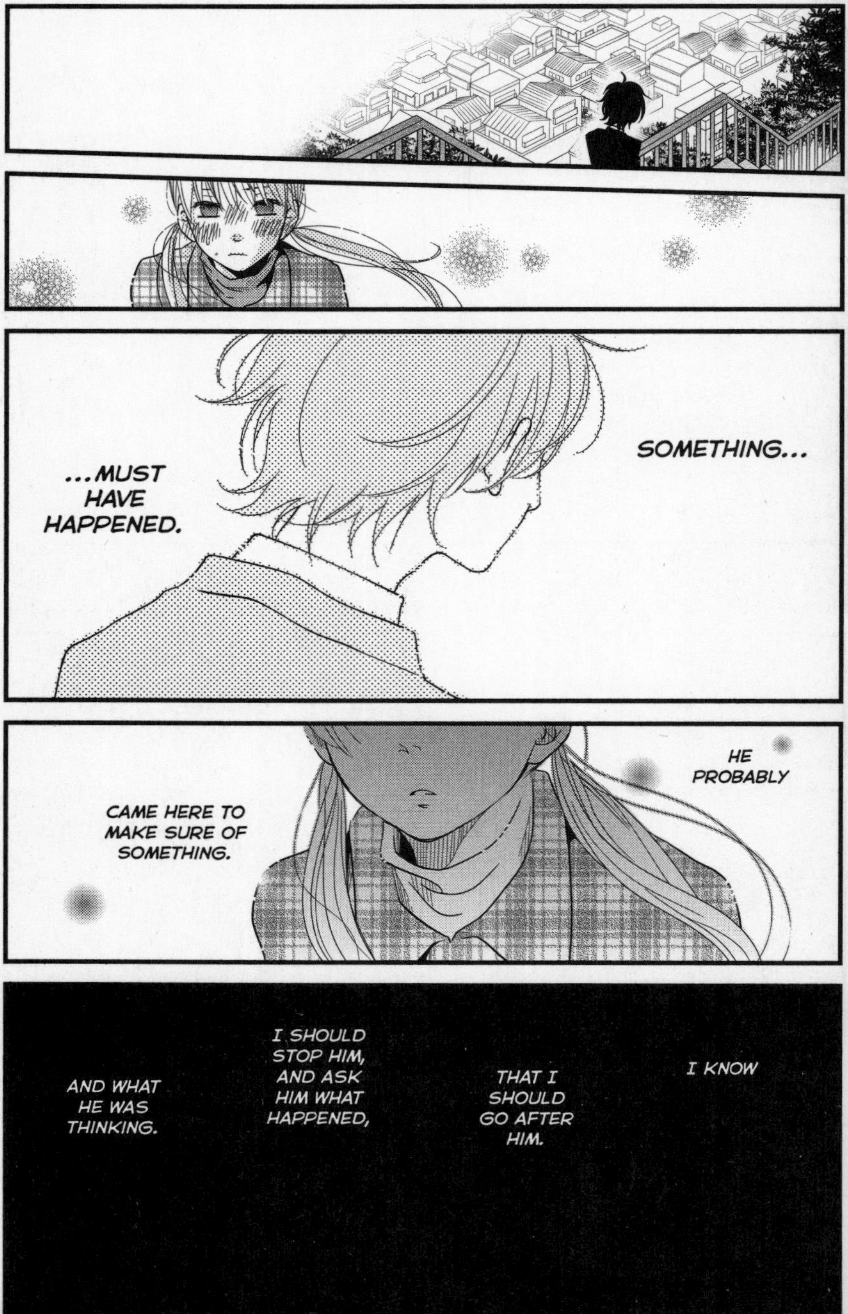
SOMETHING...
...MUST HAVE HAPPENED.
HE PROBABLY
CAME HERE TO MAKE SURE OF SOMETHING.
I KNOW
THAT I SHOULD GO AFTER HIM.
I SHOULD STOP HIM, AND ASK HIM WHAT HAPPENED,
AND WHAT HE WAS THINKING.

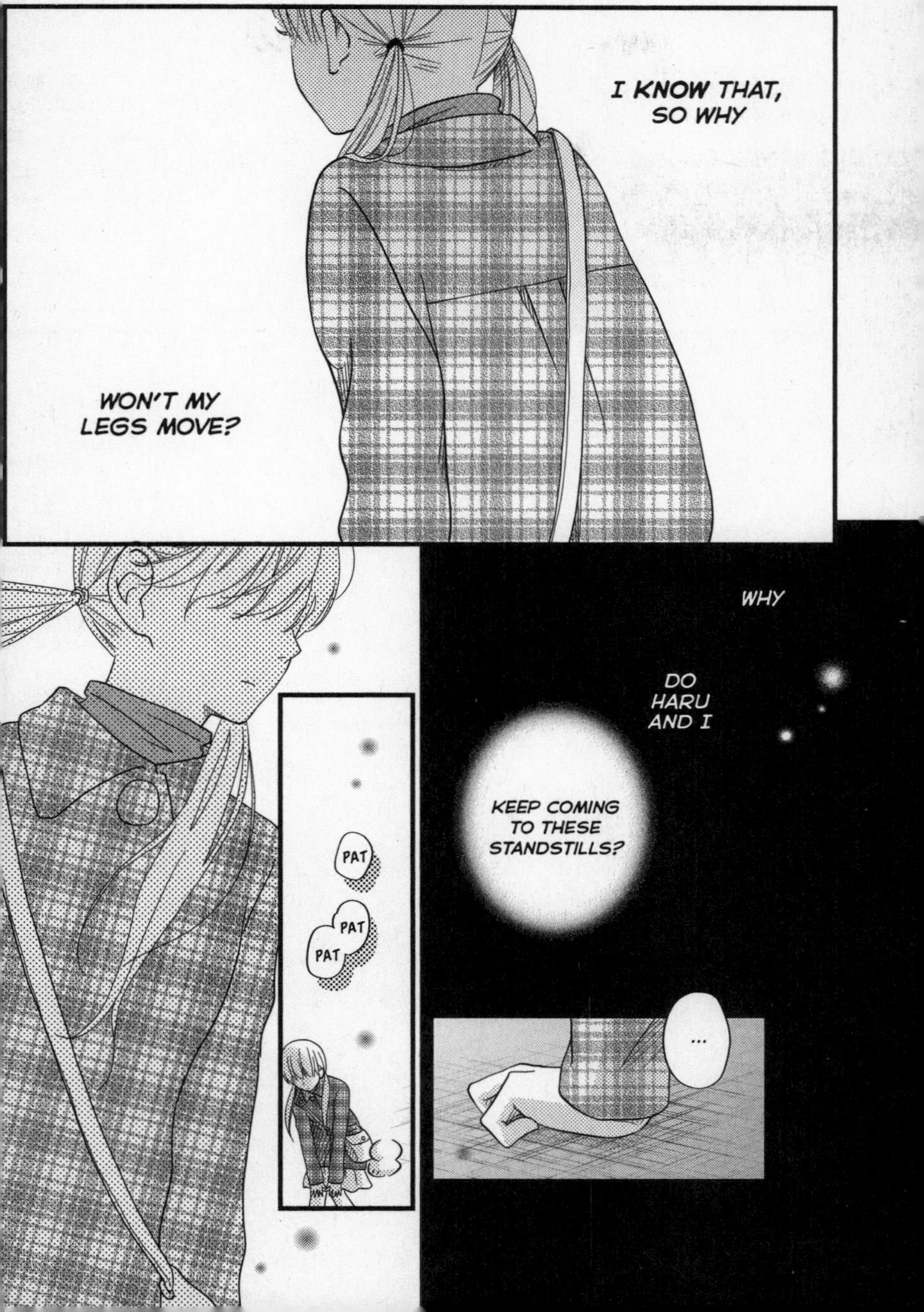
I KNOW THAT, SO WHY
WON'T MY LEGS MOVE?
WHY
DO HARU AND I
KEEP COMING TO THESE STANDSTILLS?
...
PAT
PAT
PAT

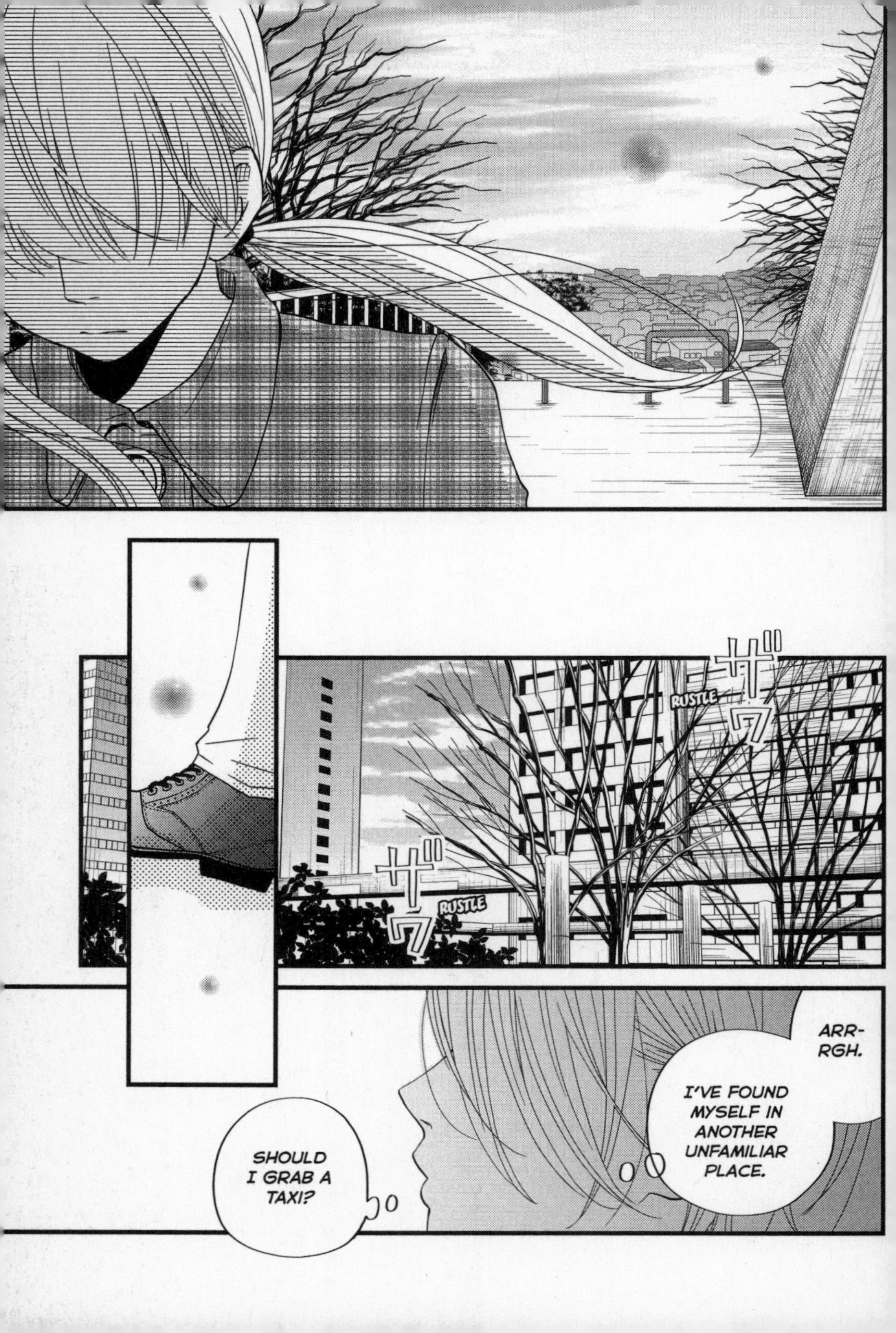
ザワ
RUSTLE
ザワ
RUSTLE
ARR-RGH.
I'VE FOUND MYSELF IN ANOTHER UNFAMILIAR PLACE.
SHOULD I GRAB A TAXI?

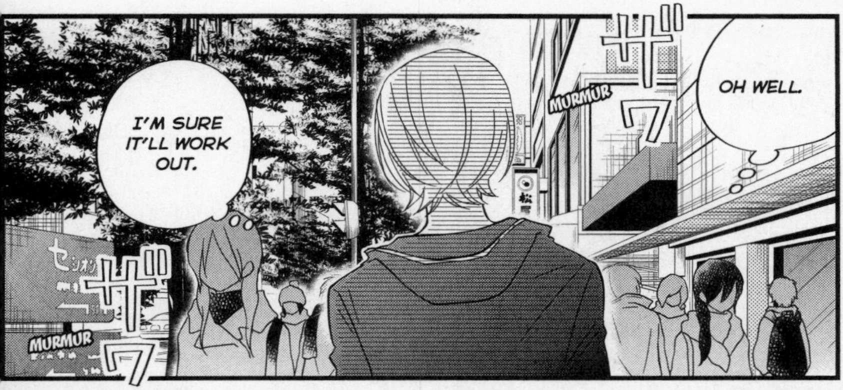
OH WELL.
ザワ
MURMUR
I'M SURE IT'LL WORK OUT.
ザワ
MURMUR

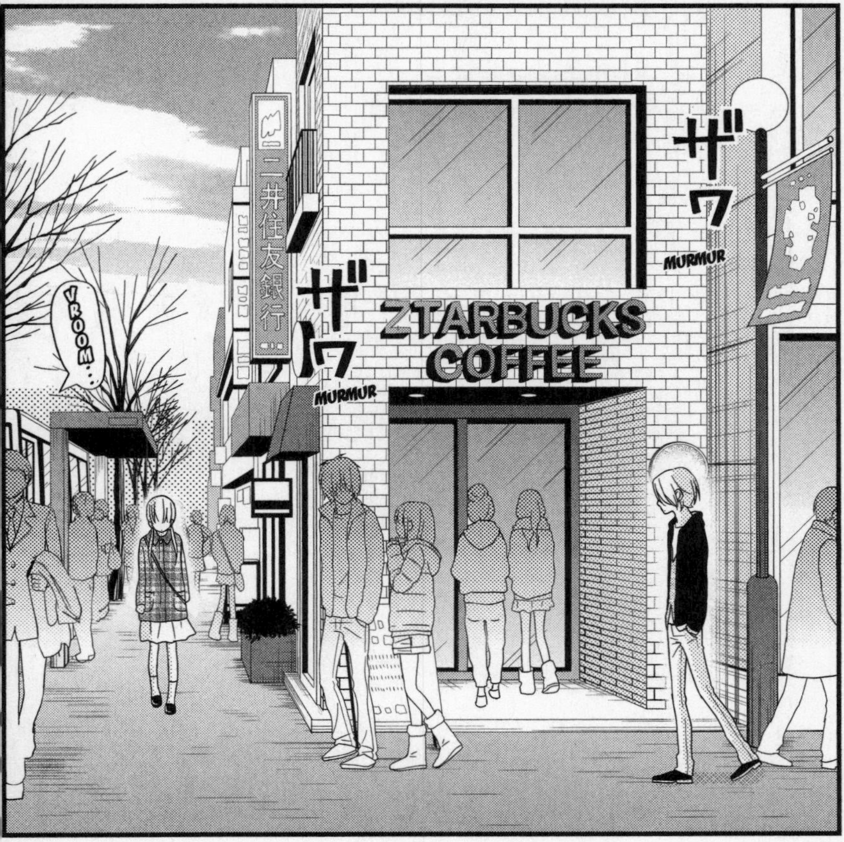
ザワ
MURMUR
ZTARBUCKS COFFEE
ザワ
MURMUR
二井住友銀行
VROOM...

Well, from Your Point of View, Yeah

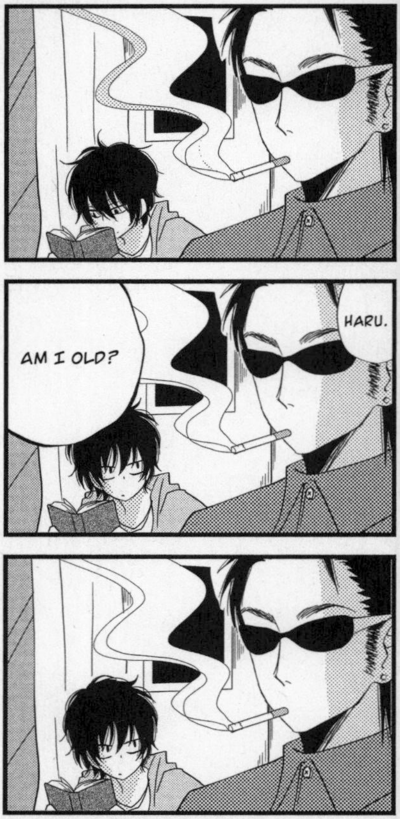
HARU.
AM I OLD?
...
AM I SUPPOSED TO TAKE A HINT HERE?
YES.
APPARENTLY IT BOTHERS HIM TO HAVE BEEN CALLED AN OLD MAN.

Natsume and Mitchan Are...

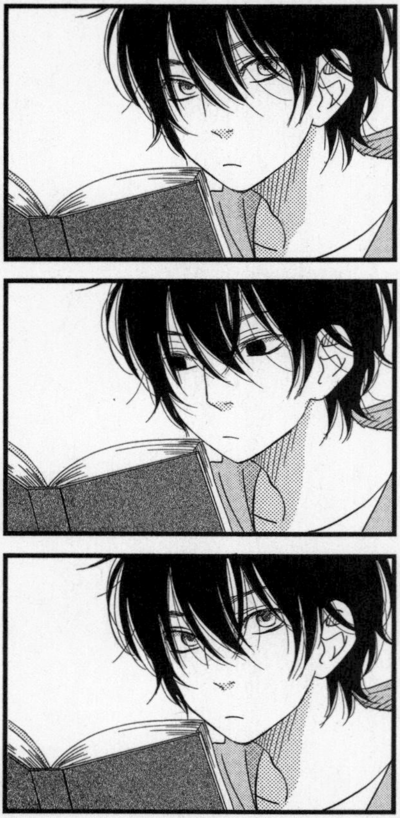
SIZZ
HEY.
I DON'T LIKE PICTURING YOU AND NATSUME.
YOU CAN THINK ABOUT IT IF YOU WANT, BUT DON'T EVER SPEAK OF IT.
SIZZLE

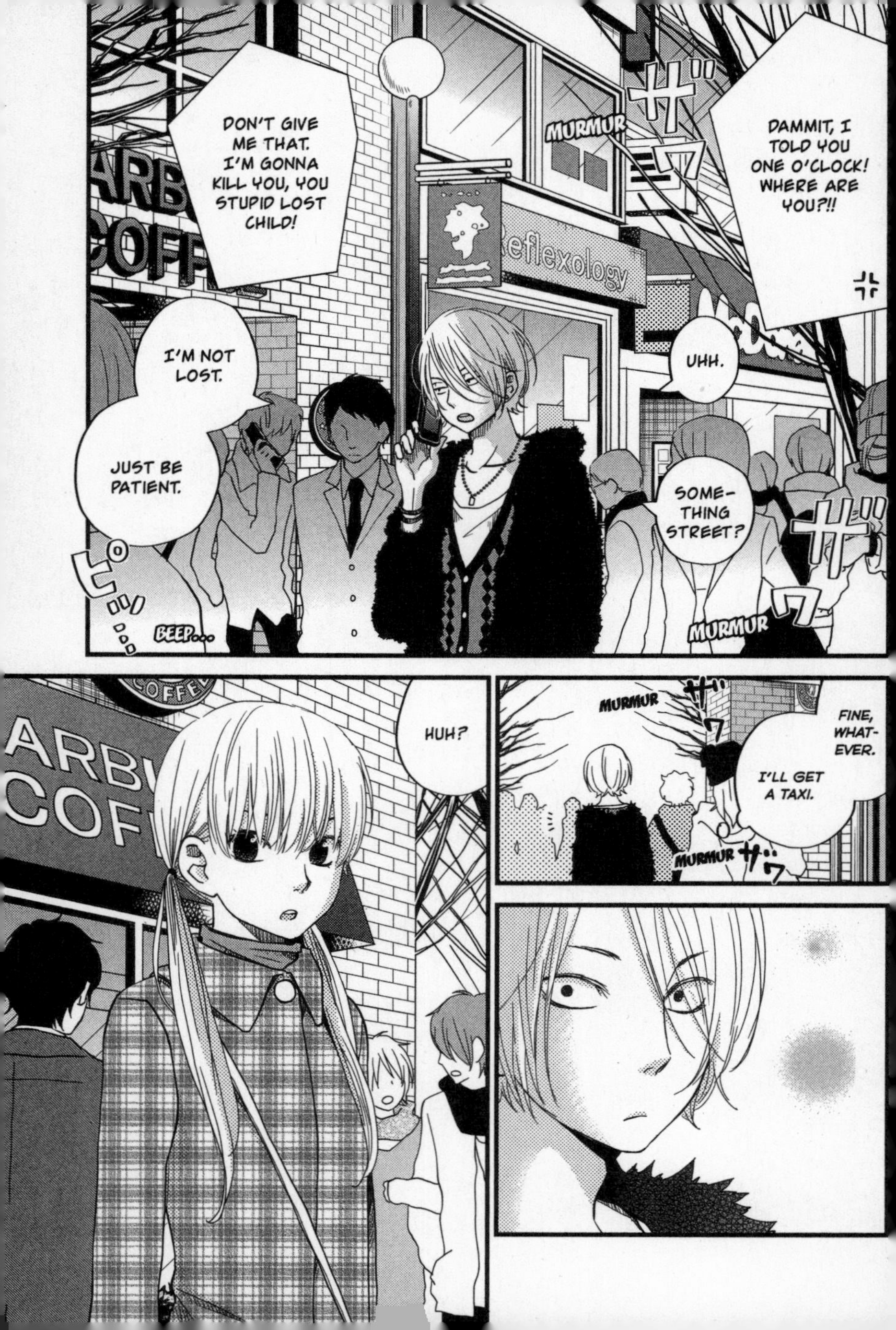

DAMMIT, I TOLD YOU ONE O'CLOCK! WHERE ARE YOU?!!
MURMUR
Reflexology
UHH.
SOME-THING STREET?
MURMUR
DON'T GIVE ME THAT. I'M GONNA KILL YOU, YOU STUPID LOST CHILD!
I'M NOT LOST.
JUST BE PATIENT.
BEEP...
FINE, WHATEVER.
I'LL GET A TAXI.
MURMUR
MURMUR
HUH?

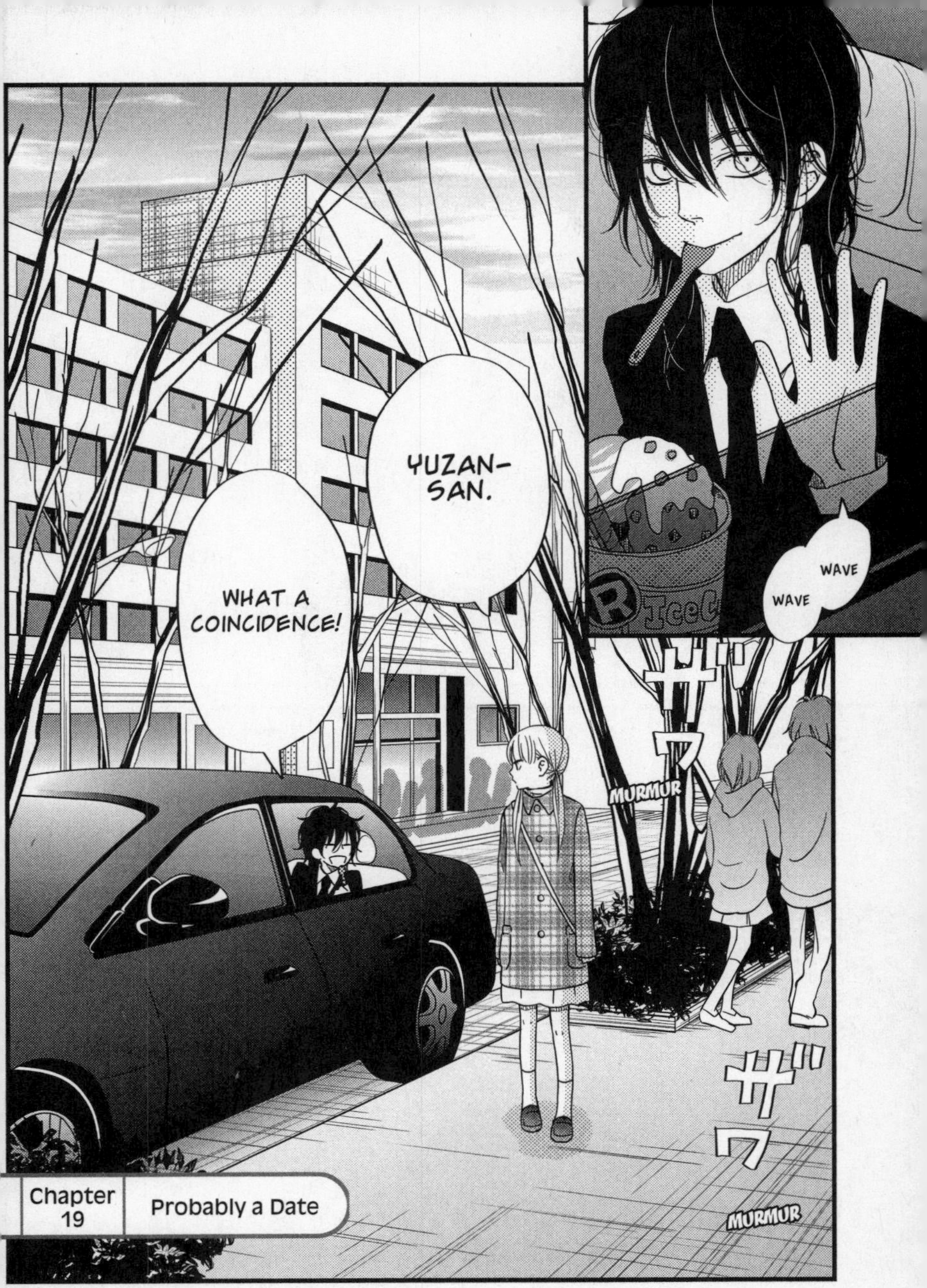
WAVE
WAVE
ザワ
MURMUR
YUZAN-SAN.
WHAT A COINCIDENCE!
ザワ
MURMUR

Chapter 19 Probably a Date

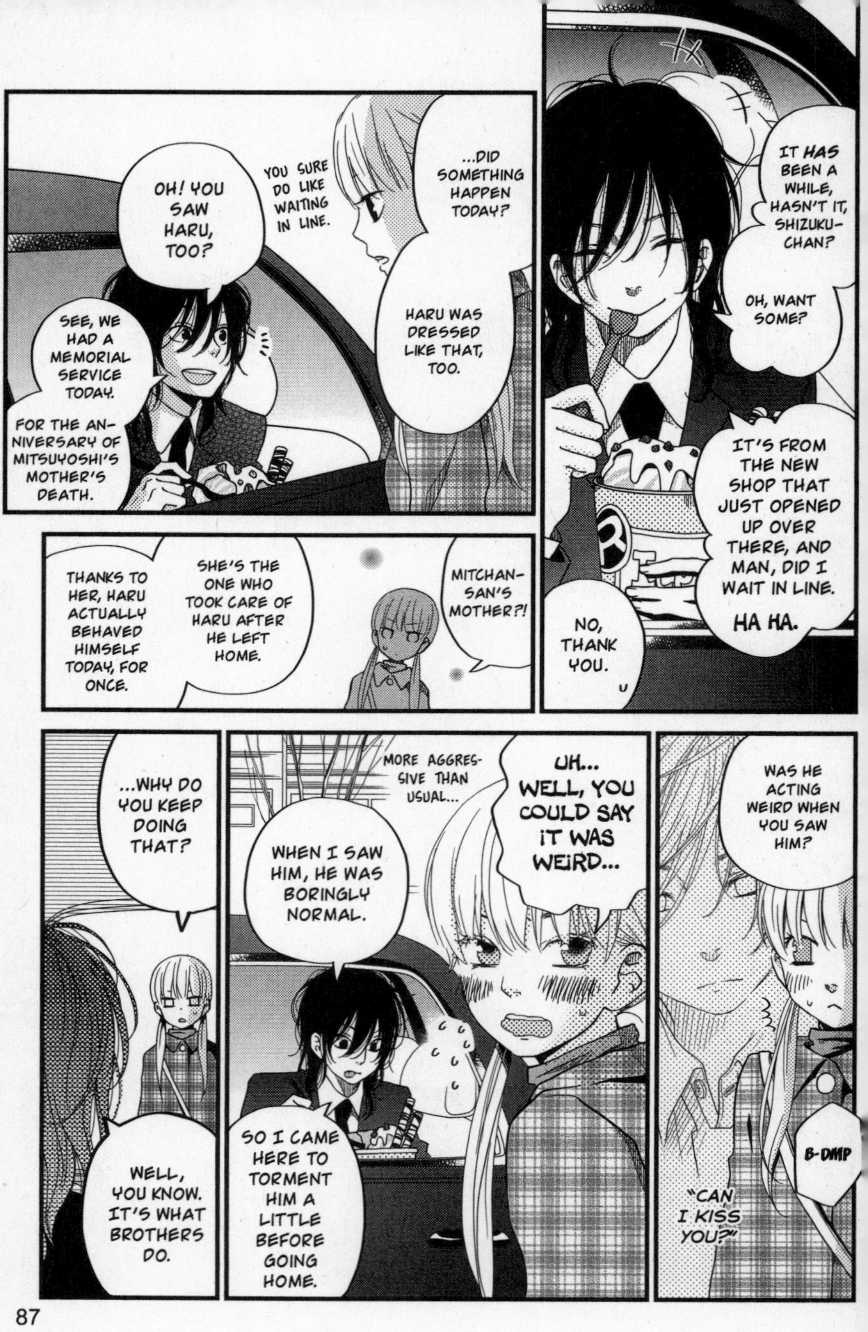
IT HAS BEEN A WHILE, HASN'T IT, SHIZUKU-CHAN?
OH, WANT SOME?
IT'S FROM THE NEW SHOP THAT JUST OPENED UP OVER THERE, AND MAN, DID I WAIT IN LINE.
HA HA.
NO, THANK YOU.
...DID SOMETHING HAPPEN TODAY?
YOU SURE DO LIKE WAITING IN LINE.
HARU WAS DRESSED LIKE THAT, TOO.
OH! YOU SAW HARU, TOO?
SEE, WE HAD A MEMORIAL SERVICE TODAY.
FOR THE ANNIVERSARY OF MITSUYOSHI'S MOTHER'S DEATH.
MITCHAN-SAN'S MOTHER?!
SHE'S THE ONE WHO TOOK CARE OF HARU AFTER HE LEFT HOME.
THANKS TO HER, HARU ACTUALLY BEHAVED HIMSELF TODAY, FOR ONCE.
WAS HE ACTING WEIRD WHEN YOU SAW HIM?
B-DMP
"CAN I KISS YOU?"
UH... WELL, YOU COULD SAY IT WAS WEIRD...
MORE AGGRESSIVE THAN USUAL...
WHEN I SAW HIM, HE WAS BORINGLY NORMAL.
SO I CAME HERE TO TORMENT HIM A LITTLE BEFORE GOING HOME.
...WHY DO YOU KEEP DOING THAT?
WELL, YOU KNOW. IT'S WHAT BROTHERS DO.

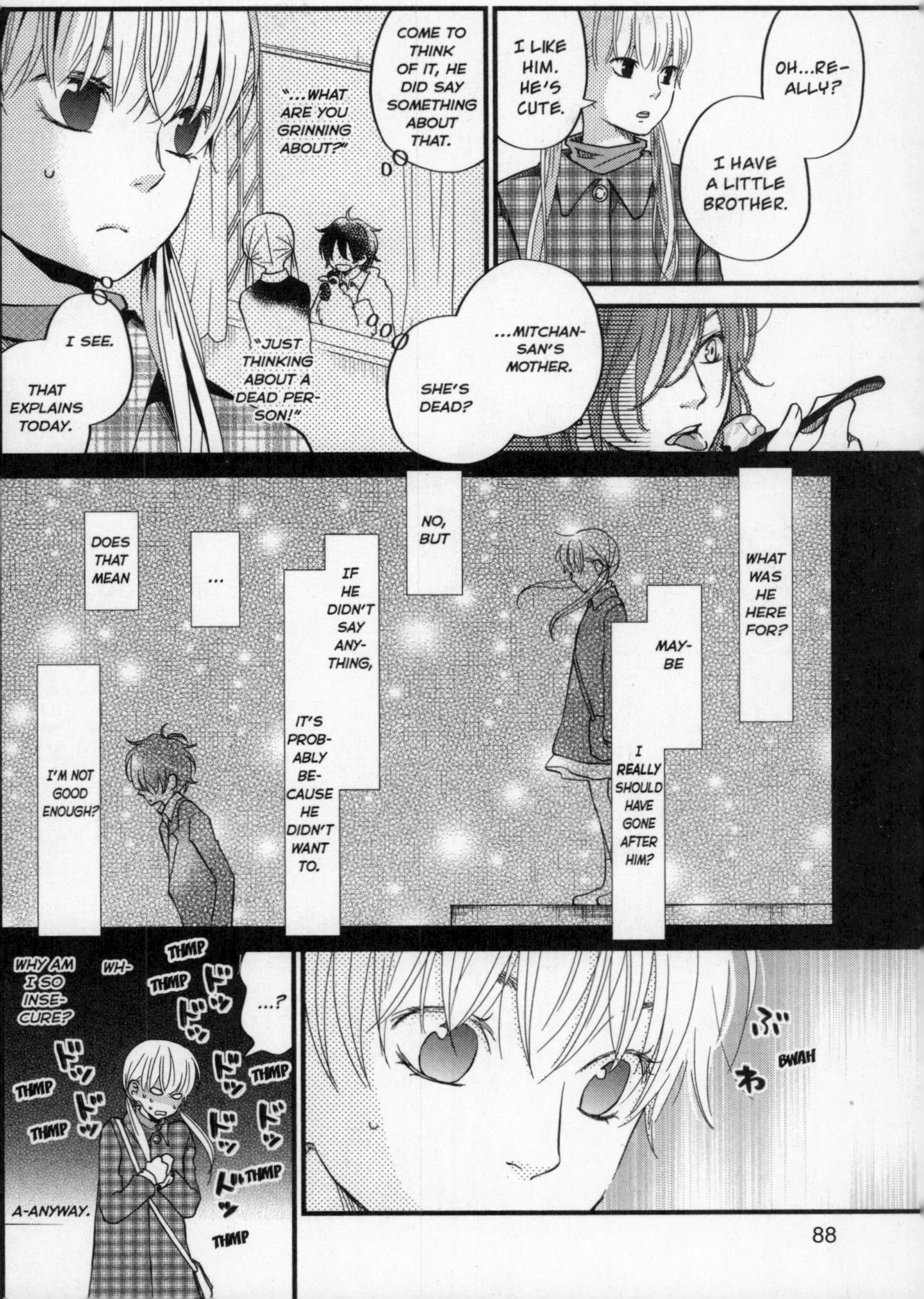
OH...RE-ALLY?
I HAVE A LITTLE BROTHER.
I LIKE HIM. HE'S CUTE.
...MITCHAN-SAN'S MOTHER.
SHE'S DEAD?
COME TO THINK OF IT, HE DID SAY SOMETHING ABOUT THAT.
"...WHAT ARE YOU GRINNING ABOUT?"
"JUST THINKING ABOUT A DEAD PER-SON!"
I SEE.
THAT EXPLAINS TODAY.
WHAT WAS HE HERE FOR?
MAY-BE
I REALLY SHOULD HAVE GONE AFTER HIM?
NO, BUT
IF HE DIDN'T SAY ANY-THING,
IT'S PROB-ABLY BE-CAUSE HE DIDN'T WANT TO.
...
DOES THAT MEAN
I'M NOT GOOD ENOUGH?
ぶわ
BWAH
...?
THMP
THMP
THMP
THMP
THMP
THMP
THMP
WH-
WHY AM I SO INSE-CURE?
A-ANYWAY.

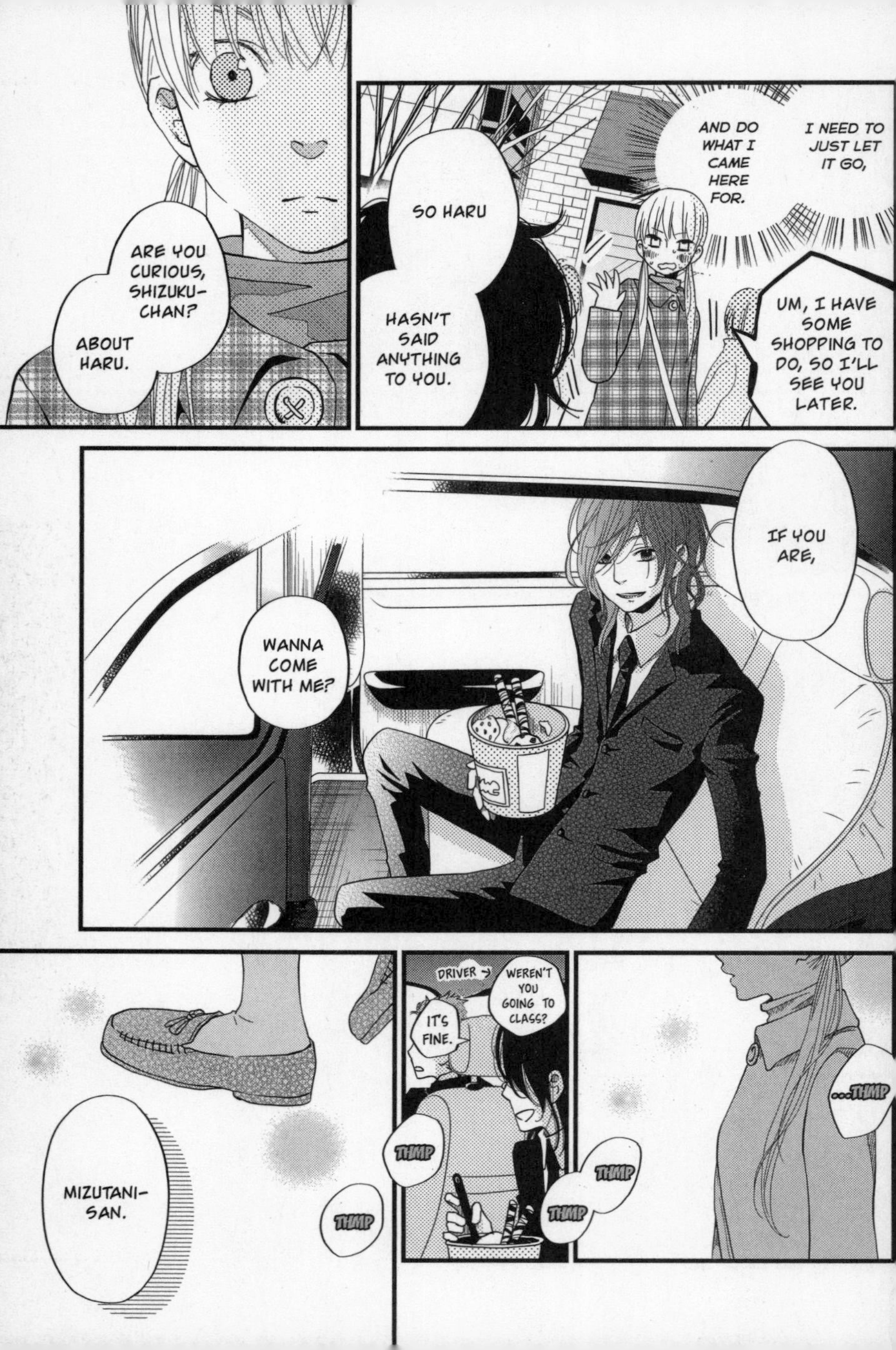
I NEED TO JUST LET IT GO,
AND DO WHAT I CAME HERE FOR.
UM, I HAVE SOME SHOPPING TO DO, SO I'LL SEE YOU LATER.
SO HARU
HASN'T SAID ANYTHING TO YOU.
ARE YOU CURIOUS, SHIZUKU-CHAN?
ABOUT HARU.
IF YOU ARE,
WANNA COME WITH ME?
...THMP
DRIVER →
WEREN'T YOU GOING TO CLASS?
IT'S FINE.
THMP
THMP
THMP
THMP
MIZUTANI-SAN.

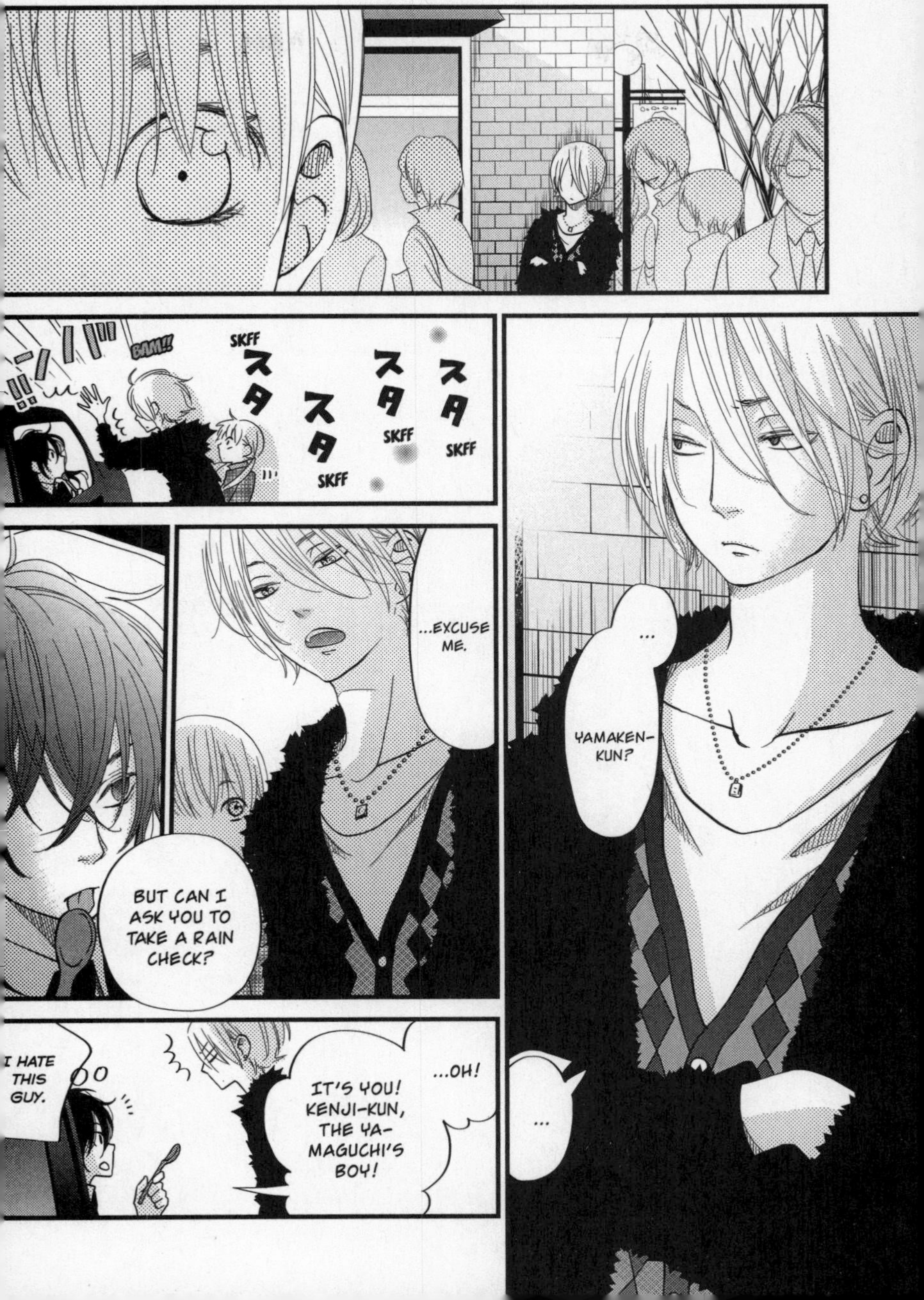

...
YAMAKEN-KUN?
...
BAM!!
SKFF
スタ
SKFF
スタ
SKFF
スタ
SKFF
スタ
...EXCUSE ME.
BUT CAN I ASK YOU TO TAKE A RAIN CHECK?
...OH!
IT'S YOU! KENJI-KUN, THE YA-MAGUCHI'S BOY!
I HATE THIS GUY.

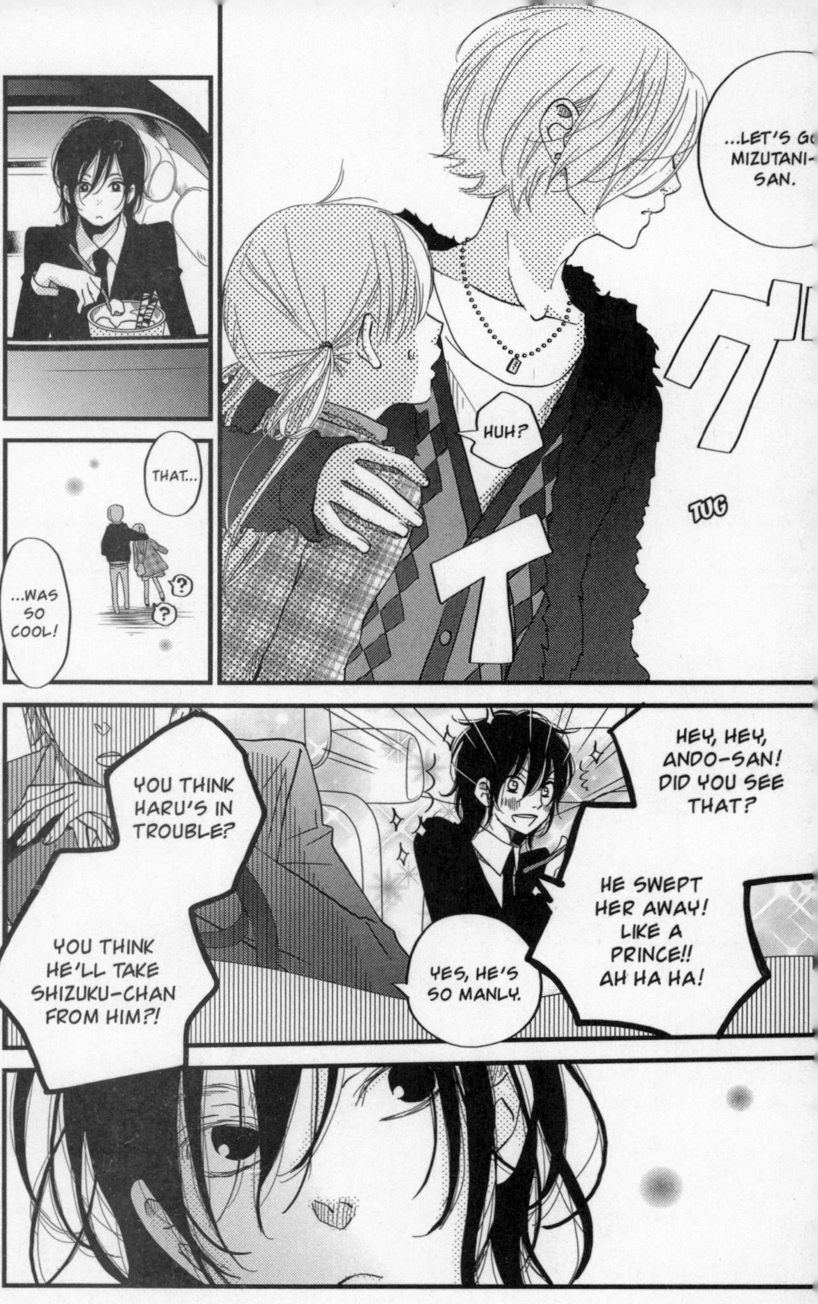

...LET'S GO MIZUTANI-SAN.
TUG
HUH?
THAT...
...WAS SO COOL!
HEY, HEY, ANDO-SAN! DID YOU SEE THAT?
HE SWEPT HER AWAY! LIKE A PRINCE!! AH HA HA!
YES, HE'S SO MANLY.
YOU THINK HARU'S IN TROUBLE?
YOU THINK HE'LL TAKE SHIZUKU-CHAN FROM HIM?!

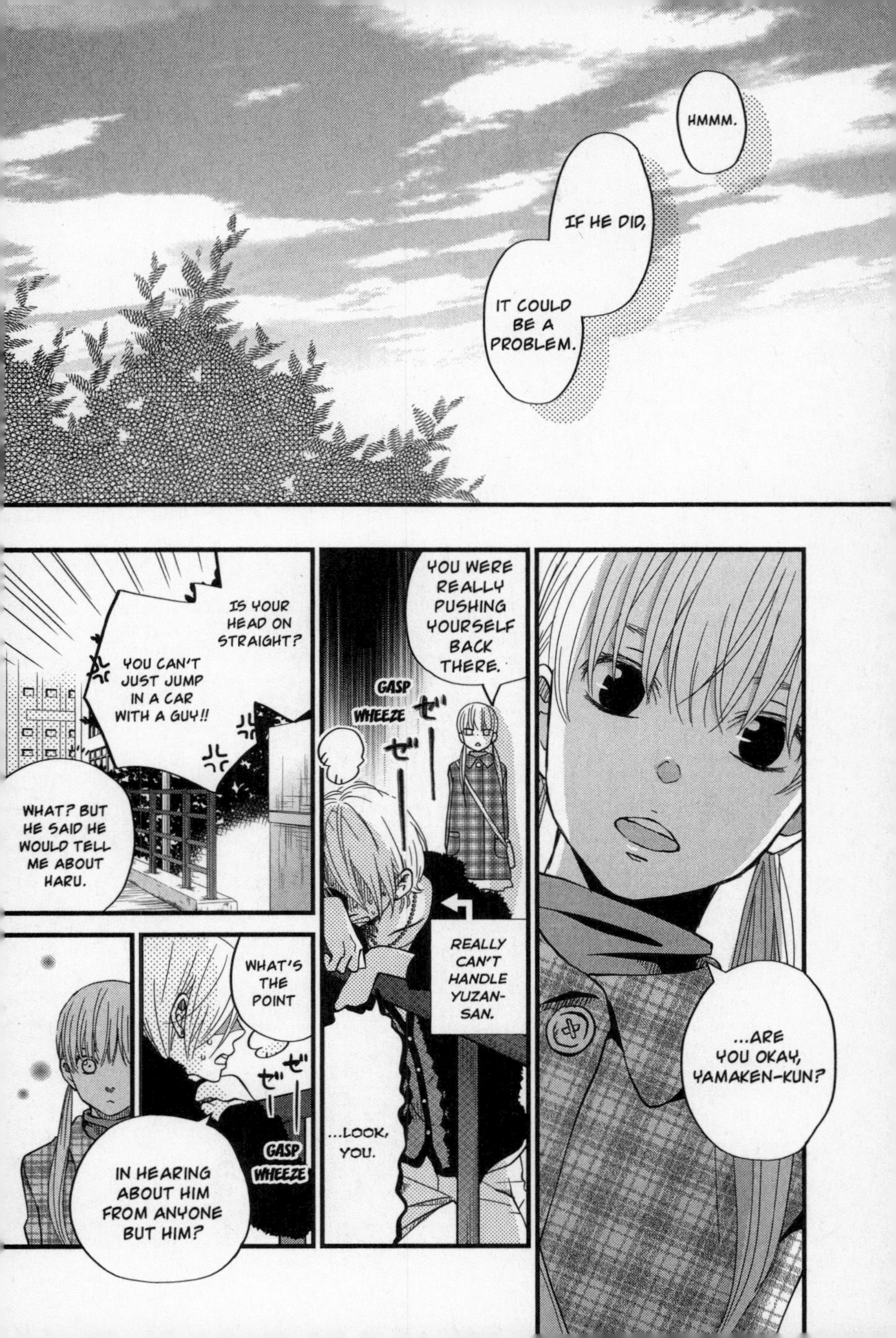
HMMM.
IF HE DID,
IT COULD BE A PROBLEM.
...ARE YOU OKAY, YAMAKEN-KUN?
YOU WERE REALLY PUSHING YOURSELF BACK THERE.
GASP
WHEEZE
ぜー
ぜー
REALLY CAN'T HANDLE YUZAN-SAN.
...LOOK, YOU.
IS YOUR HEAD ON STRAIGHT?
YOU CAN'T JUST JUMP IN A CAR WITH A GUY!!
WHAT? BUT HE SAID HE WOULD TELL ME ABOUT HARU.
WHAT'S THE POINT
ぜ
ぜ
GASP
WHEEZE
IN HEARING ABOUT HIM FROM ANYONE BUT HIM?

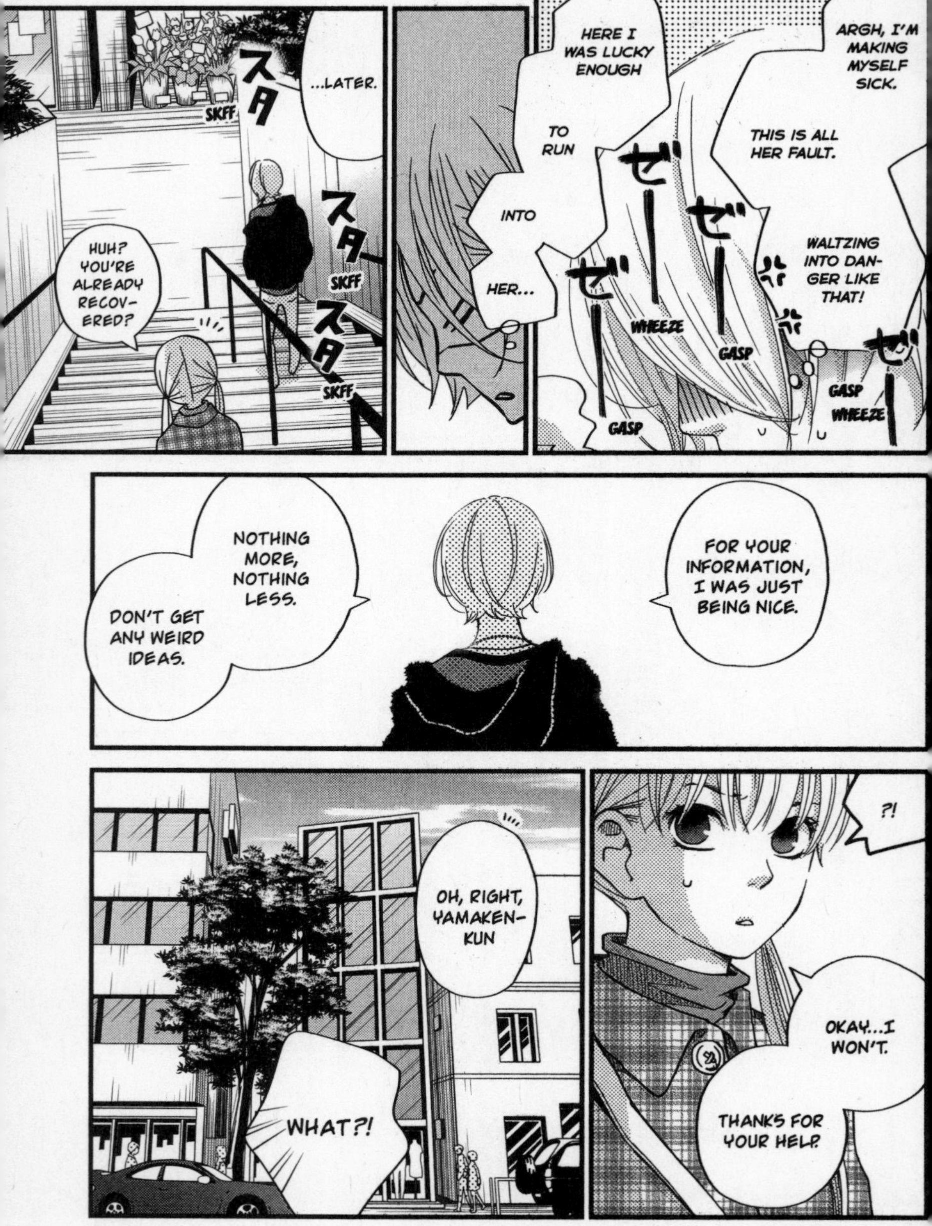
ARGH, I'M MAKING MYSELF SICK.
THIS IS ALL HER FAULT.
WALTZING INTO DANGER LIKE THAT!
GASP
WHEEZE
HERE I WAS LUCKY ENOUGH
TO RUN
INTO
HER...
GASP
WHEEZE
GASP
...LATER.
スタ
SKFF
スタ
SKFF
スタ
SKFF
HUH? YOU'RE ALREADY RECOV-ERED?
FOR YOUR INFORMATION, I WAS JUST BEING NICE.
NOTHING MORE, NOTHING LESS.
DON'T GET ANY WEIRD IDEAS.
?!
OKAY...I WON'T.
THANKS FOR YOUR HELP.
OH, RIGHT, YAMAKEN-KUN
WHAT?!

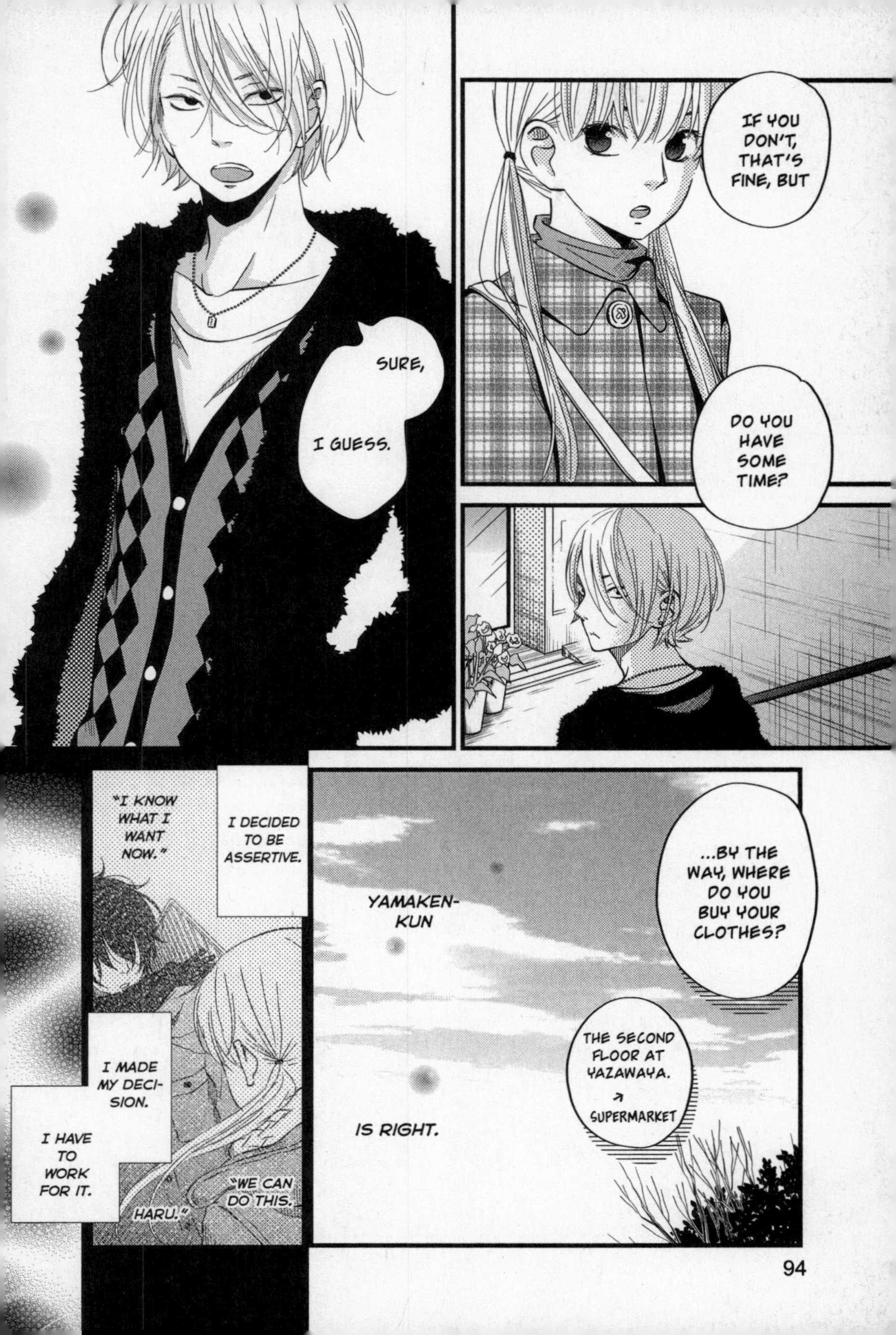
IF YOU DON'T, THAT'S FINE, BUT
DO YOU HAVE SOME TIME?
SURE,
I GUESS.
...BY THE WAY, WHERE DO YOU BUY YOUR CLOTHES?
THE SECOND FLOOR AT YAZAWAYA.
→ SUPERMARKET
YAMAKEN-KUN
IS RIGHT.
I DECIDED TO BE ASSERTIVE.
"I KNOW WHAT I WANT NOW."
I MADE MY DECI-SION.
I HAVE TO WORK FOR IT.
"WE CAN DO THIS.
HARU."

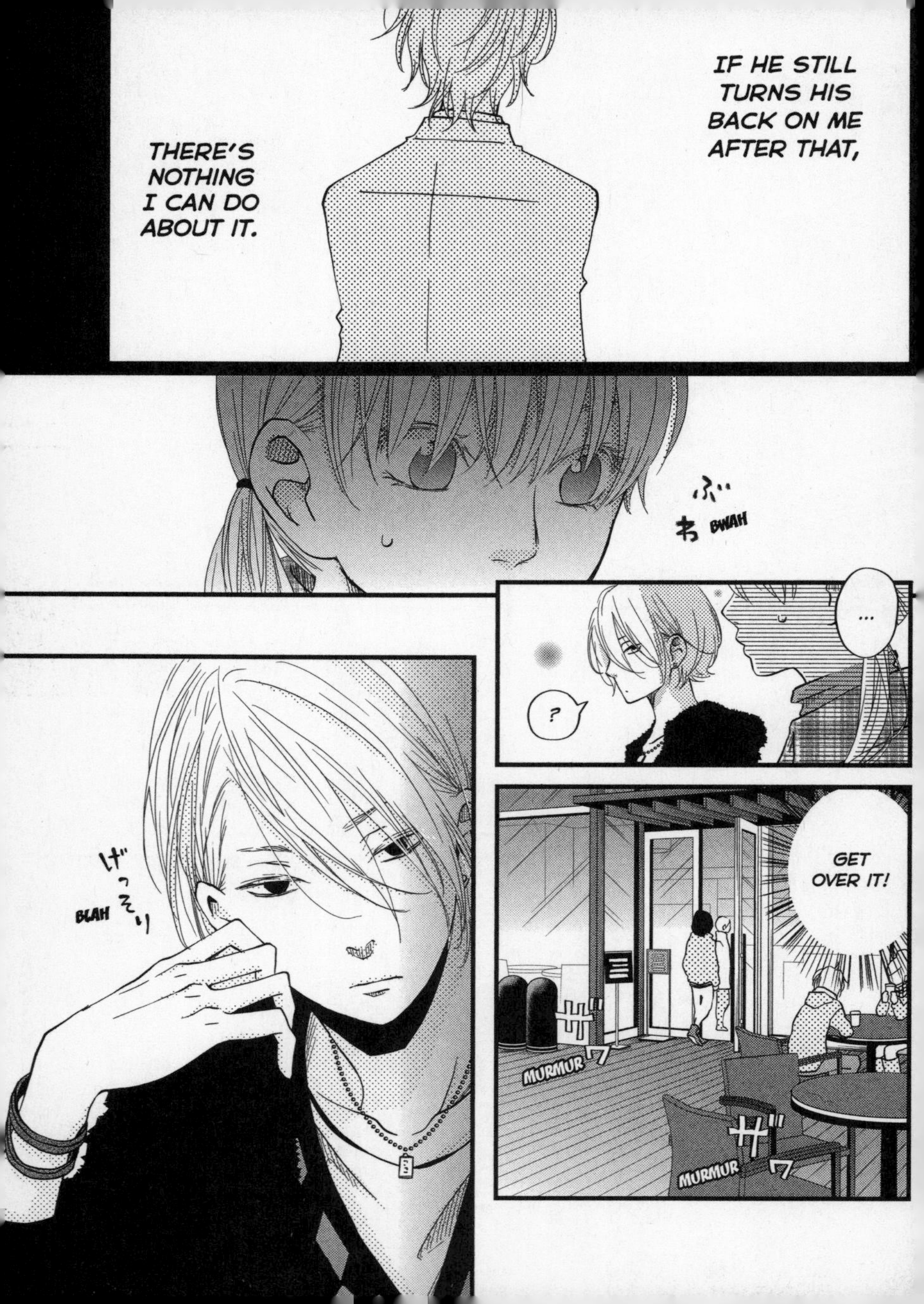
IF HE STILL TURNS HIS BACK ON ME AFTER THAT,
THERE'S NOTHING I CAN DO ABOUT IT.
ぶわ BWAH
...
?
GET OVER IT!
ザワ MURMUR
ザワ MURMUR
げっそり BLAH

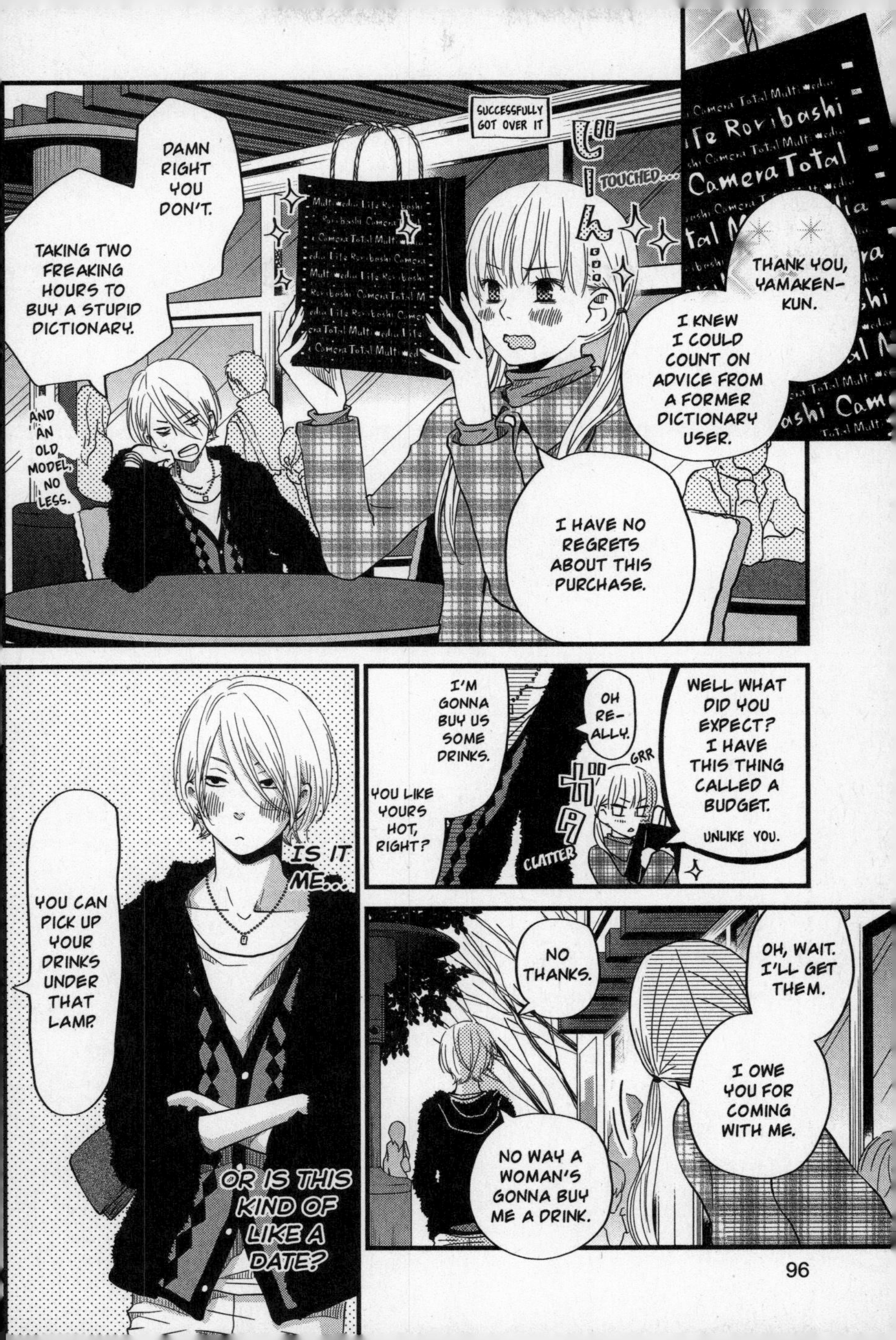
SUCCESSFULLY GOT OVER IT
TOUCHED...
THANK YOU, YAMAKEN-KUN.
I KNEW I COULD COUNT ON ADVICE FROM A FORMER DICTIONARY USER.
I HAVE NO REGRETS ABOUT THIS PURCHASE.
DAMN RIGHT YOU DON'T.
TAKING TWO FREAKING HOURS TO BUY A STUPID DICTIONARY.
AND AN OLD MODEL, NO LESS.
WELL WHAT DID YOU EXPECT? I HAVE THIS THING CALLED A BUDGET.
UNLIKE YOU.
OH RE-ALLY.
GRR
CLATTER
I'M GONNA BUY US SOME DRINKS.
YOU LIKE YOURS HOT, RIGHT?
OH, WAIT. I'LL GET THEM.
I OWE YOU FOR COMING WITH ME.
NO THANKS.
NO WAY A WOMAN'S GONNA BUY ME A DRINK.
IS IT ME...
YOU CAN PICK UP YOUR DRINKS UNDER THAT LAMP.
OR IS THIS KIND OF LIKE A DATE?

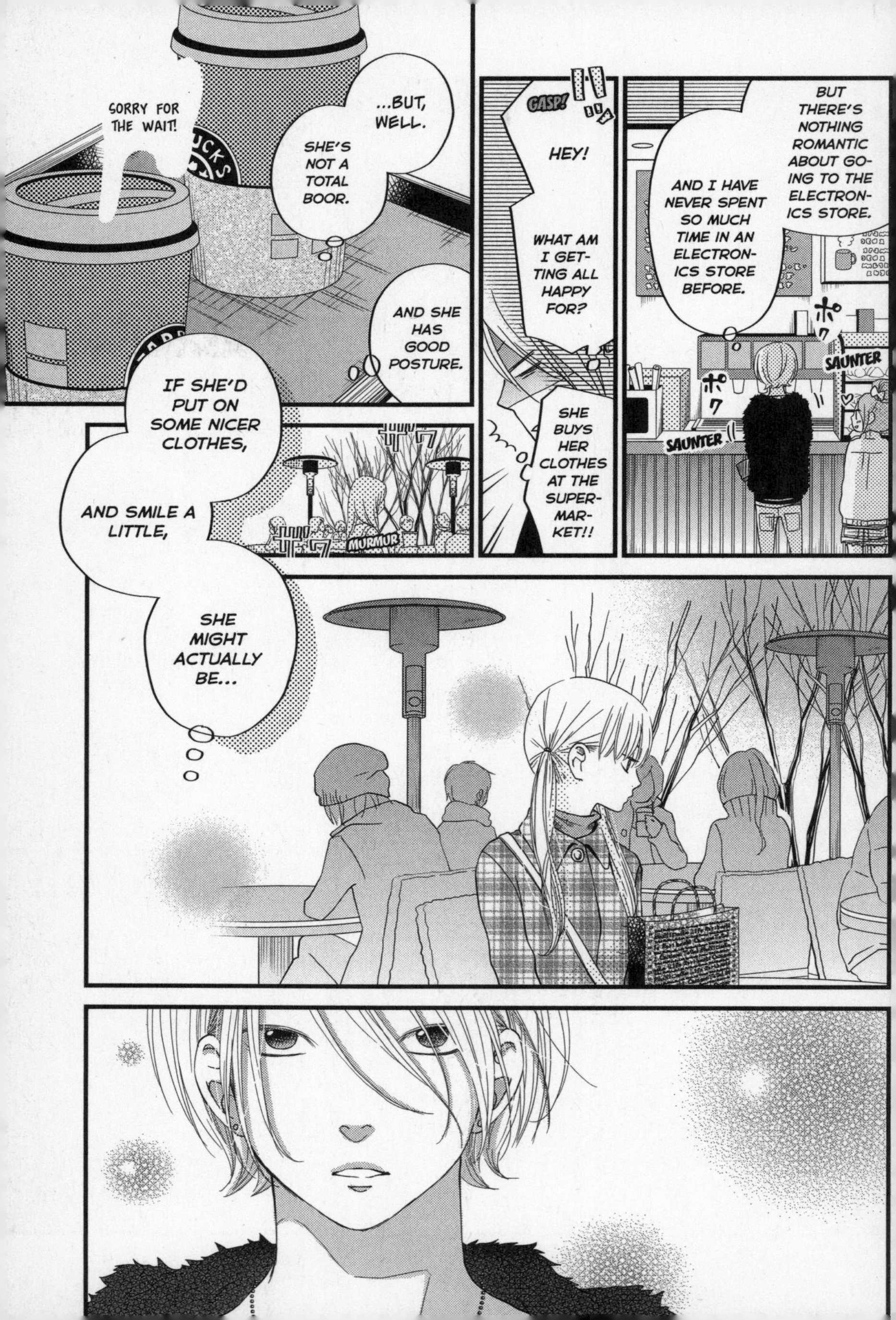
BUT THERE'S NOTHING ROMANTIC ABOUT GOING TO THE ELECTRONICS STORE.
AND I HAVE NEVER SPENT SO MUCH TIME IN AN ELECTRONICS STORE BEFORE.
SAUNTER
SAUNTER
GASP!
HEY!
WHAT AM I GETTING ALL HAPPY FOR?
SHE BUYS HER CLOTHES AT THE SUPERMARKET!!
SORRY FOR THE WAIT!
...BUT, WELL.
SHE'S NOT A TOTAL BOOR.
AND SHE HAS GOOD POSTURE.
MURMUR
IF SHE'D PUT ON SOME NICER CLOTHES,
AND SMILE A LITTLE,
SHE MIGHT ACTUALLY BE...

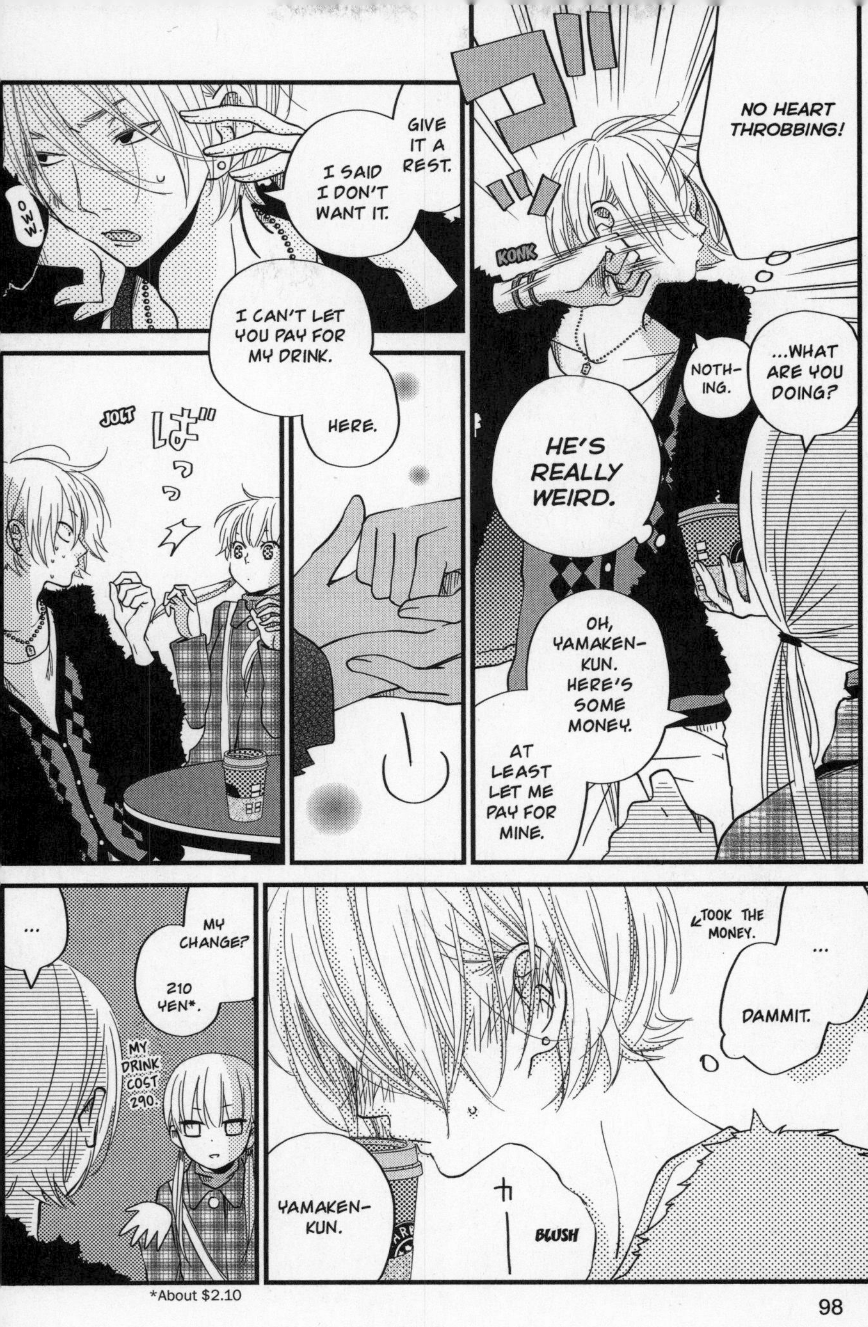
NO HEART THROBBING!
KONK
...WHAT ARE YOU DOING?
NOTH-ING.
HE'S REALLY WEIRD.
OH, YAMAKEN-KUN. HERE'S SOME MONEY.
AT LEAST LET ME PAY FOR MINE.
GIVE IT A REST.
I SAID I DON'T WANT IT.
OWW.
I CAN'T LET YOU PAY FOR MY DRINK.
HERE.
JOLT
TOOK THE MONEY.
...
DAMMIT.
YAMAKEN-KUN.
BLUSH
MY CHANGE?
210 YEN*.
MY DRINK COST 290.
...

*About $2.10

...

じったり
SLUMP

...

YAMAKEN-KUN.

era
T×1×1 Multi-media
á Camera To
T×1×1 Multi-media Li
T×1×1 Multi-media Life Rc-boshi Came

...

YOU SEEM LIKE SOMEONE WITH A WEALTH OF EXPERIENCE WITH WOMEN.

...

YOU MEAN...

I JUST KNOW YOU'RE A PLAYER, YAMAGUCHI-KUN!

...LIKE THAT?

ブッ
PFFT

HAVE-

HAVE YOU EVER KISSED A GIRL?

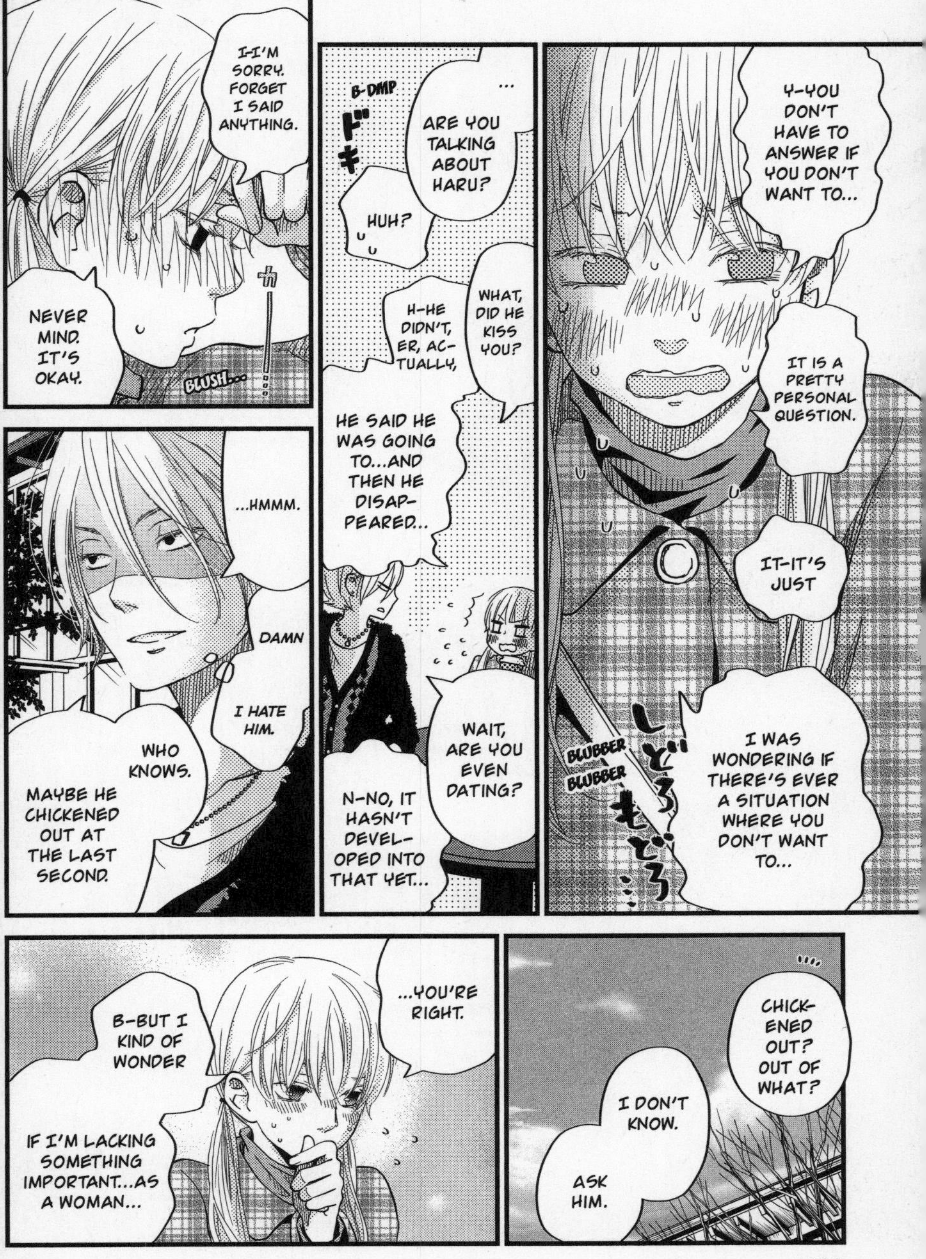
Y-YOU DON'T HAVE TO ANSWER IF YOU DON'T WANT TO...
IT IS A PRETTY PERSONAL QUESTION.
IT-IT'S JUST
I WAS WONDERING IF THERE'S EVER A SITUATION WHERE YOU DON'T WANT TO...
BLUBBER BLUBBER
しどろもどろ
...
ARE YOU TALKING ABOUT HARU?
B-DMP
ドキ
HUH?
WHAT, DID HE KISS YOU?
H-HE DIDN'T, ER, ACTUALLY,
HE SAID HE WAS GOING TO...AND THEN HE DISAPPEARED...
WAIT, ARE YOU EVEN DATING?
N-NO, IT HASN'T DEVELOPED INTO THAT YET...
I-I'M SORRY. FORGET I SAID ANYTHING.
カ
BLUSH...
NEVER MIND. IT'S OKAY.
...HMMM.
DAMN
I HATE HIM.
WHO KNOWS.
MAYBE HE CHICKENED OUT AT THE LAST SECOND.
...
CHICKENED OUT? OUT OF WHAT?
I DON'T KNOW.
ASK HIM.
...YOU'RE RIGHT.
B-BUT I KIND OF WONDER
IF I'M LACKING SOMETHING IMPORTANT...AS A WOMAN...

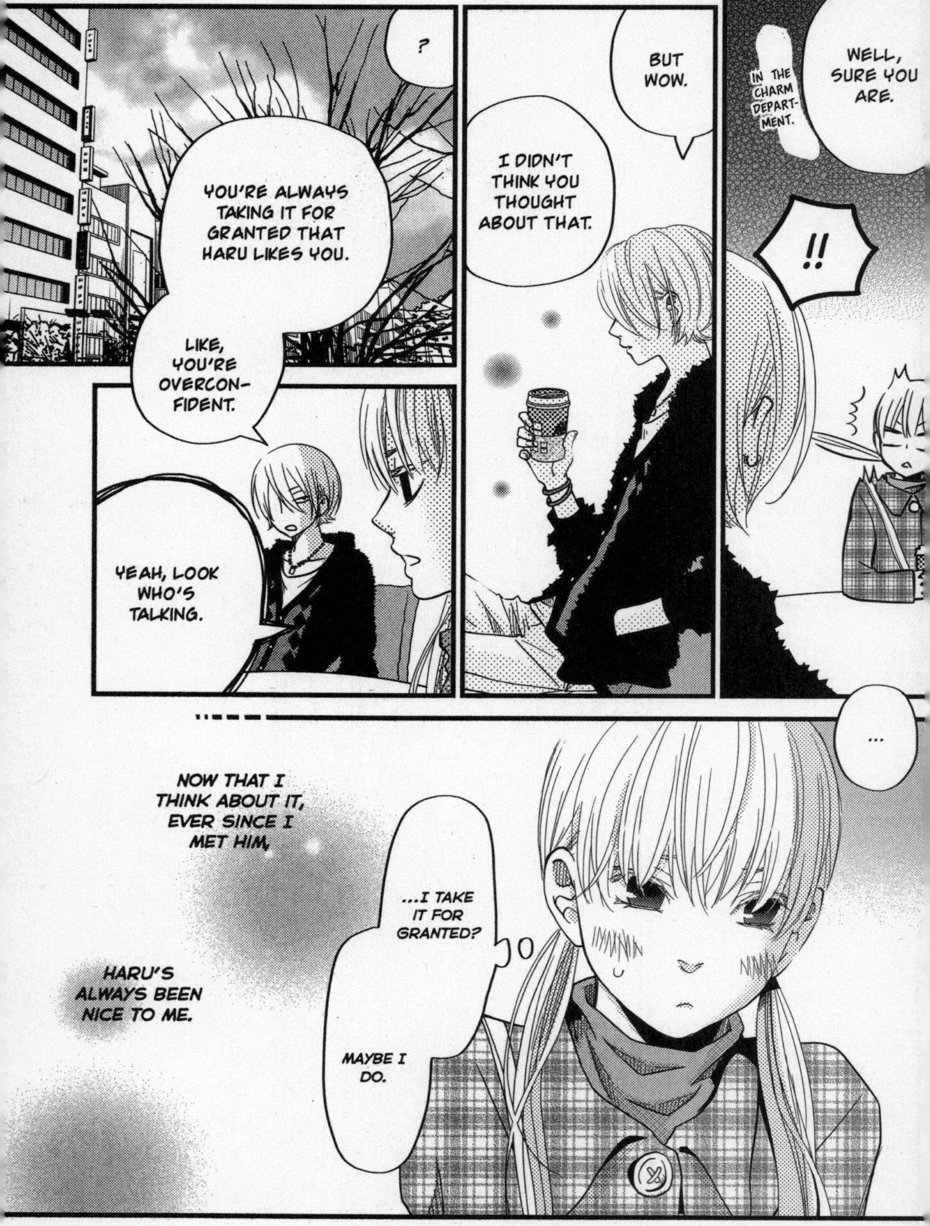
WELL, SURE YOU ARE.
IN THE CHARM DEPARTMENT.
!!
BUT WOW.
I DIDN'T THINK YOU THOUGHT ABOUT THAT.
?
YOU'RE ALWAYS TAKING IT FOR GRANTED THAT HARU LIKES YOU.
LIKE, YOU'RE OVERCON-FIDENT.
YEAH, LOOK WHO'S TALKING.
...
...I TAKE IT FOR GRANTED?
MAYBE I DO.
NOW THAT I THINK ABOUT IT, EVER SINCE I MET HIM,
HARU'S ALWAYS BEEN NICE TO ME.

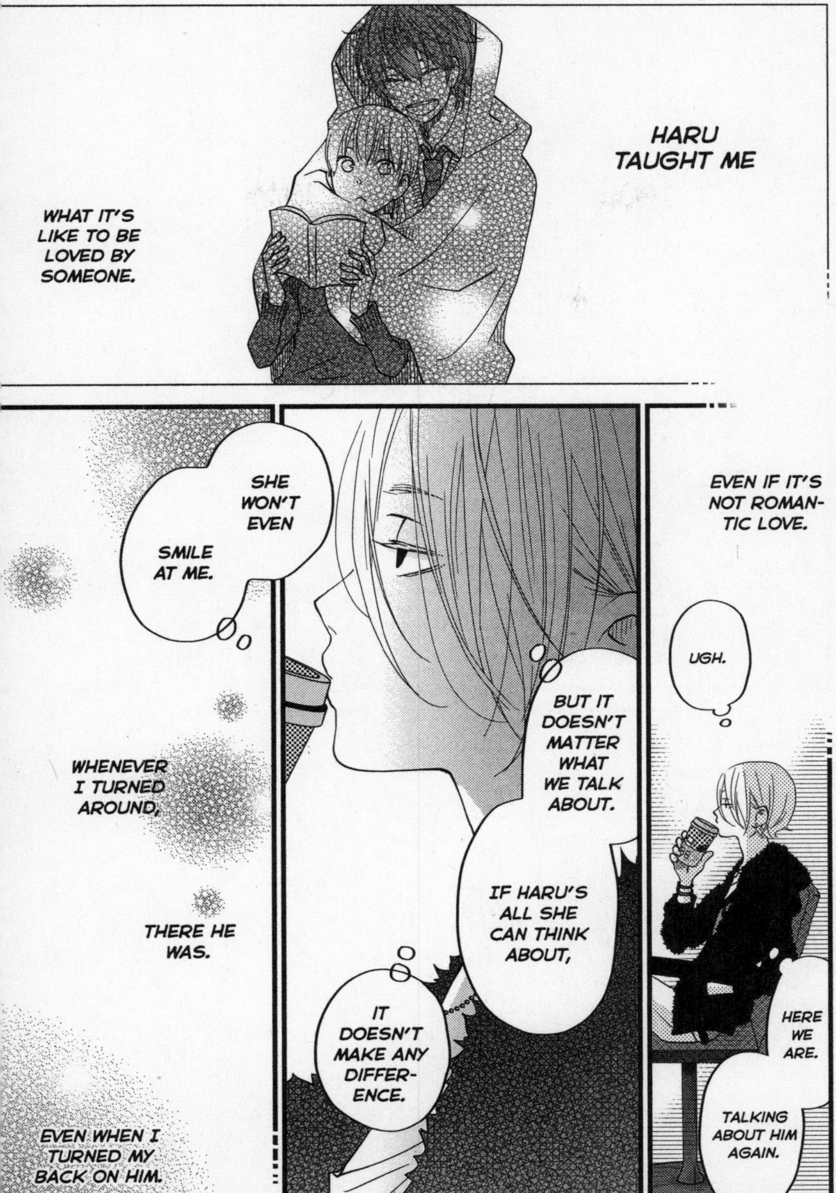
HARU TAUGHT ME
WHAT IT'S LIKE TO BE LOVED BY SOMEONE.
EVEN IF IT'S NOT ROMANTIC LOVE.
UGH.
HERE WE ARE.
TALKING ABOUT HIM AGAIN.
BUT IT DOESN'T MATTER WHAT WE TALK ABOUT.
IF HARU'S ALL SHE CAN THINK ABOUT,
IT DOESN'T MAKE ANY DIFFERENCE.
SHE WON'T EVEN SMILE AT ME.
WHENEVER I TURNED AROUND,
THERE HE WAS.
EVEN WHEN I TURNED MY BACK ON HIM.

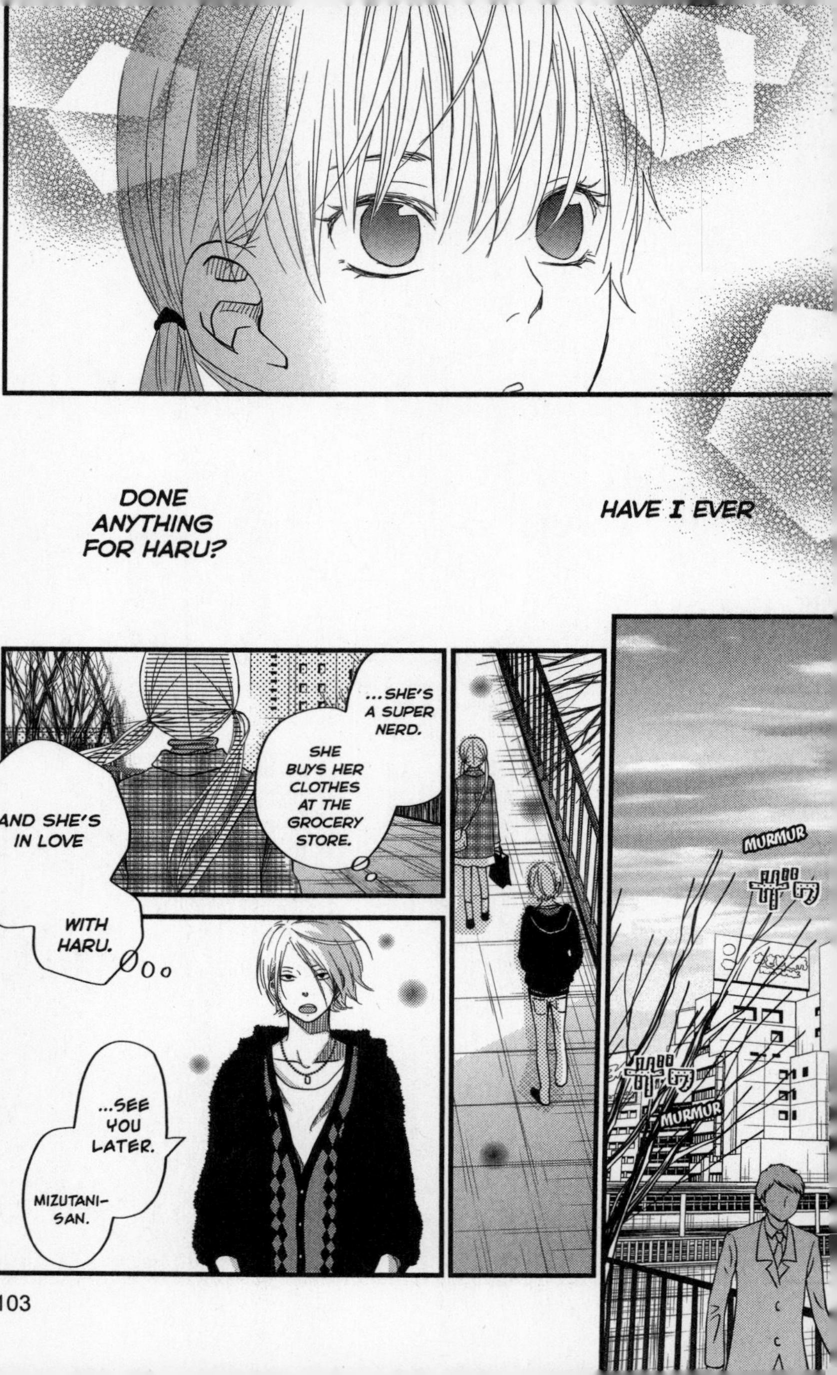
HAVE I EVER
DONE ANYTHING FOR HARU?
MURMUR
MURMUR
...SHE'S A SUPER NERD.
SHE BUYS HER CLOTHES AT THE GROCERY STORE.
AND SHE'S IN LOVE
WITH HARU.
...SEE YOU LATER.
MIZUTANI-SAN.

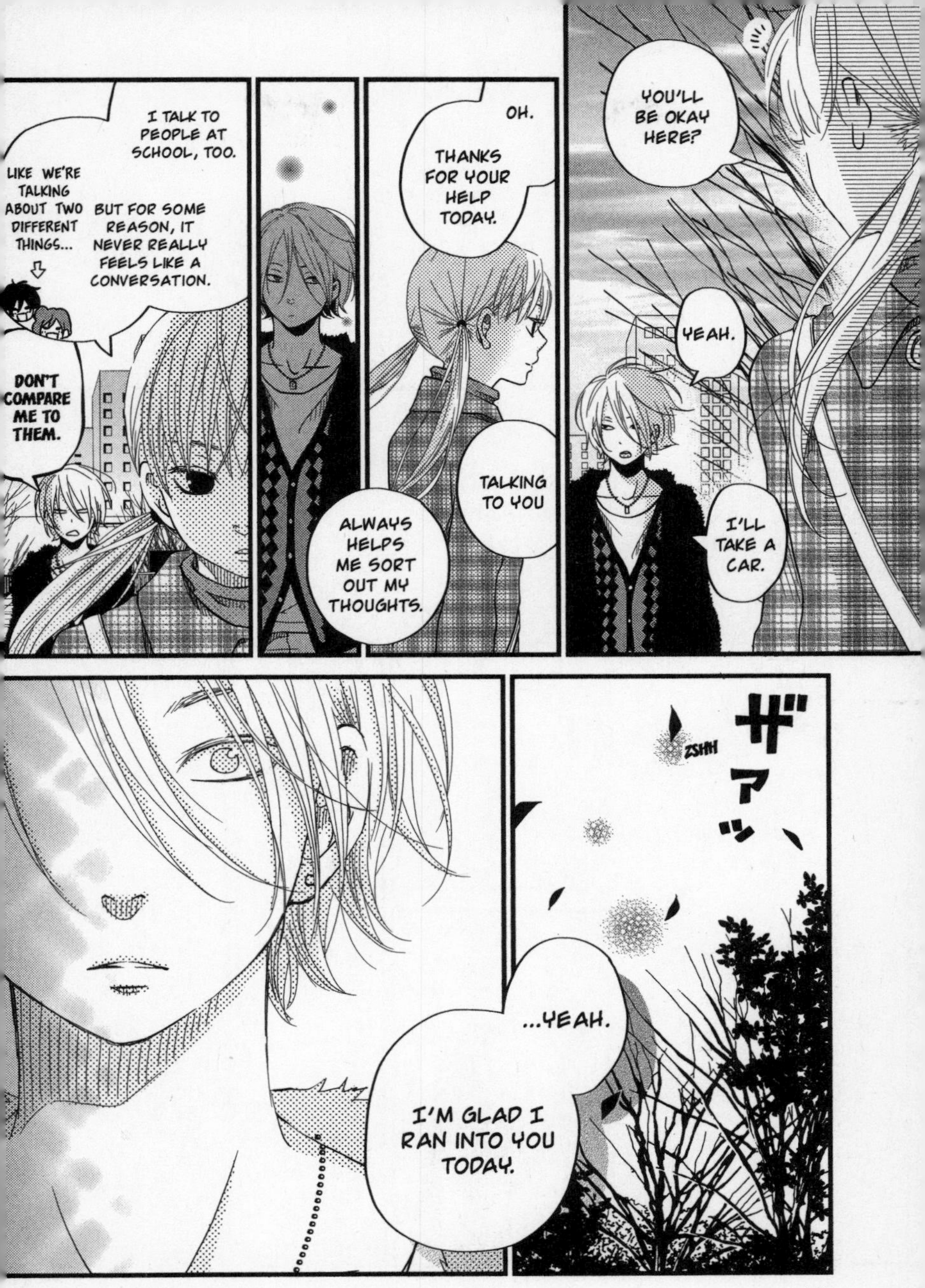
YOU'LL BE OKAY HERE?
YEAH.
I'LL TAKE A CAR.
OH.
THANKS FOR YOUR HELP TODAY.
TALKING TO YOU
ALWAYS HELPS ME SORT OUT MY THOUGHTS.
I TALK TO PEOPLE AT SCHOOL, TOO.
BUT FOR SOME REASON, IT NEVER REALLY FEELS LIKE A CONVERSATION.
LIKE WE'RE TALKING ABOUT TWO DIFFERENT THINGS...
DON'T COMPARE ME TO THEM.
ザアッ
ZSHH
...YEAH.
I'M GLAD I RAN INTO YOU TODAY.

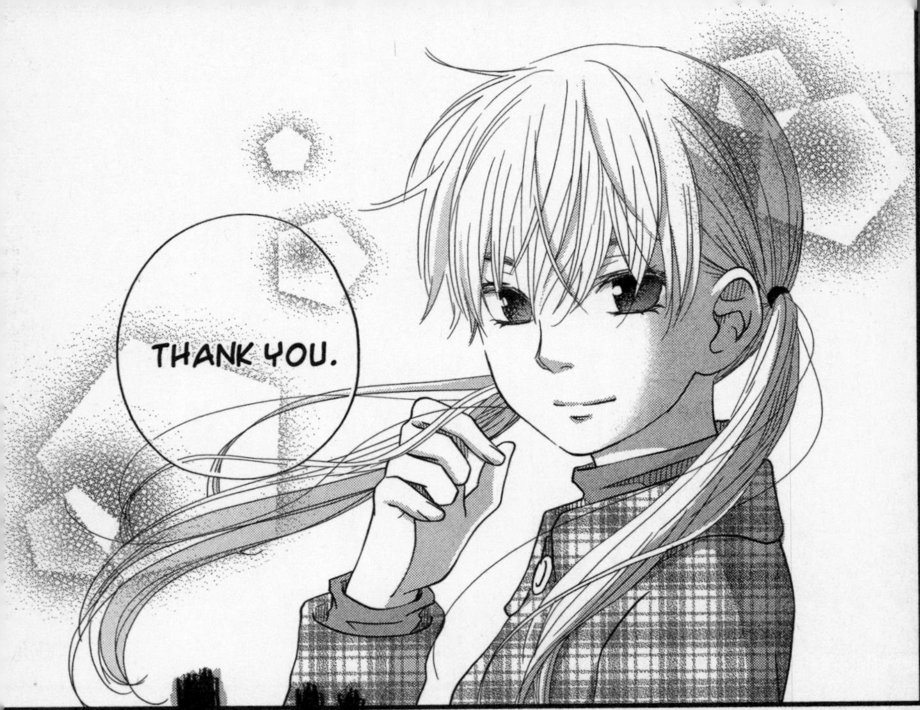
THANK YOU.
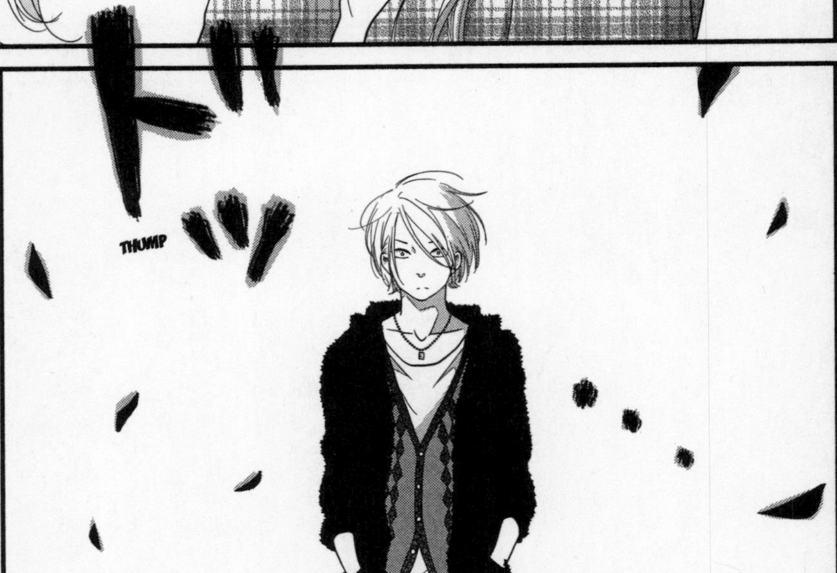
ドッ
THUMP

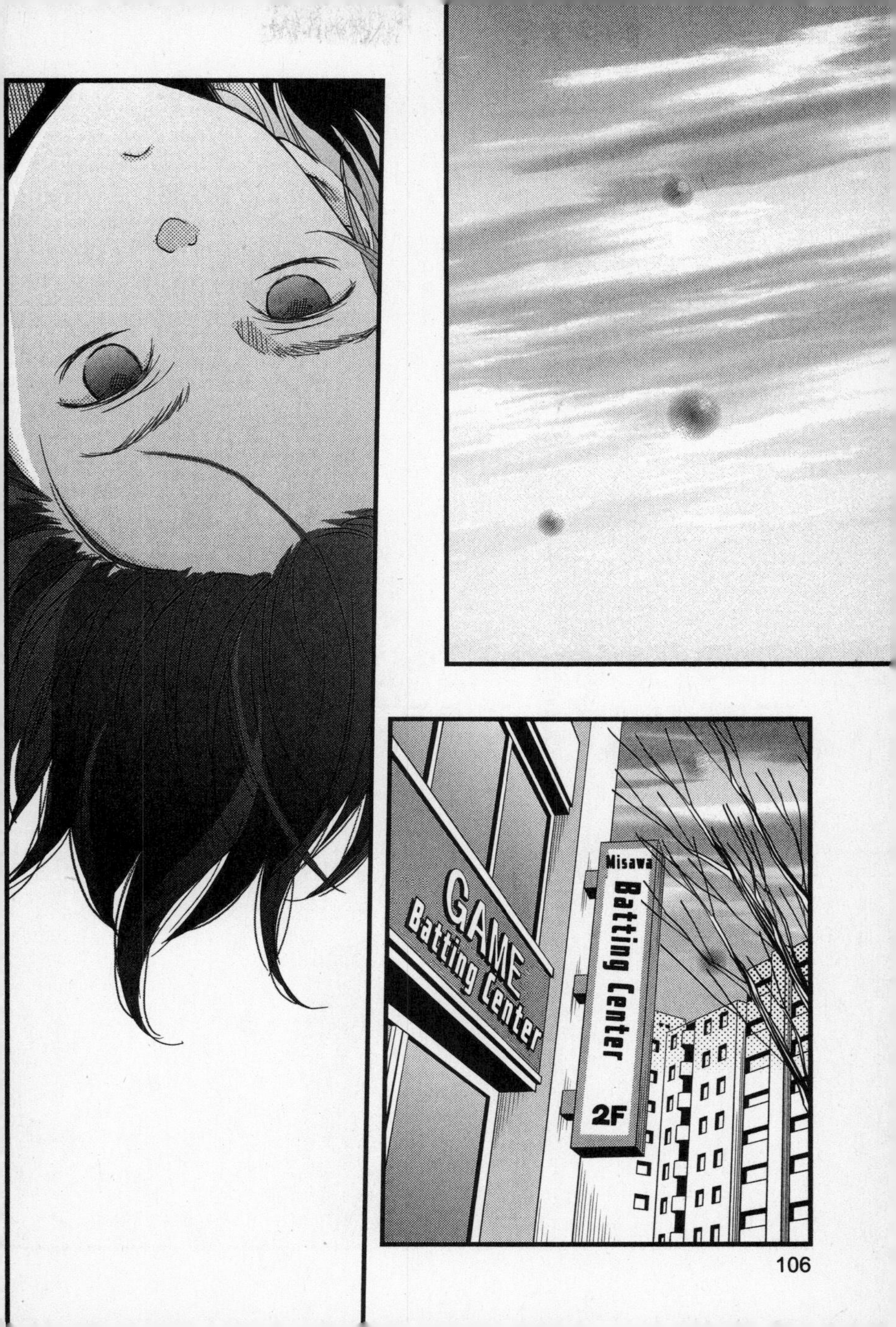
Misawa
Batting Center
2F
GAME
Batting Center

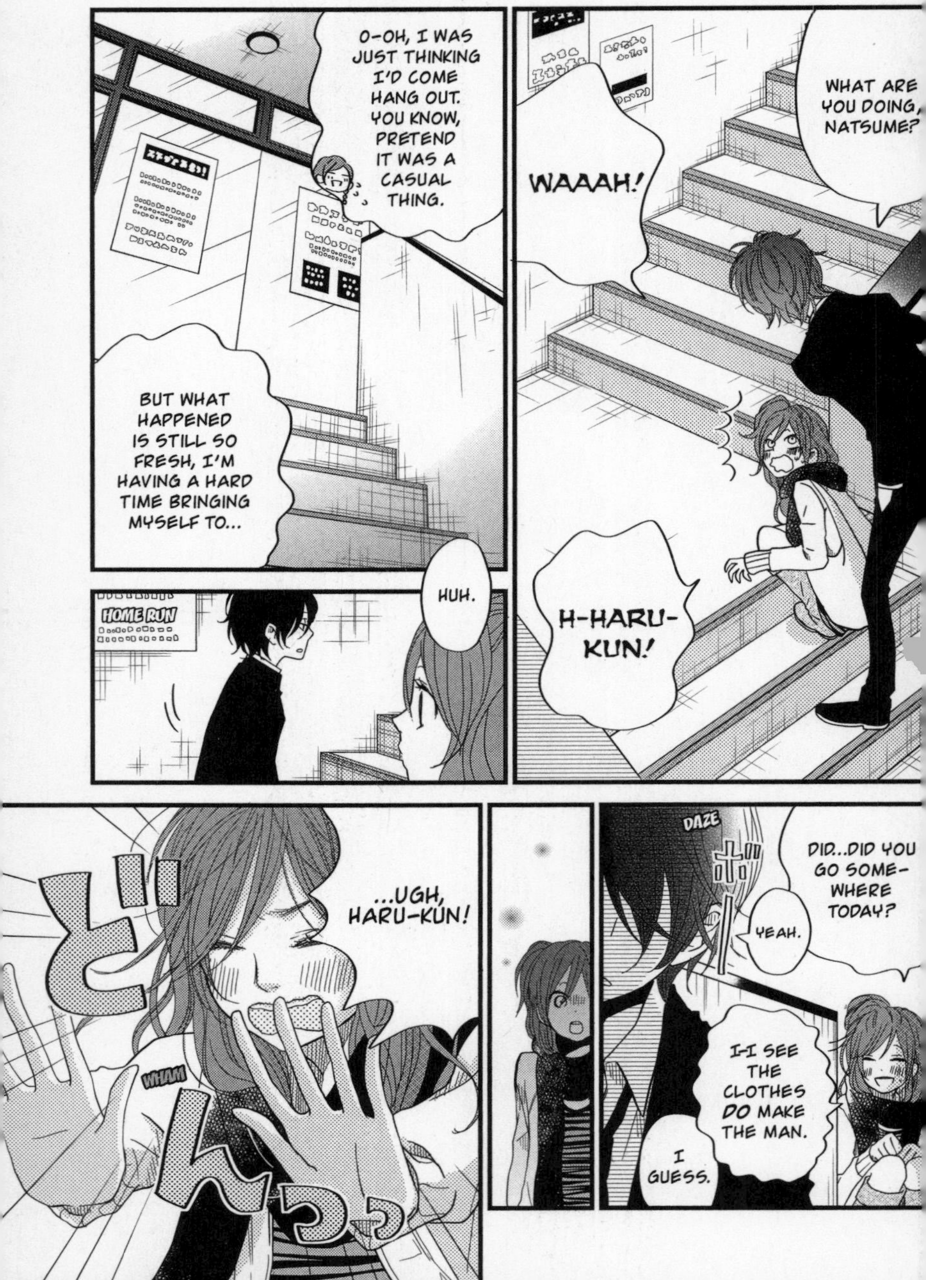
WHAT ARE YOU DOING, NATSUME?
WAAAH!
H-HARU-KUN!
O-OH, I WAS JUST THINKING I'D COME HANG OUT. YOU KNOW, PRETEND IT WAS A CASUAL THING.
BUT WHAT HAPPENED IS STILL SO FRESH, I'M HAVING A HARD TIME BRINGING MYSELF TO...
HOME RUN
HUH.
DAZE
DID...DID YOU GO SOME-WHERE TODAY?
YEAH.
I-I SEE THE CLOTHES DO MAKE THE MAN.
I GUESS.
...UGH, HARU-KUN!
どんっっ
WHAM

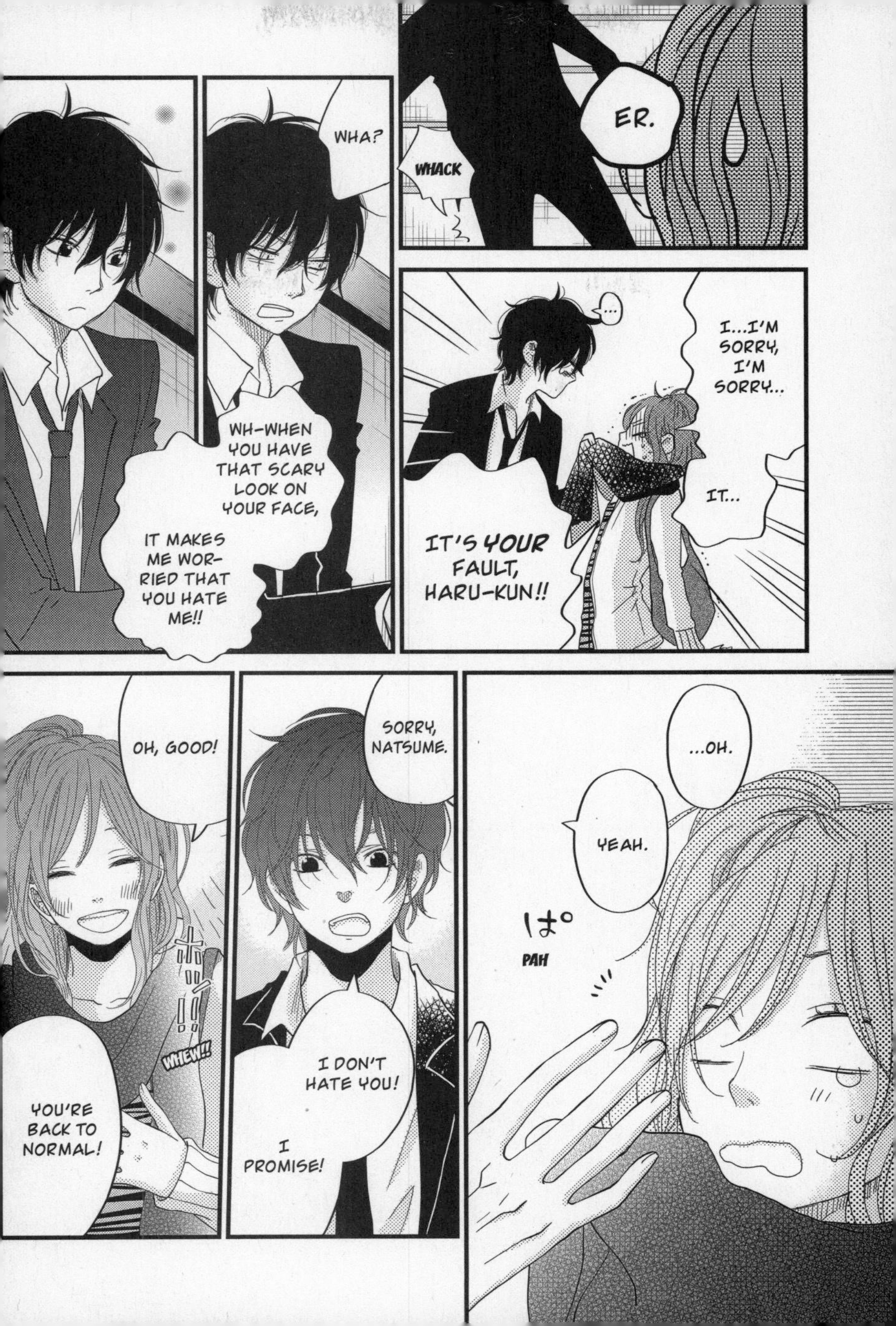
ER.
WHACK
I...I'M SORRY, I'M SORRY...
...
IT...
IT'S YOUR FAULT, HARU-KUN!!
WHA?
WH-WHEN YOU HAVE THAT SCARY LOOK ON YOUR FACE,
IT MAKES ME WORRIED THAT YOU HATE ME!!
...OH.
YEAH.
ぱ
PAH
SORRY, NATSUME.
I DON'T HATE YOU!
I PROMISE!
OH, GOOD!
WHEW!!
YOU'RE BACK TO NORMAL!

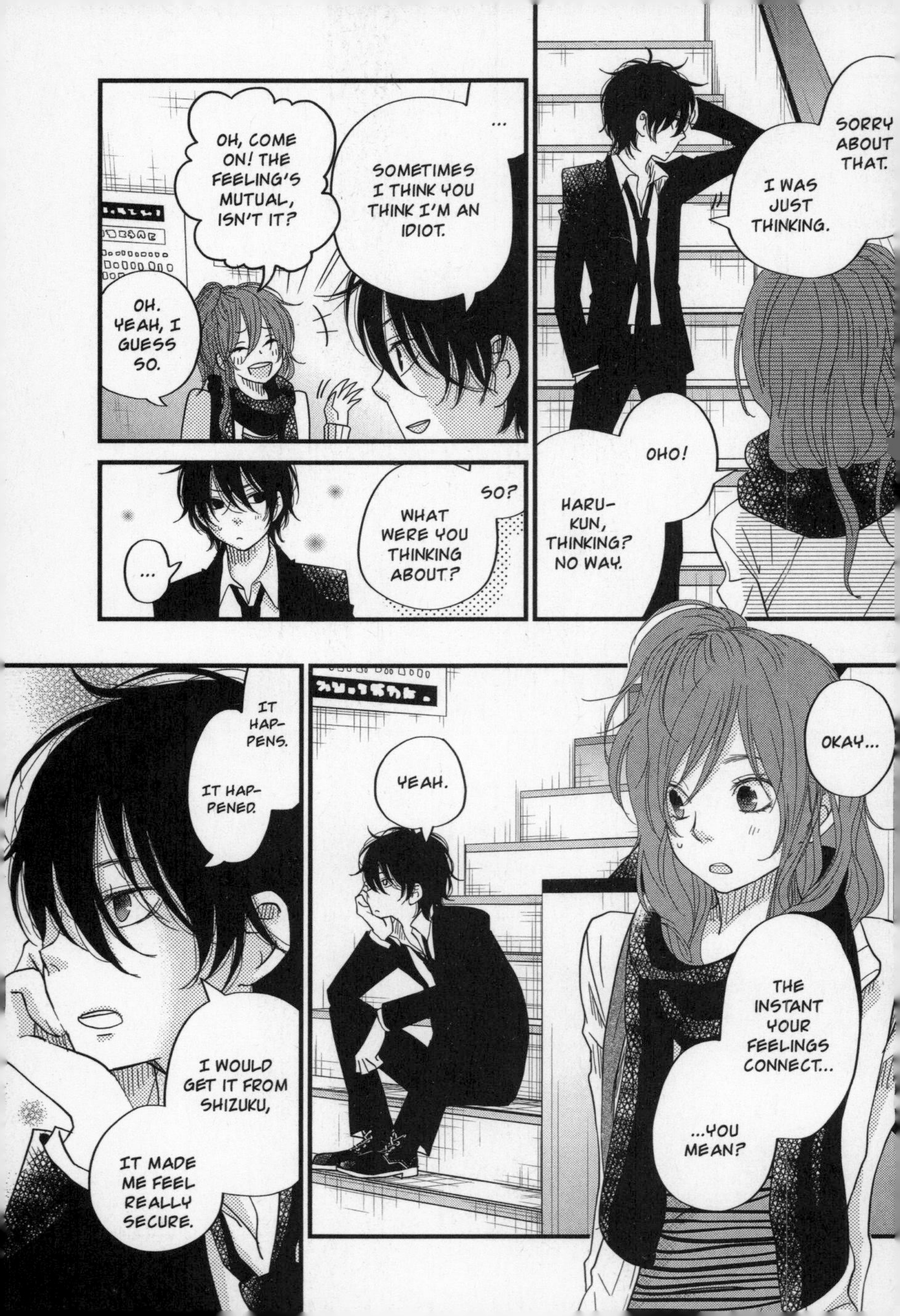
SORRY ABOUT THAT.
I WAS JUST THINKING.
OHO!
HARU-KUN, THINKING? NO WAY.
...
SOMETIMES I THINK YOU THINK I'M AN IDIOT.
OH, COME ON! THE FEELING'S MUTUAL, ISN'T IT?
OH. YEAH, I GUESS SO.
SO?
WHAT WERE YOU THINKING ABOUT?
...
OKAY...
THE INSTANT YOUR FEELINGS CONNECT...
...YOU MEAN?
YEAH.
IT HAP-PENS.
IT HAP-PENED.
I WOULD GET IT FROM SHIZUKU,
IT MADE ME FEEL REALLY SECURE.

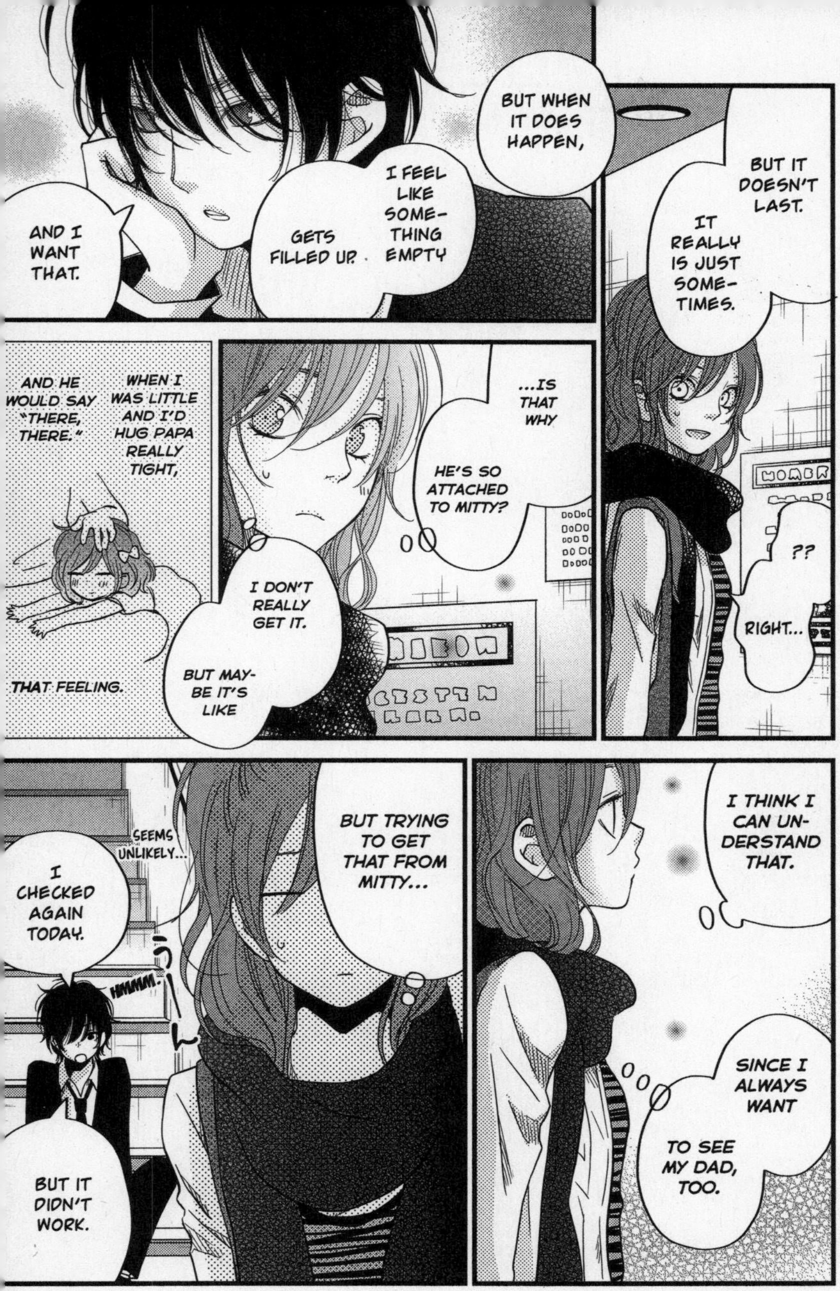
BUT WHEN IT DOES HAPPEN,
I FEEL LIKE SOME-THING EMPTY
GETS FILLED UP.
AND I WANT THAT.
BUT IT DOESN'T LAST.
IT REALLY IS JUST SOME-TIMES.
??
RIGHT...
...IS THAT WHY
HE'S SO ATTACHED TO MITTY?
I DON'T REALLY GET IT.
BUT MAY-BE IT'S LIKE
WHEN I WAS LITTLE AND I'D HUG PAPA REALLY TIGHT,
AND HE WOULD SAY "THERE, THERE."
THAT FEELING.
I THINK I CAN UN-DERSTAND THAT.
SINCE I ALWAYS WANT
TO SEE MY DAD, TOO.
BUT TRYING TO GET THAT FROM MITTY...
SEEMS UNLIKELY...
I CHECKED AGAIN TODAY.
HMMM.
BUT IT DIDN'T WORK.

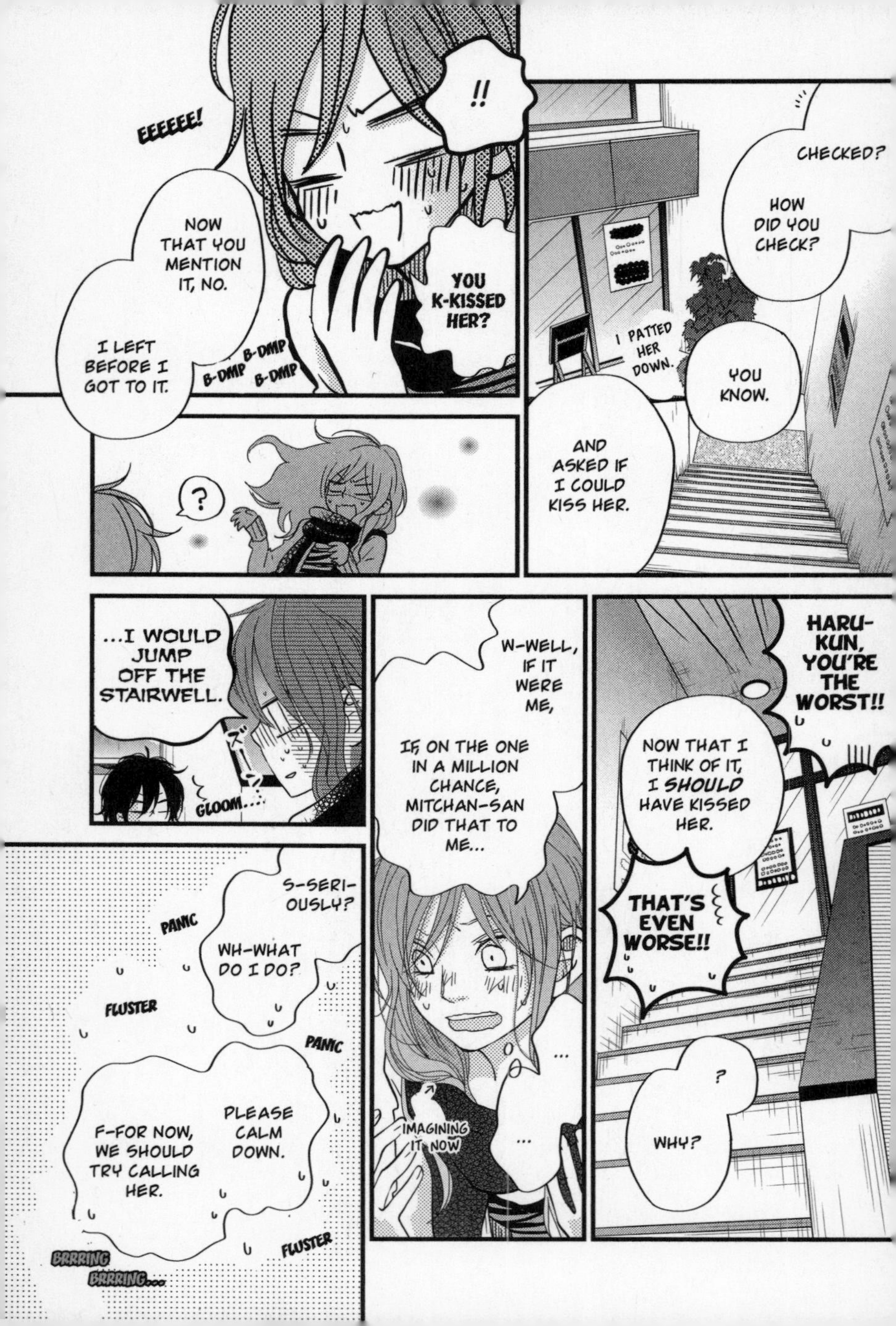
CHECKED?
HOW DID YOU CHECK?
YOU KNOW.
I PATTED HER DOWN.
AND ASKED IF I COULD KISS HER.
!!
EEEEEE!
YOU K-KISSED HER?
NOW THAT YOU MENTION IT, NO.
I LEFT BEFORE I GOT TO IT.
B-DMP B-DMP B-DMP
?
HARU-KUN, YOU'RE THE WORST!!
NOW THAT I THINK OF IT, I SHOULD HAVE KISSED HER.
THAT'S EVEN WORSE!!
?
WHY?
W-WELL, IF IT WERE ME,
IF, ON THE ONE IN A MILLION CHANCE, MITCHAN-SAN DID THAT TO ME...
...
IMAGINING IT NOW
...
...I WOULD JUMP OFF THE STAIRWELL.
GLOOM...
S-SERIOUSLY?
PANIC
WH-WHAT DO I DO?
FLUSTER
PANIC
PLEASE CALM DOWN.
F-FOR NOW, WE SHOULD TRY CALLING HER.
FLUSTER
BRRRING BRRRING...

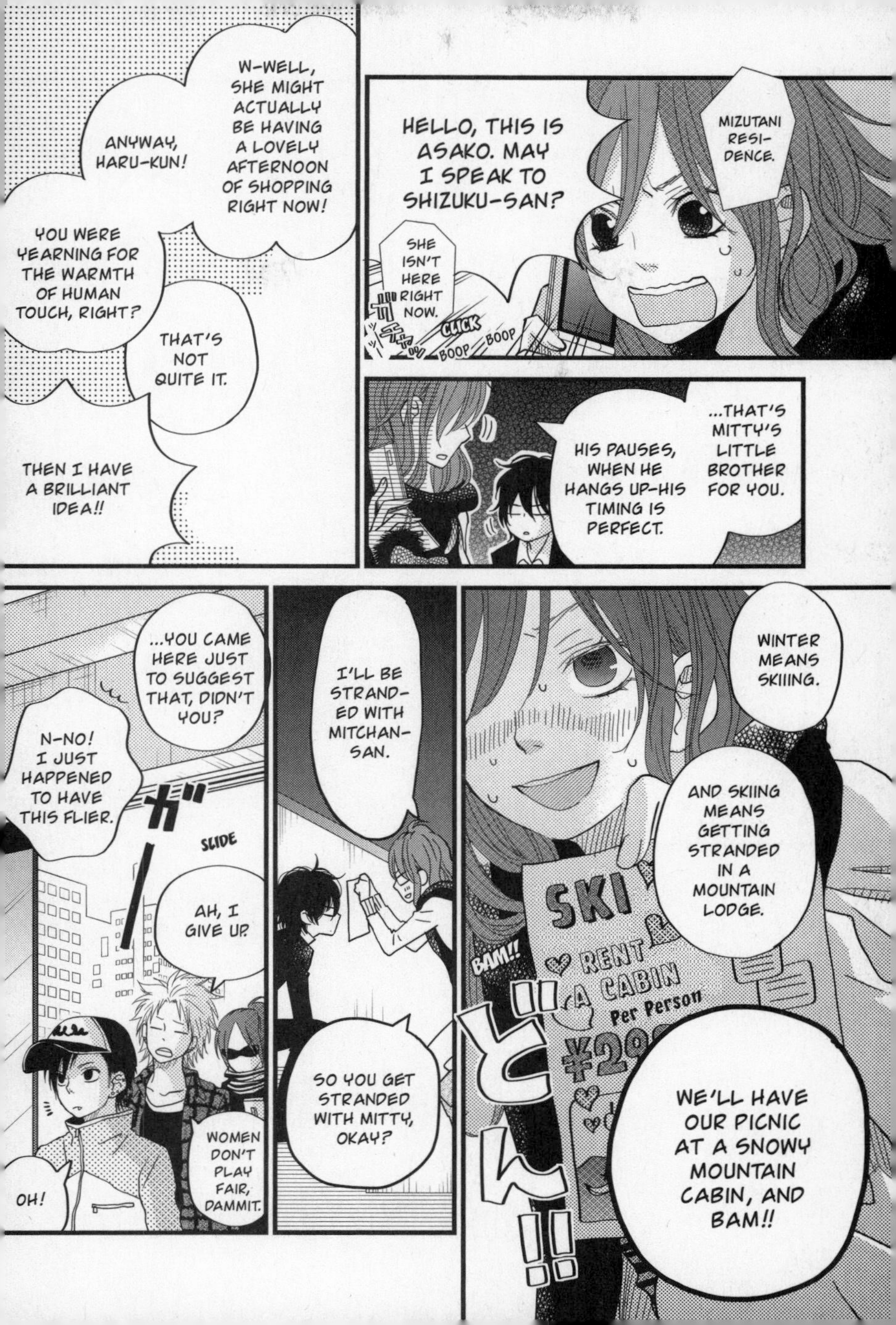
MIZUTANI RESIDENCE.
HELLO, THIS IS ASAKO. MAY I SPEAK TO SHIZUKU-SAN?
SHE ISN'T HERE RIGHT NOW.
CLICK
BOOP BOOP
...THAT'S MITTY'S LITTLE BROTHER FOR YOU.
HIS PAUSES, WHEN HE HANGS UP—HIS TIMING IS PERFECT.
W-WELL, SHE MIGHT ACTUALLY BE HAVING A LOVELY AFTERNOON OF SHOPPING RIGHT NOW!
ANYWAY, HARU-KUN!
YOU WERE YEARNING FOR THE WARMTH OF HUMAN TOUCH, RIGHT?
THAT'S NOT QUITE IT.
THEN I HAVE A BRILLIANT IDEA!!
WINTER MEANS SKIING.
AND SKIING MEANS GETTING STRANDED IN A MOUNTAIN LODGE.
SKI
RENT A CABIN
Per Person
BAM!!
どーん!!
WE'LL HAVE OUR PICNIC AT A SNOWY MOUNTAIN CABIN, AND BAM!!
I'LL BE STRANDED WITH MITCHAN-SAN.
SO YOU GET STRANDED WITH MITTY, OKAY?
...YOU CAME HERE JUST TO SUGGEST THAT, DIDN'T YOU?
N-NO! I JUST HAPPENED TO HAVE THIS FLIER.
SLIDE
AH, I GIVE UP.
WOMEN DON'T PLAY FAIR, DAMMIT.
OH!

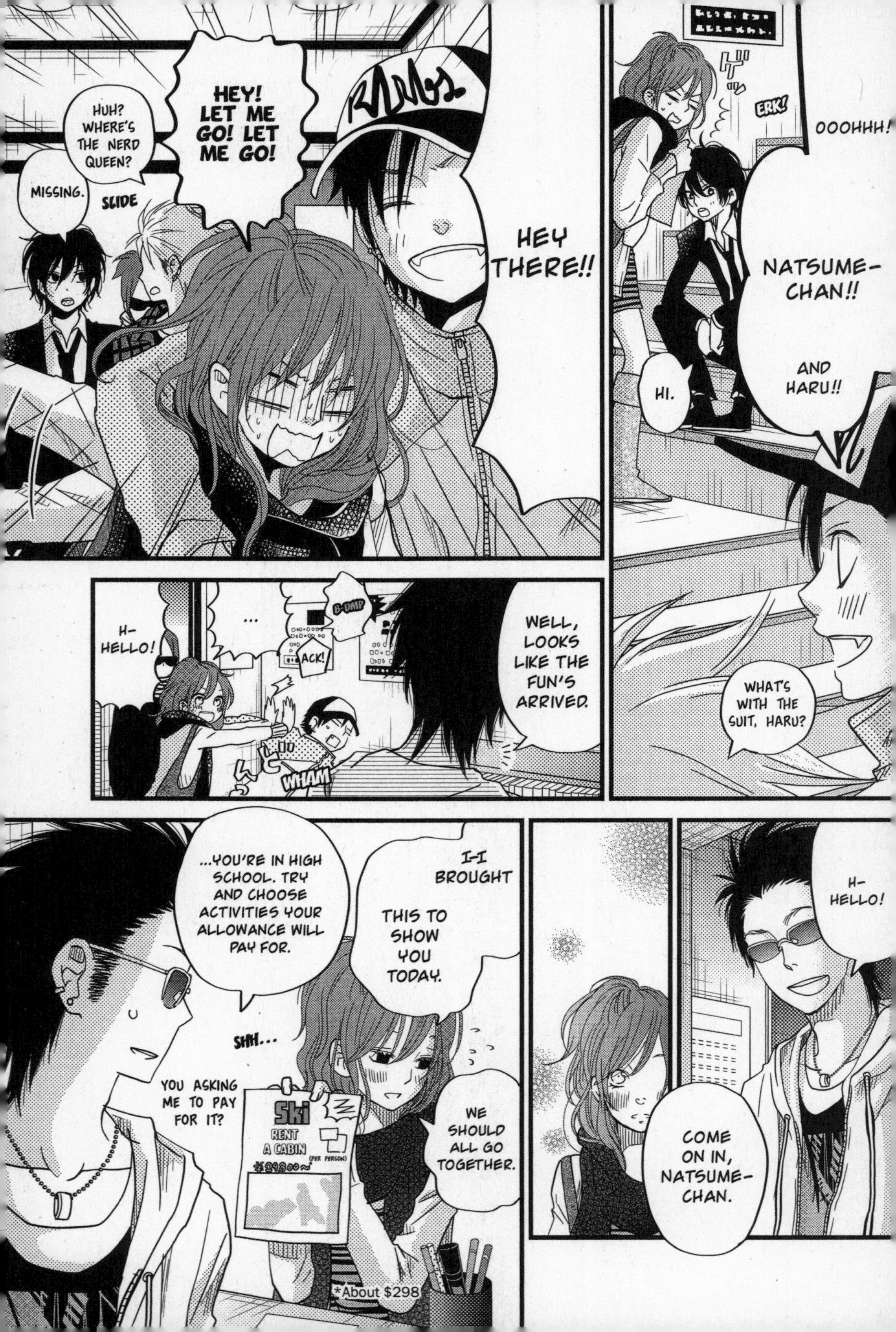

OOOHHH!
ERK!
NATSUME-CHAN!!
AND HARU!!
HI.
HEY! LET ME GO! LET ME GO!
HEY THERE!!
HUH? WHERE'S THE NERD QUEEN?
MISSING.
SLIDE
WHAT'S WITH THE SUIT, HARU?
WELL, LOOKS LIKE THE FUN'S ARRIVED.
B-DMP
...
H-HELLO!
ACK!
WHAM
H-HELLO!
COME ON IN, NATSUME-CHAN.
I-I BROUGHT
THIS TO SHOW YOU TODAY.
WE SHOULD ALL GO TOGETHER.
SHH...
YOU ASKING ME TO PAY FOR IT?
...YOU'RE IN HIGH SCHOOL. TRY AND CHOOSE ACTIVITIES YOUR ALLOWANCE WILL PAY FOR.
Ski
RENT A CABIN
(PER PERSON)

*About $298

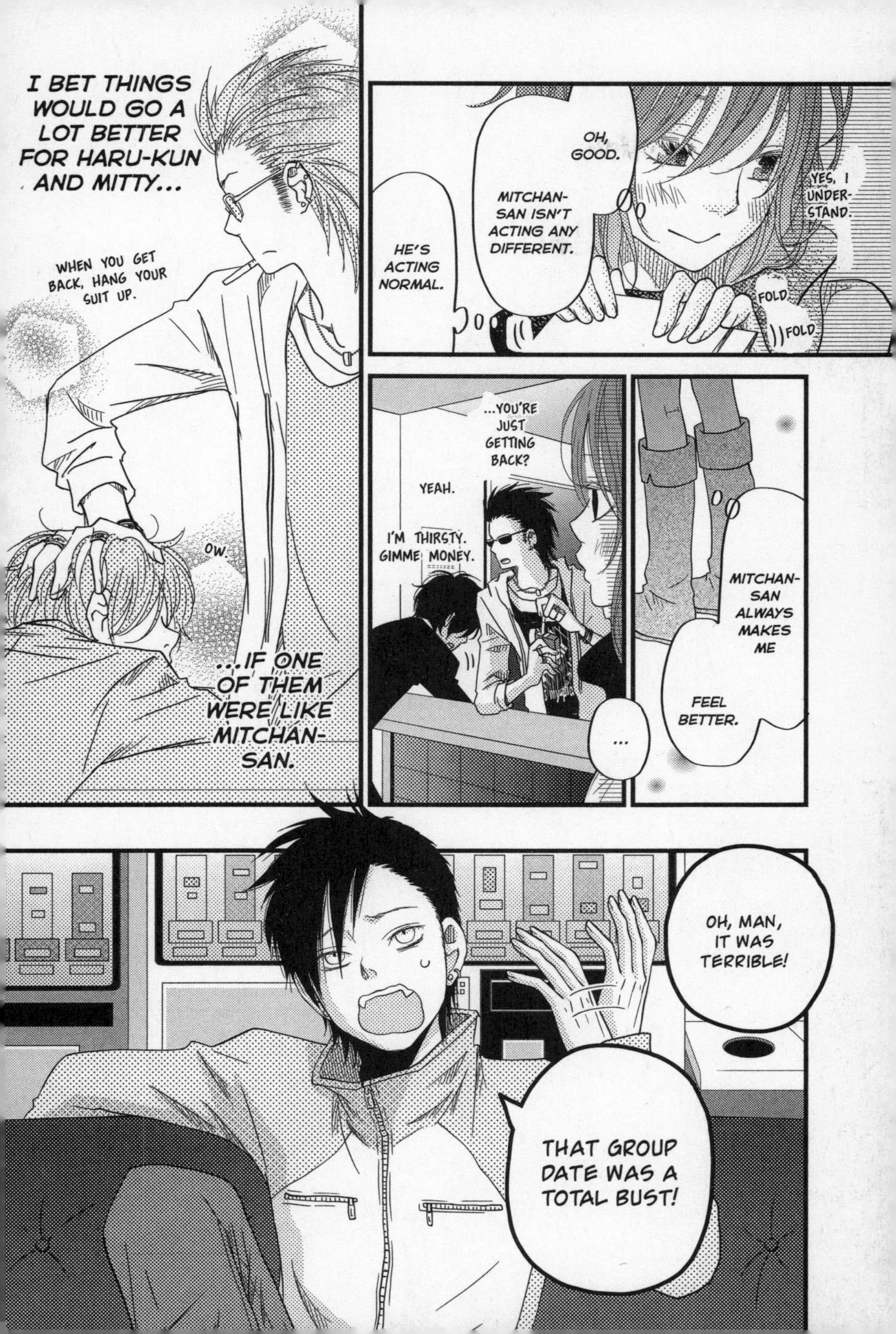
YES, I UNDERSTAND.
OH, GOOD.
MITCHAN-SAN ISN'T ACTING ANY DIFFERENT.
FOLD
FOLD
HE'S ACTING NORMAL.
MITCHAN-SAN ALWAYS MAKES ME
FEEL BETTER.
...YOU'RE JUST GETTING BACK?
YEAH.
I'M THIRSTY. GIMME MONEY.
...
I BET THINGS WOULD GO A LOT BETTER FOR HARU-KUN AND MITTY...
WHEN YOU GET BACK, HANG YOUR SUIT UP.
OW.
...IF ONE OF THEM WERE LIKE MITCHAN-SAN.
OH, MAN, IT WAS TERRIBLE!
THAT GROUP DATE WAS A TOTAL BUST!

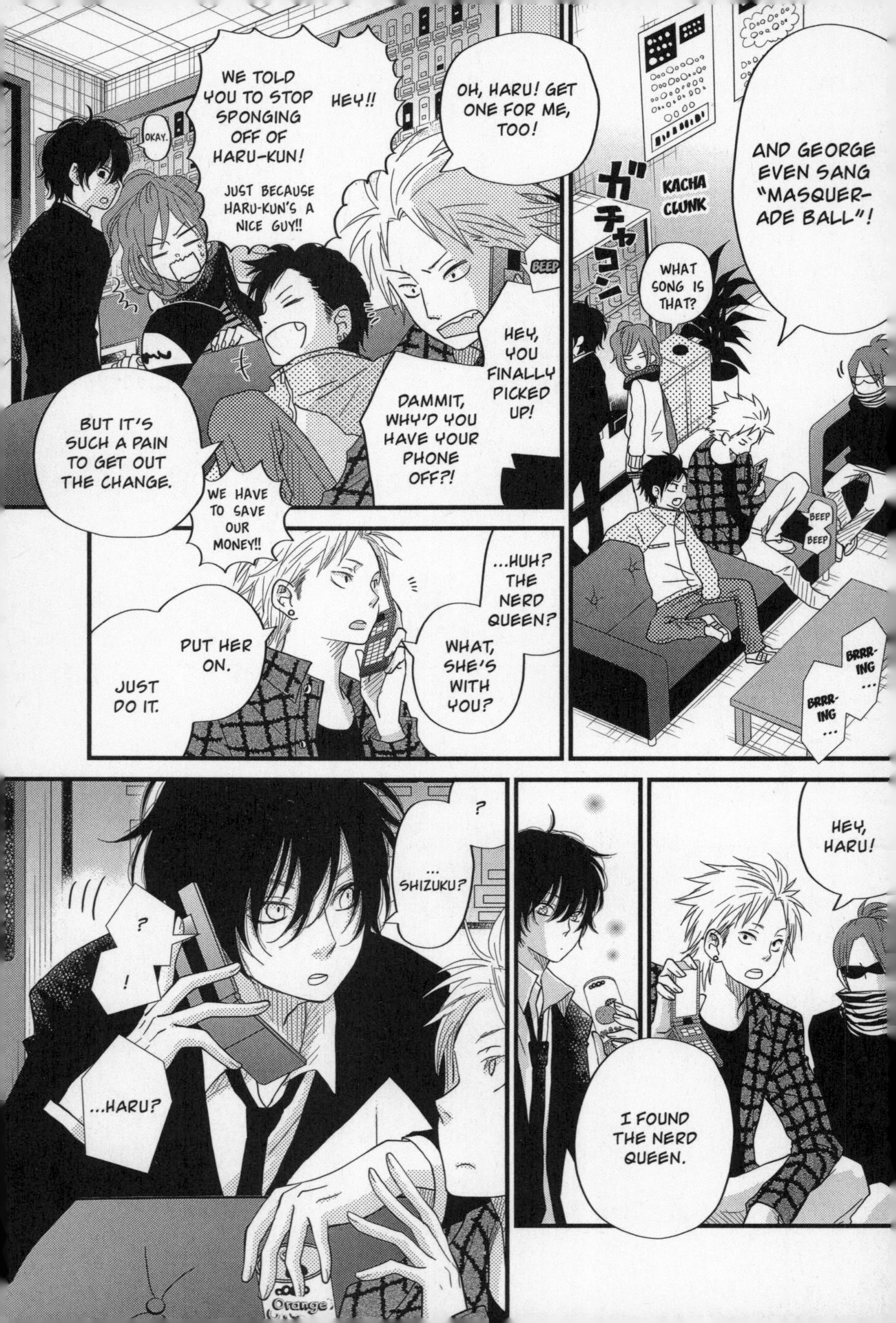
AND GEORGE EVEN SANG "MASQUER-ADE BALL"!
KACHA CLUNK
ガチャコン
WHAT SONG IS THAT?
BEEP BEEP
BRRR-ING...
BRRR-ING...
OH, HARU! GET ONE FOR ME, TOO!
HEY!!
WE TOLD YOU TO STOP SPONGING OFF OF HARU-KUN!
OKAY.
JUST BECAUSE HARU-KUN'S A NICE GUY!!
BUT IT'S SUCH A PAIN TO GET OUT THE CHANGE.
WE HAVE TO SAVE OUR MONEY!!
BEEP
HEY, YOU FINALLY PICKED UP!
DAMMIT, WHY'D YOU HAVE YOUR PHONE OFF?!
...HUH? THE NERD QUEEN?
WHAT, SHE'S WITH YOU?
PUT HER ON.
JUST DO IT.
HEY, HARU!
I FOUND THE NERD QUEEN.
?
... SHIZUKU?
?
!
...HARU?
Orange

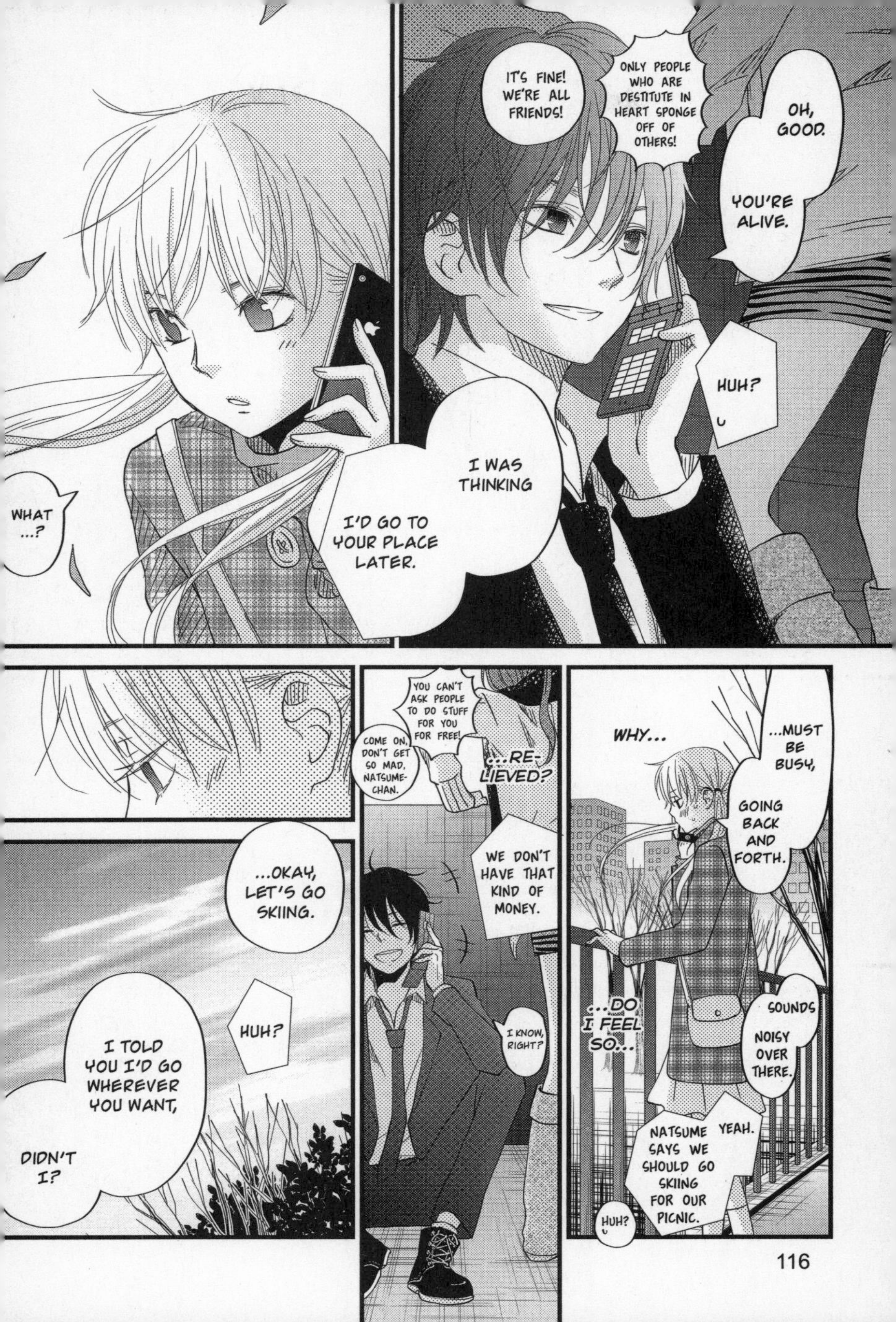
OH, GOOD.
YOU'RE ALIVE.
ONLY PEOPLE WHO ARE DESTITUTE IN HEART SPONGE OFF OF OTHERS!
IT'S FINE! WE'RE ALL FRIENDS!
HUH?
I WAS THINKING I'D GO TO YOUR PLACE LATER.
WHAT ...?
...MUST BE BUSY,
GOING BACK AND FORTH.
WHY...
SOUNDS NOISY OVER THERE.
...DO I FEEL SO...
YEAH.
NATSUME SAYS WE SHOULD GO SKIING FOR OUR PICNIC.
HUH?
YOU CAN'T ASK PEOPLE TO DO STUFF FOR YOU FOR FREE!
COME ON, DON'T GET SO MAD, NATSUME-CHAN.
...RE-LIEVED?
WE DON'T HAVE THAT KIND OF MONEY.
I KNOW, RIGHT?
...OKAY, LET'S GO SKIING.
HUH?
I TOLD YOU I'D GO WHEREVER YOU WANT,
DIDN'T I?

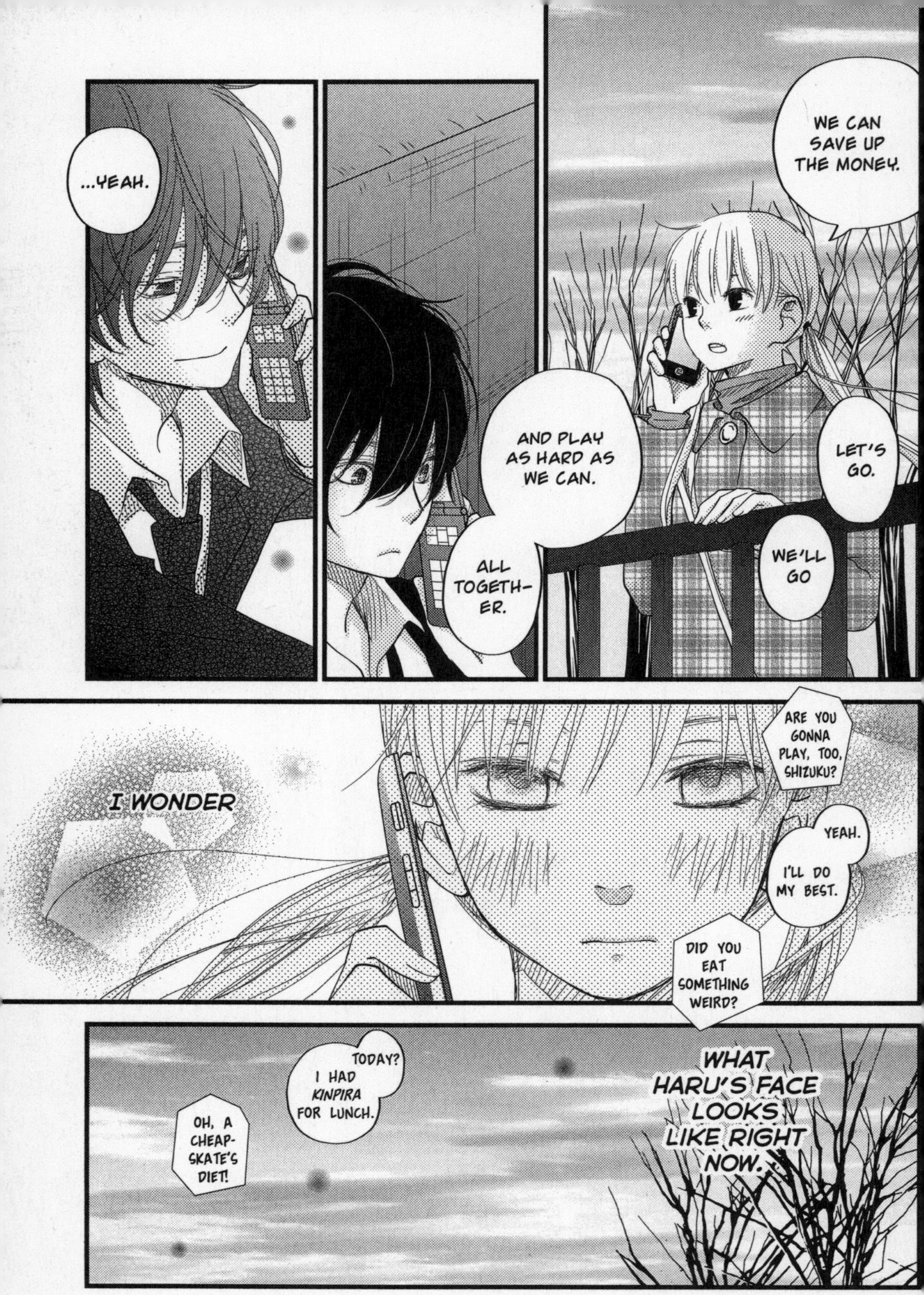
WE CAN SAVE UP THE MONEY.
AND PLAY AS HARD AS WE CAN.
LET'S GO.
WE'LL GO
ALL TOGETH-ER.
...YEAH.
ARE YOU GONNA PLAY, TOO, SHIZUKU?
YEAH.
I'LL DO MY BEST.
DID YOU EAT SOMETHING WEIRD?
I WONDER
WHAT HARU'S FACE LOOKS LIKE RIGHT NOW.
TODAY? I HAD KINPIRA FOR LUNCH.
OH, A CHEAP-SKATE'S DIET!

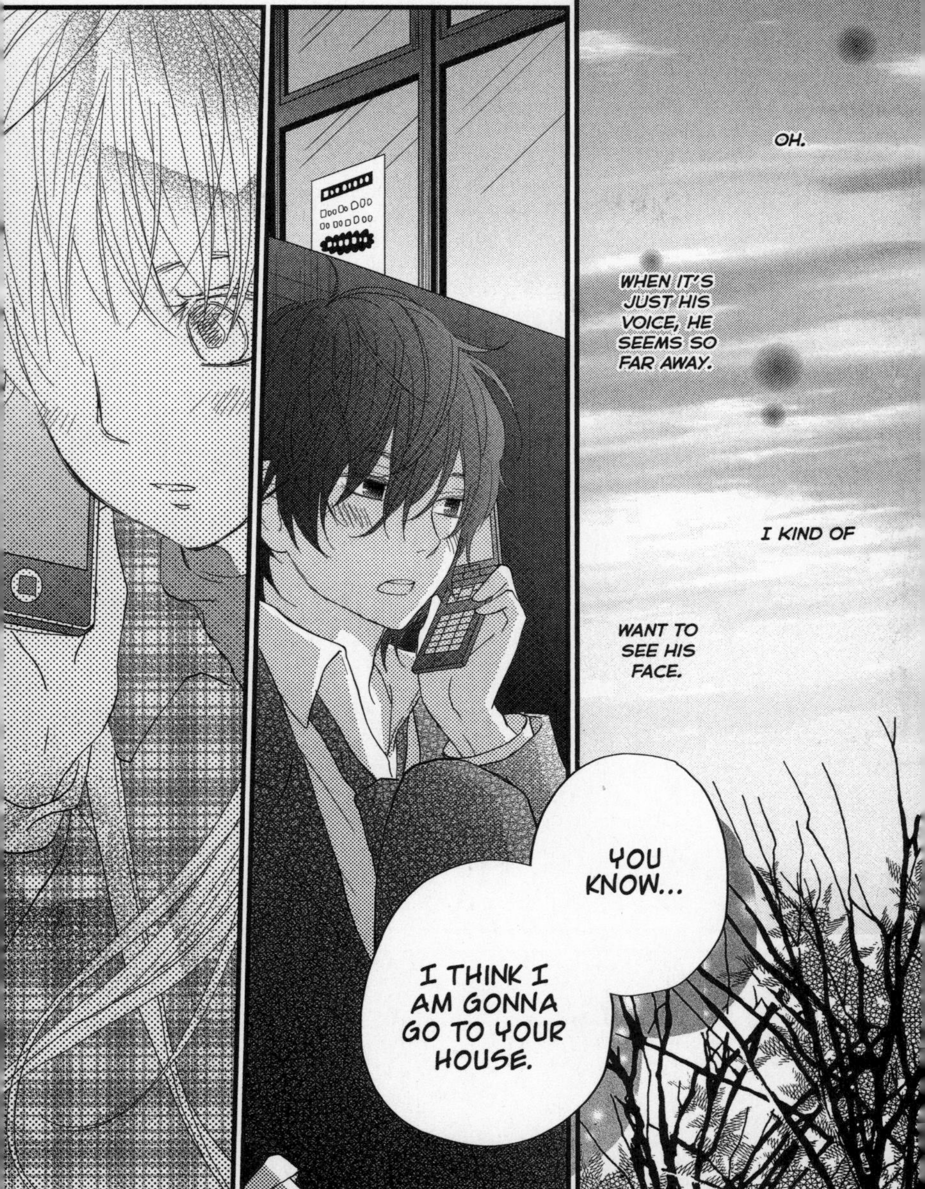
OH.
WHEN IT'S JUST HIS VOICE, HE SEEMS SO FAR AWAY.
I KIND OF
WANT TO SEE HIS FACE.
YOU KNOW...
I THINK I AM GONNA GO TO YOUR HOUSE.

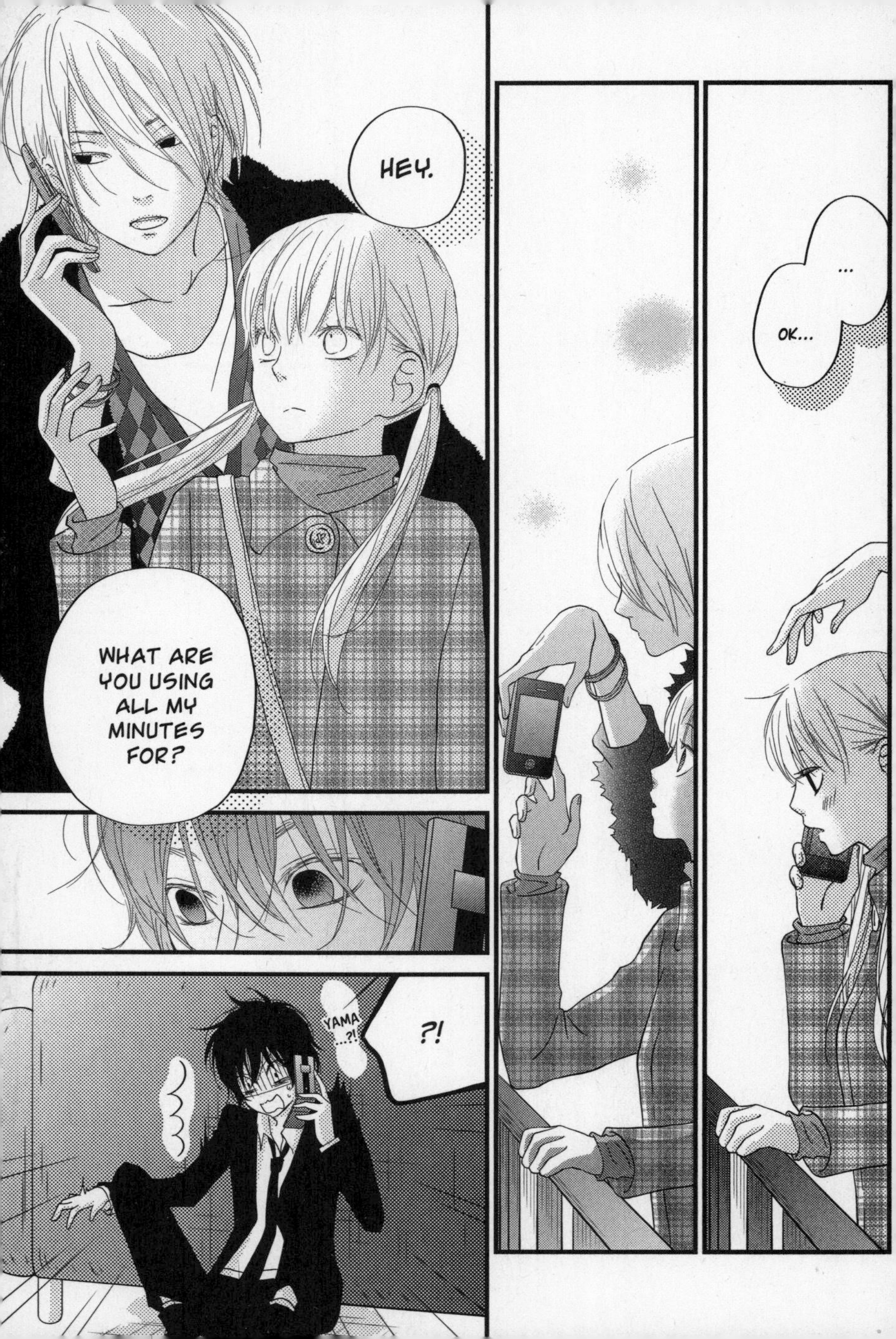
...
OK...
HEY.
WHAT ARE YOU USING ALL MY MINUTES FOR?
?!
YAMA ...?!

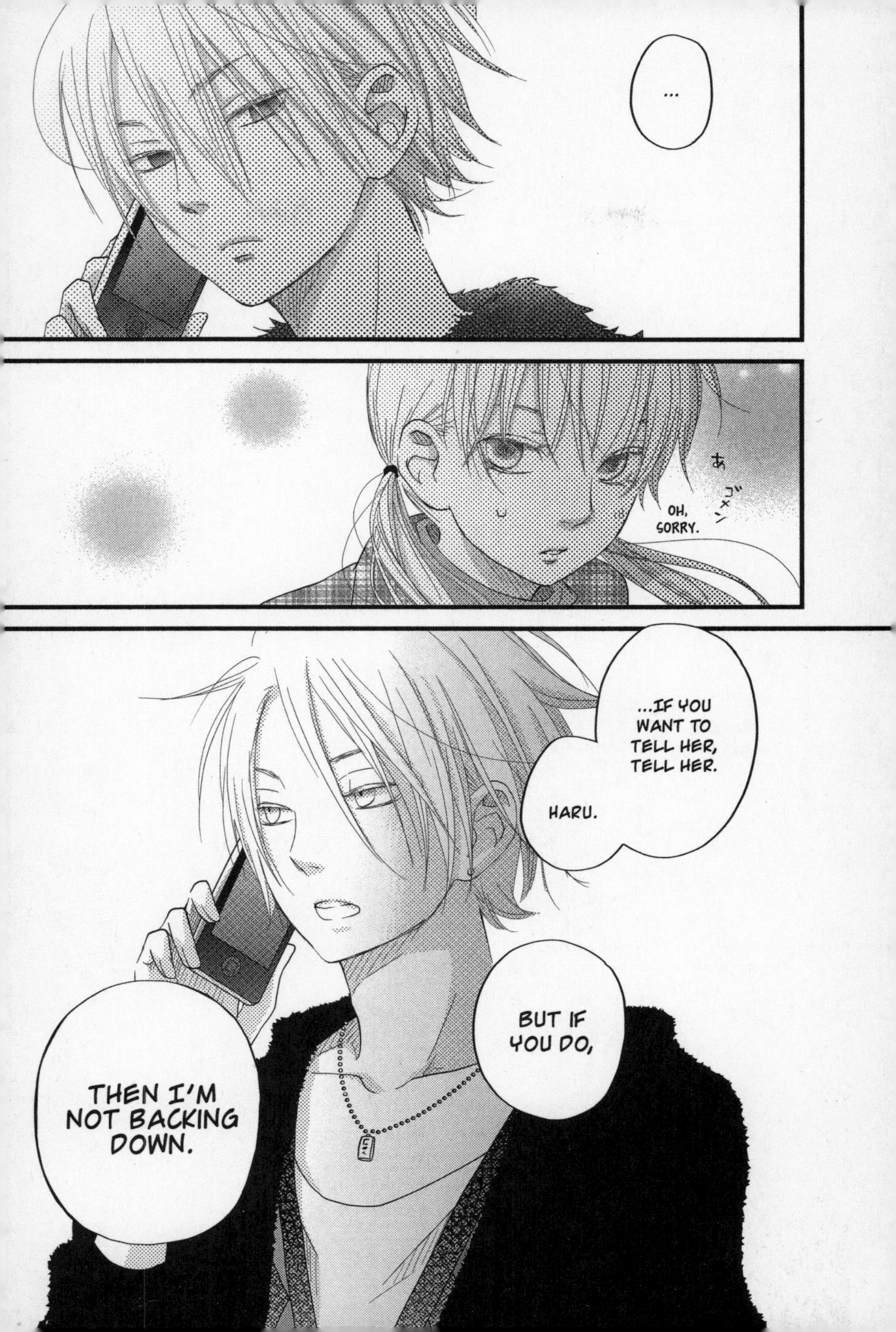
...
あゴメン
OH, SORRY.
...IF YOU WANT TO TELL HER, TELL HER.
HARU.
BUT IF YOU DO,
THEN I'M NOT BACKING DOWN.

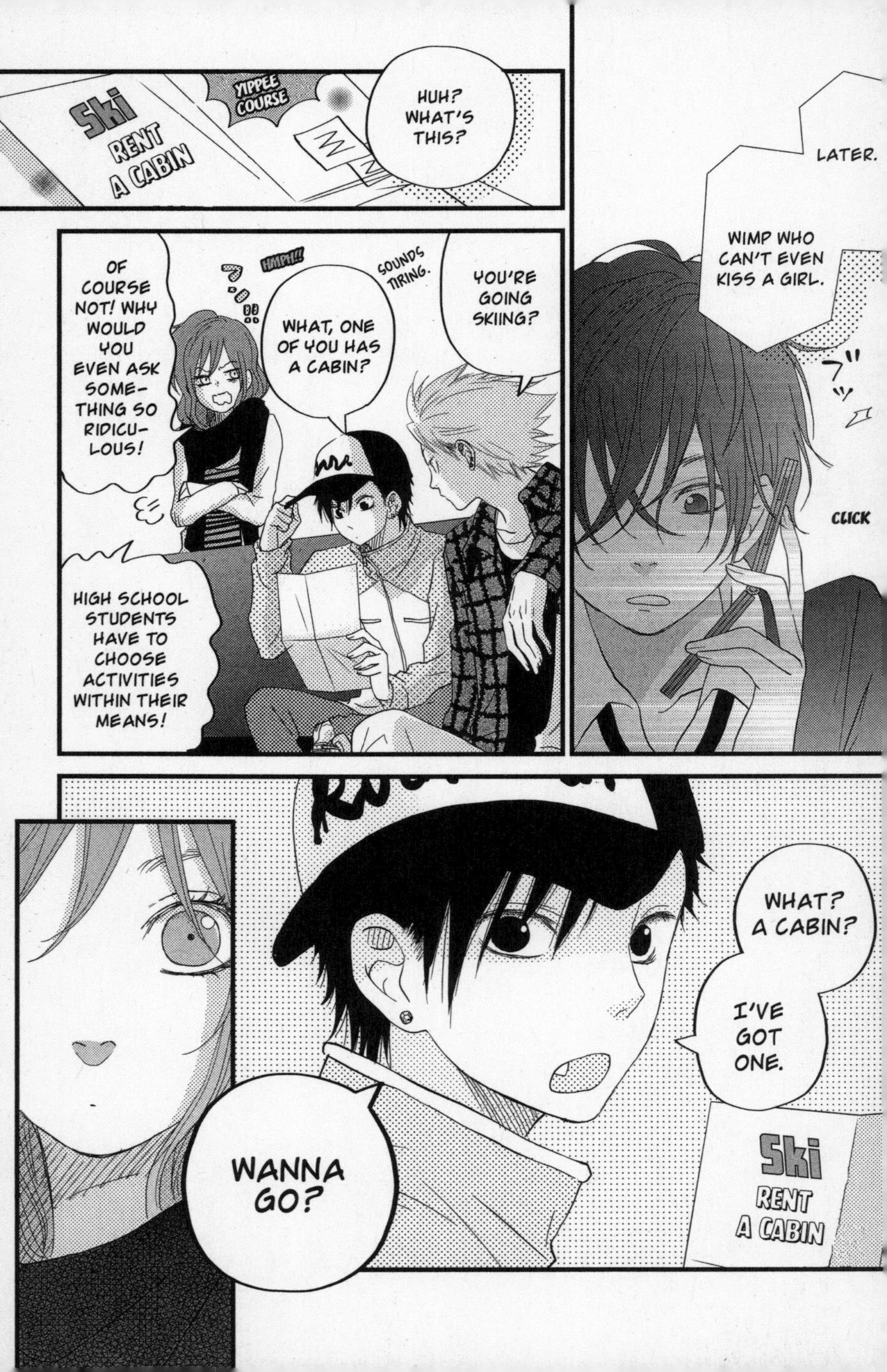
LATER.
WIMP WHO CAN'T EVEN KISS A GIRL.
CLICK
Ski
RENT A CABIN
YIPPEE COURSE
HUH? WHAT'S THIS?
YOU'RE GOING SKIING?
SOUNDS TIRING.
WHAT, ONE OF YOU HAS A CABIN?
HMPH!!
OF COURSE NOT! WHY WOULD YOU EVEN ASK SOMETHING SO RIDICULOUS!
HIGH SCHOOL STUDENTS HAVE TO CHOOSE ACTIVITIES WITHIN THEIR MEANS!
WHAT? A CABIN?
I'VE GOT ONE.
Ski
RENT A CABIN
WANNA GO?

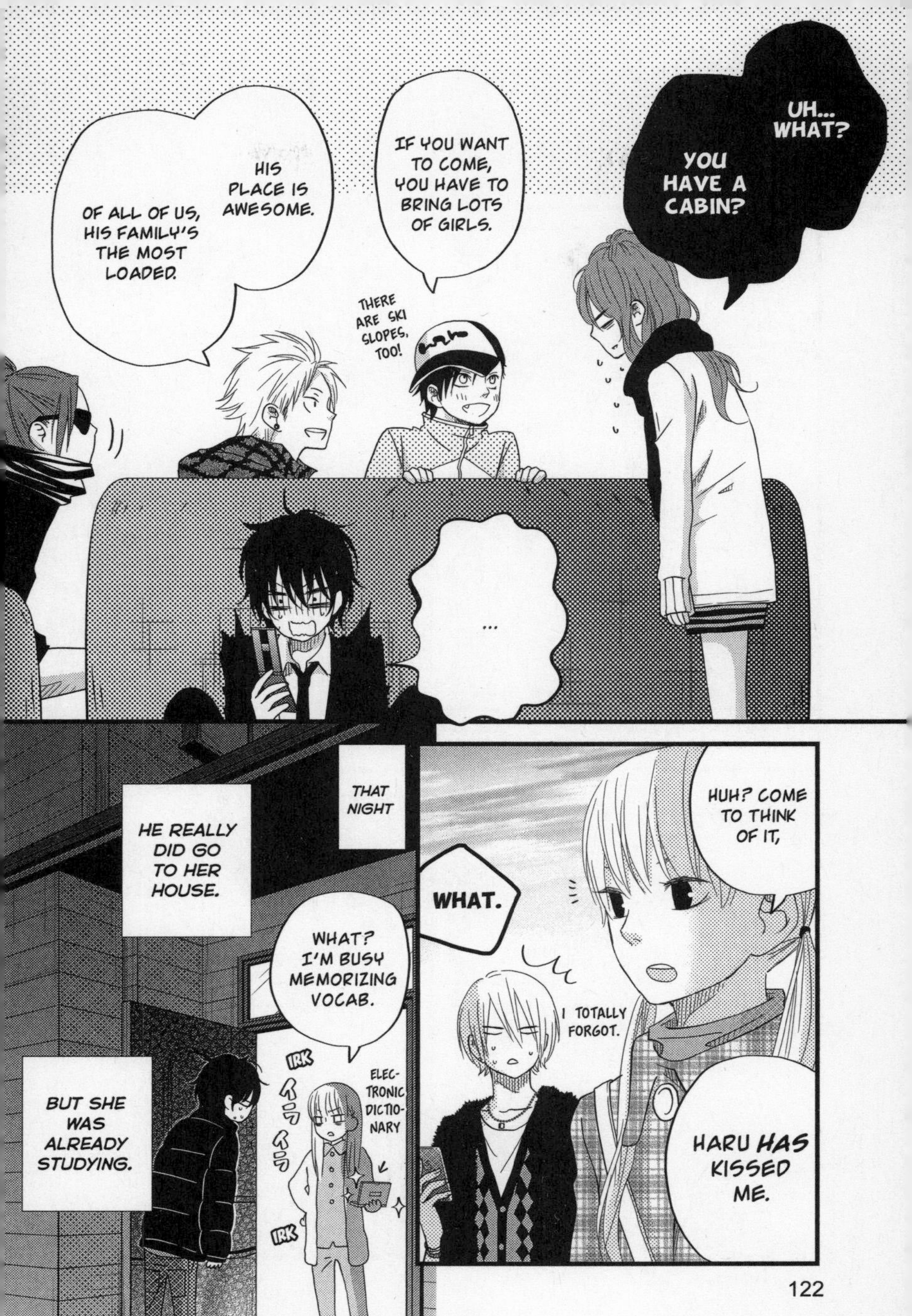
UH... WHAT?
YOU HAVE A CABIN?
IF YOU WANT TO COME, YOU HAVE TO BRING LOTS OF GIRLS.
THERE ARE SKI SLOPES, TOO!
HIS PLACE IS AWESOME.
OF ALL OF US, HIS FAMILY'S THE MOST LOADED.
...
HUH? COME TO THINK OF IT,
WHAT.
I TOTALLY FORGOT.
HARU HAS KISSED ME.
THAT NIGHT
HE REALLY DID GO TO HER HOUSE.
WHAT? I'M BUSY MEMORIZING VOCAB.
IRK
ELECTRONIC DICTIONARY
IRK
BUT SHE WAS ALREADY STUDYING.

At the Electronics Store, part 1

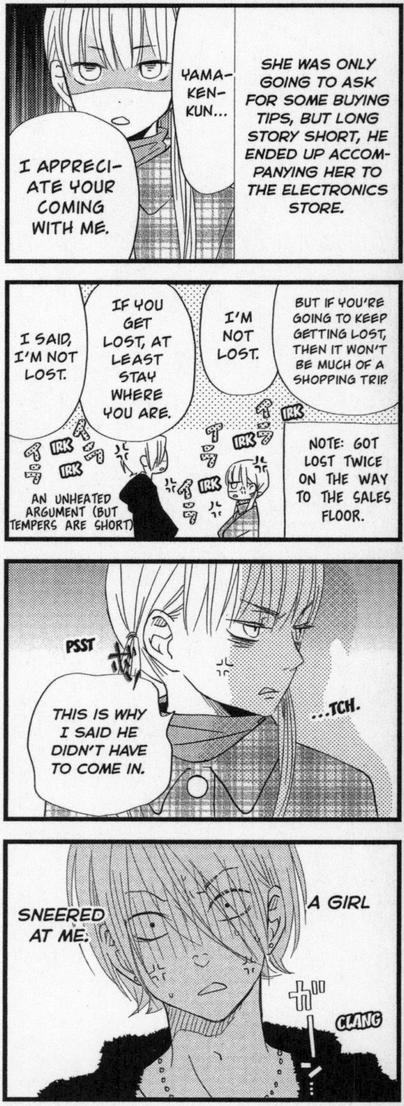
SHE WAS ONLY GOING TO ASK FOR SOME BUYING TIPS, BUT LONG STORY SHORT, HE ENDED UP ACCOMPANYING HER TO THE ELECTRONICS STORE.
YAMA-KEN-KUN...
I APPRECIATE YOUR COMING WITH ME.
BUT IF YOU'RE GOING TO KEEP GETTING LOST, THEN IT WON'T BE MUCH OF A SHOPPING TRIP.
I'M NOT LOST.
IF YOU GET LOST, AT LEAST STAY WHERE YOU ARE.
I SAID, I'M NOT LOST.
IRK IRK IRK IRK IRK IRK
NOTE: GOT LOST TWICE ON THE WAY TO THE SALES FLOOR.
AN UNHEATED ARGUMENT (BUT TEMPERS ARE SHORT)
...TCH.
PSST
THIS IS WHY I SAID HE DIDN'T HAVE TO COME IN.
A GIRL
SNEERED AT ME.
CLANG

At the Electronics Store, Part 2

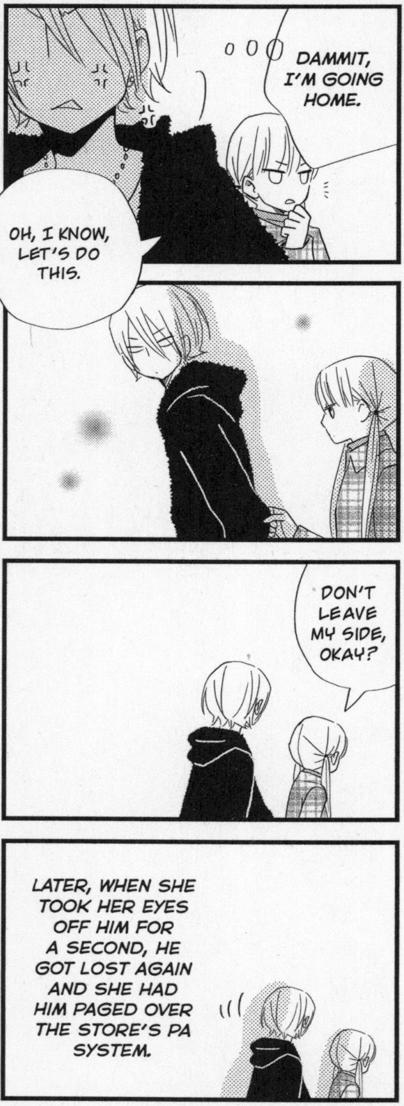
DAMMIT, I'M GOING HOME.
OH, I KNOW, LET'S DO THIS.
DON'T LEAVE MY SIDE, OKAY?
LATER, WHEN SHE TOOK HER EYES OFF HIM FOR A SECOND, HE GOT LOST AGAIN AND SHE HAD HIM PAGED OVER THE STORE'S PA SYSTEM.

Post-Chapter 19 Bonus:
"Somewhere Between Greed and Integrity"

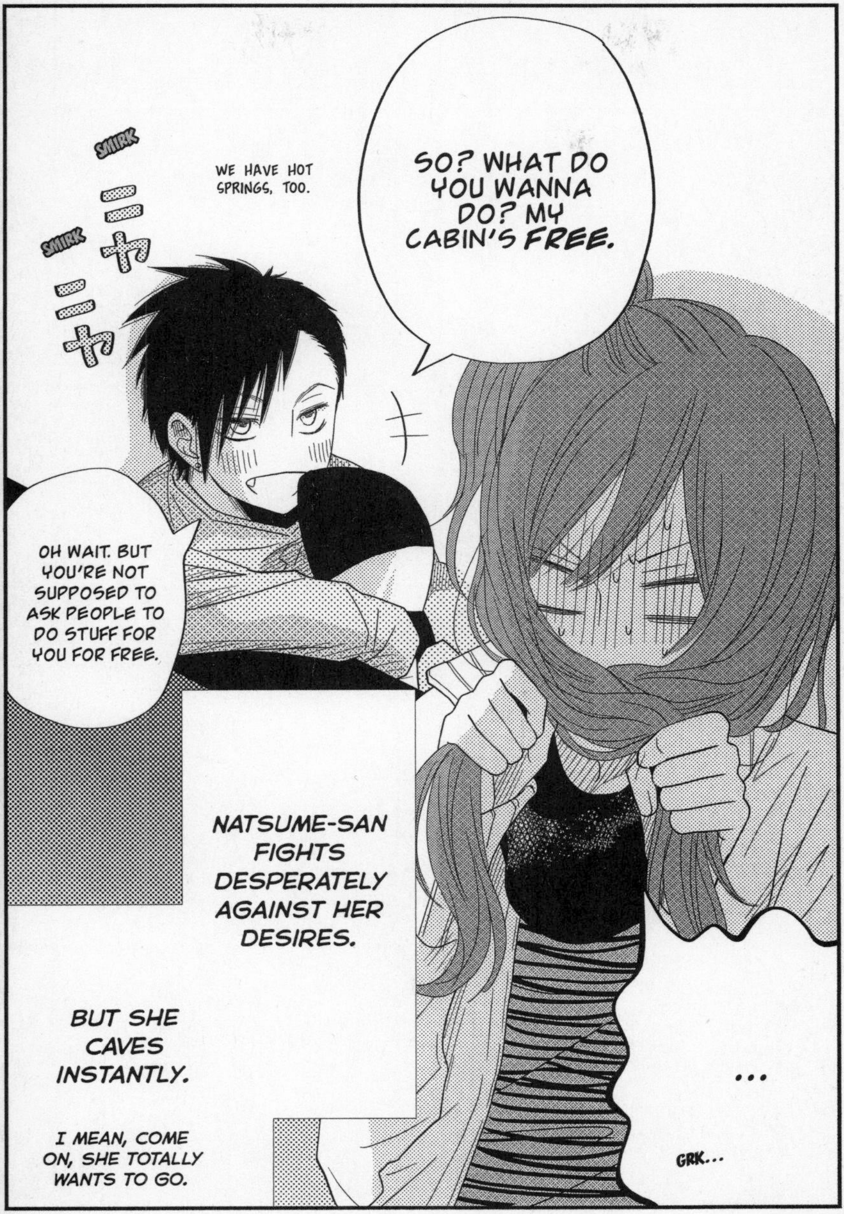

SO? WHAT DO YOU WANNA DO? MY CABIN'S FREE.
WE HAVE HOT SPRINGS, TOO.
SMIRK
SMIRK
OH WAIT. BUT YOU'RE NOT SUPPOSED TO ASK PEOPLE TO DO STUFF FOR YOU FOR FREE.
...
GRK...
NATSUME-SAN FIGHTS DESPERATELY AGAINST HER DESIRES.
BUT SHE CAVES INSTANTLY.
I MEAN, COME ON, SHE TOTALLY WANTS TO GO.

Chapter 20 Two Days, One Night

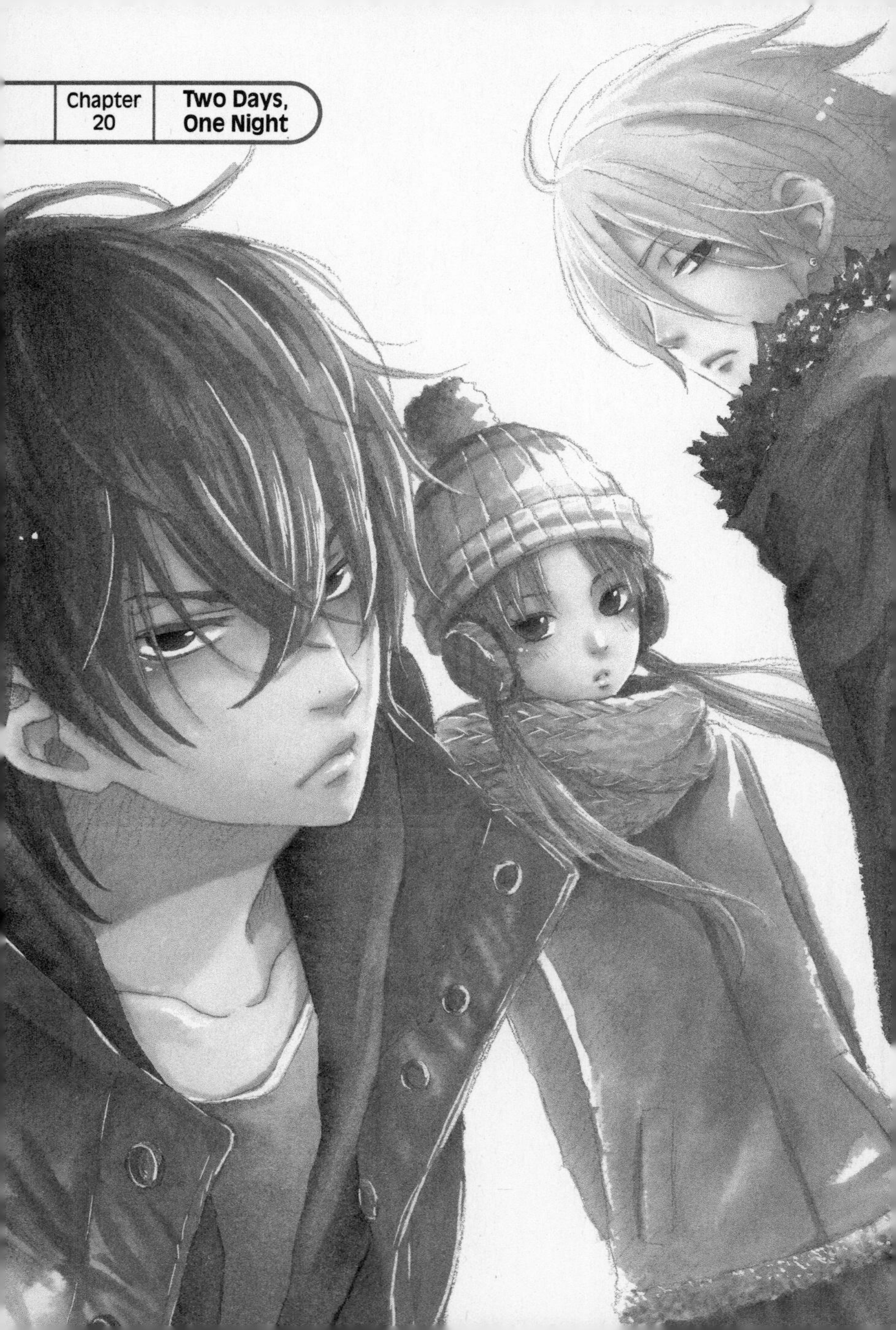

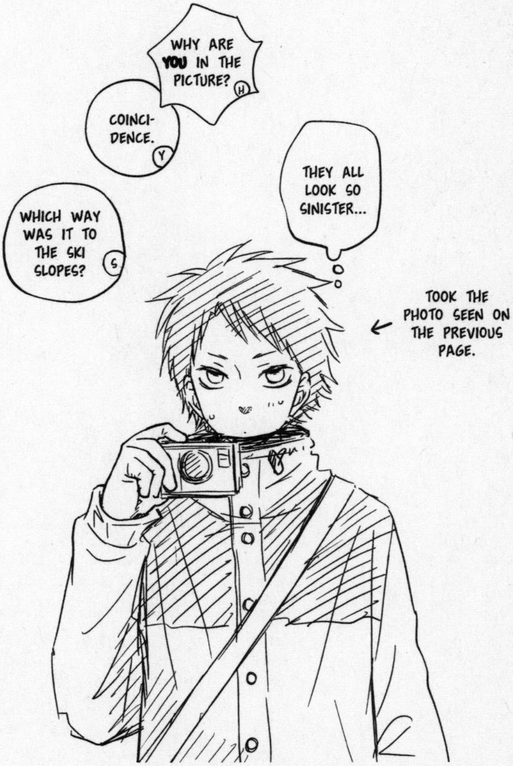
WHY ARE YOU IN THE PICTURE? H
COINCI-DENCE. Y
THEY ALL LOOK SO SINISTER...
WHICH WAY WAS IT TO THE SKI SLOPES? S
TOOK THE PHOTO SEEN ON THE PREVIOUS PAGE.

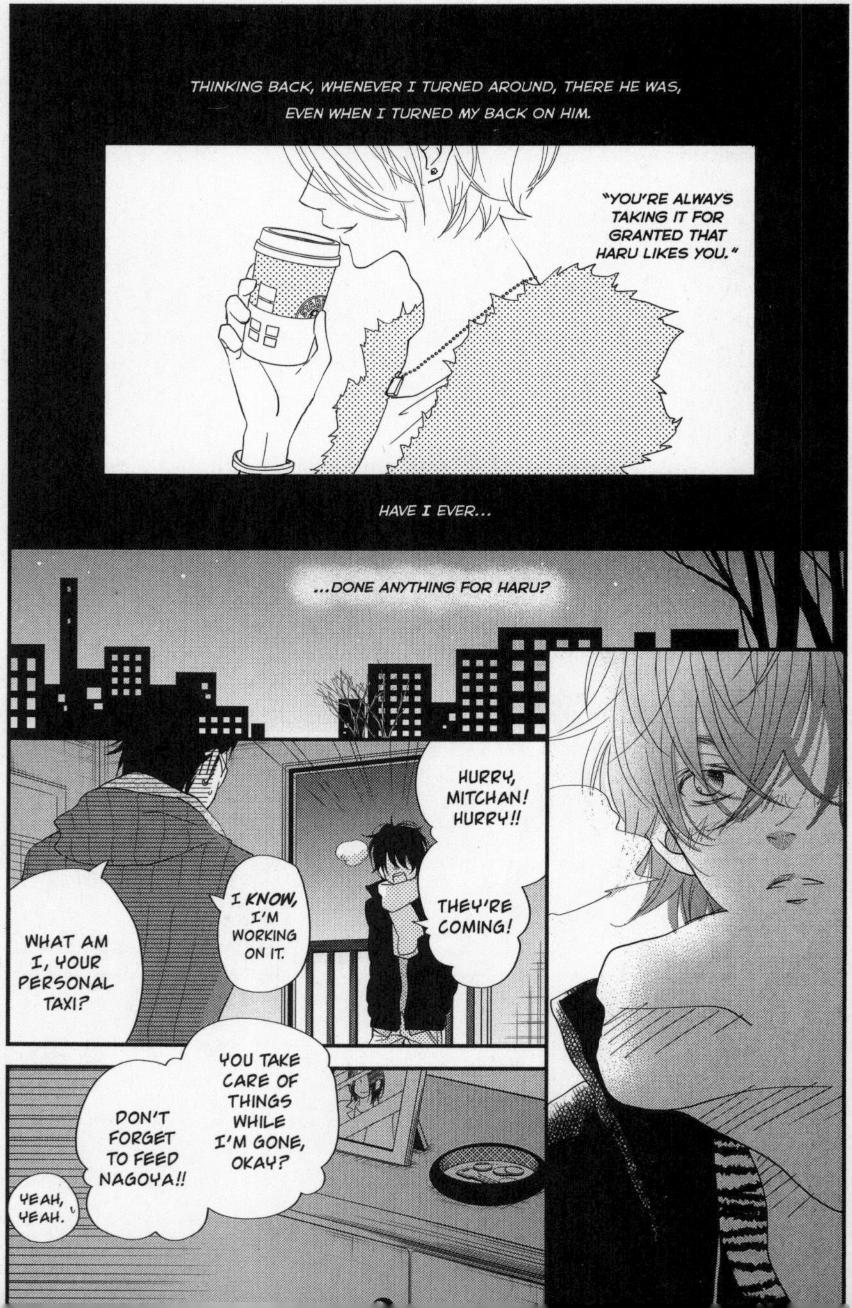
THINKING BACK, WHENEVER I TURNED AROUND, THERE HE WAS, EVEN WHEN I TURNED MY BACK ON HIM.
"YOU'RE ALWAYS TAKING IT FOR GRANTED THAT HARU LIKES YOU."
HAVE I EVER...
...DONE ANYTHING FOR HARU?
HURRY, MITCHAN! HURRY!!
THEY'RE COMING!
I KNOW, I'M WORKING ON IT.
WHAT AM I, YOUR PERSONAL TAXI?
YOU TAKE CARE OF THINGS WHILE I'M GONE, OKAY?
DON'T FORGET TO FEED NAGOYA!!
YEAH, YEAH.

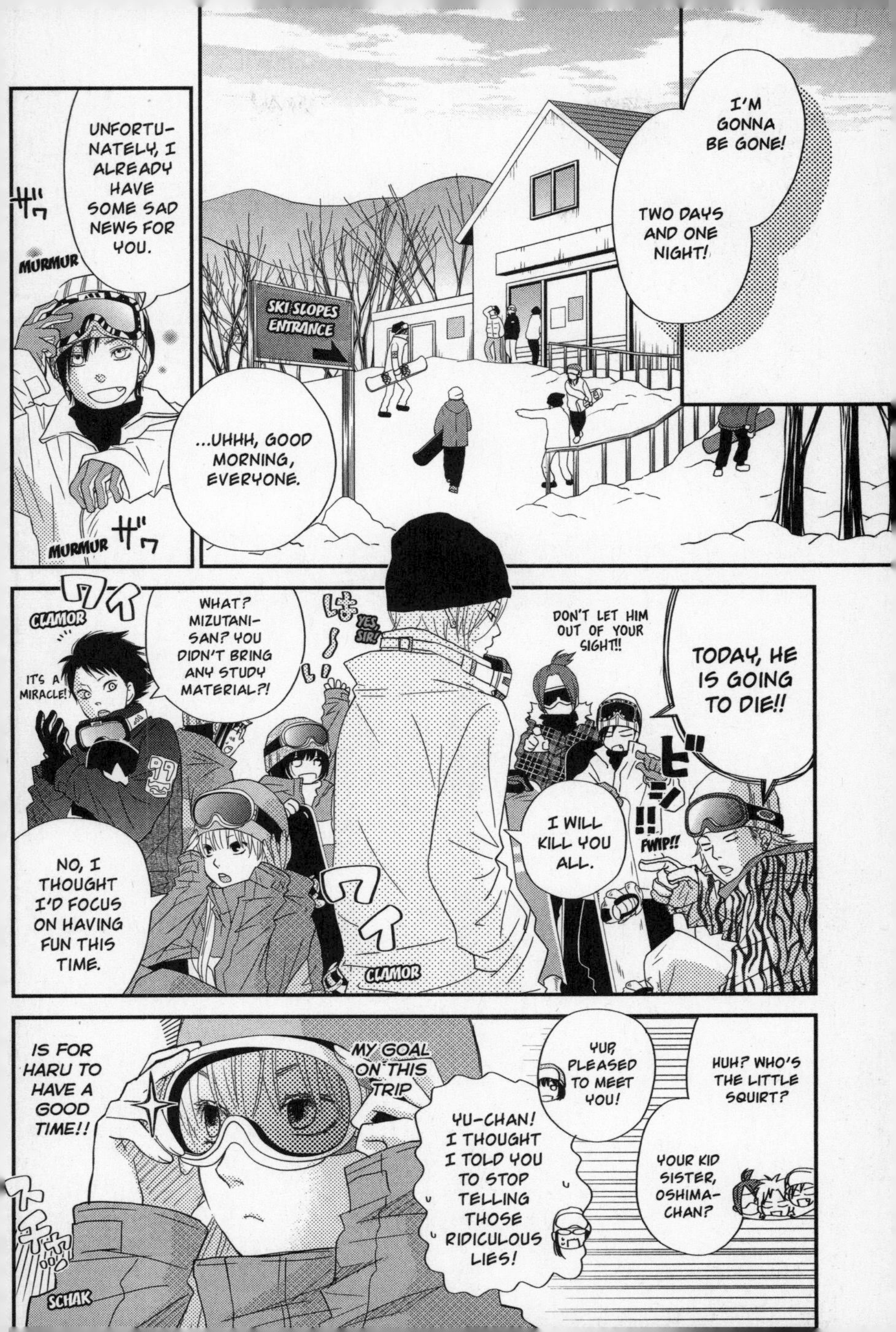
I'M GONNA BE GONE!
TWO DAYS AND ONE NIGHT!
SKI SLOPES ENTRANCE
...UHHH, GOOD MORNING, EVERYONE.
UNFORTU-NATELY, I ALREADY HAVE SOME SAD NEWS FOR YOU.
MURMUR
MURMUR
TODAY, HE IS GOING TO DIE!!
DON'T LET HIM OUT OF YOUR SIGHT!!
FWIP!!
I WILL KILL YOU ALL.
YES, SIR!
WHAT? MIZUTANI-SAN? YOU DIDN'T BRING ANY STUDY MATERIAL?!
IT'S A MIRACLE!
CLAMOR
NO, I THOUGHT I'D FOCUS ON HAVING FUN THIS TIME.
CLAMOR
HUH? WHO'S THE LITTLE SQUIRT?
YOUR KID SISTER, OSHIMA-CHAN?
YUP, PLEASED TO MEET YOU!
YU-CHAN! I THOUGHT I TOLD YOU TO STOP TELLING THOSE RIDICULOUS LIES!
MY GOAL ON THIS TRIP
IS FOR HARU TO HAVE A GOOD TIME!!
SCHAK

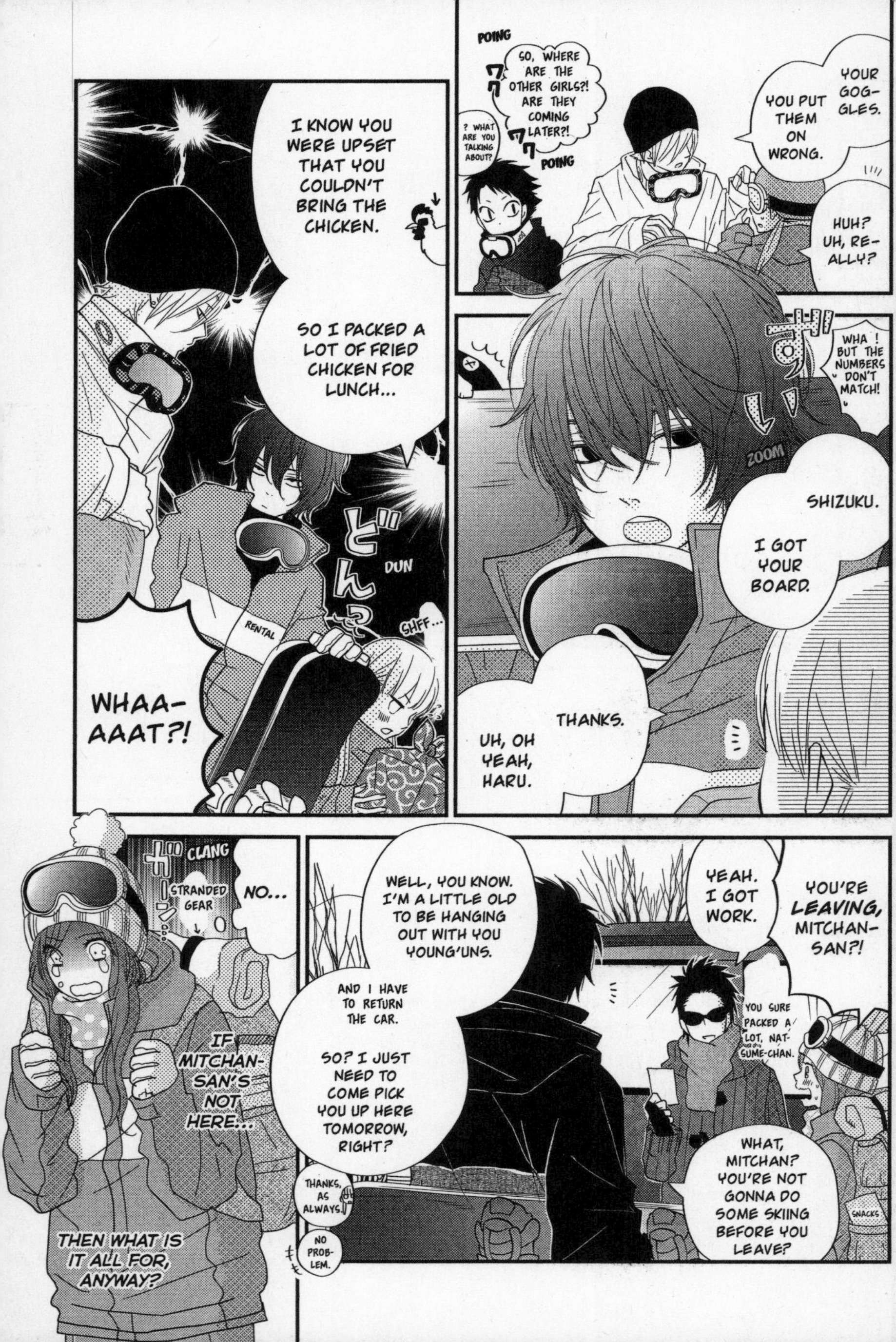
YOUR GOGGLES.
YOU PUT THEM ON WRONG.
HUH? UH, REALLY?
POING
SO, WHERE ARE THE OTHER GIRLS?! ARE THEY COMING LATER?!
POING
? WHAT ARE YOU TALKING ABOUT?
WHA! BUT THE NUMBERS DON'T MATCH!
ZOOM
SHIZUKU.
I GOT YOUR BOARD.
UH, OH YEAH, HARU.
THANKS.
I KNOW YOU WERE UPSET THAT YOU COULDN'T BRING THE CHICKEN.
SO I PACKED A LOT OF FRIED CHICKEN FOR LUNCH...
DUN
SHFF...
RENTAL
WHAA-AAAT?!
YOU'RE LEAVING, MITCHAN-SAN?!
YEAH. I GOT WORK.
WELL, YOU KNOW. I'M A LITTLE OLD TO BE HANGING OUT WITH YOU YOUNG'UNS.
AND I HAVE TO RETURN THE CAR.
YOU SURE PACKED A LOT, NATSUME-CHAN.
WHAT, MITCHAN? YOU'RE NOT GONNA DO SOME SKIING BEFORE YOU LEAVE?
SNACKS
SO? I JUST NEED TO COME PICK YOU UP HERE TOMORROW, RIGHT?
THANKS, AS ALWAYS.
NO PROBLEM.
NO...
CLANG
STRANDED GEAR
IF MITCHAN-SAN'S NOT HERE...
THEN WHAT IS IT ALL FOR, ANYWAY?

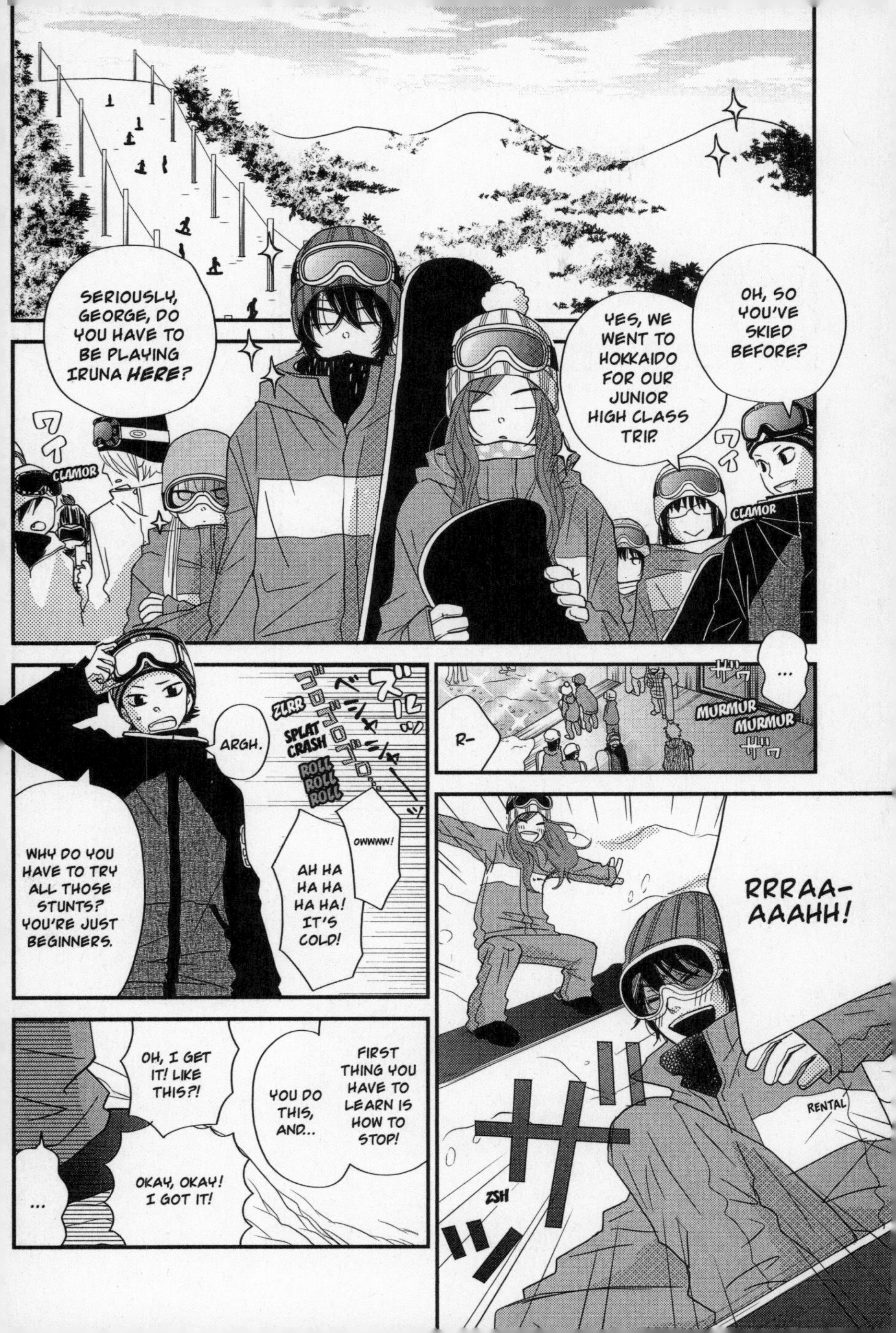
OH, SO YOU'VE SKIED BEFORE?
YES, WE WENT TO HOKKAIDO FOR OUR JUNIOR HIGH CLASS TRIP.
CLAMOR
SERIOUSLY, GEORGE, DO YOU HAVE TO BE PLAYING IRUNA HERE?
CLAMOR
...
MURMUR MURMUR
R-
RRRAA-AAAHH!
RENTAL
ZSH
ARGH.
ZLRR
SPLAT
CRASH
ROLL ROLL ROLL
OWWWW!
AH HA HA HA HA HA! IT'S COLD!
WHY DO YOU HAVE TO TRY ALL THOSE STUNTS? YOU'RE JUST BEGINNERS.
FIRST THING YOU HAVE TO LEARN IS HOW TO STOP!
YOU DO THIS, AND...
OH, I GET IT! LIKE THIS?!
OKAY, OKAY! I GOT IT!
...

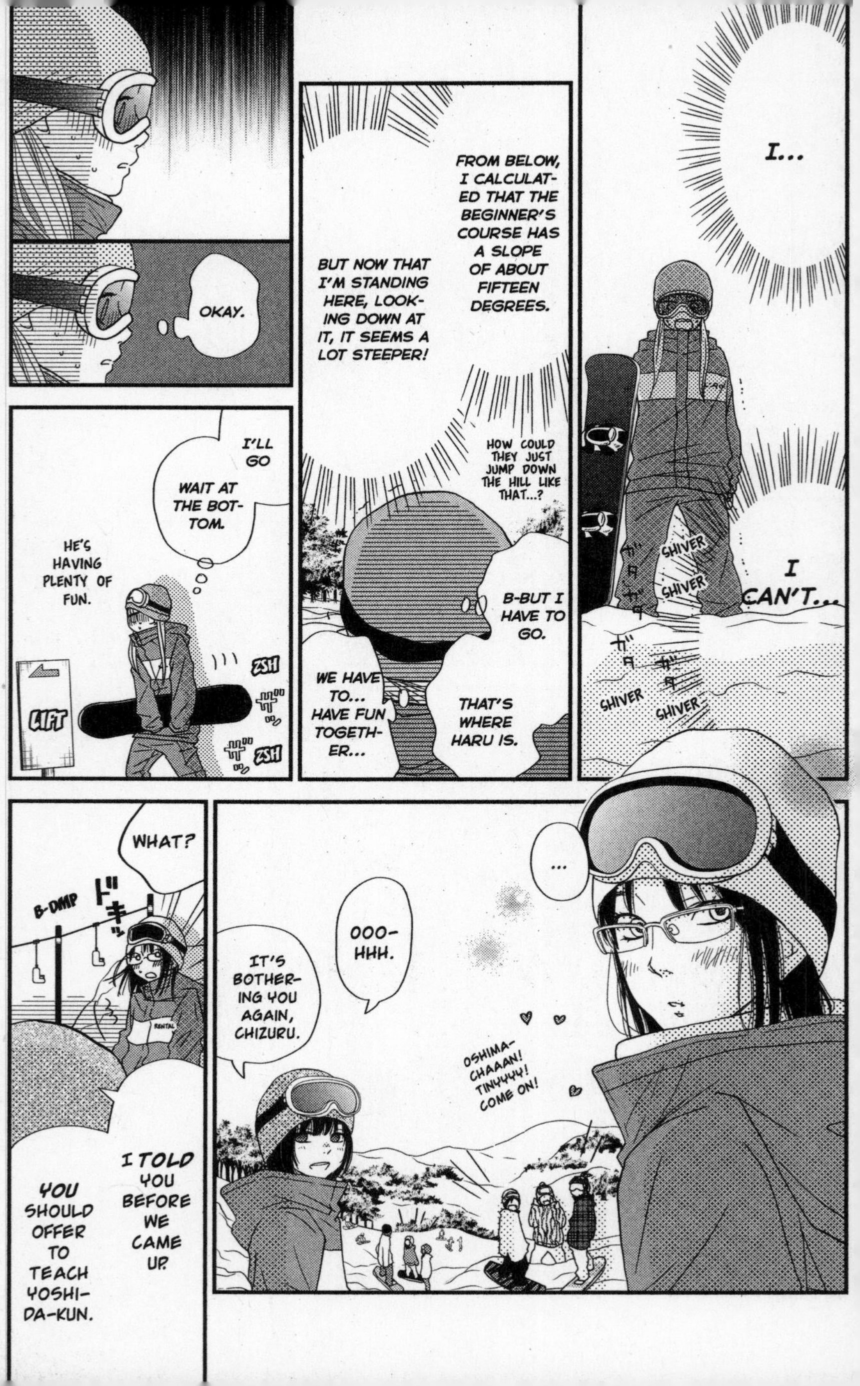
I...
SHIVER
SHIVER
I CAN'T...
SHIVER
SHIVER
FROM BELOW, I CALCULATED THAT THE BEGINNER'S COURSE HAS A SLOPE OF ABOUT FIFTEEN DEGREES.
BUT NOW THAT I'M STANDING HERE, LOOKING DOWN AT IT, IT SEEMS A LOT STEEPER!
HOW COULD THEY JUST JUMP DOWN THE HILL LIKE THAT...?
B-BUT I HAVE TO GO.
THAT'S WHERE HARU IS.
WE HAVE TO... HAVE FUN TOGETHER...
OKAY.
I'LL GO WAIT AT THE BOTTOM.
HE'S HAVING PLENTY OF FUN.
ZSH
ZSH
LIFT
...
OOO-HHH.
IT'S BOTHERING YOU AGAIN, CHIZURU.
OSHIMA-CHAAAN! TINYYYY! COME ON!
WHAT?
B-DMP
RENTAL
I TOLD YOU BEFORE WE CAME UP.
YOU SHOULD OFFER TO TEACH YOSHIDA-KUN.

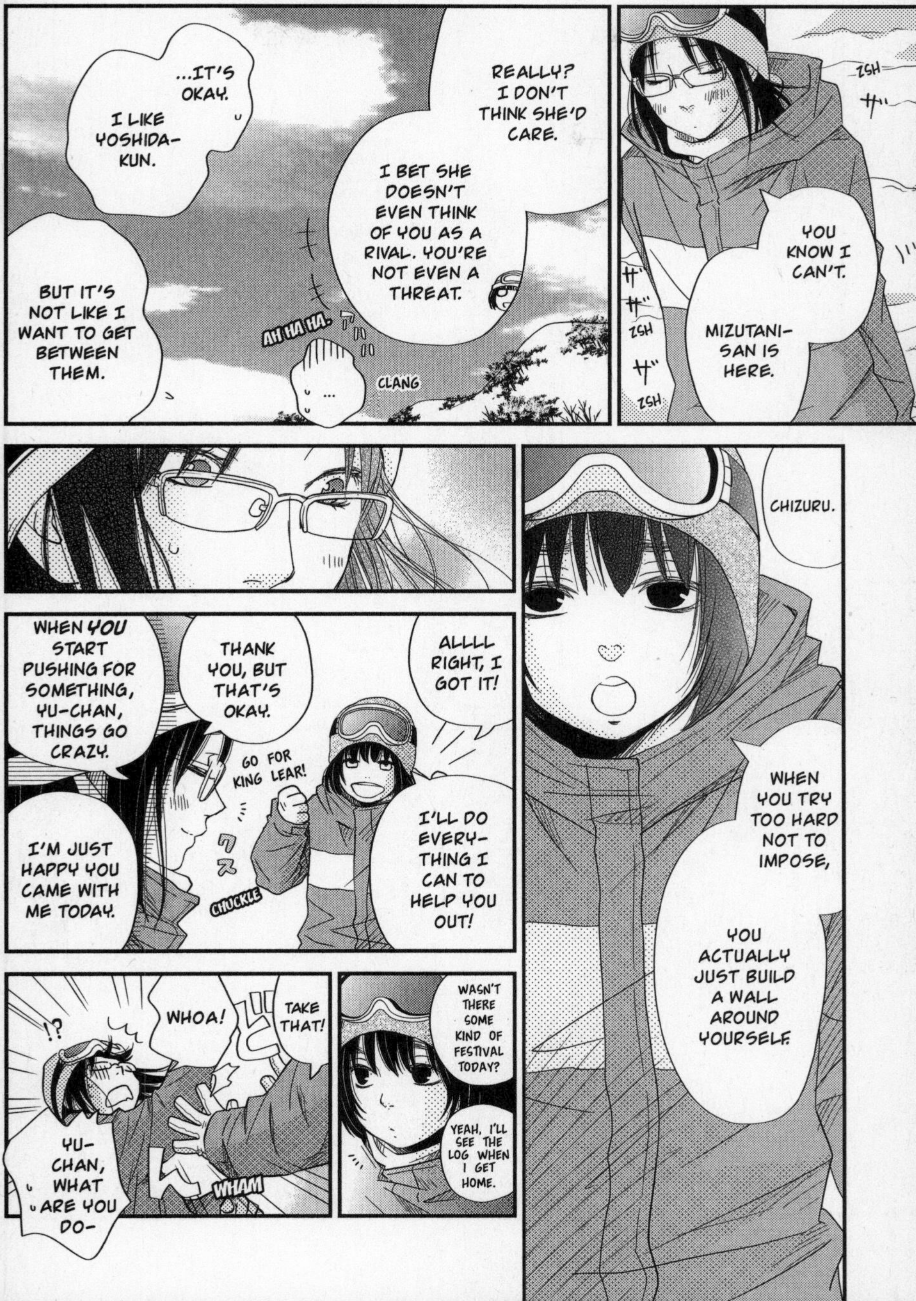
ZSH
YOU KNOW I CAN'T.
MIZUTANI-SAN IS HERE.
ZSH
ZSH
REALLY? I DON'T THINK SHE'D CARE.
I BET SHE DOESN'T EVEN THINK OF YOU AS A RIVAL. YOU'RE NOT EVEN A THREAT.
...IT'S OKAY.
I LIKE YOSHIDA-KUN.
BUT IT'S NOT LIKE I WANT TO GET BETWEEN THEM.
AH HA HA.
CLANG
...
CHIZURU.
WHEN YOU TRY TOO HARD NOT TO IMPOSE,
YOU ACTUALLY JUST BUILD A WALL AROUND YOURSELF.
ALLLL RIGHT, I GOT IT!
I'LL DO EVERYTHING I CAN TO HELP YOU OUT!
GO FOR KING LEAR!
THANK YOU, BUT THAT'S OKAY.
WHEN YOU START PUSHING FOR SOMETHING, YU-CHAN, THINGS GO CRAZY.
I'M JUST HAPPY YOU CAME WITH ME TODAY.
CHUCKLE
WASN'T THERE SOME KIND OF FESTIVAL TODAY?
YEAH, I'LL SEE THE LOG WHEN I GET HOME.
TAKE THAT!
WHOA!
!?
YU-CHAN, WHAT ARE YOU DO-
WHAM

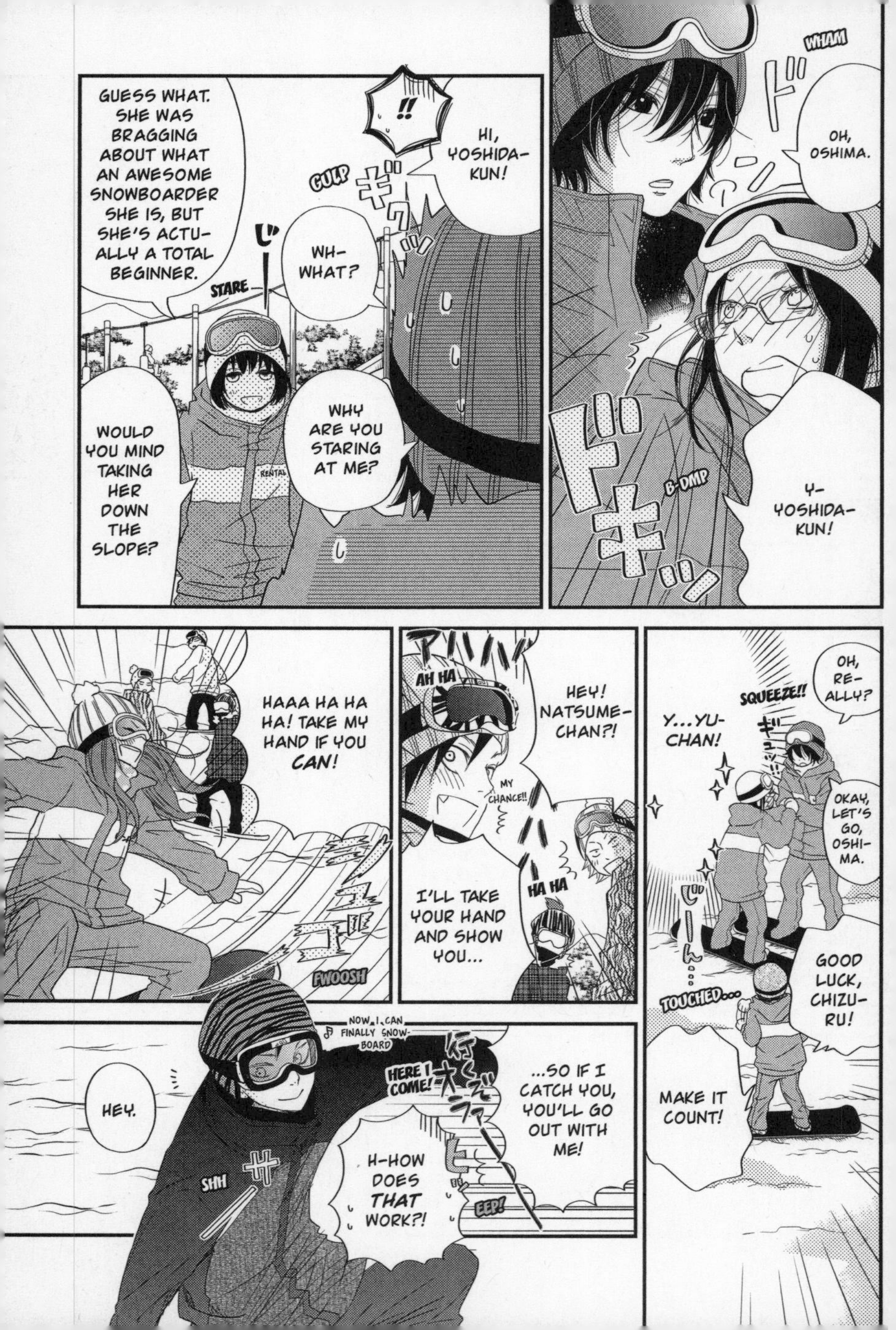
WHAM
OH, OSHIMA.
B-DMP
Y-YOSHIDA-KUN!
!!
HI, YOSHIDA-KUN!
GULP
GUESS WHAT. SHE WAS BRAGGING ABOUT WHAT AN AWESOME SNOWBOARDER SHE IS, BUT SHE'S ACTU-ALLY A TOTAL BEGINNER.
WH-WHAT?
STARE
WHY ARE YOU STARING AT ME?
WOULD YOU MIND TAKING HER DOWN THE SLOPE?
RENTAL
OH, RE-ALLY?
SQUEEZE!!
Y...YU-CHAN!
OKAY, LET'S GO, OSHI-MA.
TOUCHED...
GOOD LUCK, CHIZU-RU!
MAKE IT COUNT!
AH HA
HEY! NATSUME-CHAN?!
MY CHANCE!!
HA HA
I'LL TAKE YOUR HAND AND SHOW YOU...
HAAA HA HA HA! TAKE MY HAND IF YOU CAN!
FWOOSH
...SO IF I CATCH YOU, YOU'LL GO OUT WITH ME!
HERE I COME!
NOW I CAN FINALLY SNOW-BOARD
EEP!
H-HOW DOES THAT WORK?!
HEY.
SHH

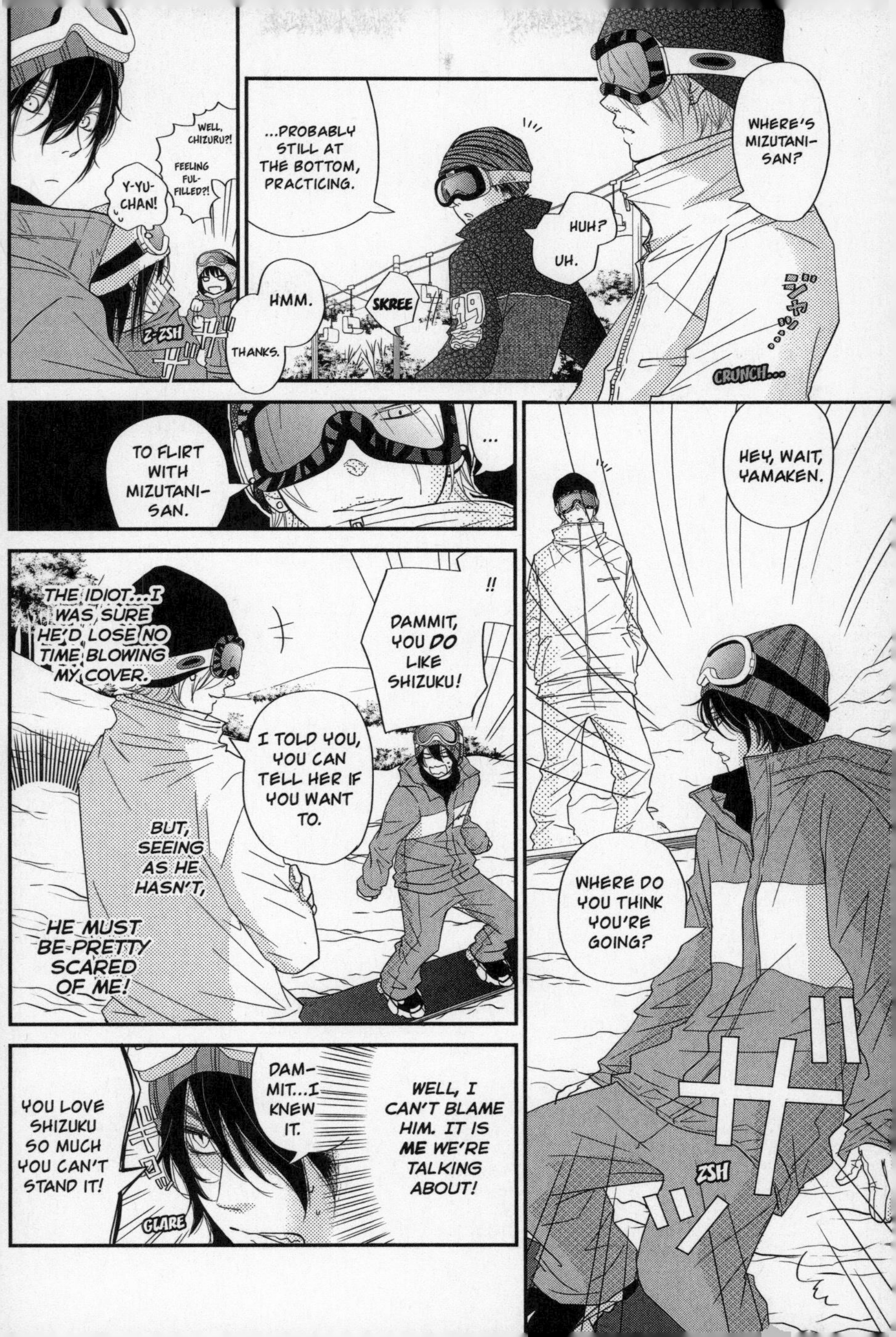
WHERE'S MIZUTANI-SAN?
HUH?
UH.
CRUNCH...
...PROBABLY STILL AT THE BOTTOM, PRACTICING.
HMM.
SKREE
THANKS.
WELL, CHIZURU?!
FEELING FUL-FILLED?!
Y-YU-CHAN!
Z-ZSH
HEY, WAIT, YAMAKEN.
WHERE DO YOU THINK YOU'RE GOING?
ZSH
...
TO FLIRT WITH MIZUTANI-SAN.
!!
DAMMIT, YOU DO LIKE SHIZUKU!
I TOLD YOU, YOU CAN TELL HER IF YOU WANT TO.
THE IDIOT...I WAS SURE HE'D LOSE NO TIME BLOWING MY COVER.
BUT, SEEING AS HE HASN'T,
HE MUST BE PRETTY SCARED OF ME!
WELL, I CAN'T BLAME HIM. IT IS ME WE'RE TALKING ABOUT!
DAM-MIT...I KNEW IT.
YOU LOVE SHIZUKU SO MUCH YOU CAN'T STAND IT!
GLARE

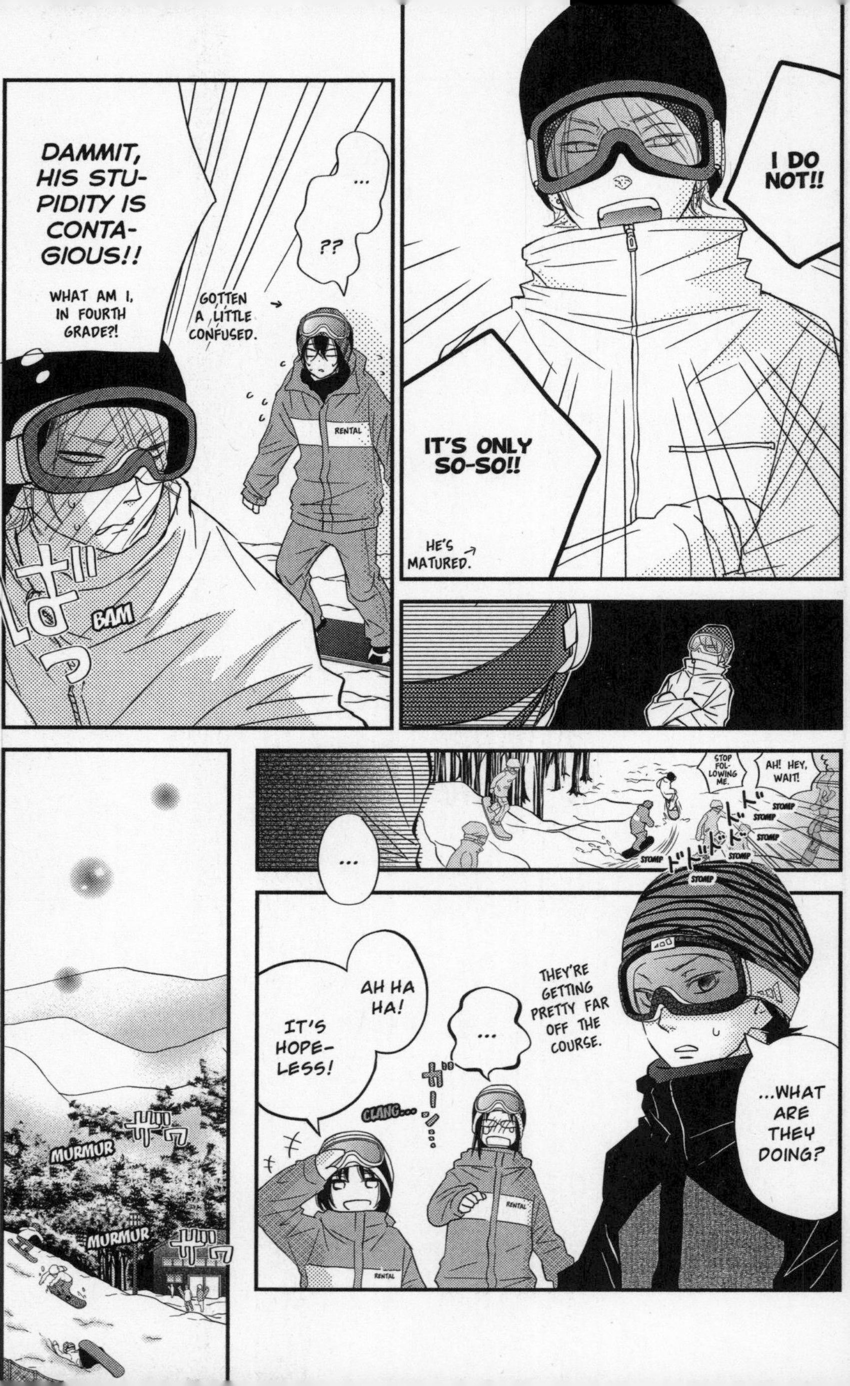
I DO NOT!!
IT'S ONLY SO-SO!!
HE'S MATURED.
DAMMIT, HIS STUPIDITY IS CONTAGIOUS!!
WHAT AM I, IN FOURTH GRADE?!
...
??
GOTTEN A LITTLE CONFUSED.
BAM
AH! HEY, WAIT!
STOP FOLLOWING ME.
STOMP
STOMP
STOMP
STOMP
STOMP
...
...WHAT ARE THEY DOING?
THEY'RE GETTING PRETTY FAR OFF THE COURSE.
...
AH HA HA!
IT'S HOPELESS!
CLANG...
RENTAL
RENTAL
RENTAL
MURMUR
MURMUR

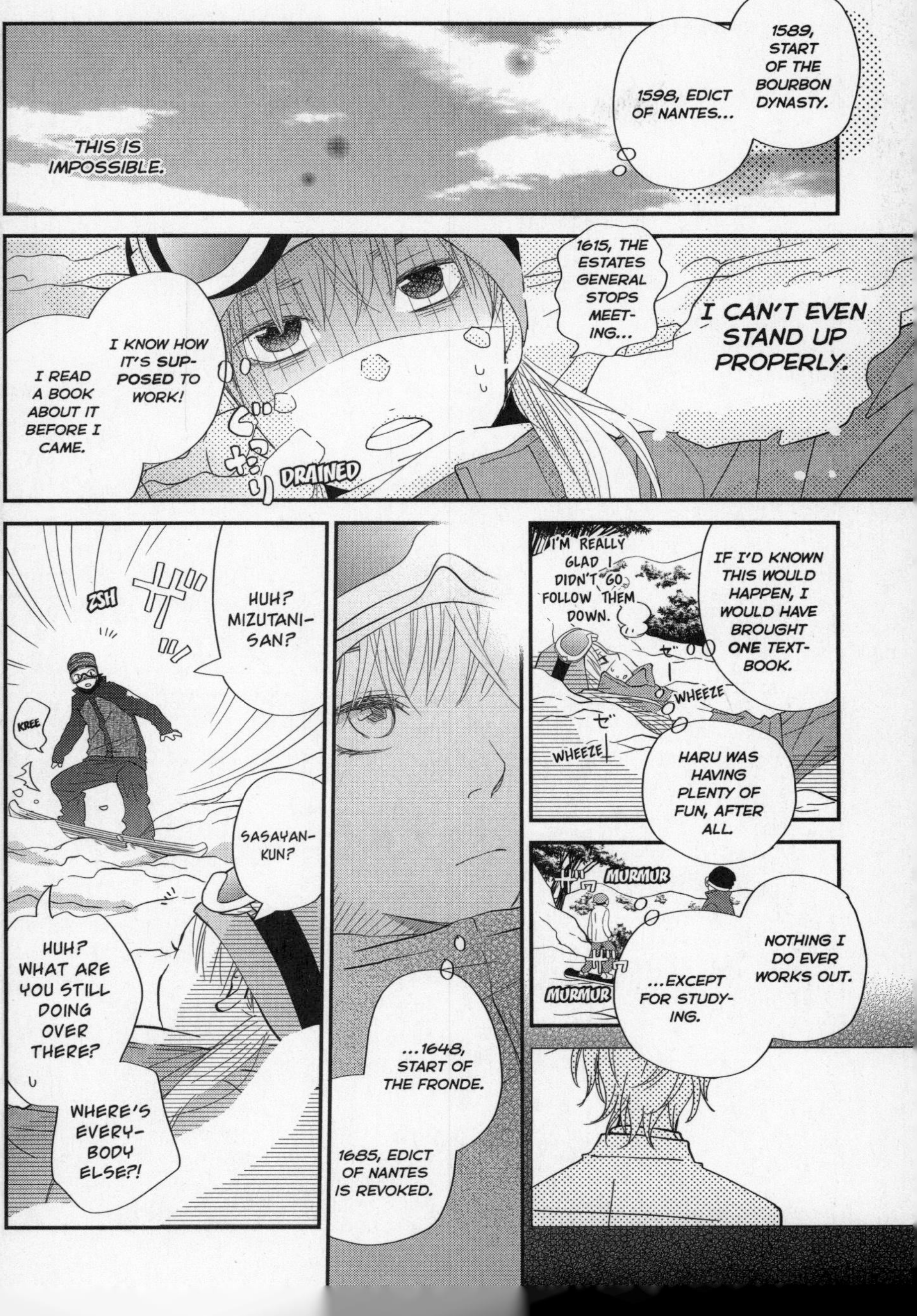
1589, START OF THE BOURBON DYNASTY.
1598, EDICT OF NANTES...
THIS IS IMPOSSIBLE.
I CAN'T EVEN STAND UP PROPERLY.
1615, THE ESTATES GENERAL STOPS MEETING...
DRAINED
I KNOW HOW IT'S SUPPOSED TO WORK!
I READ A BOOK ABOUT IT BEFORE I CAME.
IF I'D KNOWN THIS WOULD HAPPEN, I WOULD HAVE BROUGHT ONE TEXTBOOK.
I'M REALLY GLAD I DIDN'T GO FOLLOW THEM DOWN.
WHEEZE
WHEEZE
HARU WAS HAVING PLENTY OF FUN, AFTER ALL.
MURMUR
NOTHING I DO EVER WORKS OUT.
...EXCEPT FOR STUDYING.
MURMUR
...1648, START OF THE FRONDE.
1685, EDICT OF NANTES IS REVOKED.
HUH? MIZUTANI-SAN?
ZSH
KREE
SASAYAN-KUN?
HUH? WHAT ARE YOU STILL DOING OVER THERE?
WHERE'S EVERYBODY ELSE?!

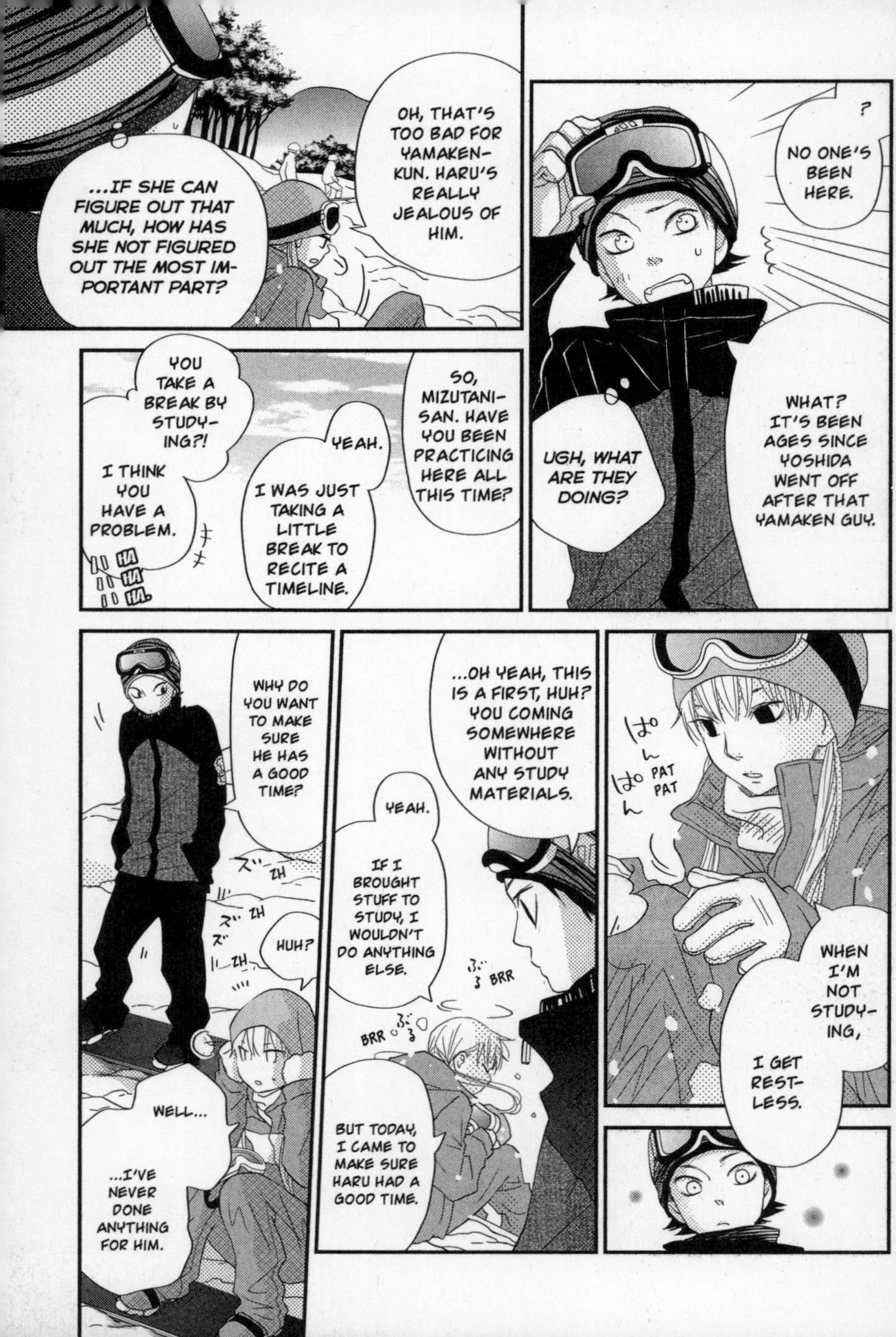
?
NO ONE'S BEEN HERE.
WHAT? IT'S BEEN AGES SINCE YOSHIDA WENT OFF AFTER THAT YAMAKEN GUY.
UGH, WHAT ARE THEY DOING?
OH, THAT'S TOO BAD FOR YAMAKEN-KUN. HARU'S REALLY JEALOUS OF HIM.
...IF SHE CAN FIGURE OUT THAT MUCH, HOW HAS SHE NOT FIGURED OUT THE MOST IMPORTANT PART?
SO, MIZUTANI-SAN. HAVE YOU BEEN PRACTICING HERE ALL THIS TIME?
YEAH.
I WAS JUST TAKING A LITTLE BREAK TO RECITE A TIMELINE.
YOU TAKE A BREAK BY STUDYING?!
I THINK YOU HAVE A PROBLEM.
HA HA HA.
ぱんぱん PAT PAT
WHEN I'M NOT STUDYING,
I GET RESTLESS.
...OH YEAH, THIS IS A FIRST, HUH? YOU COMING SOMEWHERE WITHOUT ANY STUDY MATERIALS.
YEAH.
IF I BROUGHT STUFF TO STUDY, I WOULDN'T DO ANYTHING ELSE.
ぶる BRR
BRR ぶる
BUT TODAY, I CAME TO MAKE SURE HARU HAD A GOOD TIME.
WHY DO YOU WANT TO MAKE SURE HE HAS A GOOD TIME?
ズ ZH
ズ ZH
ズ ZH
HUH?
WELL...
...I'VE NEVER DONE ANYTHING FOR HIM.

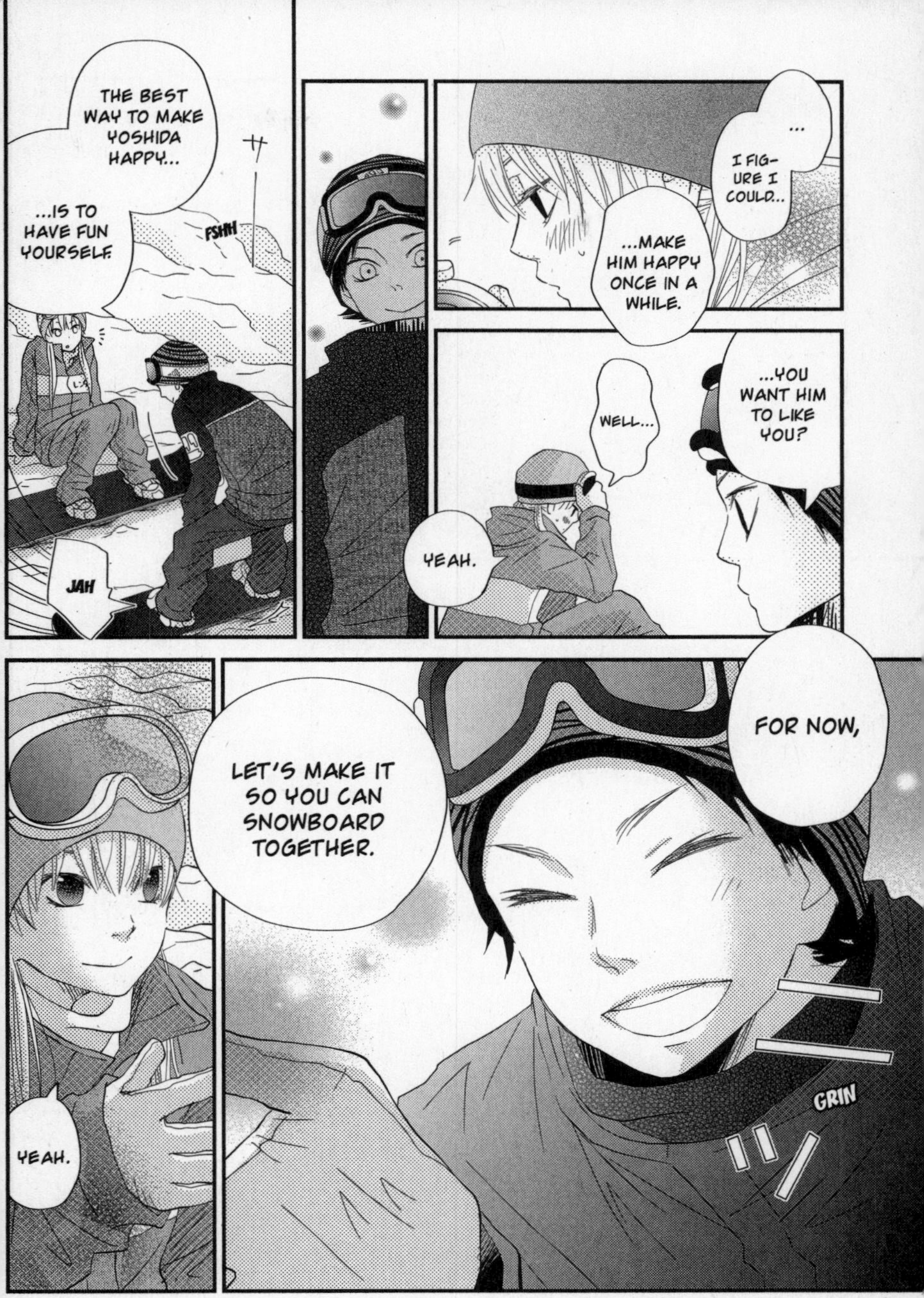
...
I FIG-URE I COULD...
...MAKE HIM HAPPY ONCE IN A WHILE.
...YOU WANT HIM TO LIKE YOU?
WELL...
YEAH.
THE BEST WAY TO MAKE YOSHIDA HAPPY...
...IS TO HAVE FUN YOURSELF.
FSHH
JAH
FOR NOW,
LET'S MAKE IT SO YOU CAN SNOWBOARD TOGETHER.
GRIN
YEAH.

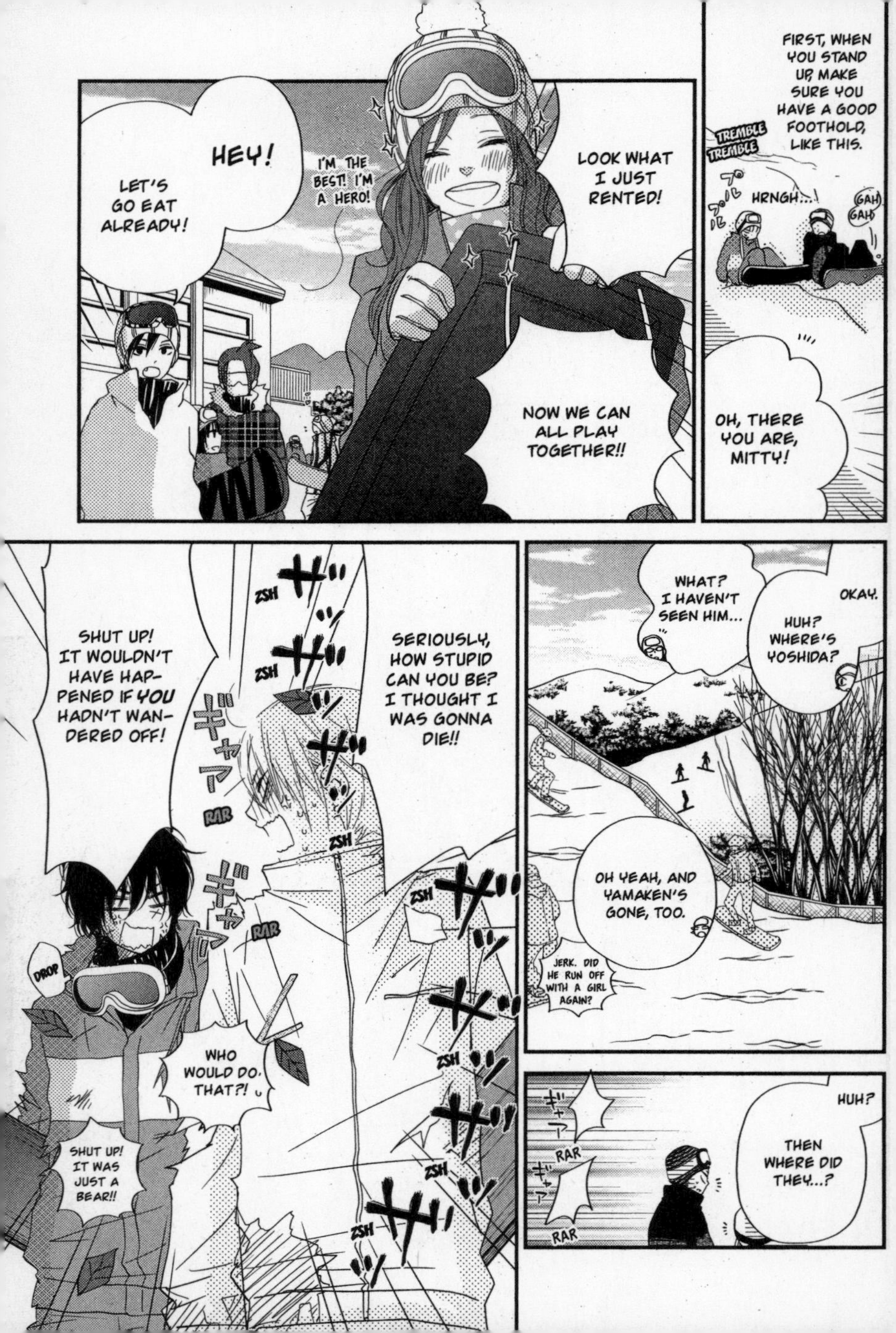
TREMBLE TREMBLE
FIRST, WHEN YOU STAND UP, MAKE SURE YOU HAVE A GOOD FOOTHOLD, LIKE THIS.
HRNGH...
GAH GAH
OH, THERE YOU ARE, MITTY!
LOOK WHAT I JUST RENTED!
NOW WE CAN ALL PLAY TOGETHER!!
I'M THE BEST! I'M A HERO!
HEY!
LET'S GO EAT ALREADY!
OKAY.
HUH? WHERE'S YOSHIDA?
WHAT? I HAVEN'T SEEN HIM...
OH YEAH, AND YAMAKEN'S GONE, TOO.
JERK. DID HE RUN OFF WITH A GIRL AGAIN?
HUH?
THEN WHERE DID THEY...?
RAR
RAR
ZSH
SERIOUSLY, HOW STUPID CAN YOU BE? I THOUGHT I WAS GONNA DIE!!
SHUT UP! IT WOULDN'T HAVE HAPPENED IF YOU HADN'T WANDERED OFF!
RAR
RAR
DROP
WHO WOULD DO THAT?!
SHUT UP! IT WAS JUST A BEAR!!

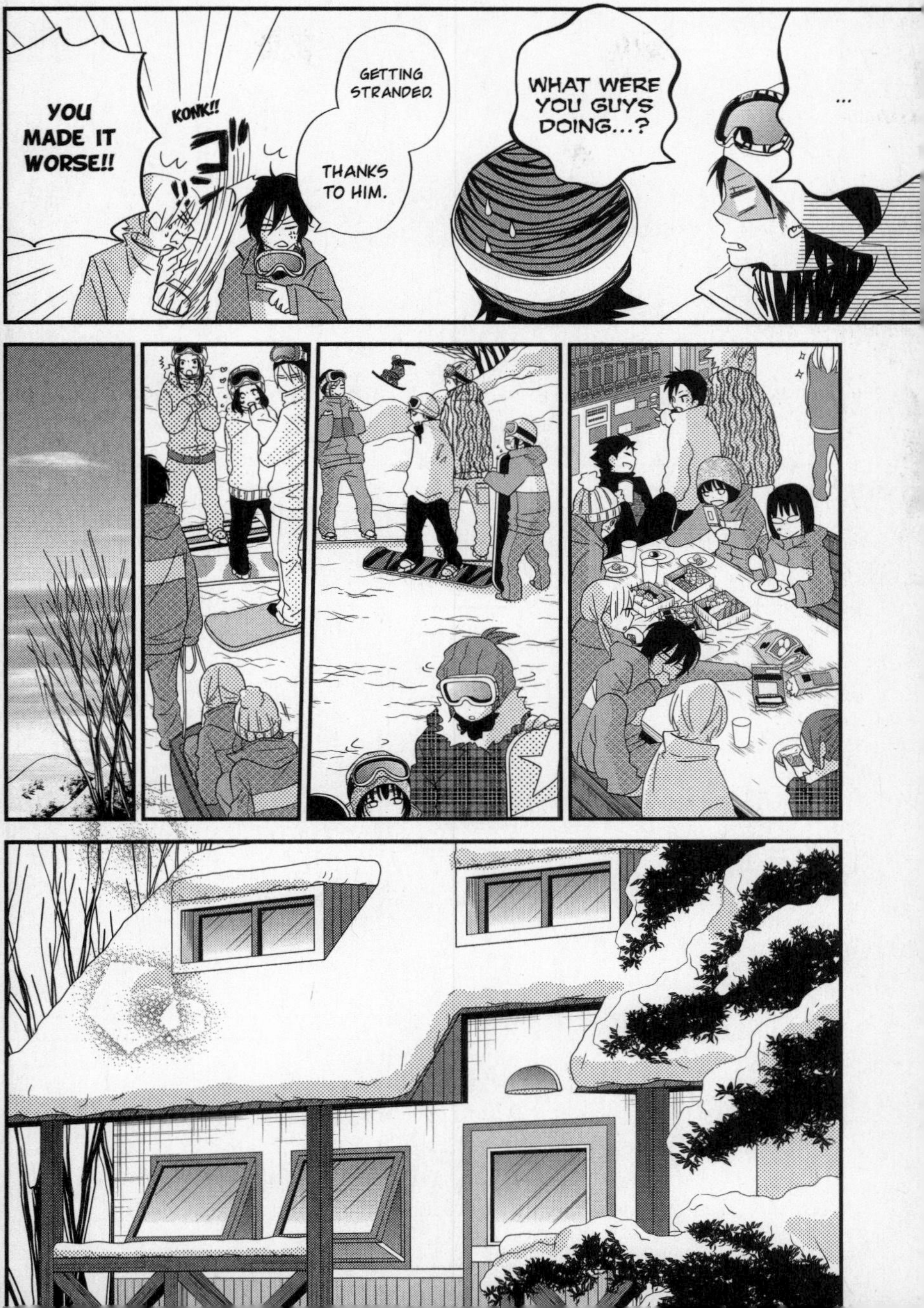
...
WHAT WERE YOU GUYS DOING...?
GETTING STRANDED.
THANKS TO HIM.
KONK!!
YOU MADE IT WORSE!!

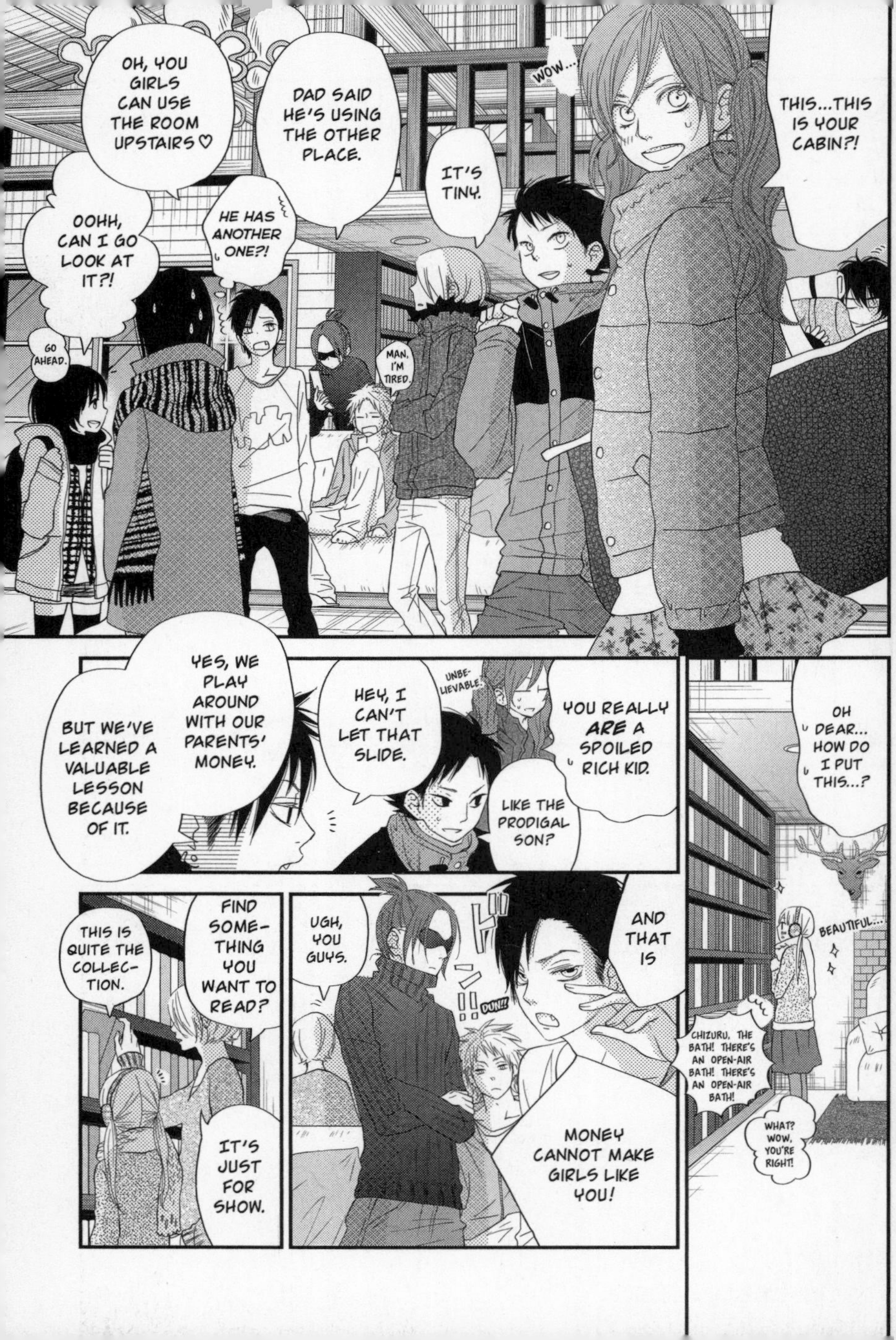
WOW...
THIS...THIS IS YOUR CABIN?!
IT'S TINY.
DAD SAID HE'S USING THE OTHER PLACE.
OH, YOU GIRLS CAN USE THE ROOM UPSTAIRS♡
HE HAS ANOTHER ONE?!
OOHH, CAN I GO LOOK AT IT?!
MAN, I'M TIRED.
GO AHEAD.
OH DEAR... HOW DO I PUT THIS...?
BEAUTIFUL...
CHIZURU, THE BATH! THERE'S AN OPEN-AIR BATH! THERE'S AN OPEN-AIR BATH!
WHAT? WOW, YOU'RE RIGHT!
YOU REALLY ARE A SPOILED RICH KID.
UNBELIEVABLE.
LIKE THE PRODIGAL SON?
HEY, I CAN'T LET THAT SLIDE.
YES, WE PLAY AROUND WITH OUR PARENTS' MONEY.
BUT WE'VE LEARNED A VALUABLE LESSON BECAUSE OF IT.
AND THAT IS
MONEY CANNOT MAKE GIRLS LIKE YOU!
DUN!!
UGH, YOU GUYS.
FIND SOMETHING YOU WANT TO READ?
THIS IS QUITE THE COLLECTION.
IT'S JUST FOR SHOW.

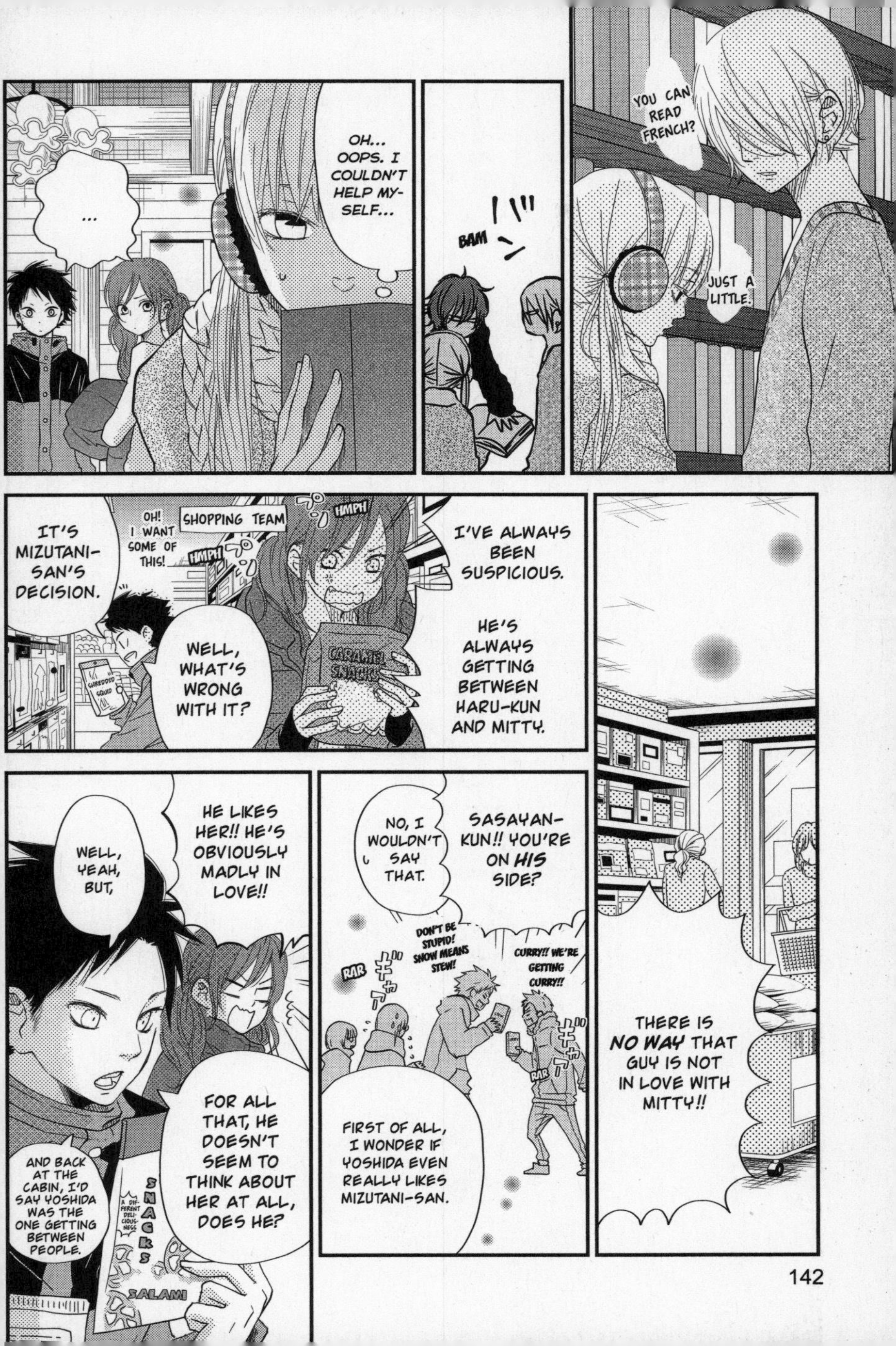

YOU CAN READ FRENCH?
JUST A LITTLE.
BAM
OH... OOPS. I COULDN'T HELP MY-SELF...
...
I'VE ALWAYS BEEN SUSPICIOUS.
HE'S ALWAYS GETTING BETWEEN HARU-KUN AND MITTY.
HMPH
SHOPPING TEAM
HMPH
OH! I WANT SOME OF THIS!
IT'S MIZUTANI-SAN'S DECISION.
WELL, WHAT'S WRONG WITH IT?
CARAMEL SNACKS
SHREDDED SQUID
THERE IS NO WAY THAT GUY IS NOT IN LOVE WITH MITTY!!
SASAYAN-KUN!! YOU'RE ON HIS SIDE?
NO, I WOULDN'T SAY THAT.
DON'T BE STUPID! SNOW MEANS STEW!
CURRY!! WE'RE GETTING CURRY!!
RAR
RAR
FIRST OF ALL, I WONDER IF YOSHIDA EVEN REALLY LIKES MIZUTANI-SAN.
HE LIKES HER!! HE'S OBVIOUSLY MADLY IN LOVE!!
WELL, YEAH, BUT,
FOR ALL THAT, HE DOESN'T SEEM TO THINK ABOUT HER AT ALL, DOES HE?
AND BACK AT THE CABIN, I'D SAY YOSHIDA WAS THE ONE GETTING BETWEEN PEOPLE.
SNACKS
A DIF-FERENT DELI-CIOUS-NESS
SALAMI

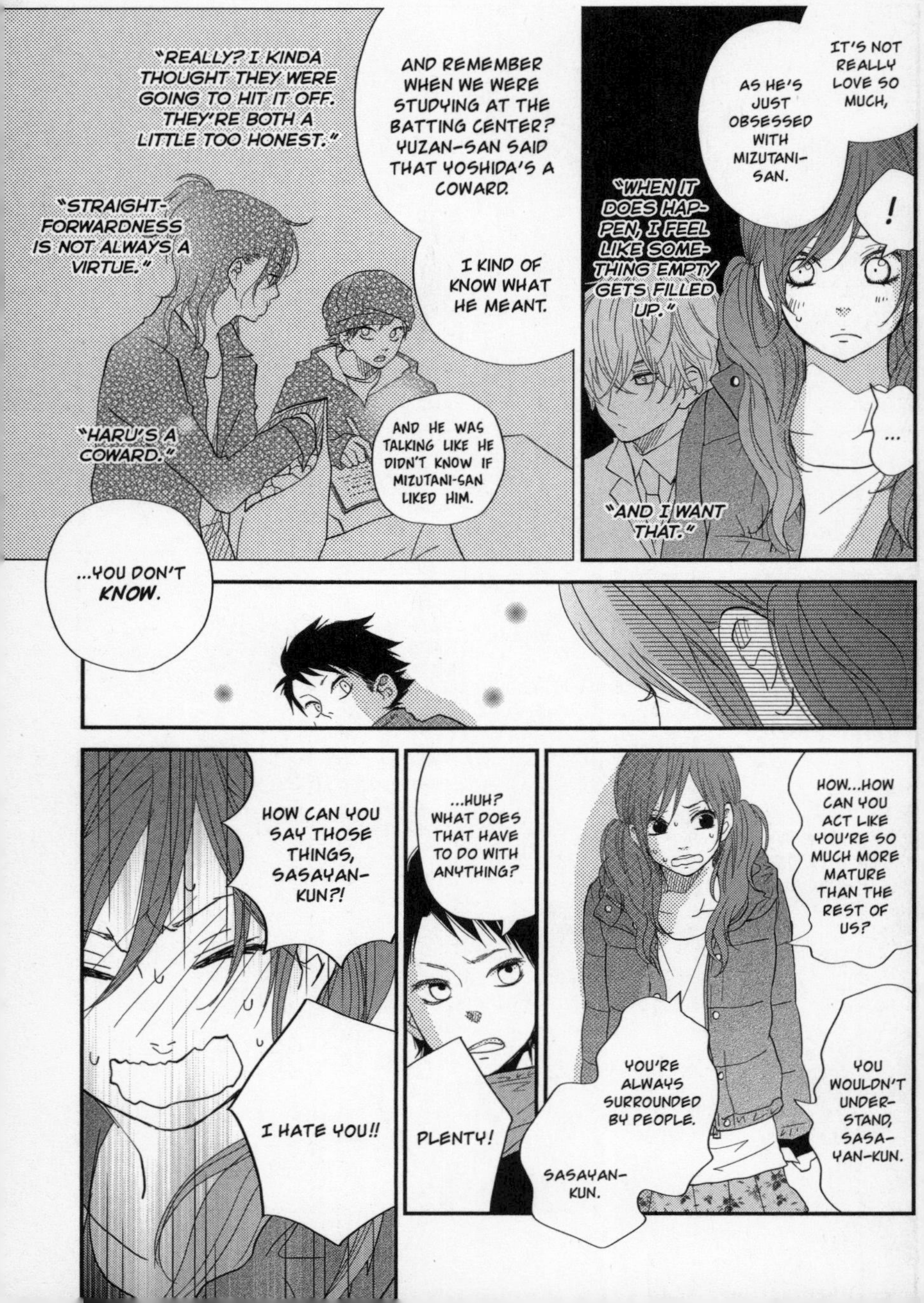
IT'S NOT REALLY LOVE SO MUCH,
AS HE'S JUST OBSESSED WITH MIZUTANI-SAN.
!
"WHEN IT DOES HAPPEN, I FEEL LIKE SOMETHING EMPTY GETS FILLED UP."
"AND I WANT THAT."
...
AND REMEMBER WHEN WE WERE STUDYING AT THE BATTING CENTER? YUZAN-SAN SAID THAT YOSHIDA'S A COWARD.
"REALLY? I KINDA THOUGHT THEY WERE GOING TO HIT IT OFF. THEY'RE BOTH A LITTLE TOO HONEST."
"STRAIGHTFORWARDNESS IS NOT ALWAYS A VIRTUE."
I KIND OF KNOW WHAT HE MEANT.
AND HE WAS TALKING LIKE HE DIDN'T KNOW IF MIZUTANI-SAN LIKED HIM.
"HARU'S A COWARD."
...YOU DON'T **KNOW**.
HOW...HOW CAN YOU ACT LIKE YOU'RE SO MUCH MORE MATURE THAN THE REST OF US?
YOU'RE ALWAYS SURROUNDED BY PEOPLE.
YOU WOULDN'T UNDERSTAND, SASAYAN-KUN.
SASAYAN-KUN.
...HUH? WHAT DOES THAT HAVE TO DO WITH ANYTHING?
PLENTY!
HOW CAN YOU SAY THOSE THINGS, SASAYAN-KUN?!
I HATE YOU!!

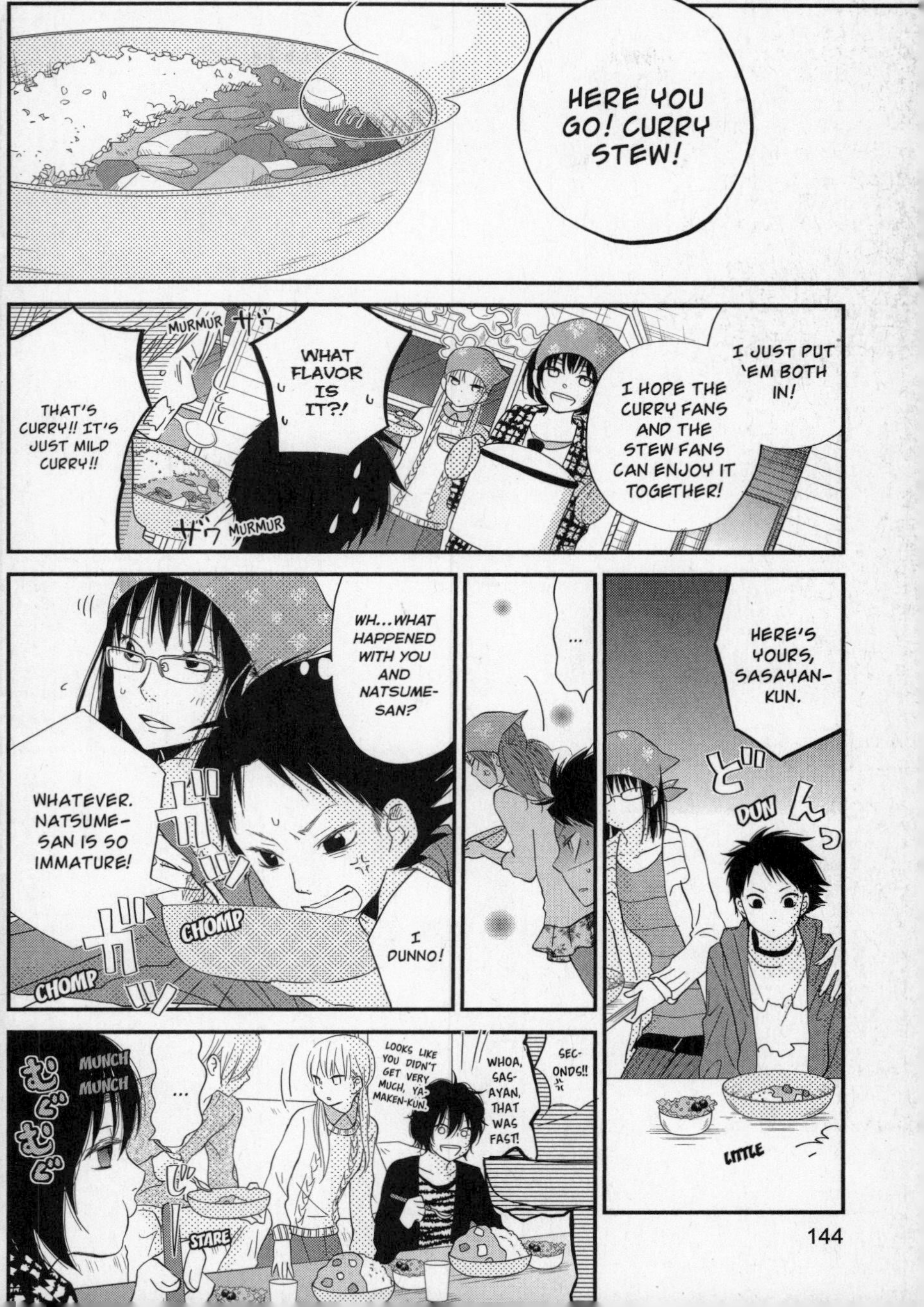
HERE YOU GO! CURRY STEW!
I JUST PUT 'EM BOTH IN!
I HOPE THE CURRY FANS AND THE STEW FANS CAN ENJOY IT TOGETHER!
WHAT FLAVOR IS IT?!
MURMUR
THAT'S CURRY!! IT'S JUST MILD CURRY!!
MURMUR
HERE'S YOURS, SASAYAN-KUN.
DUN
LITTLE
...
WH...WHAT HAPPENED WITH YOU AND NATSUME-SAN?
WHATEVER. NATSUME-SAN IS SO IMMATURE!
I DUNNO!
CHOMP
CHOMP
SEC-ONDS!!
WHOA, SASAYAN, THAT WAS FAST!
LOOKS LIKE YOU DIDN'T GET VERY MUCH, YA-MAKEN-KUN.
...
MUNCH MUNCH
STARE

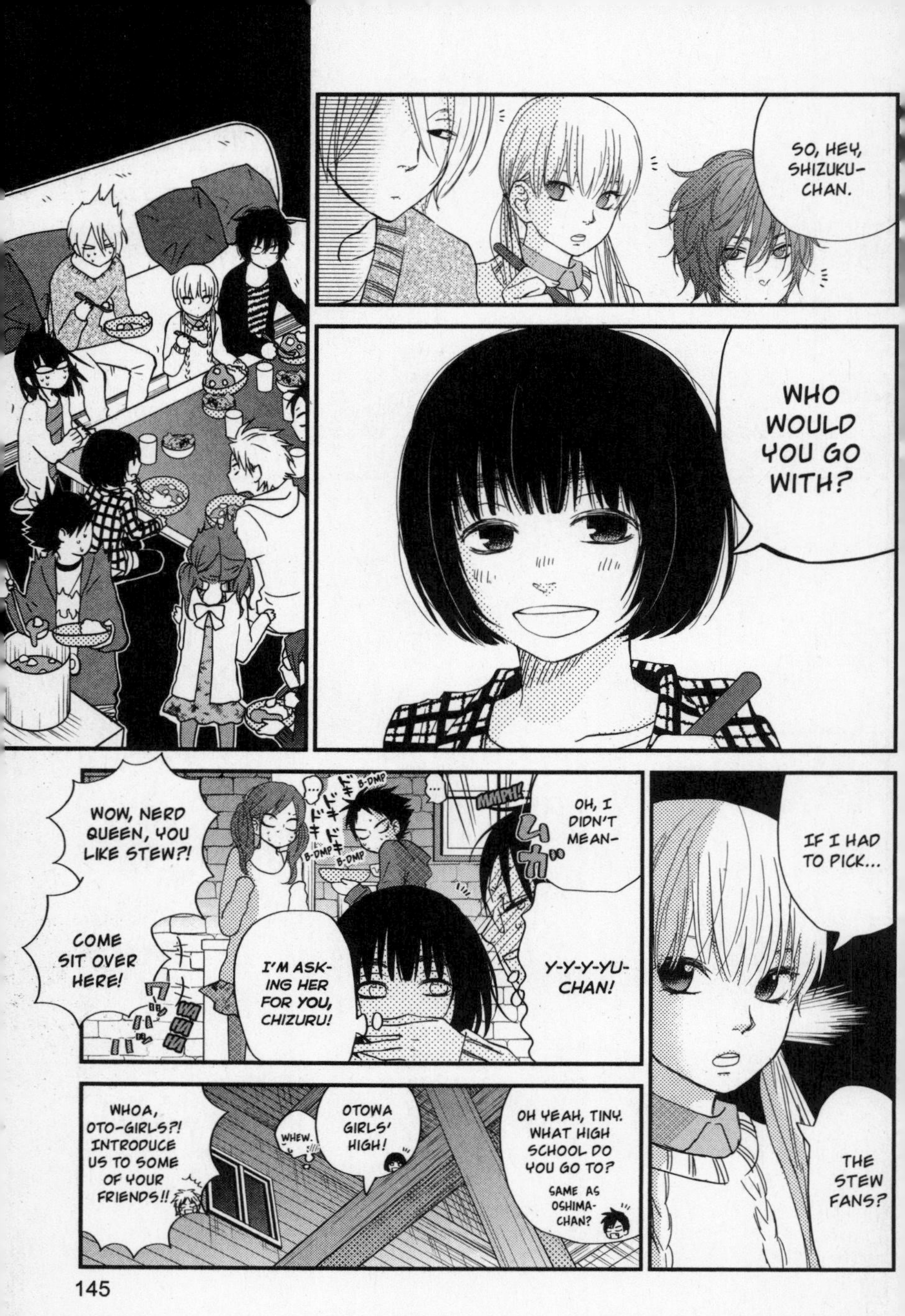
SO, HEY, SHIZUKU-CHAN.
WHO WOULD YOU GO WITH?
IF I HAD TO PICK...
THE STEW FANS?
MMPH!
OH, I DIDN'T MEAN-
Y-Y-Y-YU-CHAN!
B-DMP
B-DMP
B-DMP
I'M ASKING HER FOR YOU, CHIZURU!
WOW, NERD QUEEN, YOU LIKE STEW?!
COME SIT OVER HERE!
WA HA HA
OH YEAH, TINY. WHAT HIGH SCHOOL DO YOU GO TO?
SAME AS OSHIMA-CHAN?
OTOWA GIRLS' HIGH!
WHEW.
WHOA, OTO-GIRLS?! INTRODUCE US TO SOME OF YOUR FRIENDS!!

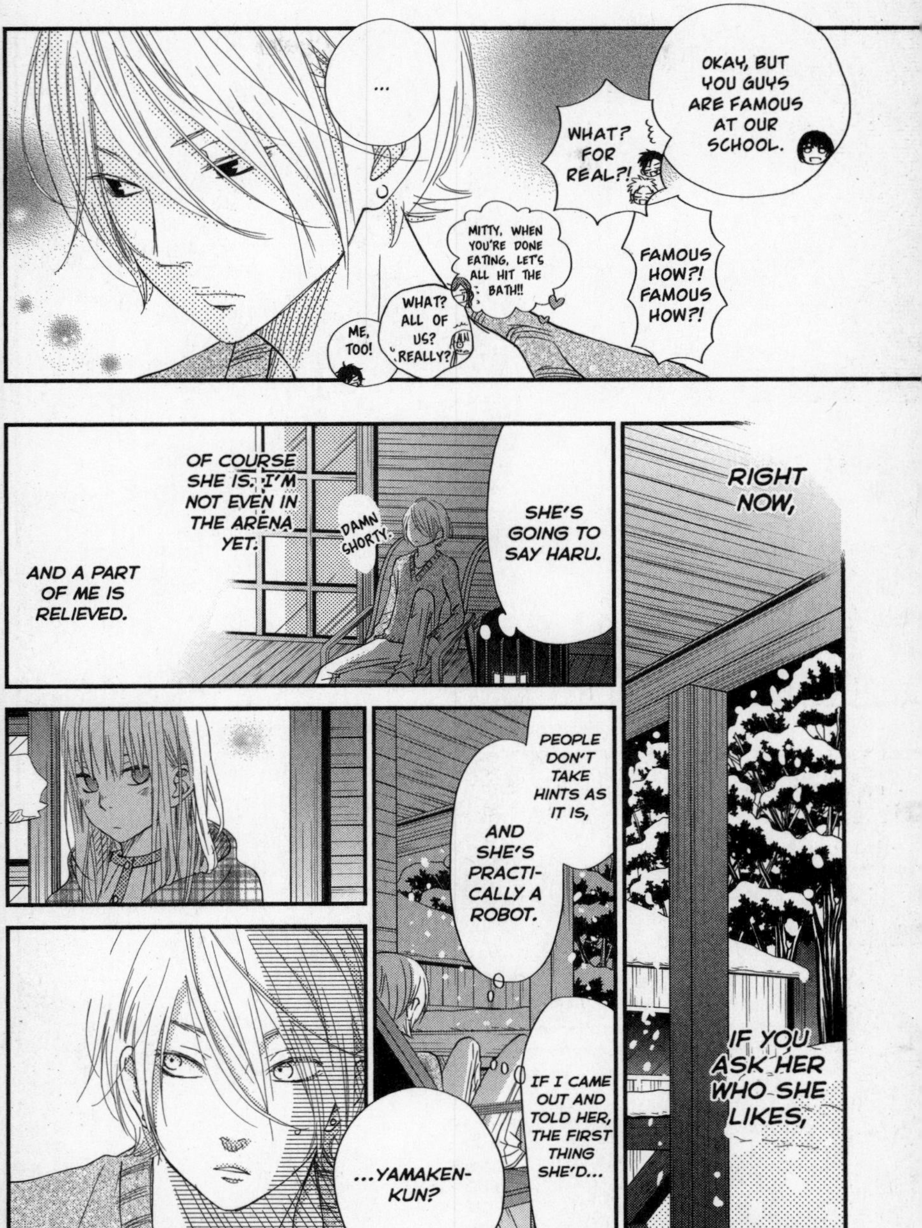
OKAY, BUT YOU GUYS ARE FAMOUS AT OUR SCHOOL.
WHAT? FOR REAL?!
FAMOUS HOW?! FAMOUS HOW?!
...
MITTY, WHEN YOU'RE DONE EATING, LET'S ALL HIT THE BATH!!
WHAT? ALL OF US? REALLY?
ME, TOO!
RIGHT NOW,
IF YOU ASK HER WHO SHE LIKES,
SHE'S GOING TO SAY HARU.
DAMN SHORTY.
OF COURSE SHE IS. I'M NOT EVEN IN THE ARENA YET.
AND A PART OF ME IS RELIEVED.
PEOPLE DON'T TAKE HINTS AS IT IS,
AND SHE'S PRACTICALLY A ROBOT.
IF I CAME OUT AND TOLD HER, THE FIRST THING SHE'D...
...YAMAKEN-KUN?

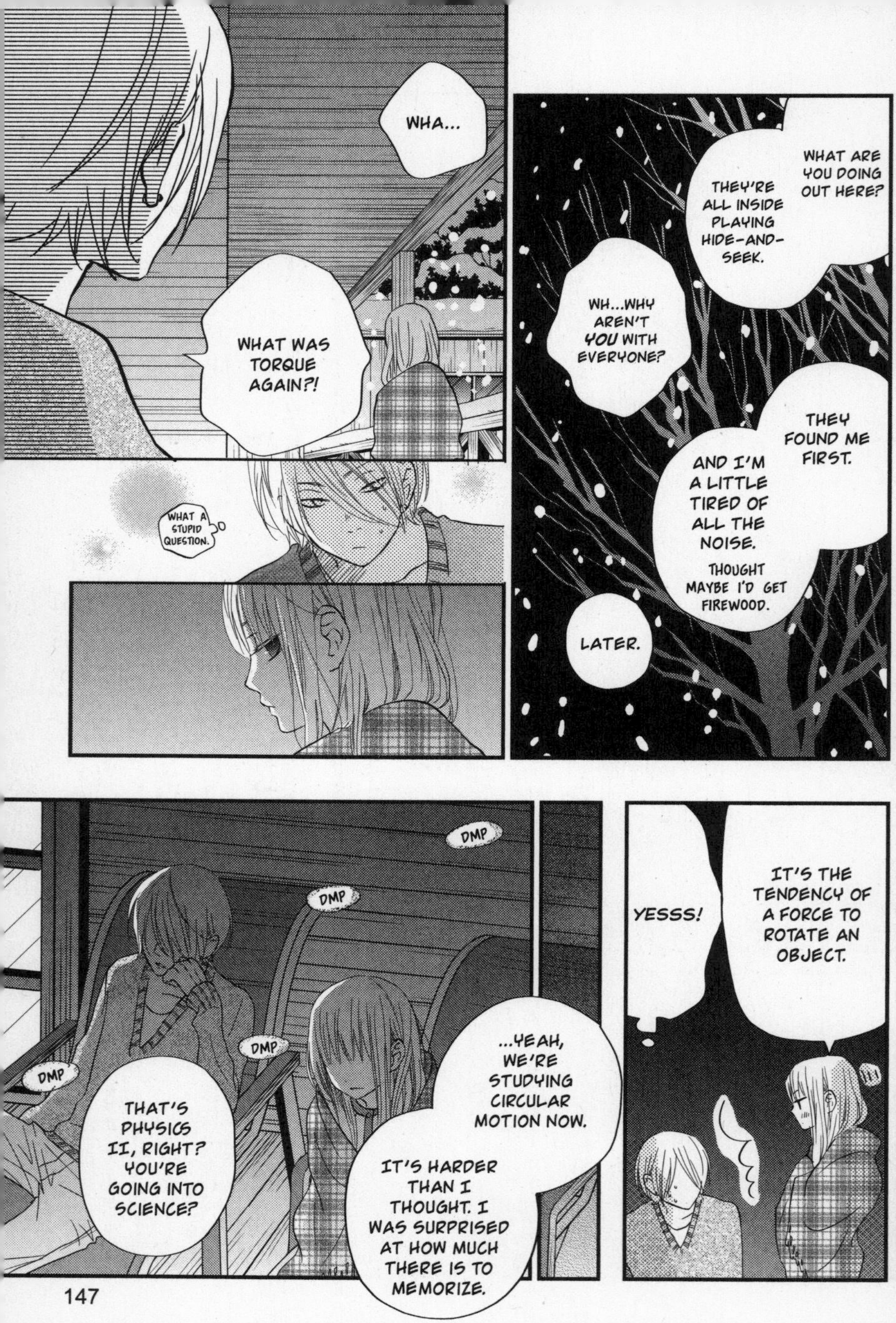
WHAT ARE YOU DOING OUT HERE?
THEY'RE ALL INSIDE PLAYING HIDE-AND-SEEK.
WH...WHY AREN'T *YOU* WITH EVERYONE?
THEY FOUND ME FIRST.
AND I'M A LITTLE TIRED OF ALL THE NOISE.
THOUGHT MAYBE I'D GET FIREWOOD.
LATER.
WHA...
WHAT WAS TORQUE AGAIN?!
WHAT A STUPID QUESTION.
IT'S THE TENDENCY OF A FORCE TO ROTATE AN OBJECT.
YESSS!
DMP
DMP
...YEAH, WE'RE STUDYING CIRCULAR MOTION NOW.
IT'S HARDER THAN I THOUGHT. I WAS SURPRISED AT HOW MUCH THERE IS TO MEMORIZE.
DMP
DMP
THAT'S PHYSICS II, RIGHT? YOU'RE GOING INTO SCIENCE?

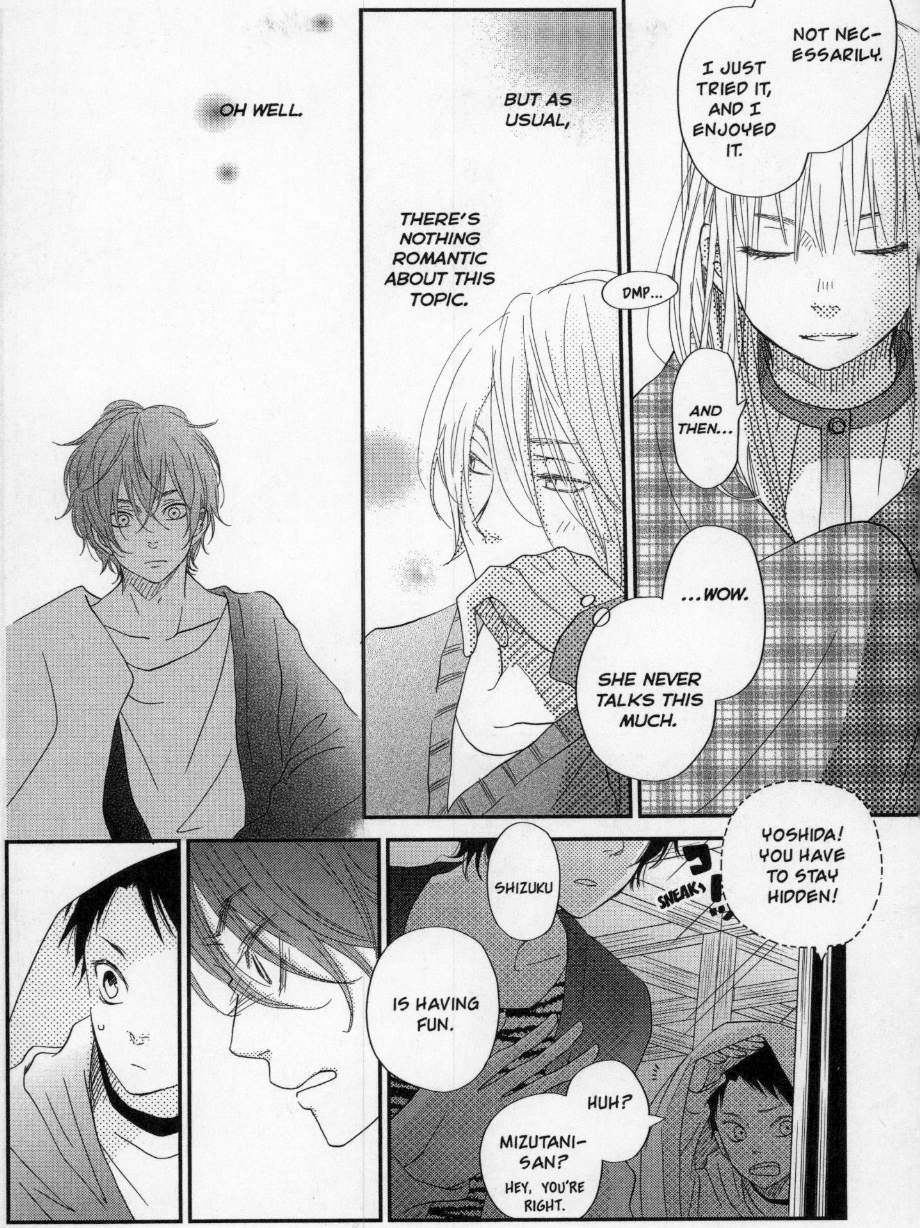
NOT NEC-ESSARILY.
I JUST TRIED IT, AND I ENJOYED IT.
DMP...
AND THEN...
...WOW.
SHE NEVER TALKS THIS MUCH.
BUT AS USUAL,
THERE'S NOTHING ROMANTIC ABOUT THIS TOPIC.
OH WELL.
YOSHIDA! YOU HAVE TO STAY HIDDEN!
SNEAK
SHIZUKU
IS HAVING FUN.
HUH?
MIZUTANI-SAN?
HEY, YOU'RE RIGHT.

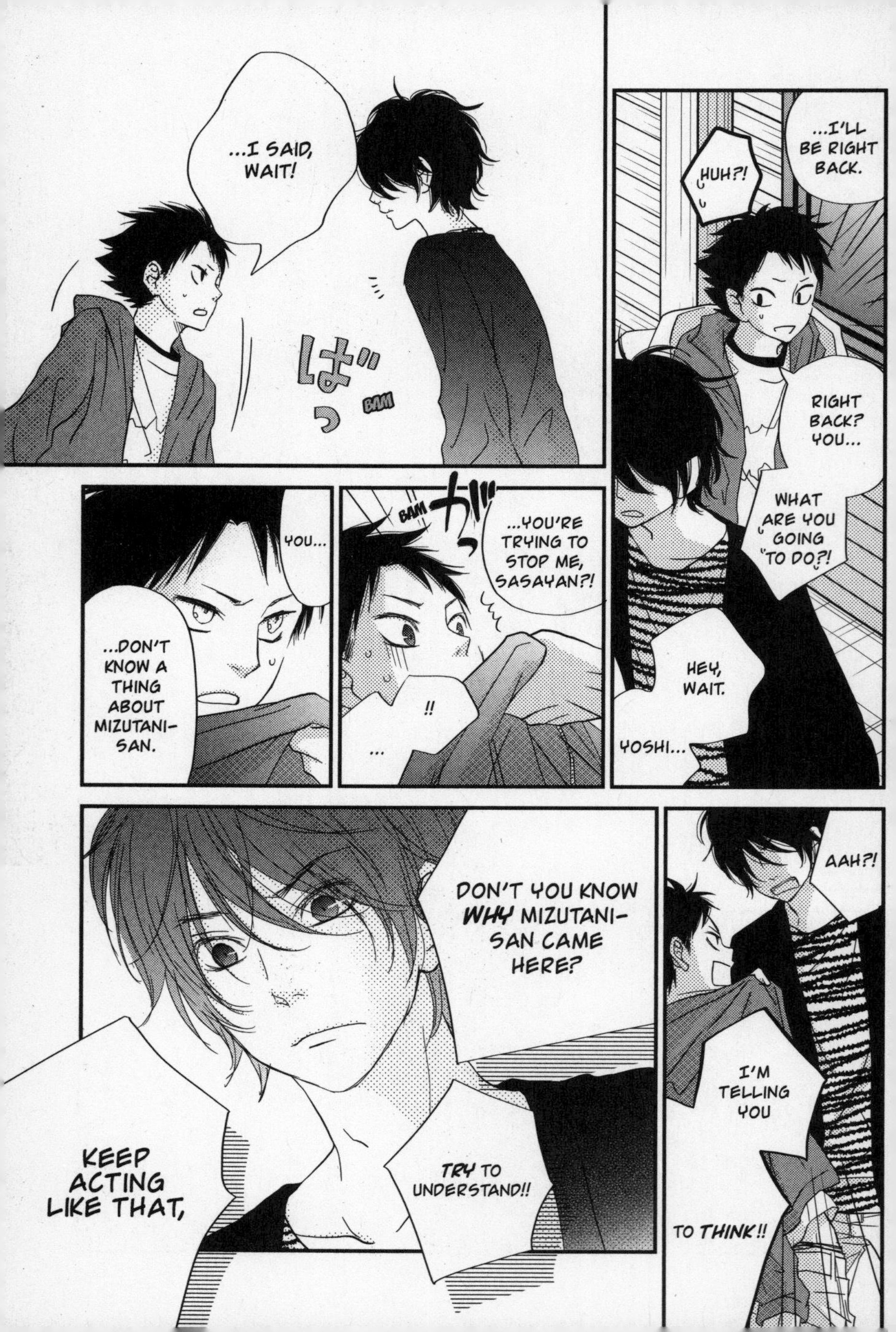

...I'LL BE RIGHT BACK.
HUH?!
RIGHT BACK? YOU...
WHAT ARE YOU GOING TO DO?!
HEY, WAIT.
YOSHI...
...I SAID, WAIT!
ばっ
BAM
がっ
BAM
...YOU'RE TRYING TO STOP ME, SASAYAN?!
!!
...
YOU...
...DON'T KNOW A THING ABOUT MIZUTANI-SAN.
AAH?!
I'M TELLING YOU
TO *THINK*!!
DON'T YOU KNOW ***WHY*** MIZUTANI-SAN CAME HERE?
TRY TO UNDERSTAND!!
KEEP ACTING LIKE THAT,

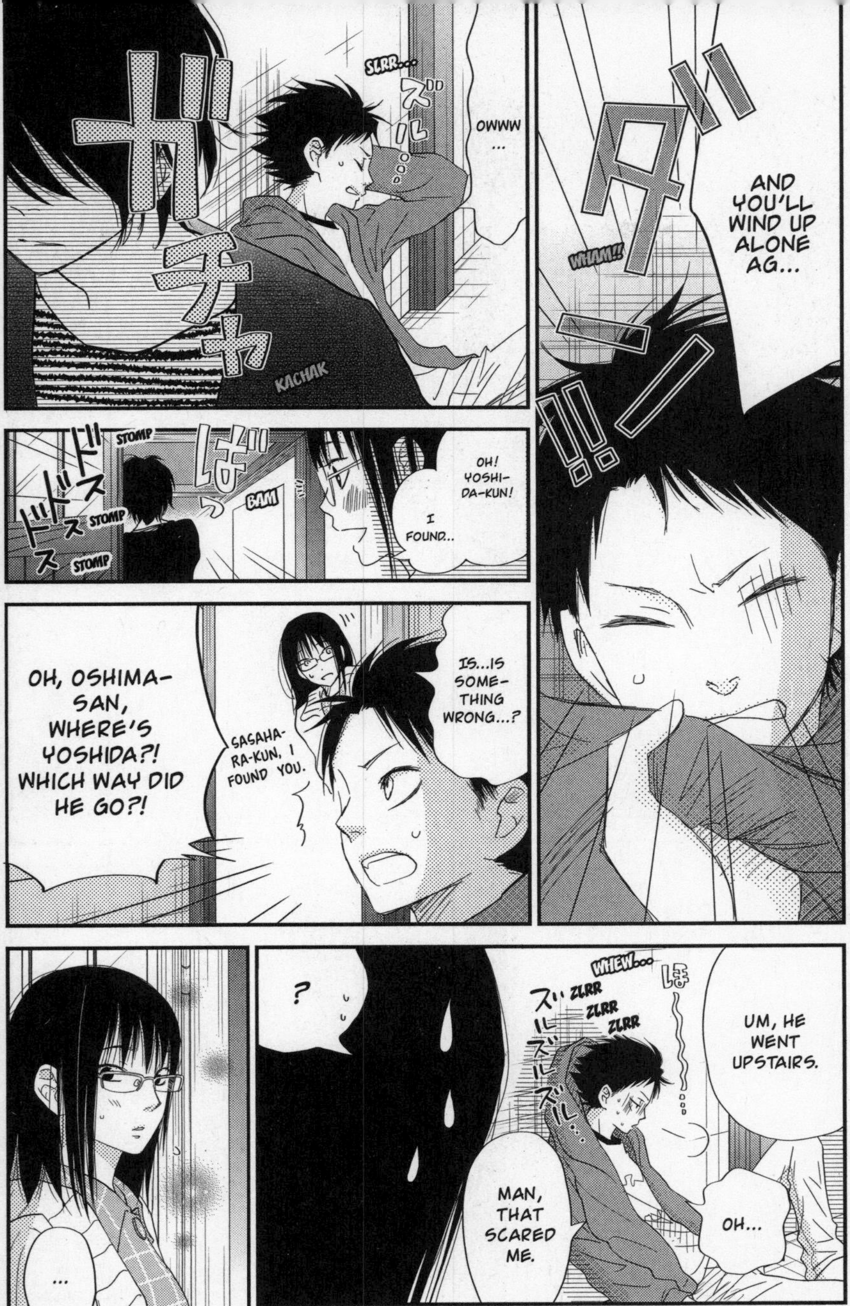
WHAM!!
AND YOU'LL WIND UP ALONE AG...
SLRR...
OWWW...
KACHAK
OH! YOSHIDA-KUN!
I FOUND...
BAM
STOMP
STOMP
STOMP
IS...IS SOMETHING WRONG...?
SASAHARA-KUN, I FOUND YOU.
OH, OSHIMA-SAN, WHERE'S YOSHIDA?! WHICH WAY DID HE GO?!
UM, HE WENT UPSTAIRS.
WHEW...
ZLRR
ZLRR
ZLRR
OH...
MAN, THAT SCARED ME.
?
...

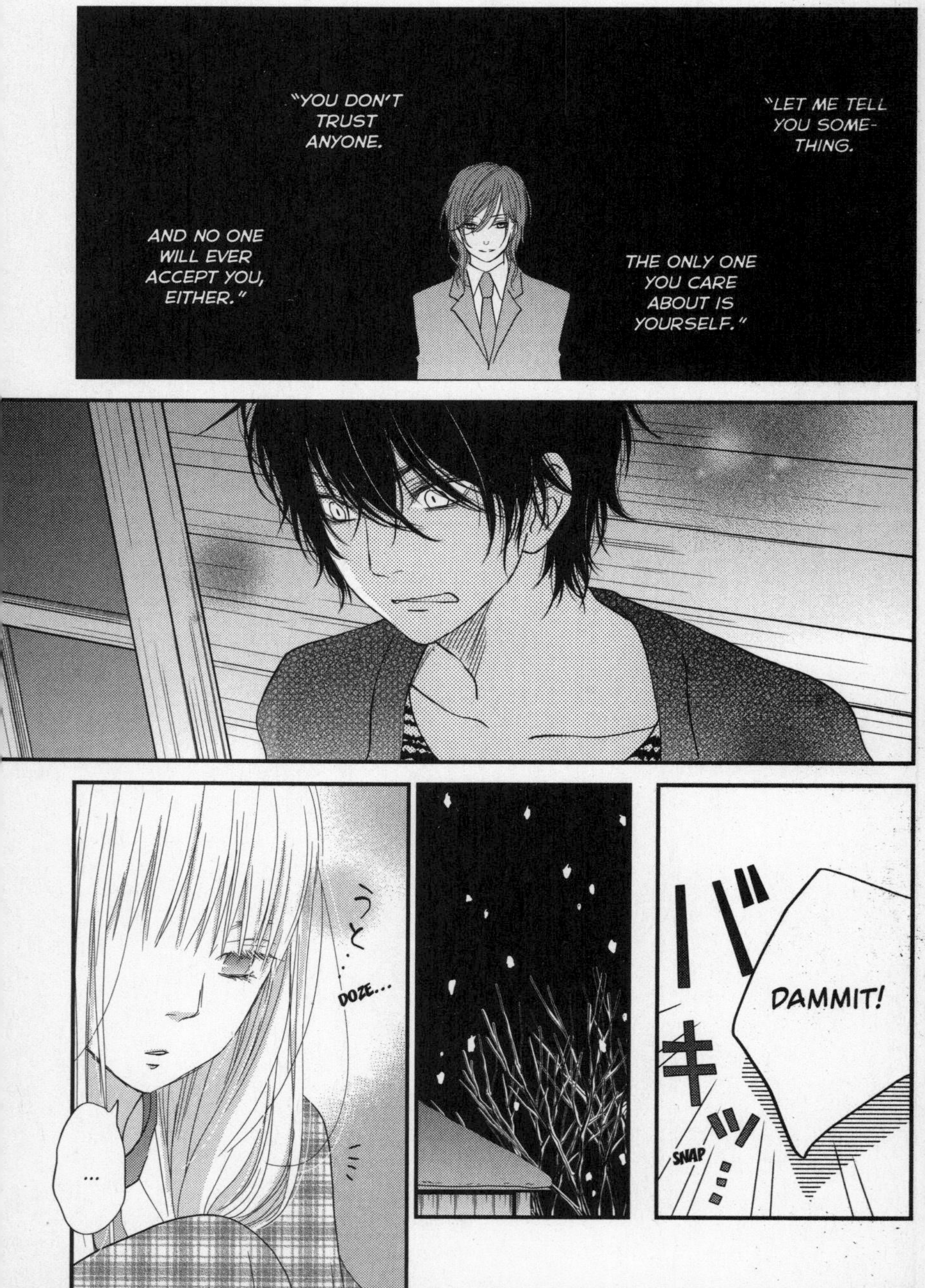
"LET ME TELL YOU SOME-THING.
THE ONLY ONE YOU CARE ABOUT IS YOURSELF."
"YOU DON'T TRUST ANYONE.
AND NO ONE WILL EVER ACCEPT YOU, EITHER."
DAMMIT!
バキッ
SNAP
うと
DOZE...
...

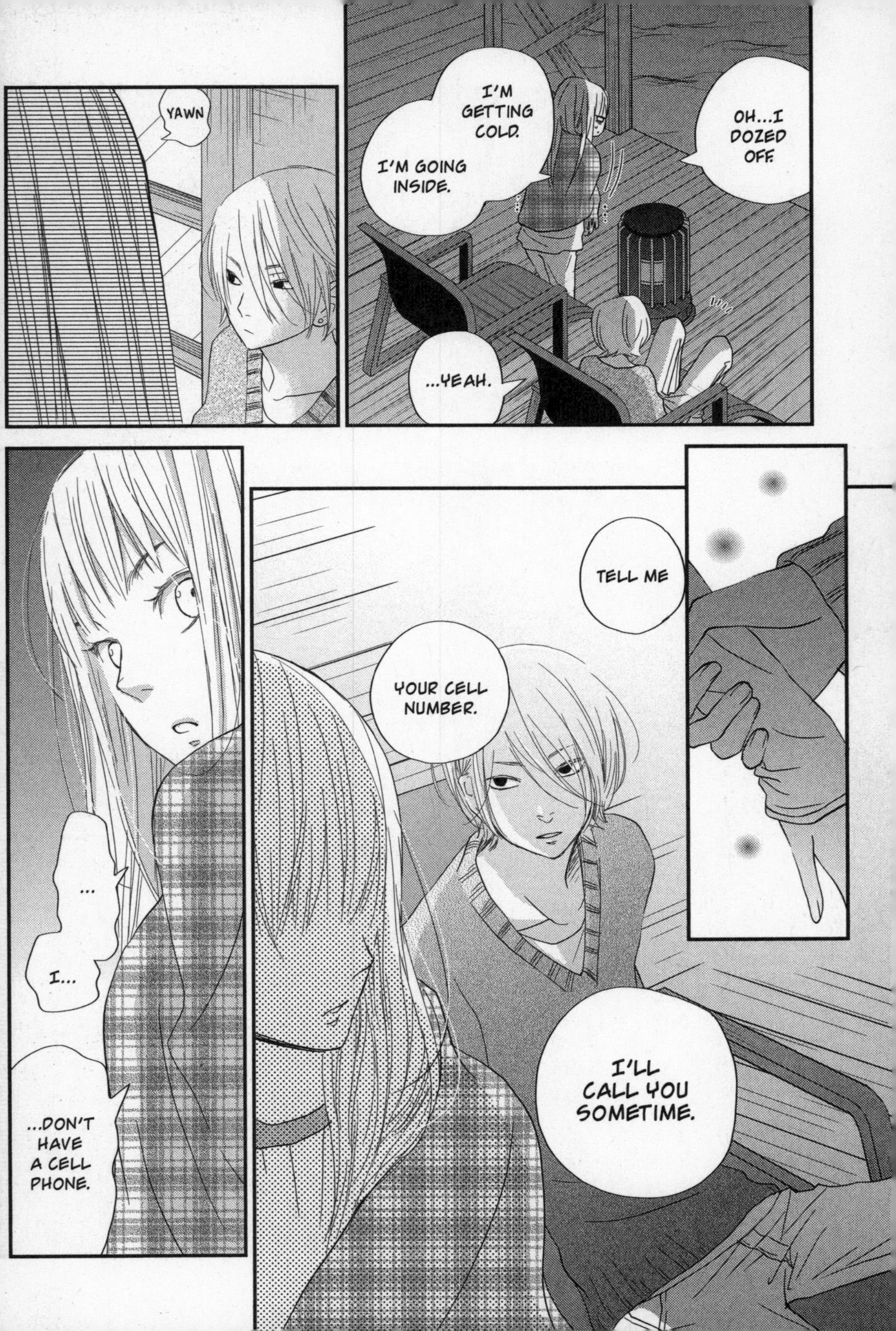
OH...I DOZED OFF.
I'M GETTING COLD.
I'M GOING INSIDE.
...YEAH.
YAWN
TELL ME
YOUR CELL NUMBER.
I'LL CALL YOU SOMETIME.
...
I...
...DON'T HAVE A CELL PHONE.

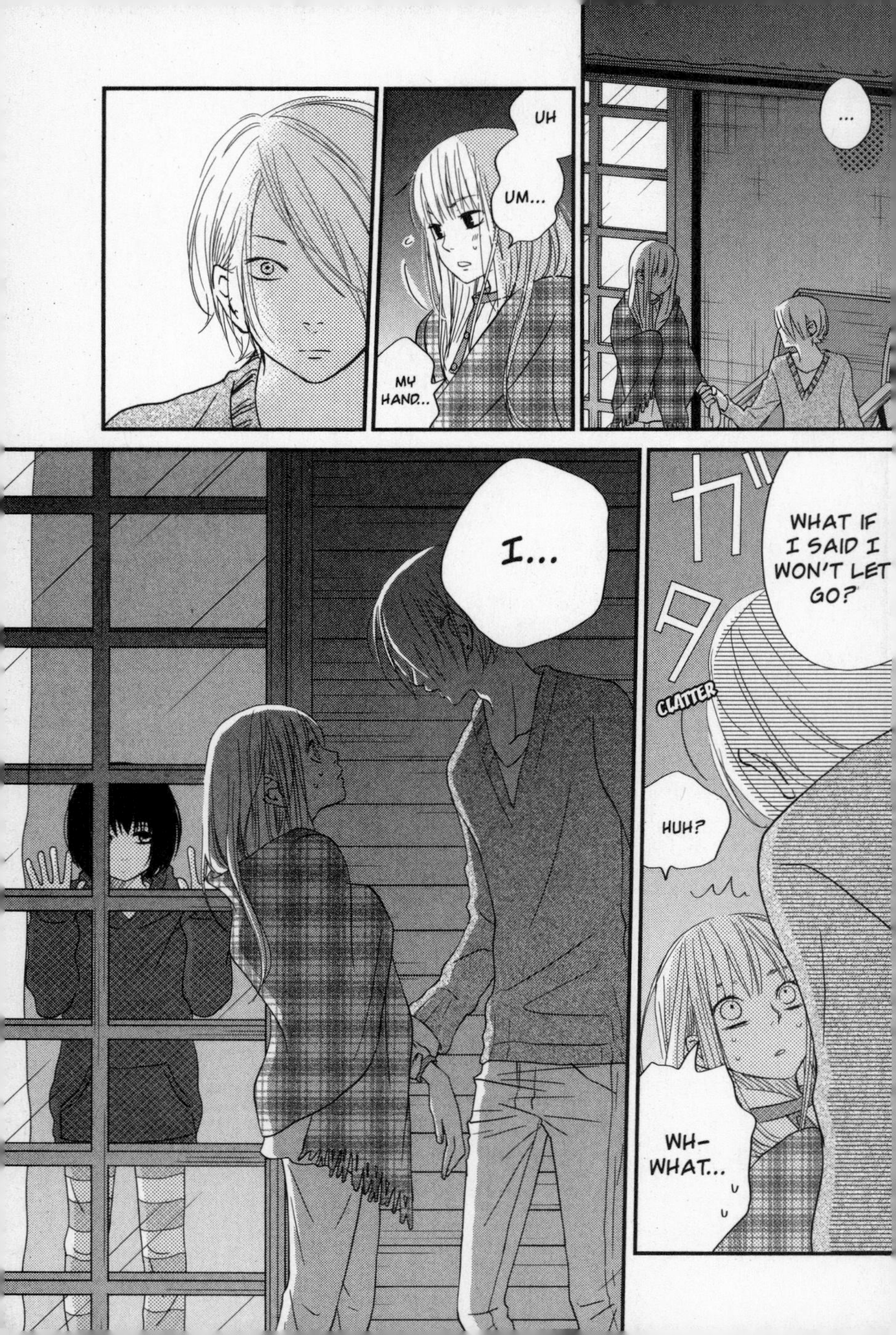
...
UH
UM...
MY HAND...
ガタ
CLATTER
WHAT IF I SAID I WON'T LET GO?
HUH?
WH-WHAT...
I...

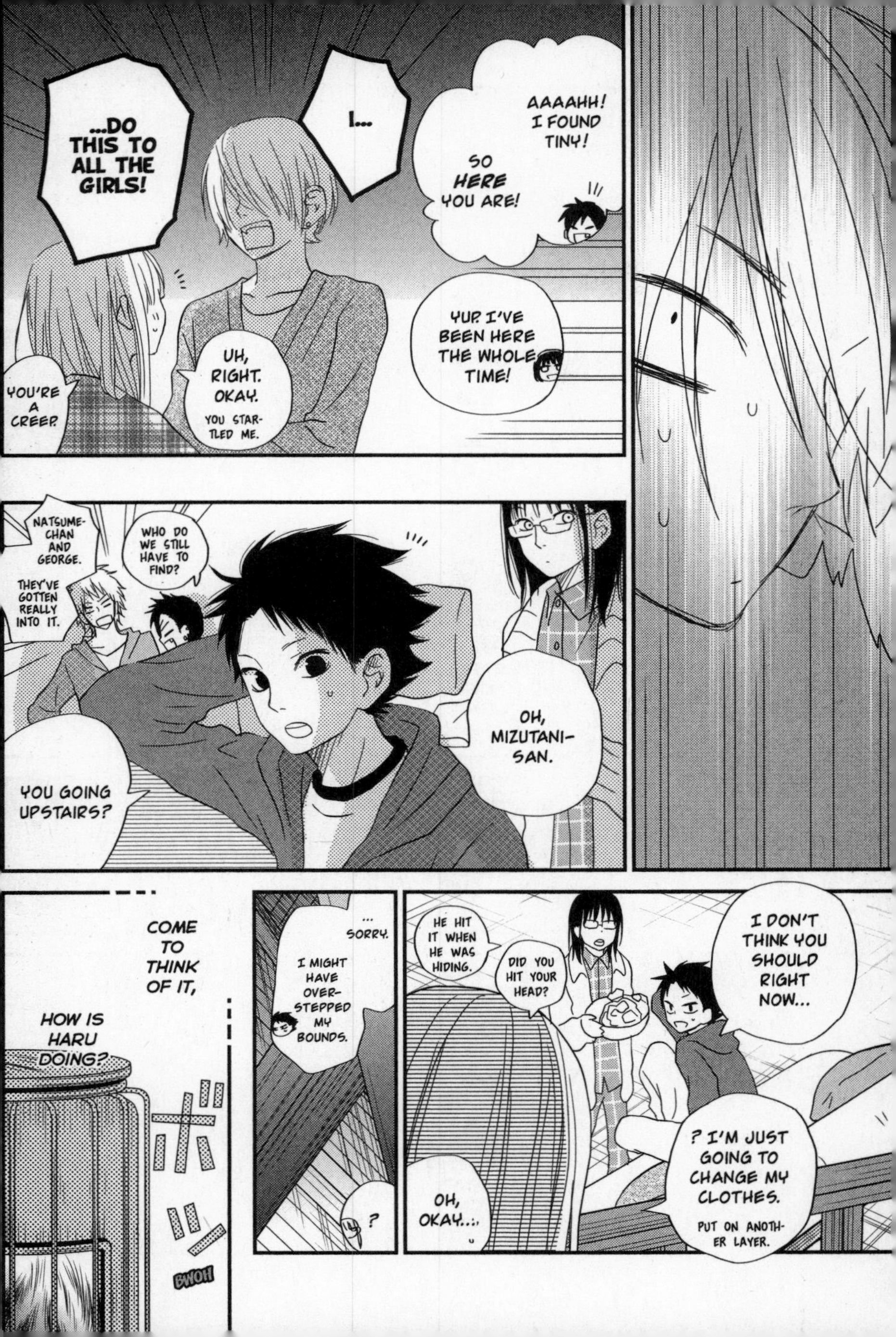
AAAAHH! I FOUND TINY!
SO HERE YOU ARE!
YUP. I'VE BEEN HERE THE WHOLE TIME!
I...
...DO THIS TO ALL THE GIRLS!
UH, RIGHT. OKAY.
YOU STARTLED ME.
YOU'RE A CREEP.
OH, MIZUTANI-SAN.
YOU GOING UPSTAIRS?
WHO DO WE STILL HAVE TO FIND?
NATSUME-CHAN AND GEORGE.
THEY'VE GOTTEN REALLY INTO IT.
I DON'T THINK YOU SHOULD RIGHT NOW...
DID YOU HIT YOUR HEAD?
HE HIT IT WHEN HE WAS HIDING.
? I'M JUST GOING TO CHANGE MY CLOTHES.
PUT ON ANOTHER LAYER.
OH, OKAY...
...SORRY.
I MIGHT HAVE OVERSTEPPED MY BOUNDS.
?
COME TO THINK OF IT,
HOW IS HARU DOING?
BWOH

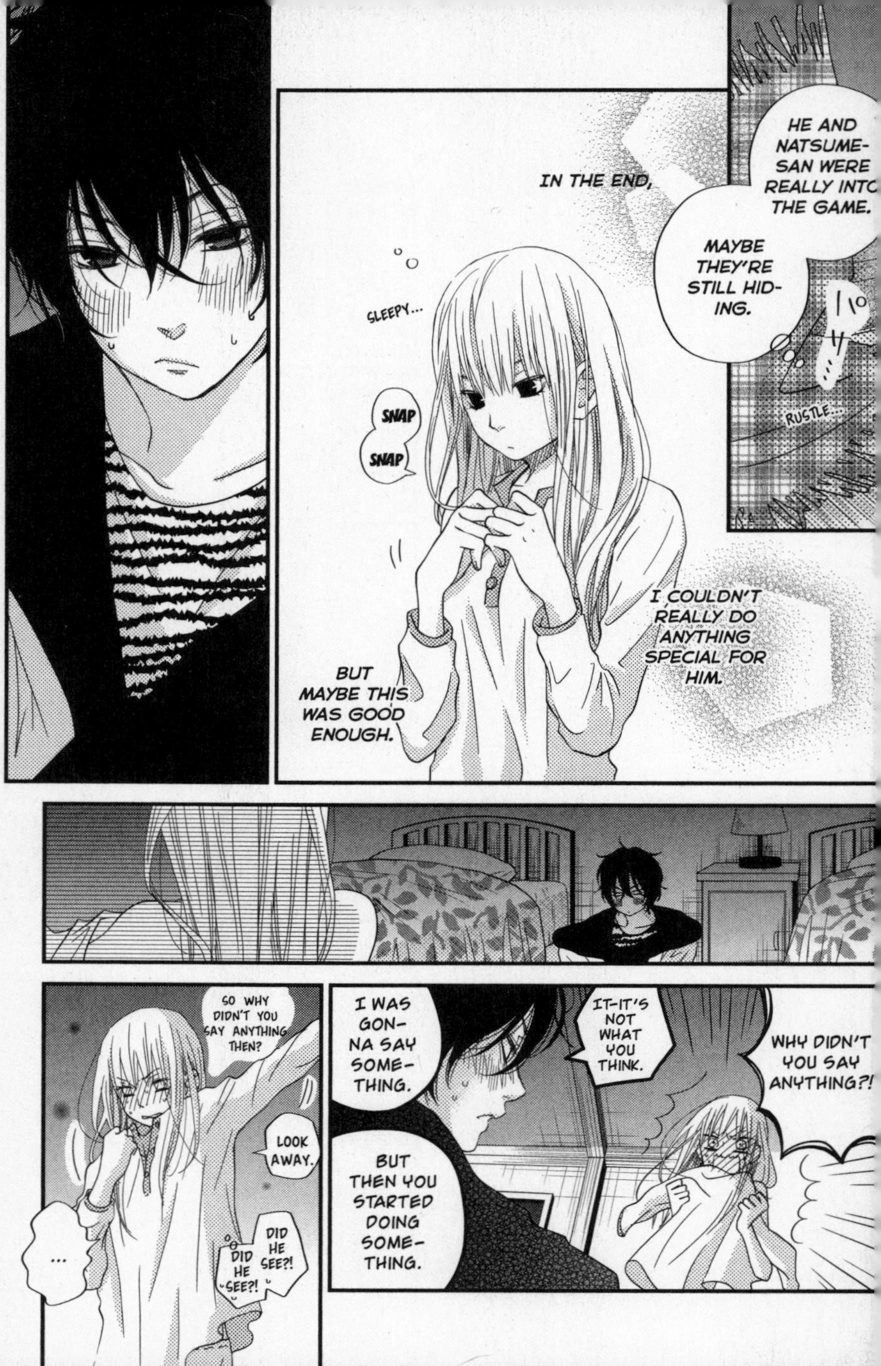

HE AND NATSUME-SAN WERE REALLY INTO THE GAME.
MAYBE THEY'RE STILL HIDING.
RUSTLE...
IN THE END,
SLEEPY...
SNAP
SNAP
I COULDN'T REALLY DO ANYTHING SPECIAL FOR HIM.
BUT MAYBE THIS WAS GOOD ENOUGH.
WHY DIDN'T YOU SAY ANYTHING?!
IT-IT'S NOT WHAT YOU THINK.
I WAS GONNA SAY SOMETHING.
BUT THEN YOU STARTED DOING SOMETHING.
SO WHY DIDN'T YOU SAY ANYTHING THEN?
LOOK AWAY.
DID HE SEE?!
DID HE SEE?!
...

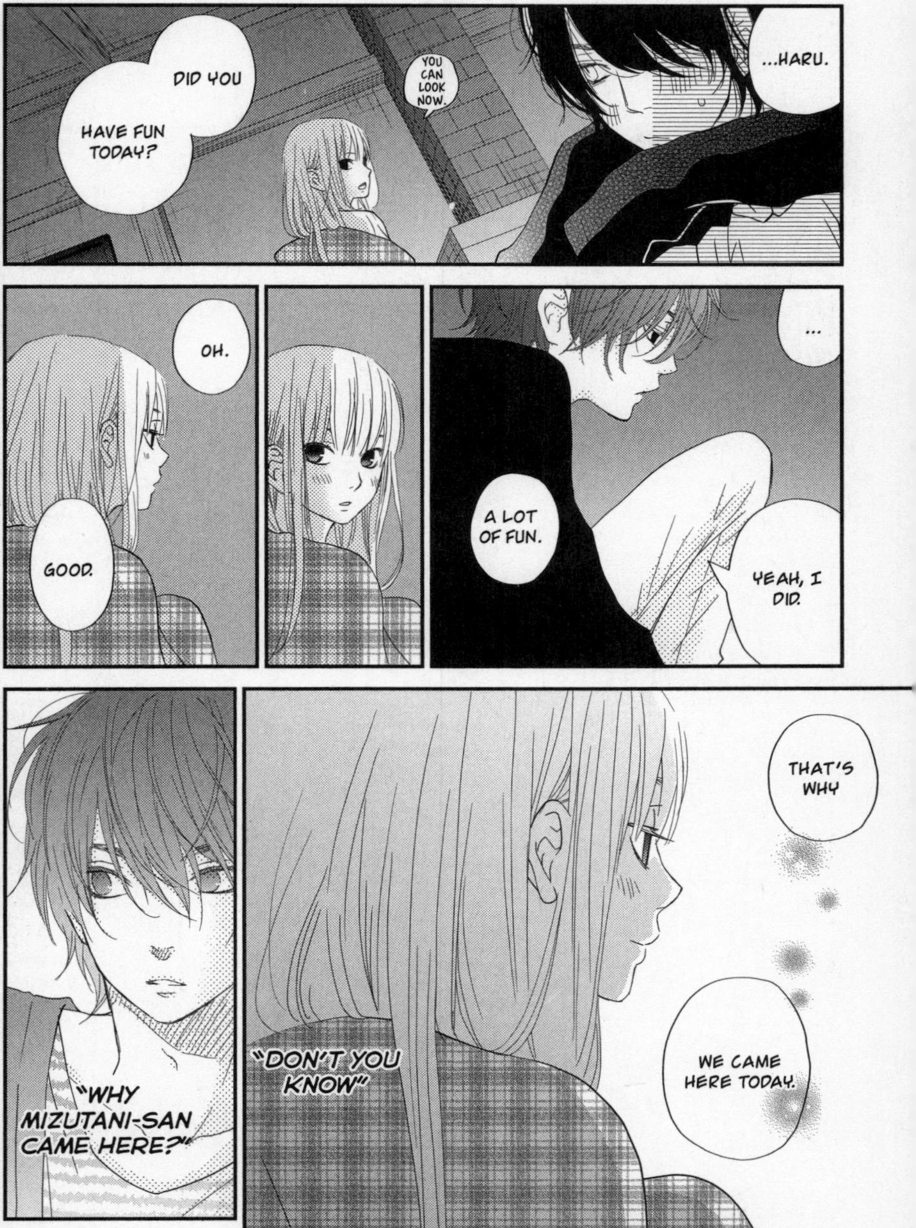
...HARU.
YOU CAN LOOK NOW.
DID YOU HAVE FUN TODAY?
...
YEAH, I DID.
A LOT OF FUN.
OH.
GOOD.
THAT'S WHY
WE CAME HERE TODAY.
"DON'T YOU KNOW"
"WHY MIZUTANI-SAN CAME HERE?"

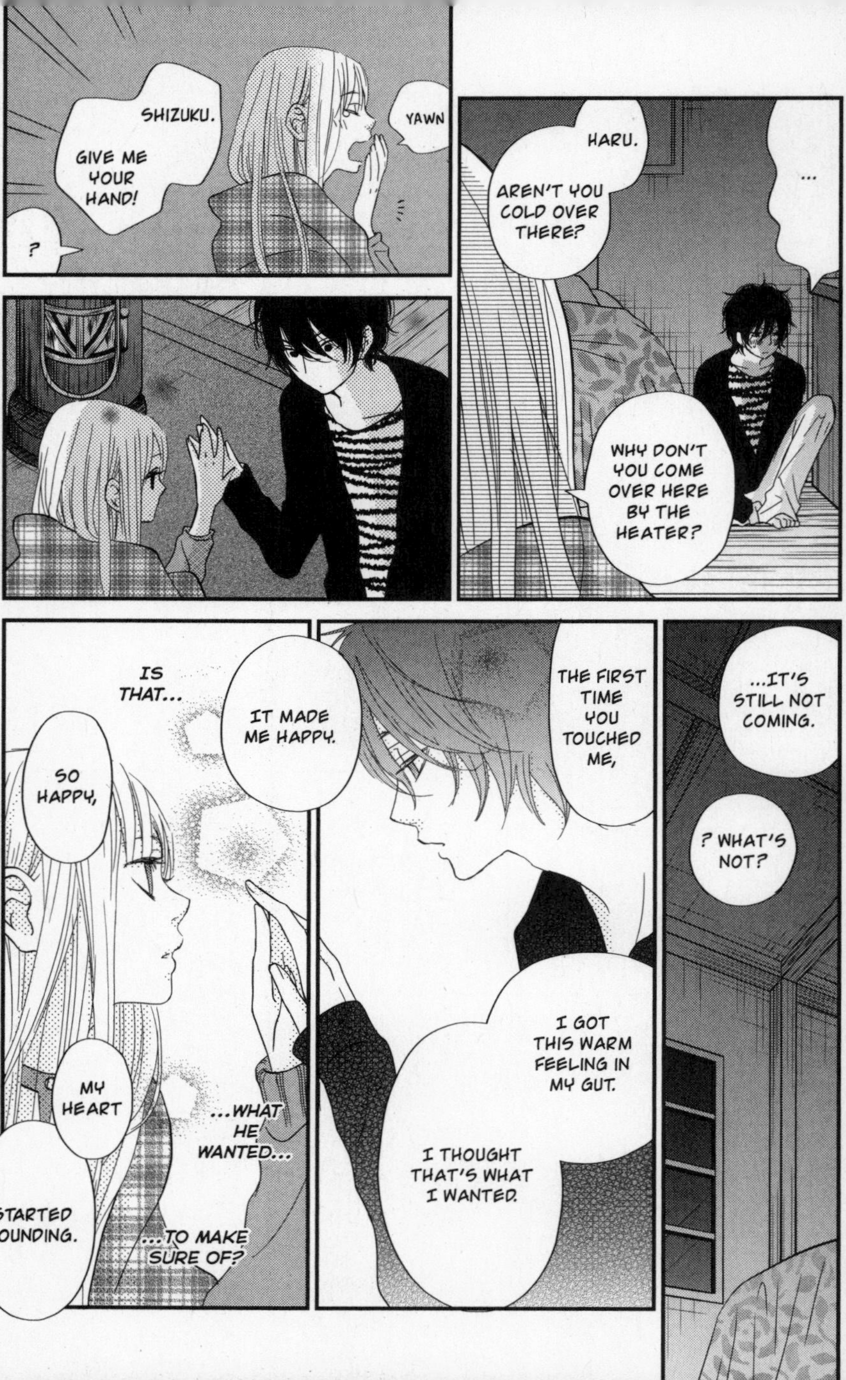
HARU.
AREN'T YOU COLD OVER THERE?
...
WHY DON'T YOU COME OVER HERE BY THE HEATER?
YAWN
SHIZUKU.
GIVE ME YOUR HAND!
?
...IT'S STILL NOT COMING.
? WHAT'S NOT?
THE FIRST TIME YOU TOUCHED ME,
IT MADE ME HAPPY.
I GOT THIS WARM FEELING IN MY GUT.
I THOUGHT THAT'S WHAT I WANTED.
IS THAT...
SO HAPPY,
MY HEART
STARTED POUNDING.
...WHAT HE WANTED...
...TO MAKE SURE OF?

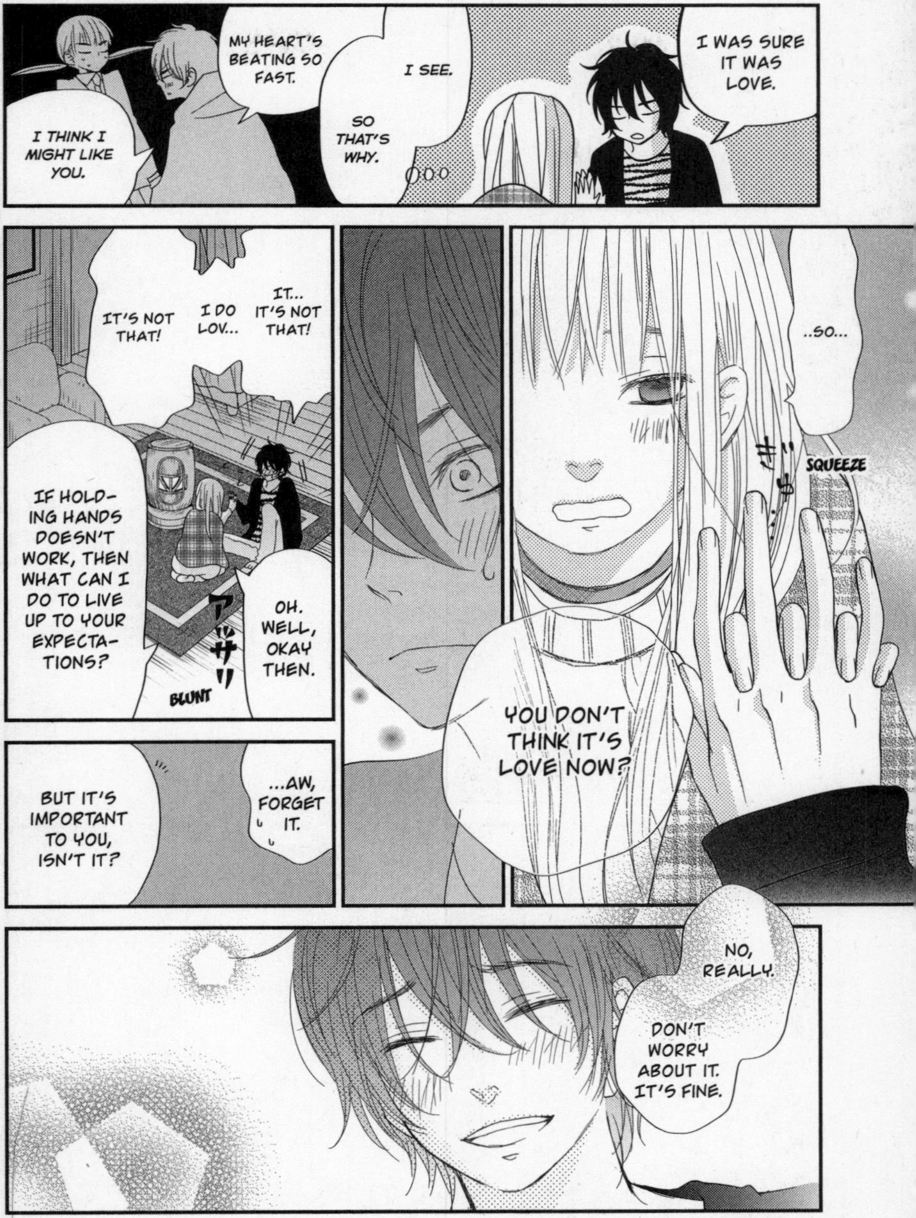
I WAS SURE IT WAS LOVE.
I SEE.
SO THAT'S WHY.
MY HEART'S BEATING SO FAST.
I THINK I MIGHT LIKE YOU.
..SO...
SQUEEZE
YOU DON'T THINK IT'S LOVE NOW?
IT... IT'S NOT THAT!
I DO LOV...
IT'S NOT THAT!
OH. WELL, OKAY THEN.
BLUNT
IF HOLDING HANDS DOESN'T WORK, THEN WHAT CAN I DO TO LIVE UP TO YOUR EXPECTATIONS?
...AW, FORGET IT.
BUT IT'S IMPORTANT TO YOU, ISN'T IT?
NO, REALLY.
DON'T WORRY ABOUT IT. IT'S FINE.

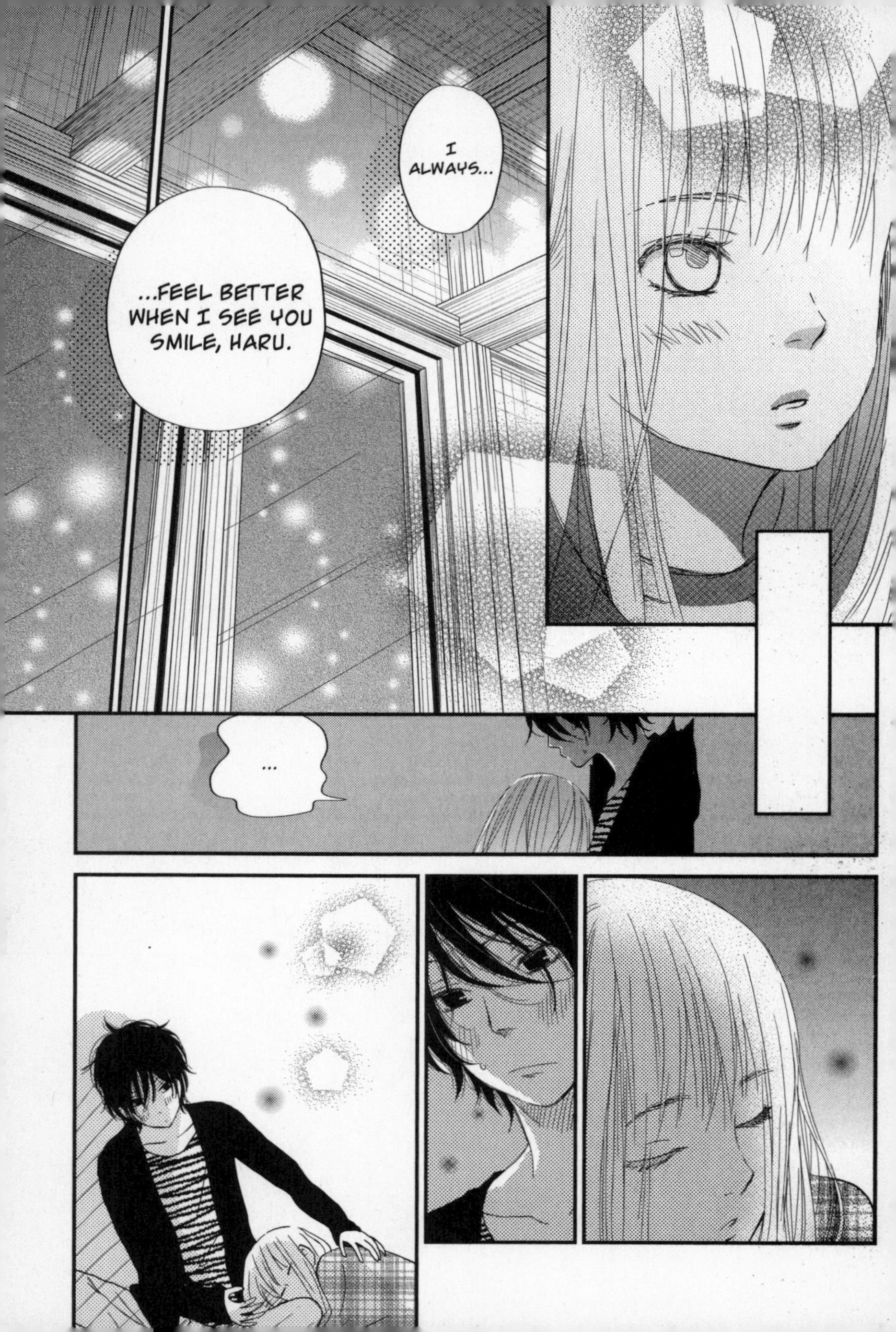
I ALWAYS...
...FEEL BETTER WHEN I SEE YOU SMILE, HARU.
...

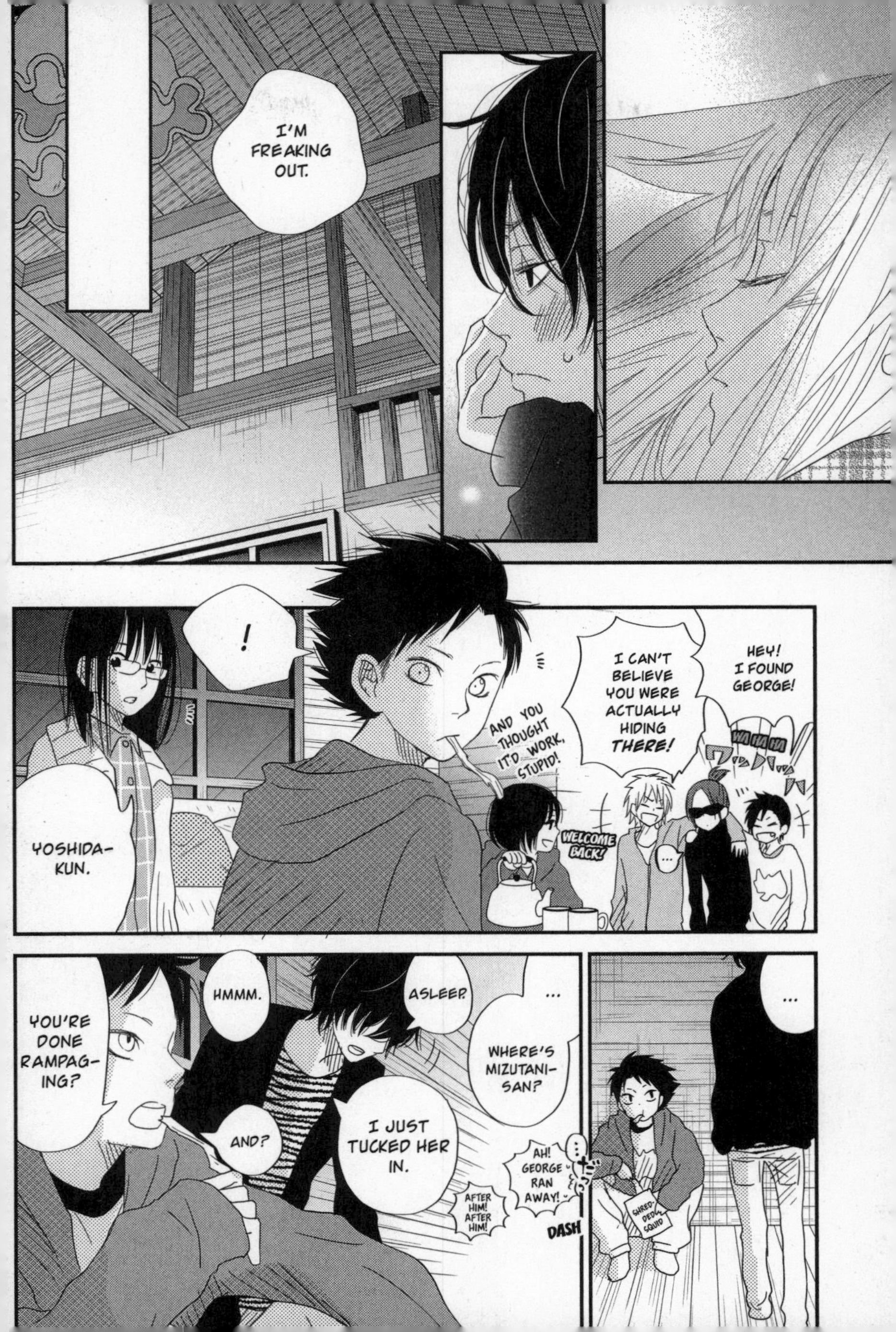
I'M FREAKING OUT.
HEY! I FOUND GEORGE!
WA HA HA
I CAN'T BELIEVE YOU WERE ACTUALLY HIDING THERE!
AND YOU THOUGHT IT'D WORK, STUPID!
WELCOME BACK!
...
!
YOSHIDA-KUN.
...
AH! GEORGE RAN AWAY!
AFTER HIM! AFTER HIM!
DASH
SHRED-DED SQUID
...
WHERE'S MIZUTANI-SAN?
ASLEEP?
I JUST TUCKED HER IN.
HMMM.
YOU'RE DONE RAMPAGING?
AND?

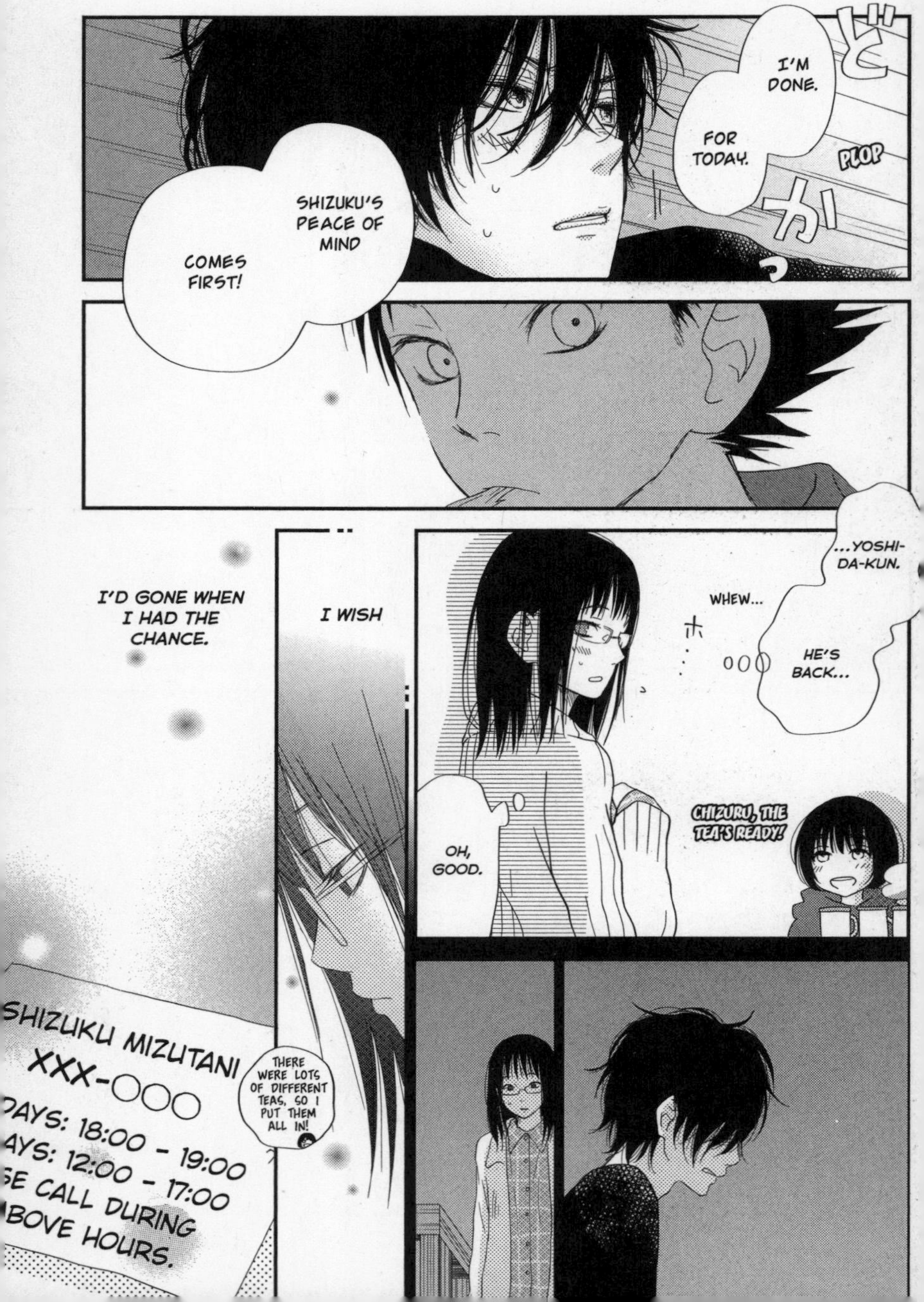

I'M DONE.
FOR TODAY.
どか
PLOP
SHIZUKU'S PEACE OF MIND COMES FIRST!
...YOSHI-DA-KUN. HE'S BACK...
WHEW...
ホ
CHIZURU, THE TEA'S READY!
OH, GOOD.
I WISH
I'D GONE WHEN I HAD THE CHANCE.
SHIZUKU MIZUTANI
XXX-○○○
DAYS: 18:00 - 19:00
AYS: 12:00 - 17:00
SE CALL DURING
BOVE HOURS.
THERE WERE LOTS OF DIFFERENT TEAS, SO I PUT THEM ALL IN!

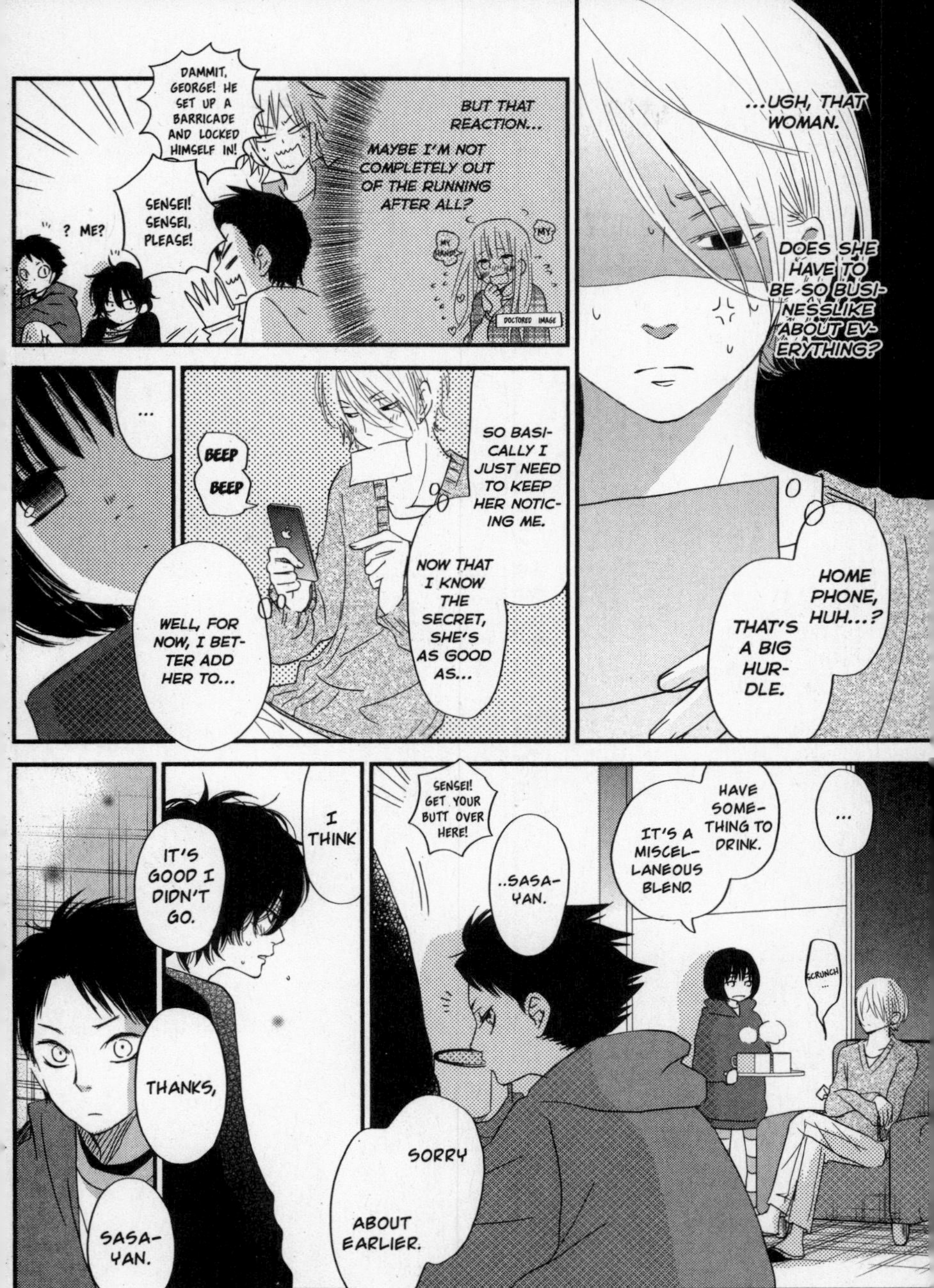
...UGH, THAT WOMAN.
DOES SHE HAVE TO BE SO BUSINESSLIKE ABOUT EVERYTHING?
HOME PHONE, HUH...?
THAT'S A BIG HURDLE.
BUT THAT REACTION...
MAYBE I'M NOT COMPLETELY OUT OF THE RUNNING AFTER ALL?
MY
MY HANDS
DOCTORED IMAGE
DAMMIT, GEORGE! HE SET UP A BARRICADE AND LOCKED HIMSELF IN!
SENSEI! SENSEI, PLEASE!
? ME?
SO BASICALLY I JUST NEED TO KEEP HER NOTICING ME.
NOW THAT I KNOW THE SECRET, SHE'S AS GOOD AS...
BEEP
BEEP
WELL, FOR NOW, I BETTER ADD HER TO...
...
...
HAVE SOMETHING TO DRINK.
IT'S A MISCELLANEOUS BLEND.
SCRUNCH...
SENSEI! GET YOUR BUTT OVER HERE!
..SASA-YAN.
SORRY
ABOUT EARLIER.
I THINK
IT'S GOOD I DIDN'T GO.
THANKS,
SASA-YAN.

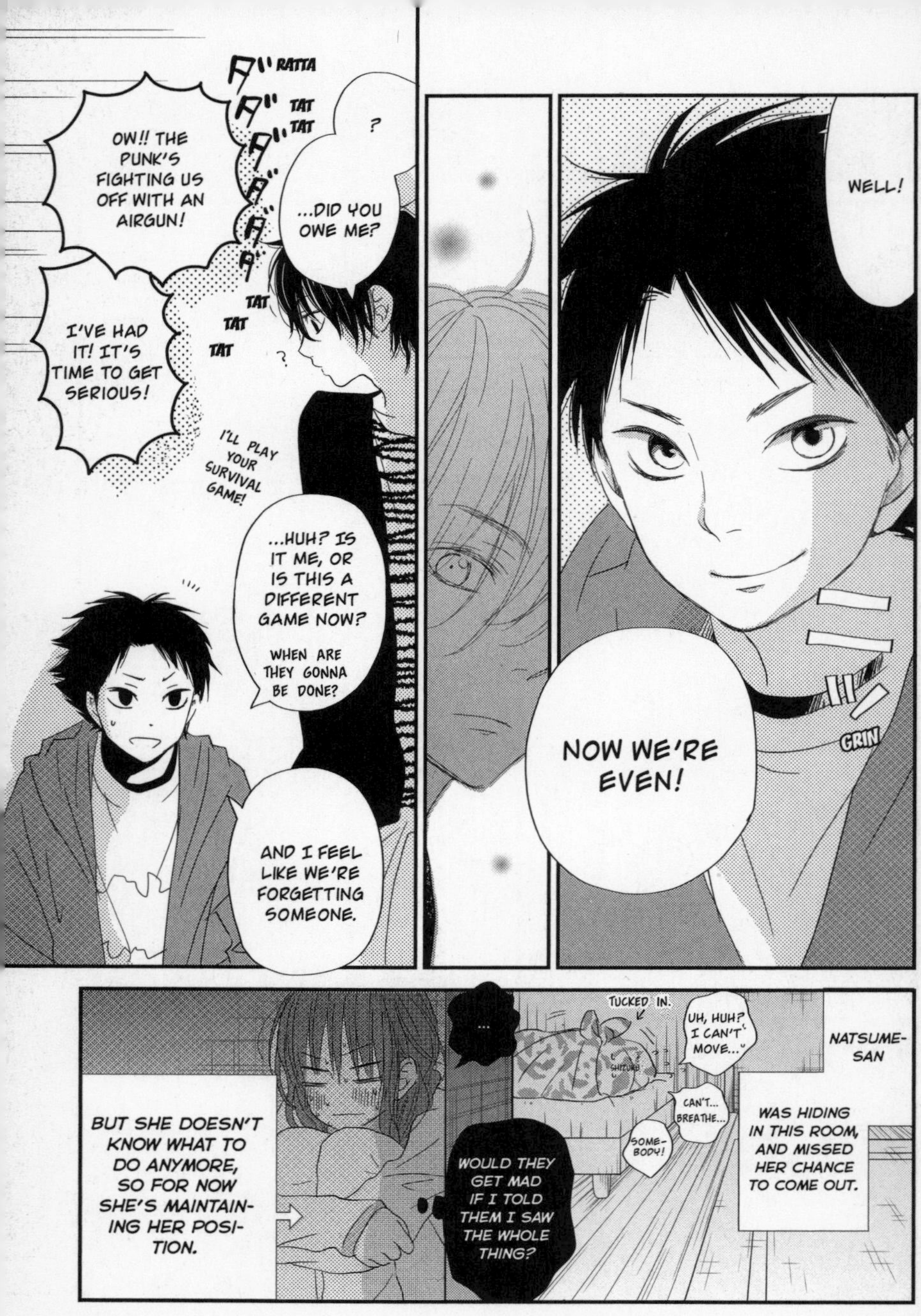
WELL!
NOW WE'RE EVEN!
GRIN
...DID YOU OWE ME?
?
RATTA TAT TAT
OW!! THE PUNK'S FIGHTING US OFF WITH AN AIRGUN!
TAT TAT TAT
I'VE HAD IT! IT'S TIME TO GET SERIOUS!
?
I'LL PLAY YOUR SURVIVAL GAME!
...HUH? IS IT ME, OR IS THIS A DIFFERENT GAME NOW?
WHEN ARE THEY GONNA BE DONE?
AND I FEEL LIKE WE'RE FORGETTING SOMEONE.
NATSUME-SAN
WAS HIDING IN THIS ROOM, AND MISSED HER CHANCE TO COME OUT.
TUCKED IN.
UH, HUH? I CAN'T MOVE...
CAN'T... BREATHE...
SOME-BODY!
...
WOULD THEY GET MAD IF I TOLD THEM I SAW THE WHOLE THING?
BUT SHE DOESN'T KNOW WHAT TO DO ANYMORE, SO FOR NOW SHE'S MAINTAIN-ING HER POSI-TION.

Continued in Volume 6!!

Close Call

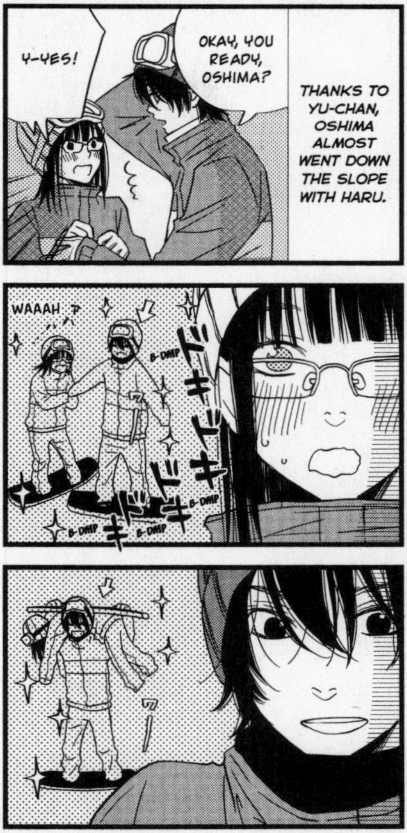
THANKS TO YU-CHAN, OSHIMA ALMOST WENT DOWN THE SLOPE WITH HARU.
OKAY, YOU READY, OSHIMA?
Y-YES!
B-DMP
WAAAH
B-DMP
B-DMP
B-DMP
AH! YAMAKEN!
WAIT, DAMMIT!
N-NO...
BUT IN REALITY, OSHIMA-SAN NARROWLY ESCAPED DANGER.
CLANG

Well, It's Cold

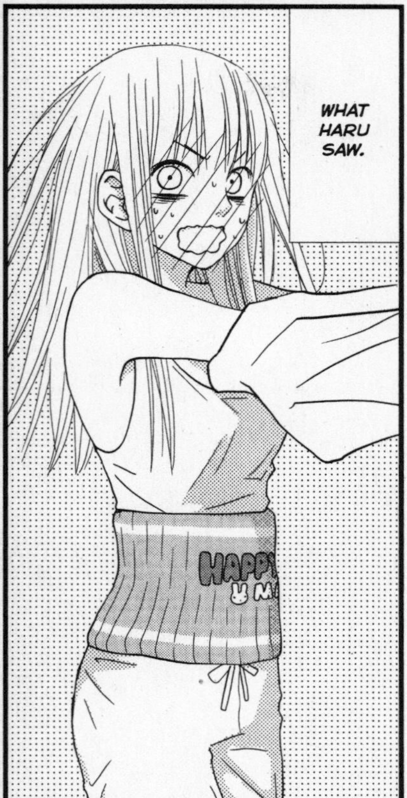
WHAT HARU SAW.
KIND OF HAPPY, KIND OF...NOT.
DID HE SEE?
DID HE SEE?

★ Special Bonus Manga ★

We Asked Yu-chan! The Gang's Reputatoin

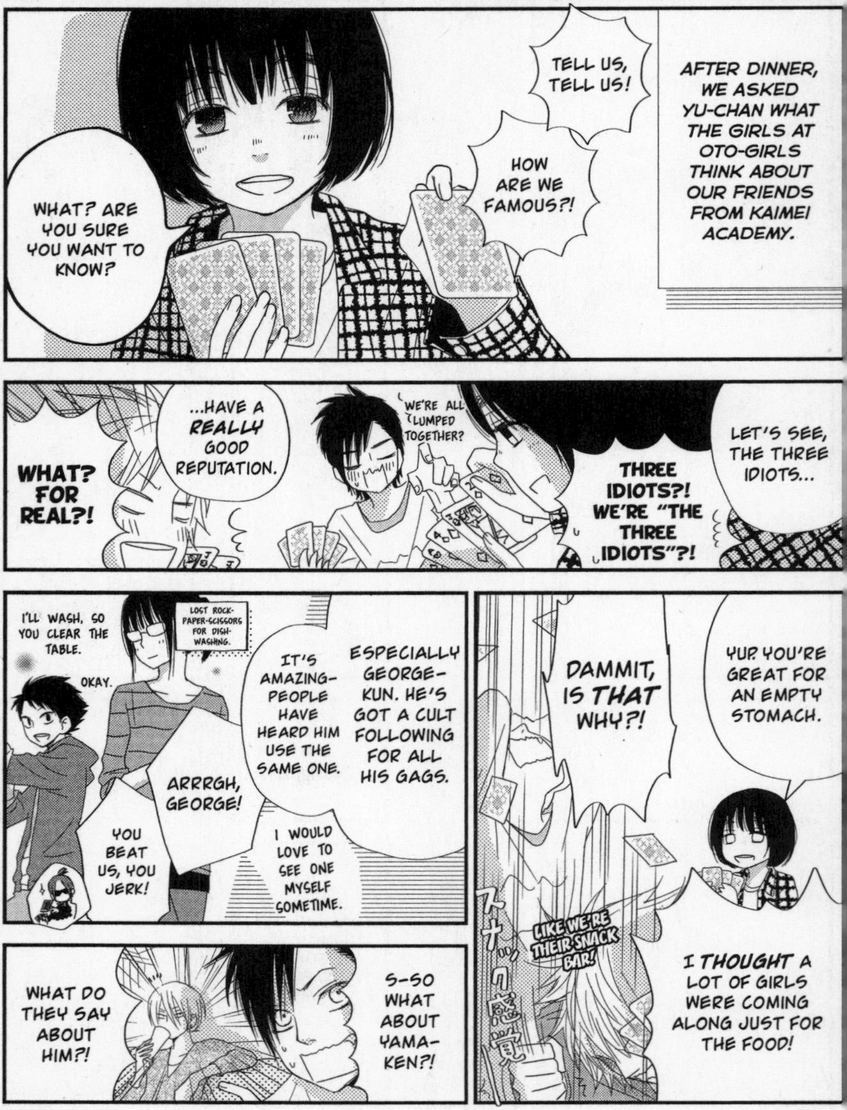
AFTER DINNER, WE ASKED YU-CHAN WHAT THE GIRLS AT OTO-GIRLS THINK ABOUT OUR FRIENDS FROM KAIMEI ACADEMY.
TELL US, TELL US!
HOW ARE WE FAMOUS?!
WHAT? ARE YOU SURE YOU WANT TO KNOW?
LET'S SEE, THE THREE IDIOTS...
THREE IDIOTS?! WE'RE "THE THREE IDIOTS"?!
WE'RE ALL LUMPED TOGETHER?
...HAVE A REALLY GOOD REPUTATION.
WHAT? FOR REAL?!
YUP. YOU'RE GREAT FOR AN EMPTY STOMACH.
DAMMIT, IS THAT WHY?!
LIKE WE'RE THEIR SNACK BAR!
I THOUGHT A LOT OF GIRLS WERE COMING ALONG JUST FOR THE FOOD!
ESPECIALLY GEORGE-KUN. HE'S GOT A CULT FOLLOWING FOR ALL HIS GAGS.
IT'S AMAZING- PEOPLE HAVE HEARD HIM USE THE SAME ONE.
I WOULD LOVE TO SEE ONE MYSELF SOMETIME.
ARRRGH, GEORGE!
LOST ROCK-PAPER-SCISSORS FOR DISH-WASHING.
I'LL WASH, SO YOU CLEAR THE TABLE.
OKAY.
YOU BEAT US, YOU JERK!
S-SO WHAT ABOUT YAMA-KEN?!
WHAT DO THEY SAY ABOUT HIM?!

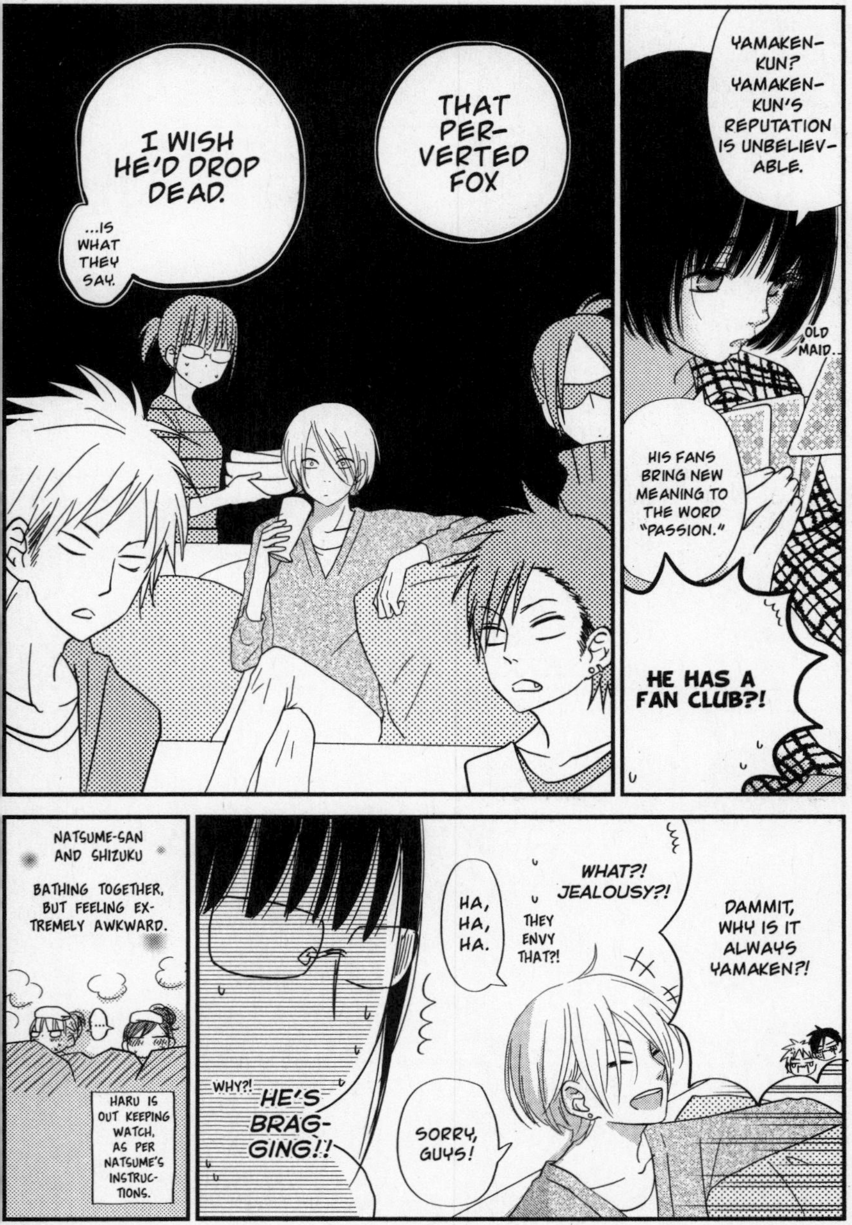
YAMAKEN-KUN? YAMAKEN-KUN'S REPUTATION IS UNBELIEV-ABLE.
OLD MAID...
HIS FANS BRING NEW MEANING TO THE WORD "PASSION."
HE HAS A FAN CLUB?!
THAT PER-VERTED FOX
I WISH HE'D DROP DEAD.
...IS WHAT THEY SAY.
DAMMIT, WHY IS IT ALWAYS YAMAKEN?!
WHAT?! JEALOUSY?!
THEY ENVY THAT?!
HA, HA, HA.
SORRY, GUYS!
HE'S BRAG-GING!!
WHY?!
NATSUME-SAN AND SHIZUKU
BATHING TOGETHER, BUT FEELING EX-TREMELY AWKWARD.
...
HARU IS OUT KEEPING WATCH, AS PER NATSUME'S INSTRUC-TIONS.

★ The End ★

C O M M E N T

Robico

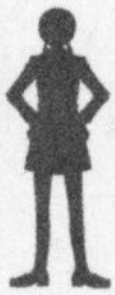

A LOT OF PEOPLE TELL ME THAT THIS MANGA IS FULL OF WEIRDOS, BUT I DOUBT ANY ONE OF THE PEOPLE IN THE MANGA THINKS OF THEMSELVES AS WEIRD. BUT I DO WONDER IF EVERYONE IS ACTUALLY LIKE THAT. WELL, ANYWAY, THIS IS VOLUME 5. I HOPE YOU ENJOYED IT.

Translation Notes

Japanese is a tricky language for most Westerners, and translation is often more art than science. For your edification and reading pleasure, here are notes on some of the places where we could have gone in a different direction with our translation of this book, or where a Japanese cultural reference is used.

Lion dance, page 10

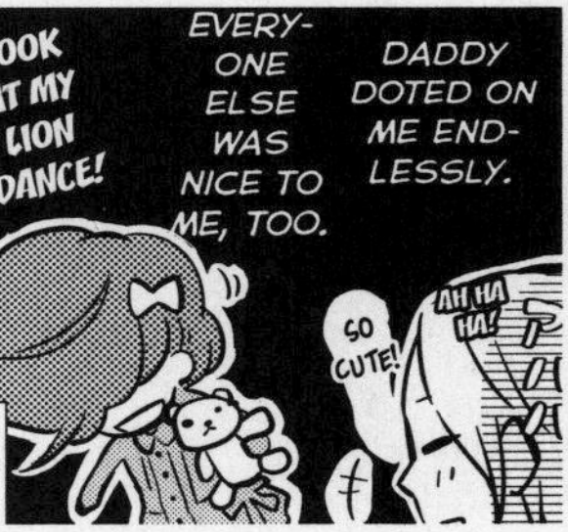
DADDY DOTED ON ME END-LESSLY.
EVERY-ONE ELSE WAS NICE TO ME, TOO.
LOOK AT MY LION DANCE!
AH HA HA!
SO CUTE!

The lion dance is a traditional dance performed at the New Year. The dance is supposed to be performed in a special lion costume, which, as you can see, little Asako is not wearing. She may be trying to imitate the lion mask by using her hair.

The vaulting horse, page 28

More accurately, this should be called the "vaulting box." It's a piece of gymnastics equipment used in Japanese physical education classes. It is a set of long wooden boxes placed on top of each other, creating different height levels, and students are supposed to leap over them after a running start.

Does-ky dolphin, page 31

For the curious, the animal that Asako nonsensically brings into the Japanese conversation is an anteater. When she tells Shizuku that her junior high crimes do have something to do with her problem, the word she uses is *ari*. For emphasis, she adds *ō* (roughly translated, it means "majorly"), and just keeps going to make the word *ōarikui*, which means "giant anteater." This may be an attempt on her part to sound smarter by using a bigger word.

The Nago Roost, page 44

Haru named his snow fort after Nagoya the chicken. The word he uses for "roost" is ya, so it's the Nago *Ya*.

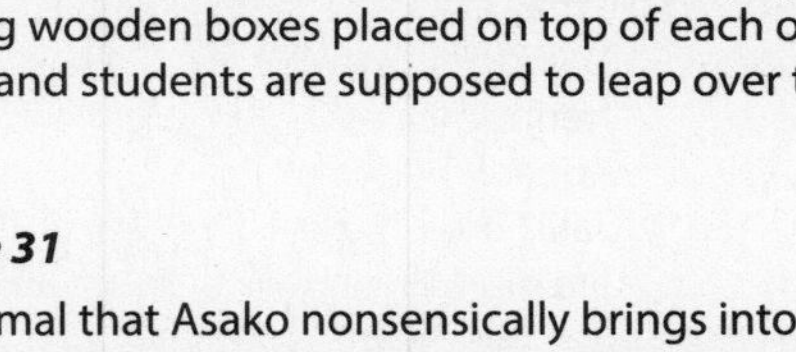

Konaki-jiji, page 52

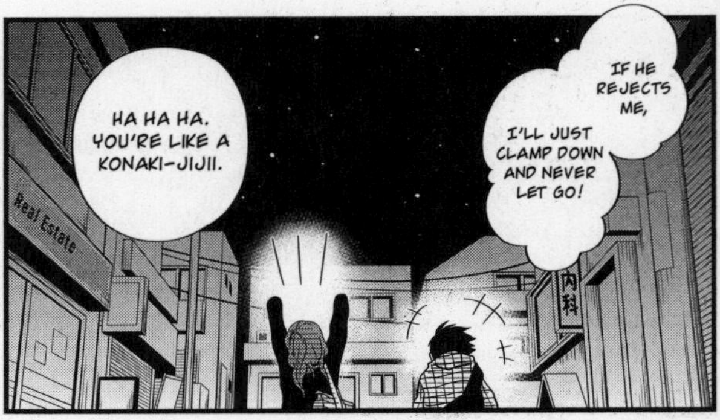
IF HE REJECTS ME,
I'LL JUST CLAMP DOWN AND NEVER LET GO!
HA HA HA. YOU'RE LIKE A KONAKI-JIJII.
Real Estate
内科

Meaning roughly "old man that cries like a child," a konaki-jiji is a creature from Japanese folklore. As the name suggests, the creature looks like an old man, but cries like a baby. If a passerby takes pity on the creature and picks it up to comfort it, it will latch on and refuse to let go. It can also make itself as heavy as a rock, to either crush its victim or prevent him or her from running away.

Group date and "Masquerade Ball," page 114

In their never-ending quest to find girlfriends, Ma-bo and his friends had a *gōkon*, which is roughly equivalent to a group date; it's a little get together with equal numbers of boys and girls who may or may not have all known each other previously. The idea is for people to pair up and, in the perfect situation, become official couples. A common venue for such gatherings is a karaoke box—a private room rented by the hour or half hour for karaoke. Apparently at this particular date, George performed "*Kamen Butōkai* (Masquerade Ball)," the 1985 breakout hit from the boy band Shonentai. Ma-bo and the others must have thought this a surefire way to win the heart of any girl.

Kinpira, page 117

Kinpira is a dish of root vegetables (carrots, daikon radish, etc.), sauteed in sugar and soy sauce. It may be a cheap dish, but it probably isn't weird enough to change Shizuku's behavior.

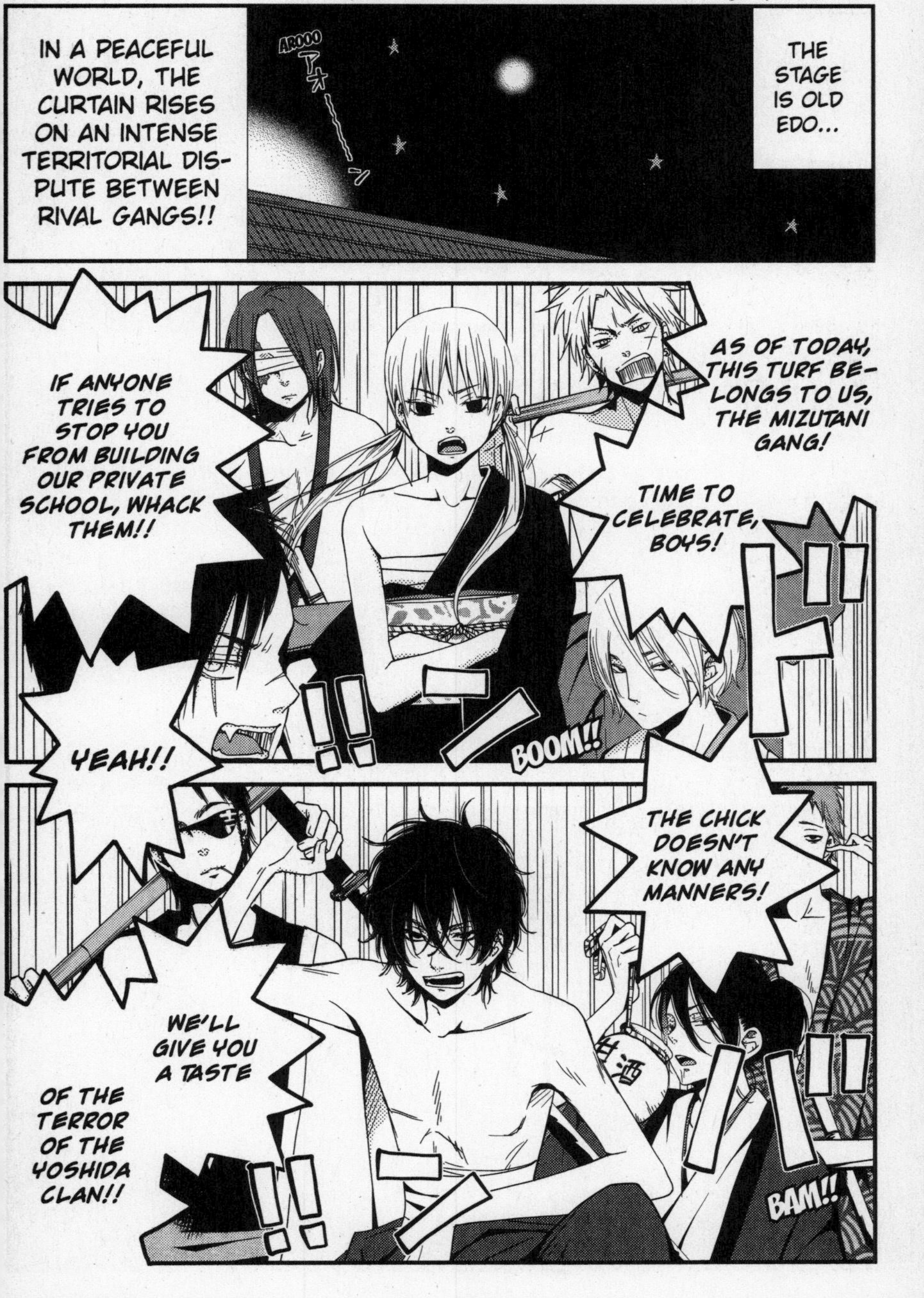
THE STAGE IS OLD EDO...
AROOO
IN A PEACEFUL WORLD, THE CURTAIN RISES ON AN INTENSE TERRITORIAL DIS-PUTE BETWEEN RIVAL GANGS!!
AS OF TODAY, THIS TURF BE-LONGS TO US, THE MIZUTANI GANG!
IF ANYONE TRIES TO STOP YOU FROM BUILDING OUR PRIVATE SCHOOL, WHACK THEM!!
TIME TO CELEBRATE, BOYS!
BOOM!!
YEAH!!
THE CHICK DOESN'T KNOW ANY MANNERS!
甘酒
BAM!!
WE'LL GIVE YOU A TASTE
OF THE TERROR OF THE YOSHIDA CLAN!!

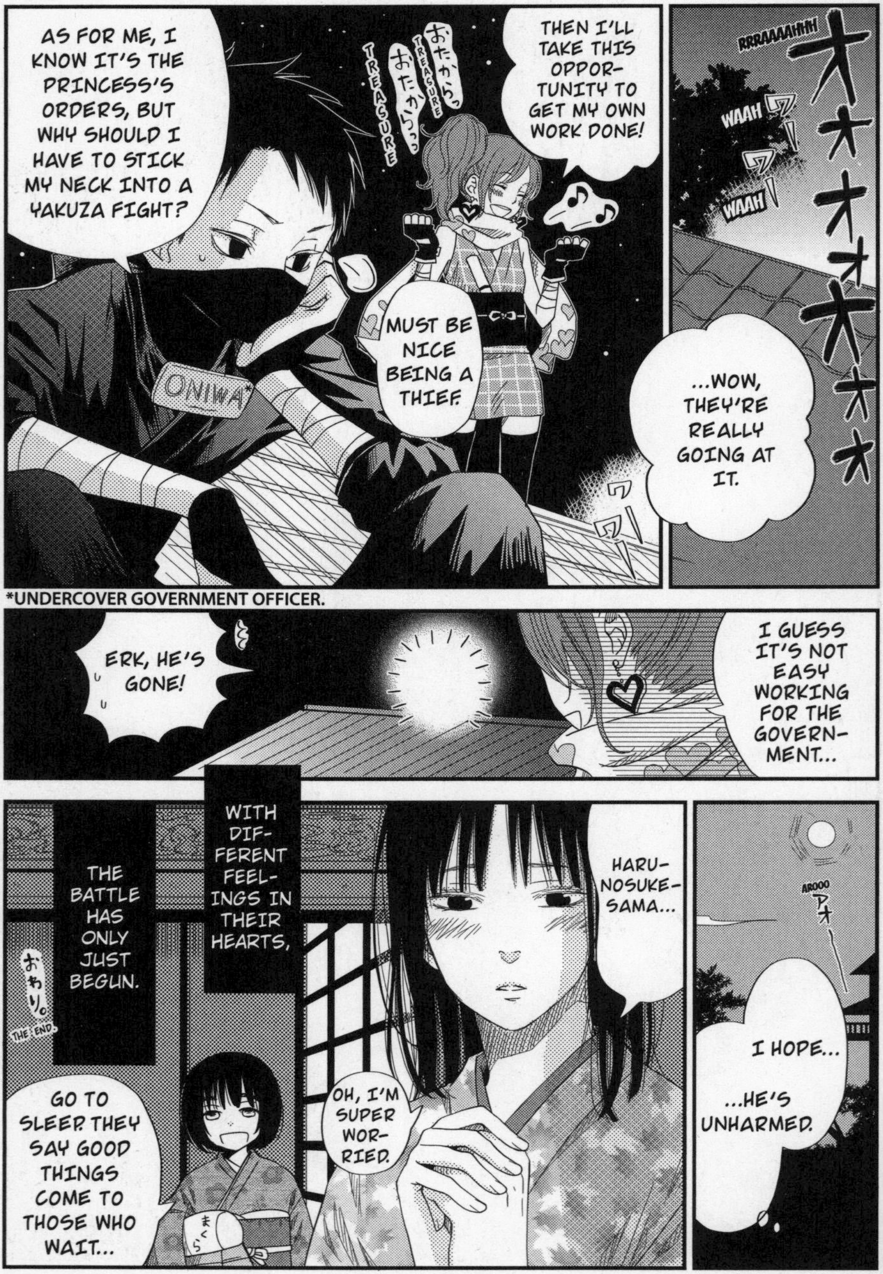
RRRAAAAHHH
WAAH
WAAH
...WOW, THEY'RE REALLY GOING AT IT.
THEN I'LL TAKE THIS OPPORTUNITY TO GET MY OWN WORK DONE!
おたからっ TREASURE
おたからっっ TREASURE
AS FOR ME, I KNOW IT'S THE PRINCESS'S ORDERS, BUT WHY SHOULD I HAVE TO STICK MY NECK INTO A YAKUZA FIGHT?
MUST BE NICE BEING A THIEF.
ONIWA*
I GUESS IT'S NOT EASY WORKING FOR THE GOVERNMENT...
ERK, HE'S GONE!
AROOO
I HOPE...
...HE'S UNHARMED.
HARUNOSUKE-SAMA...
WITH DIFFERENT FEELINGS IN THEIR HEARTS,
THE BATTLE HAS ONLY JUST BEGUN.
おわり。 THE END.
OH, I'M SUPER WORRIED.
GO TO SLEEP. THEY SAY GOOD THINGS COME TO THOSE WHO WAIT...
まくら

*UNDERCOVER GOVERNMENT OFFICER.

The Pretty Guardians
are back!

★

Kodansha Comics is proud to present
Sailor Moon with all new translations.

For more information, go to **www.kodanshacomics.com**

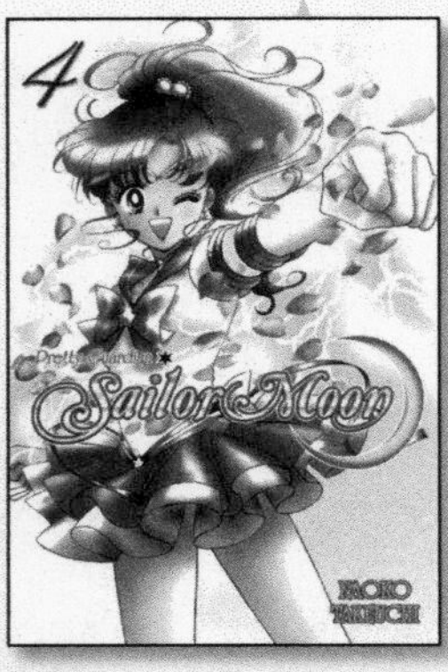
4
Pretty Guardian
Sailor Moon
NAOKO TAKEUCHI
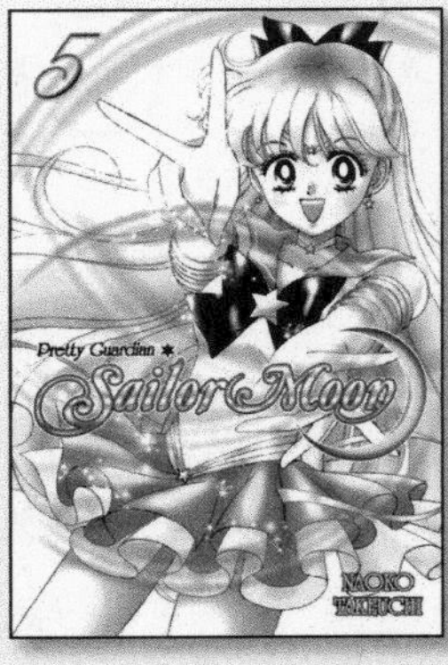
5
Pretty Guardian
Sailor Moon
NAOKO TAKEUCHI
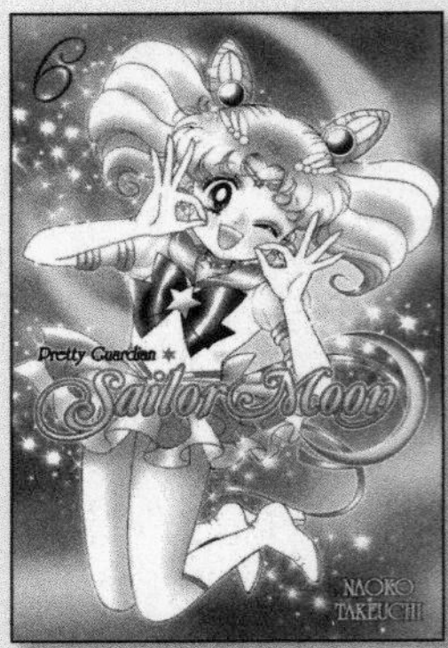
6
Pretty Guardian
Sailor Moon
NAOKO TAKEUCHI
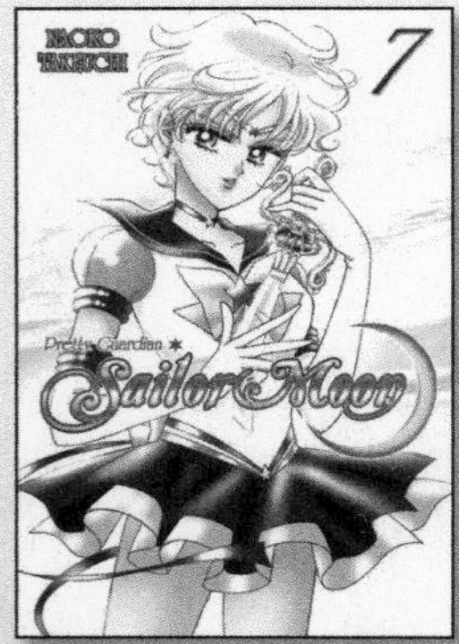
NAOKO TAKEUCHI
7
Pretty Guardian
Sailor Moon
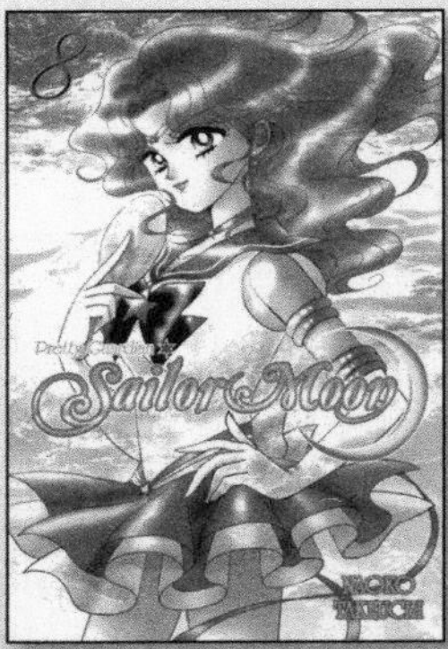
8
Sailor Moon
NAOKO TAKEUCHI
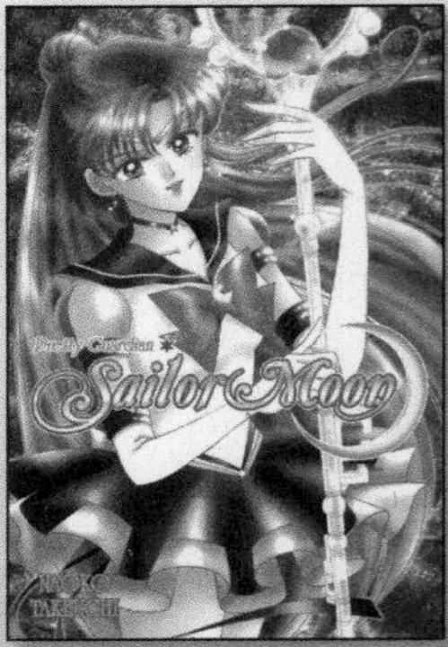
Pretty Guardian
Sailor Moon
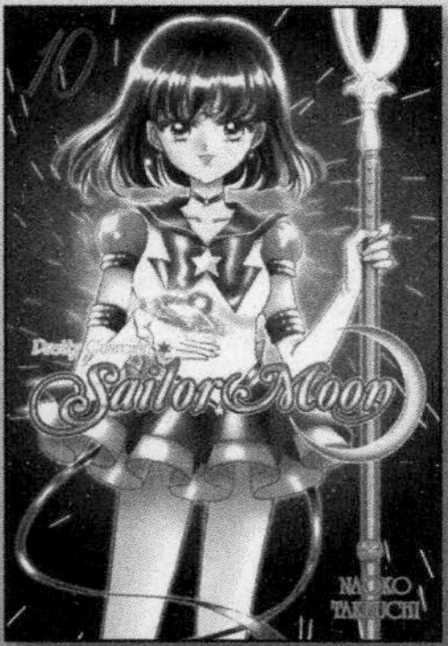
10
Sailor Moon
NAOKO TAKEUCHI
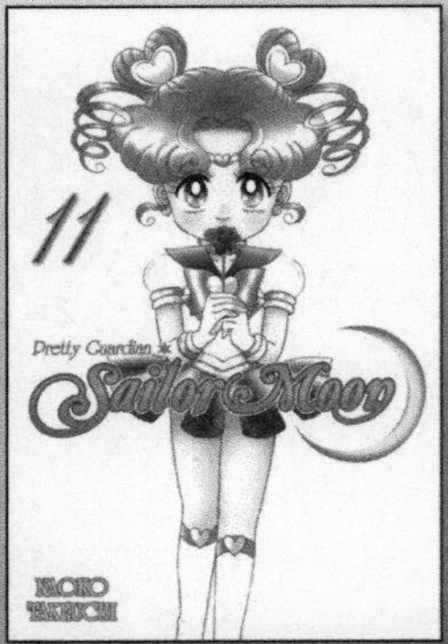
11
Pretty Guardian
Sailor Moon
NAOKO TAKEUCHI
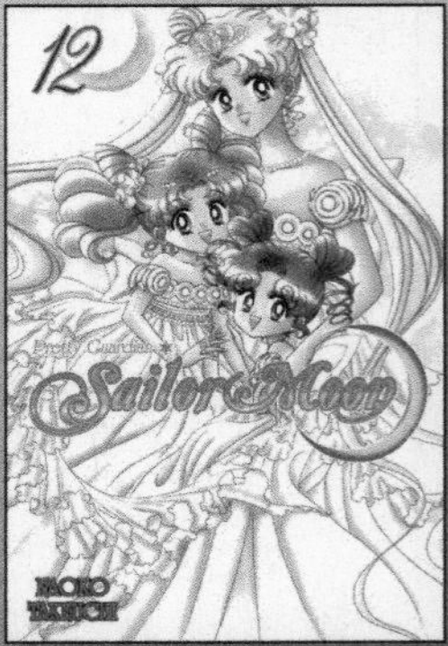
12
Pretty Guardian
Sailor Moon
NAOKO TAKEUCHI

KC
KODANSHA
COMICS

Say I Love You.

KC
KODANSHA COMICS

Mei Tachibana has no friends — and says she doesn't need them!

But everything changes when she accidentally roundhouse kicks the most popular boy in school! However, Yamato Kurosawa isn't angry in the slightest—in fact, he thinks his ordinary life could use an unusual girl like Mei. But winning Mei's trust will be a tough task. How long will she refuse to say, "I love you"?

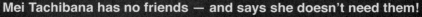

NO.6

A PERFECT LIFE
IN A PERFECT CITY

For Shion, an elite student in the technologically sophisticated city No. 6, life is carefully choreographed. One fateful day, he takes a misstep, sheltering a fugitive his age from a typhoon. Helping this boy throws Shion's life down a path to discovering the appalling secrets behind the "perfection" of No. 6.

KC
KODANSH
COMICS

My Little Monster volume 5 is a work of fiction. Names, characters, places, and incidents are the products of the author's imagination or are used fictitiously. Any resemblance to actual events, locales, or persons, living or dead, is entirely coincidental.

A Kodansha Comics Trade Paperback Original.

My Little Monster volume 5 copyright © 2010 Robico
English translation copyright © 2014 Robico

Published in the United States by Kodansha Comics, an imprint of Kodansha USA Publishing, LLC, New York.

Publication rights for this English edition arranged through Kodansha Ltd., Tokyo.

First published in Japan in 2010 by Kodansha Ltd., Tokyo as *Tonari no Kaibutsu-kun*, volume 5.

ISBN 978-1-61262-601-7

Printed in the United States of America.

www.kodanshacomics.com

9 8 7 6 5 4 3 2 1

Translator: Alethea Nil
Lettering: Kiyoko Shir